MORAL OBLIGATION

MORAL OBLIGATION

Edited by

**Ellen Frankel Paul, Fred D. Miller, Jr.,
and Jeffrey Paul**

CAMBRIDGE
UNIVERSITY PRESS

PUBLISHED BY THE PRESS SYNDICATE OF THE UNIVERSITY OF CAMBRIDGE
The Pitt Building, Trumpington Street, Cambridge, United Kingdom

CAMBRIDGE UNIVERSITY PRESS
The Edinburgh Building, Cambridge CB2 8RU, UK
32 Avenue of the Americas, New York, NY 10013-2473, USA
477 Williamstown Road, Port Melbourne, VIC 3207, Australia
Ruiz de Alarcón 13, 28014 Madrid, Spain
Dock House, The Waterfront, Cape Town 8001, South Africa

http://www.cambridge.org

First published 2010

Printed in the United States of America

Typeface Palatino 10/12 pt.

A catalog record for this book is available from the British Library

Library of Congress Cataloging-in-Publication Data
Moral Obligation
edited by Ellen Frankel Paul, Fred D. Miller, Jr., and Jeffrey Paul.   p. cm.
"The essays . . . have also been published without introduction and index, in the
semiannual journal Social Philosophy & Policy, volume 27, number 2"–T.p. verso.
Includes bibliographical references and index.
ISBN 978-0-521-16896-0

1. Ethics. 2. Duty. 3. Responsibility.
I. Paul, Ellen Frankel. II. Miller, Fred Dycus, 1944- III. Paul, Jeffrey. IV. Title.

BJ21.M585 2010
170--dc22

2010022185

The essays in this book have also been published,
without introduction and index, in the semiannual journal
Social Philosophy & Policy, Volume 27, Number 2,
which is available by subscription.

CONTENTS

INTRODUCTION

The notion of obligation—of what an agent owes to himself, to others, or to society generally—occupies a central place in morality. But what are the sources of our moral obligations, and what are their limits? To what extent do obligations vary in their stringency and severity, and does it make sense to talk about imperfect obligations, that is, obligations that leave the individual with a broad range of freedom to determine how and when to fulfill them? Moreover, does moral obligation always override individual self-interest, and, if not, how should we handle situations in which an agent's obligations come into conflict with his personal goals and commitments?

The twelve essays in this volume address these questions and explore related issues. Some of them discuss broad theoretical questions: they ask, for example, whether moral obligations can be derived from underlying moral or nonmoral facts; or they seek to determine whether, in some cases, an action might be judged objectively wrong but subjectively right. Some essays look at moral reasons for action, characterizing moral obligation in terms of our reasons for assigning blame, or considering whether the fact that an action is wrong provides an additional reason not to perform it. Other essays discuss specific moral obligations, such as the obligation not to waste scarce resources or the obligation to work toward resolving international conflicts and establishing peace. Still others examine the tensions that may exist between our obligations and our other concerns, including our desires to pursue our own aims and projects and to secure our own interests and the interests of those who are close to us.

The collection opens with four essays that explore theoretical issues regarding moral obligation. In "Reflection and Morality," Charles Larmore examines the role that impersonal reflection plays in our understanding of our obligations to one another. One of our distinctive traits as human beings is our capacity to distance ourselves from our individual concerns—the capacity of each individual to view himself as one person among others. Larmore argues that this capacity is essential to our ability to think in moral terms: it allows us to turn our attention from our own happiness to the happiness of another, and to take the same interest in the other person's good (just because it is his or hers) as we naturally take in our own. Reflection, on Larmore's view, is a practical enterprise: we reflect on what we have reason to do, in order to discover how we should live. In the course of the essay, Larmore touches on a range of subjects, including the nature of reasons for action and the relationship between moral reasons and reasons of prudence. In particular, he rejects the notion that prudential reasons are more basic than moral ones, and he denies the possibility that morality can be grounded in considerations of prudence or mutual advantage. Larmore contends that moral reasons are *sui generis* and cannot be derived from any other sorts of considerations; they are, moreover, universal (that is, valid for all agents under similar circumstances) and impersonal (binding without regard to our own interests and attachments). He concludes that reflection plays a vital role in our development as moral beings, since it allows us to see another person's good, in and of itself, as making a claim on our moral attention.

Terry Horgan and Mark Timmons look at the category of supererogatory actions, actions that go "beyond the call of duty," in their essay, "Untying a Knot from the Inside Out: Reflections on the 'Paradox' of Supererogation." They take as their starting-point a famous 1958 essay by the philosopher J. O. Urmson entitled "Saints and Heroes." In that essay, Urmson challenged the then-prevailing view that sorted actions into three categories: those that were morally obligatory; those that were morally indifferent, and therefore optional; and those that were morally wrong. To these, Urmson added a fourth category: supererogatory acts, which were morally praiseworthy, but which individuals had no moral obligation to perform. As Horgan and Timmons note, the concept of supererogation seems to be a paradoxical one. On the one hand, supererogatory actions are (by definition) supposed to be morally good, indeed the morally best, actions. But on the other hand, if they are morally best, why aren't they morally required? In short, how can an action that is morally best for a person to perform fail to be what the person is morally required to do? The source of this alleged paradox is the so-called "good-ought tie-up": the idea that the moral goodness of an action tends to entail an obligation to perform it. Horgan and Timmons address the alleged paradox in two stages. First, they examine the moral phenomenology of several purported cases of supererogatory actions, in order to show that they are, indeed, genuine cases of actions that are morally good yet beyond the call of duty. Second, the authors analyze this moral phenomenology in order to explain why there is no real paradox involved in cases of supererogation. Their explanation appeals to the idea that moral reasons can play what they call a "merit-conferring role"; that is, moral reasons that favor supererogatory actions function to confer merit on the actions they favor, but they do this without also *requiring* the actions in question. Hence, supererogatory actions can be good and morally meritorious, yet still be morally optional. Horgan and Timmons conclude that the recognition of a merit-conferring role unties the "good-ought tie-up," and that there are good grounds, independent of helping to resolve the alleged paradox, for recognizing this sort of role that moral reasons can play.

A different kind of paradox is the focus of Holly M. Smith's contribution to this volume, "Subjective Rightness." In many cases, an agent's actions are guided by mistaken beliefs about his circumstances, and in such cases we may be tempted to judge that his action is both right and wrong. That is, an action may seem right in view of the agent's beliefs, but wrong in light of the actual circumstances. As Smith notes, twentieth-century philosophers such as Bertrand Russell, C. D. Broad, and others introduced a distinction between objective and subjective rightness in order to deal with cases of this sort. Yet, historically, the idea of subjective rightness has been understood in at least four different ways: the subjectively right act might be defined as (1) the act that is most likely to be objectively right; (2) the act that has the highest expected value; (3) the act that would be objectively right if the facts were as the agent believed them to be; or (4) the act that is best in light of the agent's beliefs at the time when he performs it. Smith discusses each of these definitions in turn and judges each to be deficient. She goes on to propose a different approach to defining subjective rightness, an approach that centers on defining *principles* of subjective rightness rather than subjectively right *acts*. The crucial point, she argues, is that a normative principle can be characterized as a principle of subjective rightness only relative to a governing principle of objective rightness. For example, a moral theory might include an objective principle stating that an action is wrong if it involves killing an innocent person. But in some cases an agent may be uncertain as to whether the action he is contemplating involves the killing of an innocent, and to handle those cases, a moral theory must include various principles of subjective rightness to guide the agent's actions in situations of uncertainty. Smith sets out her account in detail and concludes that, since we must often make moral decisions without complete knowledge, any comprehensive moral theory must include multiple principles of subjective rightness to address the different degrees of knowledge that moral decision-makers possess.

The question of whether our moral obligations can be justified on the basis of more fundamental, nonmoral facts lies at the center of Thomas Hurka's essay, "Underivative Duty: Prichard on Moral Obligation." Hurka explores the early-twentieth-century philosopher H. A. Prichard's defense of the view that moral duty is underivative, a view reflected in Prichard's argument that it is a mistake to ask, "Why ought I to do what I morally ought?" because the only possible answer is, "Because you morally ought to." Hurka notes that this view was shared by other philosophers of Prichard's time, including Henry Sidgwick and A. C. Ewing, but he believes Prichard stated the view most forcefully and defended it best. The claim that moral obligation is underivative can be understood on three different levels. On the broadest level, it expresses the idea that normative truths are not reducible to or derivable from non-normative truths (such as scientific facts). On the level of moral judgments, the idea is that truths about how we ought to act are also underivative: moral "oughts" cannot be grounded in any more fundamental considerations, either normative or non-normative. Finally, on the level of specific deontological duties (such as the duty to keep promises), the idea is that these duties are not derived from a more general duty to promote good consequences. Using these three levels as a framework, Hurka offers a detailed discussion of Prichard's views, with particular emphasis on Prichard's critique of consequentialism. According to this critique, the attempt to justify moral duties based on their consequences (whether for the satisfaction of the agent's interests, or for the good of others) has the tendency to distort those duties. If a duty is justified instrumentally by the fact that it promotes the agent's advantage, for example, then it is, in effect, reduced to a duty to promote the agent's advantage. Hurka concludes his essay with a discussion of Prichard's critique of ancient ethics and, in particular, the ethics of Aristotle: the fundamental flaw of these ethical systems, Hurka suggests, is that they are grounded in a picture of the moral agent as essentially self-concerned.

The collection's next three essays explore the links between our moral obligations and moral reasons for action. In "'But It Would Be Wrong,'" Stephen Darwall asks whether the fact that an action would be wrong is itself a reason not to perform it. If we suppose that an action is morally wrong because it has certain wrong-making features, and that these features provide us with reasons not to perform the action, then it seems natural to assume that the fact that the action is wrong does not provide us with an *additional* reason not to perform it. But Darwall argues that this view is mistaken. The concepts of moral obligation and moral wrong, he argues, are connected in an important way to our reactive attitudes (e.g., indignation or blame), attitudes through which we hold agents responsible for their actions. On his analysis, moral obligation and moral wrong conceptually involve authoritative demands that we make of one another as members of a moral community. Moral obligation is conceptually linked to accountability: an agent who has an obligation is morally answerable if he fails to fulfill it. To say that an action is morally wrong is to say that we would be justified in blaming an agent who performed it without an adequate excuse. Darwall sets out this view and relates it to views of moral obligation held by John Stuart Mill, P. F. Strawson, Bernard Williams, and others. In the end, Darwall concludes, the fact that an action is morally wrong does indeed provide a reason not to perform it (in addition to whatever features make the act wrong). This additional reason consists in the fact that a morally wrong action violates a legitimate demand that we make of one another, and therefore disrespects the authority we have, as members of a moral community, to make such demands.

In "Moral Obligation, Blame, and Self-Governance," John Skorupski argues that our judgments about moral obligations are rooted in the rationality of our feelings. He begins with a discussion of evaluative reasons—the reasons we have for feeling sentiments such as admiration, gratitude, anger, or fear—reasons which are not reducible to epistemic ones (reasons to believe something) or practical ones (reasons to do something). The key to understanding our moral obligations, on Skorupski's view, is the sentiment of blame: an action is understood to be morally wrong if it is blameworthy. Blame, in turn, can be understood in terms of the objects that typically give rise to it (for example, stealing, acting cruelly) and in terms of the actions it prompts toward the person who is blamed (the withdrawal of recognition or the cutting off of relations, either temporarily or permanently). The proper object of the sentiment of blame is some action that the agent had warranted reason not to do and could have refrained from doing. Skorupski goes on to contend that the categorical nature of moral obligation is consistent with, and indeed follows from, his analysis of moral concepts in terms of reasons for blame. In the remainder of his essay, he draws out the implications of his analysis for moral agency. Given that moral agency essentially involves susceptibility to blame, it follows that moral agency is a species of self-governing agency. Self-governing agents must, at the very least, be able to think about what reasons they have, in order to assess what they have sufficient reason to believe, feel, or do, and this notion of self-governance implies that an agent's moral obligations are always relative to the agent's warranted beliefs. Skorupski concludes by considering whether moral agents, in addition to being self-governing, must also be autonomous in the strong sense intended by Immanuel Kant: that is, whether they must be capable of knowing their moral obligations by means of their own personal insight.

The relationship between practical reasons and imperfect moral duties or obligations is the subject of Patricia Greenspan's contribution to this volume, "Making Room for Options: Moral Reasons, Imperfect Duties, and Choice." Drawing on a distinction made by Kant, contemporary philosophers understand imperfect duties as those that leave some room for choice as to the time, place, and manner of their fulfillment (as opposed to perfect duties, which specify precisely what we must do, given particular circumstances). The classic example of an imperfect duty, as Greenspan notes, is the duty to aid those in need, which leaves individuals with some leeway regarding whom to aid, when, and how much. Yet the notion of an imperfect duty seems to stand in tension with the contemporary understanding of practical reasons for action: practical reasons are taken to be prima facie requirements of action, which may be overridden by other reasons, but are otherwise taken to constrain an agent's choices. On this view, it would be irrational for an individual to recognize a particular reason as the strongest reason for action he has, and yet make no attempt to act on it. If one has a strong reason to aid a particular victim of a natural disaster, for example, then one is morally required to aid him, unless one has an equally strong (or stronger) reason to perform some other action. This view seems to undermine the very idea of imperfect duties—duties that leave the agent with the freedom to choose how to fulfill them—and Greenspan defends an alternative conception of practical reasons that is designed to preserve this freedom. She distinguishes between *critical reasons,* which count against a potential action, and *favoring reasons,* which highlight valuable features of a potential action (or answer criticisms against it). She goes on to argue that only reasons that offer criticism of alternatives can yield binding moral requirements, and that reasons for particular ways of satisfying imperfect duties merely count in favor of the acts in question. If we conceive of practical reasons in this way, Greenspan concludes, we can understand imperfect duties as having genuine moral force, and yet preserve the freedom of individuals to determine precisely how and when to fulfill them.

The collection continues with three essays that focus on particular moral obligations. The general obligation to be virtuous is the subject of Paul Guyer's essay, "The Obligation to Be Virtuous: Kant's Conception of the *Tugendverpflichtung.*" Guyer asks whether it makes sense to distinguish, as Kant does, between specific duties (such as the duty of beneficence toward others) and a general obligation to be virtuous. We might suppose that this general obligation is entirely reducible to the obligation to fulfill one's specific duties, and thus has no content of its own. But Guyer argues that Kant understands the obligation to be virtuous as calling on agents to strengthen their commitment to fulfilling their particular duties. On Kant's view, we have a natural disposition to be moral, as well as a natural disposition toward self-love, and the obligation to be virtuous calls on us to strive to strengthen the former and control the latter. We strengthen our disposition to be moral in two ways: by cultivating moral feeling, which makes it possible for us to be moved to act by the thought of our moral duties; and by cultivating our individual conscience, the internal judge that prompts us to recognize our duties in particular situations. Guyer contends that Kant's general obligation to be virtuous amounts to an obligation to develop one's moral character so as to be ready to conduct oneself virtuously when one is presented with moral choices. With the identification of this general obligation, Guyer concludes, Kant has captured an important element of the genuinely moral life: living such a life does not merely require fulfilling a series of particular duties; rather, it requires preparing oneself to be moral by developing the resources of character that enable one to act virtuously.

In "A Conceptual and (Preliminary) Normative Exploration of Waste," Andrew Jason Cohen asks whether we have an obligation to refrain from wasting resources. He begins by defending a definition of waste as a process wherein something useful becomes less useful, and less benefit is produced than is lost. Employing this definition, Cohen goes on to consider various arguments designed to show that waste is immoral. One line of argument holds that waste is immoral because it harms the person who wastes: an agent who wastes his resources will be less able to preserve himself and pursue his goals. The problem with this argument, Cohen notes, is that some agents (e.g., the super-rich) will be able to engage in wasteful behavior without seriously impairing their chances of surviving and achieving their goals. A second line of argument is one that Cohen calls the "disgust argument": when confronted with instances of waste, we typically react with disgust, and this visceral (and widely shared) reaction gives us reason to believe that waste is immoral. Cohen rejects this second argument as well, on the grounds that, historically, people have found many perfectly moral activities disgusting; not long ago, for example, people used their disgust with the idea of interracial marriage to justify making the practice illegal. A far more promising line of argument, Cohen maintains, is one that frames the issue of waste in terms of toleration: When should we tolerate waste, and when should we not? That is, when should it be permissible to interfere with wasteful behavior, and when should it be impermissible? Cohen argues that interference should be permissible when wasteful behavior causes genuine harm to others, understood as the wrongful setting back of their interests. He fills in the details of this argument in the remainder of his essay, and he concludes that we do indeed have an obligation not to waste, at least in certain circumstances: for example, if an agent is wasting a resource that a second agent needs for his preservation, then the former has an obligation to give up the resource and allow the latter to make better use of it.

In "The Duty to Seek Peace," Bernard R. Boxill examines Kant's claim that we have an obligation to seek to establish peace between nations. Kant's view stands in contrast to the views of other theorists such as Thomas Hobbes, whose work casts doubt on the very possibility of achieving peace and seems to suggest that the best we can hope for is an uneasy truce between countries that refrain from attacking one another out of fear of retaliation. As Boxill notes, however, Kant's conception of peace involves more than the absence of open war: it requires the establishment of conditions that would foster the full development of human talents. In his essay *Perpetual Peace* (1795), Kant sets out a plan for securing peace which requires the establishment of three important institutions: a republican constitution for every state in the world; a federation of all states; and a cosmopolitan right that entitles individuals to visit foreign countries and establish relations (including economic relations) with their inhabitants on mutually agreeable terms. The prospects for securing these three institutions may seem remote, yet Kant believed their establishment was possible, and even likely, given historical trends. In the course of his essay, Boxill looks at each of these institutions and argues that Kant failed to show that they would be sufficient to secure peace. For example, Kant believed that republican states would remain at peace with one another because their citizens would be reluctant to authorize war, knowing that they would bear the costs. But this argument fails, Boxill points out, if we recognize that a majority within a republic can shift the costs of war onto a minority. He goes on to argue that the prospects for peace in today's world seem bleaker than they were even in Kant's time, since the contemporary trend toward globalization tends to increase international conflicts over the control of natural resources. Nonetheless, Boxill suggests that it may be possible to devise a plan for securing peace in a world of globalization. As we attempt to do so, he concludes, we should draw on our fear of war and our compassion for the victims of war in order to strengthen our resolve to seek peace.

The collection concludes with two essays that focus, in different ways, on tensions between moral obligations and other values. In "Goals, Luck, and Moral Obligation," R. G. Frey draws on the work of the philosopher Bernard Williams in order to explore situations in which our individual goals and projects conflict with our moral obligations. As Frey notes, Williams rejected a particular view that he held to be central to much of modern moral philosophy: namely, the view that obligation lies at the core of ethics and that the only thing that can override a moral obligation is another, stronger moral obligation. According to Williams, this view tends to impoverish our moral experience and fails to take into account things that are obviously important to our lives. Taking Williams as his inspiration, Frey sets out to discuss a number of cases in which an individual's personal goals and commitments come into conflict with his obligations. Suppose, for example, that a son makes a promise to his dying father that he will pursue a particular career; later, the son discovers that he is unsuited to that career, and that his pursuit of it has made a mess of his life, leaving him miserable. Frey maintains that the son's unhappiness, in this case, is a factor that weighs against his obligation to keep his promise, and indeed may justify his breaking it. Drawing on this case and a number of others, Frey argues that our desire to pursue goals and live lives of our own choosing may sometimes outweigh particular moral obligations. In the course of his essay, he considers the role that luck plays in our lives and the relationship between luck and moral responsibility. He concludes that any account of morality that omits or trivializes personal projects and goals is insufficient for understanding the complexity of our moral lives.

H. Tristram Engelhardt, Jr. explores the tension between morality and prudence in the collection's final essay, "Moral Obligation after the Death of God: Critical Reflections on Concerns from Immanuel Kant, G. W. F. Hegel, and Elizabeth Anscombe." In particular, Engelhardt focuses on the character of moral obligations in contemporary secular societies, in which God is no longer recognized as the source and enforcer of morality. Since the Enlightenment, Western nations have moved away from a theocentric moral culture toward a culture which views the universe as ultimately without meaning and which recognizes a diversity of moral opinions and practices. Without a unifying theological perspective, Engelhardt argues, it becomes impossible to get beyond moral diversity and discover moral truth. Moreover, without a God who punishes wrongdoing and rewards virtue, it becomes impossible to show that moral concerns should always trump concerns of prudence (that is, concerns for one's own nonmoral interests and the interests of those to whom one is close). Engelhardt looks at how the problem of anchoring morality in the absence of God has been treated in the work of a number of theorists. He offers a lengthy analysis of Kant's attempt to establish the absolute force of moral obligation by making the idea of God central to morality, while at the same time rejecting the possibility that we can know whether a God exists. Engelhardt goes on to discuss Hegel's account of morality, which emphasizes the importance of moral customs and holds that moral obligations are contingent and sociohistorically situated within particular communities and nations (with the implication that moral truth is subject to change over time). Engelhardt concludes that the "death of God" in modern secular societies comes with a significant cost: without an appeal to God, there is no clear basis for claiming that morality should take precedence over self-interest.

Questions about what we owe to one another—about the extent and limits of the demands that morality places on us—are of perennial concern in moral theory. The essays in this volume, written from a variety of perspectives, offer important insights concerning the nature, sources, and implications of our moral obligations.

ACKNOWLEDGMENTS

The editors wish to acknowledge several individuals at the Social Philosophy and Policy Center, Bowling Green State University, who provided invaluable assistance in the preparation of this volume. They include Program Manager John Milliken, Brandon Byrd, Mary Dilsaver, and Terrie Weaver.

The editors also extend special thanks to Administrative Editor Tamara Sharp, for attending to innumerable day-to-day details of the book's preparation, and to Managing Editor Harry Dolan, for providing dedicated assistance throughout the editorial and production process.

CONTRIBUTORS

Charles Larmore is W. Duncan MacMillan Family Professor in the Humanities, and Professor of Philosophy, at Brown University. Previously, he taught at Columbia University and at the University of Chicago. His work is centered in the areas of moral and political philosophy, though he has also written on the nature of the self and on various topics in metaphysics and epistemology. Among his recent books are *Les pratiques du moi* (2004), for which he received the Grand Prix de Philosophie from the Académie Française; *The Autonomy of Morality* (2008); and *Dernières nouvelles du moi* (with Vincent Descombes, 2009).

Terry Horgan is Professor of Philosophy at the University of Arizona. He is the author, with Matjaž Potrč, of *Austere Realism: Contextual Semantics Meets Minimal Ontology* (2008), and the editor, with Mark Timmons, of *Metaethics after Moore* (2006). His essays have appeared in such journals as *Philosophical Studies, Philosophy of Science, Mind,* and the *Southern Journal of Philosophy*.

Mark Timmons is Professor of Philosophy at the University of Arizona. He is editor of *Oxford Studies in Normative Ethics*, a newly inaugurated annual whose first volume will be published in 2011. He and Terry Horgan have coauthored many papers in metaethics, including "What Does Moral Phenomenology Tell Us about Moral Objectivity?" *Social Philosophy and Policy* (2008).

Holly M. Smith is Professor of Philosophy at Rutgers University. She has published widely on topics in normative ethics and biomedical ethics, and is currently working on a book manuscript (forthcoming, Oxford University Press) exploring how moral theories should accommodate the errors, ignorance, and misunderstandings that all too frequently impede us when we confront occasions for moral decision-making. Her essays have appeared in a number of journals, including *Ethics*, the *Philosophical Review, Noûs,* and the *Journal of Philosophy*.

Thomas Hurka is Chancellor Henry N.R. Jackman Distinguished Professor of Philosophical Studies at the University of Toronto, where he has taught since 2002. He is the author of *Perfectionism* (1993), *Principles: Short Essays on Ethics* (1993), and *Virtue, Vice, and Value* (2001), as well as of many articles on topics in normative ethics and political philosophy. He is currently finishing a trade book on the theory of value entitled *The Good Things in Life*, and is preparing to write a scholarly book entitled *British*

Moral Philosophers from Sidgwick to Ewing. His contribution to this volume grows out of his research for the latter book.

Stephen Darwall is Andrew Downey Orrick Professor of Philosophy at Yale University and John Dewey Distinguished University Professor Emeritus at the University of Michigan. He has written widely on the foundations and history of ethics. His books include *Impartial Reason* (1983), *The British Moralists and the Internal "Ought": 1640–1740* (1995), *Philosophical Ethics* (1998), *Welfare and Rational Care* (2002), and *The Second-Person Standpoint: Morality, Respect, and Accountability* (2006). He is a member of the American Academy of Arts and Sciences, a past president of the Central Division of the American Philosophical Association, and a founding coeditor (with David Velleman) of *The Philosophers' Imprint*.

John Skorupski is Professor of Moral Philosophy and Head of Graduate Studies at the University of St. Andrews. He studied philosophy and economics at Cambridge University. Previously, he has been a lecturer at the University of Glasgow, as well as the Chair of Philosophy at Sheffield University. He is the author of *Ethical Explorations* (1999) and *Why Read Mill Today?* (2006).

Patricia Greenspan is Professor of Philosophy at the University of Maryland, College Park. She has published articles on ethics and philosophy of action in the *Journal of Philosophy*, *Philosophical Review*, *Philosophy and Public Affairs*, *Ethics*, and other leading journals, as well as essays in various anthologies. She is the author of *Emotions and Reasons: An Inquiry into Emotional Motivation* (1988) and *Practical Guilt: Moral Dilemmas, Emotions, and Social Norms* (1995). Her most recent work focuses on practical rationality.

Paul Guyer is Professor of Philosophy and Florence R.C. Murray Professor in the Humanities at the University of Pennsylvania. He is the author, editor, and translator of numerous works about and by Immanuel Kant, including most recently *Kant* (2006), *Kant's Groundwork for the Metaphysics of Morals: A Reader's Guide* (2007), and *Knowledge, Reason, and Taste: Kant's Response to Hume* (2008). He is currently completing a history of modern aesthetics and is a Fellow of the American Academy of Arts and Sciences and a Research Prize Winner of the Alexander von Humboldt Foundation.

Andrew Jason Cohen is Associate Professor of Philosophy at Georgia State University in Atlanta, Georgia. He has published articles in *Ethics*, *The Canadian Journal of Philosophy*, and elsewhere. Most of his current work revolves around toleration—what it is, why it is a value, and what it requires. He seeks to determine the normative limits of toleration of individuals, families, cultural groups, business entities, and states. He has also examined issues relating to individualism, communitarianism, and the nature of exchange.

Bernard R. Boxill is Pardue Distinguished Professor of Philosophy at the University of North Carolina at Chapel Hill. His essays on moral and political issues have appeared in leading philosophical journals since 1972, and have centered mainly on African American political thought, including theories of reparation, affirmative action, and race, as well as on peace, war, and related topics. He is the author of *Blacks and Social Justice* (revised edition, 1992) and the editor of *Race and Racism* (2001).

R. G. Frey is Professor of Philosophy at Bowling Green State University. He is the author or editor of numerous books and articles in moral and political philosophy, including, with Christopher Heath Wellman, one of the standard contemporary works on applied ethics, *A Companion to Applied Ethics* (2003), and, with Gerald Dworkin and Sissela Bok, one of the seminal works on euthanasia, *Euthanasia and Physician-Assisted Suicide* (1998). He is the former editor of Cambridge University Press's series in applied ethics, *For and Against*, and the editor, with Tom L. Beauchamp, of the forthcoming *Handbook on Ethics and Animals*.

H. Tristram Engelhardt, Jr., is Professor of Philosophy at Rice University, and Professor Emeritus of Medicine and Community Medicine at Baylor College of Medicine in Houston, Texas. He is senior editor of the *Journal of Medicine and Philosophy* and the journal *Christian Bioethics*, both published by Oxford University Press. He is also senior editor of the book series *Philosophy and Medicine*, with over one hundred volumes in print, and of the book series *Philosophical Studies in Contemporary Culture*. His publications include *The Foundations of Bioethics* (second edition, 1996), *Bioethics and Secular Humanism* (1991), and *The Foundations of Christian Bioethics* (2000). His recent edited volumes include *Global Bioethics: The Collapse of Consensus* (2006) and *Innovation and the Pharmaceutical Industry: Critical Reflections on the Virtues of Profit* (2008).

REFLECTION AND MORALITY

By Charles Larmore

I. Our Humanity

Morality is what makes us human. One meaning of this common saying is plain enough. Refraining from injury to others, keeping our word, and helping those in need constitute the elementary decencies of society. If most of us did not observe these practices most of the time, or at least give one another the impression of doing so, no one would have the security to pursue a flourishing life. Even a life of basic dignity would be impossible if we found ourselves continually at the mercy of aggression, treachery, and indifference. Morality makes us human by providing rules of mutual respect without which there can be neither social cooperation nor individual achievement.

However, another meaning suggests itself as well. It has to do not with morality's function, but with its source. Other animals are like us in being able to show deference and feel affection, even to the point of sacrificing themselves for those whom they love. But morality, insofar as it involves looking beyond our own concerns and allegiances in order to respect others in and of themselves, lies beyond their ken. Does not then our very ability to think morally point to a peculiarly human power of self-transcendence, a power that we alone among the animals have of regarding ourselves from the outside as but one among others, and that finds in morality, if not its only, then certainly its most striking expression? This question engages our attention far less than it should. When people, philosophers included, wonder about the nature of morality, they tend to focus on what reasons there may be to be moral, what acting morally entails, or in what sense, if any, moral judgments count as true or false. All of these are important issues. But often the taken-for-granted deserves the greatest scrutiny. That we should be able at all to view the world impersonally, recognizing the independent and equal standing of others, involves an overcoming of self that is no less remarkable for having become largely second-nature.

Among philosophers, Immanuel Kant was one of the few, and certainly the most famous, to argue directly that morality is, in this sense, what makes us human. "Duty! Sublime and mighty name, what is an origin worthy of you?" Only a freedom, he replied, that "elevates man above himself as a part of the world of sense . . . a freedom and independence from the mech-

anism of all of nature." [1] Our moral consciousness, according to Kant, tes-
tifies to the freedom we alone have to rise above all that experience has
made of us, so that we may act in accord with demands we understand as
binding on us independently of our given interests and desires. I believe,
like many, that Kant was on the track of an essential truth. But, like many
too, I do not believe that the source of morality can be anything so extravagant (if morality itself is not to be an illusion) as a freedom unshaped by
the course of experience. Freedom, in any form we can conceive, depends
not only on external conditions proving conducive to our ends, but also on
our having acquired, through training and effort, the abilities necessary for
exercising control over ourselves and the world. After all, we have to learn
how to think morally, which means developing a sense of social expectations as well as the self-discipline needed to distinguish the good of others
from our own, or from what we wish their good would be.

Thus, Kant's intuition needs to be brought down to earth. One proposal
might be that the capacity for self-transcendence to which morality gives
expression consists in our nature as normative beings, responsive not
merely to the causal impress of the environment, but to the authority of
reasons as well. To see that we have a reason to think or act in a certain
way is to see that we ought to do so, all other things being equal, and
heeding an "ought"—as is clear with the moral "ought"—means holding
ourselves to a demand we regard as binding upon us. Why is not this
subordination of self the self-transcendence at issue?

Certainly morality is not possible except for beings that can respond to
reasons. Yet the "ought" is not limited to the moral realm, any more than
it is true that the only reasons for action we have are moral in character.
Most importantly, the subordination of self involved in the recognition of
reasons as such falls importantly short of the way that morality asks us to
look beyond ourselves.

Suppose, for instance, that we are pursuing some interest of our own or
the good of some people we hold dear, and doing so solely because that
interest or those people matter to us. The reasons we then perceive to act
one way rather than another are ones we would have to agree that anyone
similarly disposed would have in such circumstances. All reasons are
universal, binding on one person only if binding on all of whom the same
conditions are true that make them applicable to the first. That is what it
is for reasons to be binding, and why responding to reasons means holding ourselves responsible to the authority of an "ought," distinct from our
individual will. Nonetheless, this subordination of self is not the self-
transcendence that morality demands. For the reasons in question only
apply to us because we care about those ends. Their authority, though
real, remains conditional.

---

[1] Immanuel Kant, *Kritik der praktischen Vernunft* (*Critique of Practical Reason*) (1788),
Akademie-Ausgabe (Berlin: Reimer, 1900–), vol. V, 86–87.

Imagine, however, that we think we ought to help someone simply because that person is in distress. Perhaps it is someone whom we happen to hold dear, but we are attending, not to the love we feel, but only to the person's suffering. Reasons of this sort are not just universal, as all reasons are. They are *impersonal* as well, applying to us in abstraction from our own interests and affections. Or, more exactly, their applicability does not depend on any such personal factors insofar as the latter are identified as ours, since it is possible to have an impersonal reason to satisfy a desire of ours if the desire, understood solely as belonging to a person like any other, turns out to warrant attention.[2] In short, impersonal reasons derive from the way things are in and of themselves—as, in the imagined case, from another person's actual condition. And it is just this impersonal element that constitutes the hallmark of moral reasons for action. Thus, acknowledging the force of reasons is not by itself sufficient to impel us to look beyond ourselves in the way that morality requires. Nor is it, incidentally, a distinctively human capacity. Many of the higher animals also have, or can be trained to have, a sense of how they ought to behave. Yet moral thinking, the grasping of impersonal reasons, remains beyond their reach.

This last point suggests the direction of a more promising approach. Though other animals can respond to reasons, they appear for the most part unable to reflect about what they ought to do, evaluating and weighing the reasons they see to favor one option or another. Reflection seems basically beyond their reach, if by "reflection" is meant standing back so as to regard ourselves from the outside, as we regard someone else, in order to figure out who we are or what we really ought to think or do. Why is it not then our capacity for reflection to which morality gives special expression? Are we not better able to consider others as persons in their own right, apart from the personal concerns that color our perception of the world, the more reflective distance we achieve toward ourselves? Of course, as that question implies, reflection need not always be impersonal. Sometimes we reflect by asking ourselves what someone close to us would think about our situation. But herein lies a strength of the approach I propose. For now the freedom that is integral to morality becomes intelligible. It is the ability to overcome the hold that a natural absorption in our own affairs exercises over our thinking in order to see the intrinsic value in the good of others, and it manifestly grows out of the less impartial ways we have of standing back from ourselves. Impersonal reflection is a creature of experience, and

---

[2] Impersonal reasons are what Thomas Nagel, in *The Possibility of Altruism* (Princeton, NJ: Princeton University Press, 1970), chapter 10, called "objective" reasons, whose "defining predicate" contains no free, unbound, occurrence of the variable referring to the agent whose reasons they are. (If I jump out of the way of an oncoming truck because that will preserve my life—and not just someone's life, that "someone" happening to be me—then my reason will count as "subjective," not "objective" or impersonal.) I prefer my terminology, since reasons that are not impersonal are, in my view, nonetheless real.

a more sensible answer than Kant's to the question of what constitutes our peculiar power of self-transcendence.

Morality is not, of course, the only example of impersonal reflection (any more than it could be the only example of the nonempirical freedom that Kant postulated). When we reflect upon what we should believe about a certain matter, and ask not what we are inclined to suppose or what our friends or community would conclude, but rather what the facts themselves require, we are reflecting impersonally. For our target then consists in impersonal reasons for belief—reasons (in parallel to impersonal reasons for action) that we grasp as binding on us independently of our desires and loyalties in virtue of being based on what we know to be true about the subject matter itself. Morality, however, provides a privileged illustration of our capacity for impersonal reflection. For what could be a more conspicuous expression of our ability to stand back from our own attachments, as though we were merely one person among many, than to consider other people's good as of equal moment with ours, particularly when it is to our personal disadvantage?

In this essay, I want to examine more deeply the way reflection serves as the source of our moral thinking. How is it that by viewing ourselves from without, we can learn to see others as having an equal claim on our attention? Reflection, as I have said, need not always assume an impersonal form. What, then, is involved in its coming to exhibit the sort of self-transcendence that morality demands? Obviously, the place to begin is the nature of reflection itself.

As may already be apparent, and will become plainer as I proceed, reflecting about what to believe does not, to my mind, differ substantially from reflecting about how to act—except, of course, in subject matter. Grand distinctions are often made between theoretical and practical reason, particularly in the Kantian tradition. But they are largely overdrawn. (In this regard too, as in many others, the rationalism I espouse departs radically from Kant's.) Reason is best understood as the ability to respond to reasons, be they reasons for belief or for action, and the point of reflection, as I shall explain, is to consider explicitly what we have reason to think or do in regard to some problem that has disrupted our settled routines. Though the relation between reflection and morality is my ultimate concern, the next two sections will therefore look at the nature of reflection along quite general lines. I will not be losing sight, however, of what is involved in reflecting about how to act. It is precisely this comprehensive approach that reveals the true character of practical reflection, the common structure and function it shares with reflection about what to think and believe. So far from the practical and the theoretical constituting two disparate realms, all reflection is essentially cognitive in nature, aiming at a knowledge of the reasons there are. This general account will guide the more specific analysis of moral thinking to which I then return in Sections IV and V. There my concern will be to show how our capacity for impersonal reflection shapes the makeup of the moral point of view, its preconditions and implications. Because this capacity sets us off so dramatically from all the other animals, morality can indeed be said to form a signal expression of our humanity.

II. The Nature of Reflection

It is characteristic of the human condition that we rarely exist at one with ourselves. Often we feel torn between competing commitments. Or no sooner do we make some decision of moment than we recall our doubts about whether a different option might not be better. To deliberate honestly is to risk having a mind divided, for our inner conflicts seldom amount to mere confusions, vanishing in the wake of a more careful scrutiny. Generally, they mirror the real complexity of our situation, the multiplicity of demands that rightly exercise a hold on our attention. Even when we conclude that we have good reason to take one path rather than another, we leave behind something of ourselves in the possibilities we reject.

Yet conflict is not the only or the deepest way in which we fail to coincide with ourselves. Even more fundamental is our continual alternation between doing and reflecting. We move back and forth between two standpoints, the view from within and the view from without. Because each of us has a life that is ours alone to live, we naturally approach the world in the light of the interests and allegiances that happen to be ours. So long as everything goes its customary way, we think and act from within our own perspective. Yet we are also often moved to reflect on our thought and action—not for the pure pleasure of doing so, but because some problem has emerged that puts into question the way we have been proceeding. We are no longer clear about the sort of person we are or about what we should believe or do with regard to some other matter. Reflection is the response to a problem, the attempt to reestablish a fit between expectation and reality.

Reflecting also means, however, ceasing to live our lives from within in order to look at ourselves from without. To be sure, we stand back so as to examine the particular difficulty that has arisen. But even if it is something quite circumscribed (some trait of ours and not the shape of our life as a whole), and even if it concerns an object distinct from us (the real character of someone else or the confusing nature of some natural or social phenomenon), it is still ourselves, and not merely the difficulty, that we regard from the outside. As a response to a problem that has disturbed our routine, reflection is always a turning back upon ourselves, since it aims to figure out what *we* are to do about the difficulty before us. It requires us, moreover, to look at ourselves *from without,* since ascertaining what we ought to do means discovering what solution we have *reason* to adopt. Because reasons are necessarily universal (if they are binding on one, then they are binding on all under similar conditions), we cannot determine how we should proceed except by considering what anyone in our shoes ought to do. Naturally, we do not forget that in the case at hand we are the target, since our question remains, "What should we do?" But we approach this question (in effect, if not in so many words) by asking ourselves how anyone like us ought to think or act. When we simply respond to reasons, without reflecting, we do not take this sort of detour. But deliberating about what reasons we may have is a different matter. That is the essence of reflection, and it requires us to regard ourselves as one person among others—from without, though not necessarily, as will become clear, from an impersonal distance.

Reflection, therefore, always involves self-distancing. It requires us to adopt a third-person attitude toward ourselves, as though we were a "him" or a "her." This fact, incidentally, points to an important truth about the pursuit of self-knowledge. Reflection need not have self-knowledge as its aim, of course, since often we reflect in order to discover what we should do or what we should believe about other matters in the world. When we do seek to know ourselves better, it is because some conflict has appeared between our conception of who we are and the behavior we notice, the desires we feel, or the unsettling remarks that others have made. And since we can only handle this problem by considering how someone like us ought to revise or deepen his self-understanding, we have no choice but to study ourselves as we would any other person, by collecting evidence and drawing inferences. Our knowledge of ourselves is then built up in the same empirical, trial-and-error way as our knowledge of others. We have no privileged access to the makeup of our own minds, which is why others can sometimes know us better than we do ourselves.[3]

There are, in fact, two distinct dimensions along which we objectify ourselves whenever we reflect. First, in order to get hold of the problem we have encountered, we must adopt toward our own person the same sort of observational stance we occupy toward others when, living our lives from within, we regard their thoughts and feelings as among the elements of our environment. We look at ourselves as someone with a certain problem to solve, and we may have to study its ins and outs with care. But, second, we cannot determine what we, as such a person, ought to do in response except from a standpoint of evaluation that consists, not in everything we happen to believe and want, but in the standards and assumptions we think ought to govern our decision. This is as much as to say that, in deliberating about how we are to proceed, we examine ourselves through the eyes of someone we imagine as embodying just such an evaluative standpoint. In effect, we ask what such a person would conclude that we should do. The two kinds of self-distancing are quite

[3] In my book *Les pratiques du moi* (Paris: Presses Universitaires de France, 2004), I discuss at greater length the nature of reflection and self-knowledge.

distinct, of course: in the one, we describe ourselves as we are; in the other, we figure out what we are to do. It is in the way they work together that reflection functions as it does. To reflect is not simply to contemplate our own person, as though gazing at our reflection in a mirror, which is what the first kind of self-distancing alone would entail. We turn our attention toward ourselves in order to handle some obstacle that has disrupted our relation to the world.

Despite these differences between living our lives from within and reflecting on them from without, it would obviously be wrong to suppose that reflection stands opposed to life, or that it constitutes a luxury we might choose to forgo. We become the persons we are through the problems we confront. There is no end to the need for standing back, and we live as much outside ourselves, thinking about what we should do, as within the various activities we do pursue. Indeed, little in the way we see the world around us fails to show the mark of what we have learned by reflecting. That is why a concern for others, though it has its roots in reflection, forms an important part of our everyday lives. Internalizing what we have learned, we come to act with an eye to the well-being of those—family, friends, and associates—about whom we care enough to have considered how they feel. Similarly, we incorporate into our dealings with others moral principles we have acquired by reflecting impartially on how one should, in general, treat one's fellow man. What I am calling the view from within is not essentially self-interested.

Nonetheless, the business of living easily keeps us in the pull of our own orbit. This we often discover if we happen to reflect anew. For reflection knows no inherent limits. It allows us to make out the ways in which the very habits of mind we have acquired by reflecting still remain tied to the particularities of our life. Thus, we recognize, on taking a broader view, that our various loyalties and loves are likely to matter little to others with their own lives to live, their own ties and causes. Even the moral principles we espouse may appear a bit parochial or biased, once we consider the extent to which they have been shaped by culture or class.

As I have previously remarked, reflection can proceed from more than one type of standpoint of evaluation. It need not aim at being impersonal—that is, at judging how we ought to think or act irrespective of our own interests and attachments. We may, for instance, base our evaluation of the options before us on what we imagine some individual (real or fictional) whom we hold dear would do in our place, or would want us to do. Philosophers tend to neglect this mode of reflection, perhaps because they believe themselves to be above it, but they are certainly wrong to do so. All of us lean from time to time on various exemplars, internalized heroes and idols, to figure out how we ought to think and act. Moreover, modeling ourselves on others is not in itself a vice, as though the proper course were always to think on our own. Everything depends on the worth of the models to which we appeal. Though it is often simple chance, or some special allure, that has led them to represent for us a kind of person we would like to be, this too is not necessarily deplorable. We may not have the time or the means to check their reliability. And even when we do, some particular trait of theirs may later prove instructive in ways we could not anticipate when confirming their general value.

So little is identifying with others an appropriate object of disapproval, it plays an essential role in our coming to grasp the impersonal point of view.[4] The capacity for reflection does not spring full-blown from any-one's head. It develops over time. In early life, reflection upon who we are and what we should do consists, quite naturally, in imagining what those who are close to us would say. As our horizons broaden and we discover that parents and friends disagree, we find ourselves impelled to devise more abstract angles of evaluation: thus, we come to examine ourselves by the standards of some larger community to which we feel bound. But the same factors tend to push us beyond that perspective as well. And thus we may eventually fashion the idea of a fully informed and perfectly rational standpoint, transcending the limitations in the attitudes of par-ticular individuals and societies—though, even then, identification is not at an end, since generally we do so by looking in our own culture for exemplars of such a standpoint to take as our models. Only through this sort of process do we learn what it is to hold ourselves accountable to an impersonal standard of thought and action. Only thus can we come to grasp the specifically moral point of view, which is to see in another's good, separately from our own interests and attachments, a reason for action on our part.

Nonetheless, whether we assume the outlook of some other individual, or reflect instead from an impersonal standpoint, certain elements remain constant. One is that reflection aims, in response to a problem, at deter-mining what we have reason to think or do. Reasons, as I have pointed out, are universal in character: if they are binding on us, then they are binding on all who find themselves in conditions similar to those that make them applicable to us. It follows that even when we reflect, not impersonally, but by identifying with the standpoint of someone we esteem, our conclusions are still ones we must assume that anyone like us ought to endorse in such a situation. That is not an awkward implication. For would we adopt that standpoint if we did not presume it to be attuned to how people should really behave who have interests like those that impel us to take it up? If I pattern my wardrobe on what some movie star wears, I am assuming that he knows how people who want to be cool ought to dress.

[4] Cf. Adam Smith, *The Theory of Moral Sentiments* (1759, 1790; Indianapolis, IN: Liberty Classics, 1976), part III, chapters 2–3, as well as George Herbert Mead, *Mind, Self, and Society* (Chicago: University of Chicago Press, 1934), part III.

Another constant is that, in reflecting, we have to rely on our current understanding of the world. We cannot regard ourselves from without except by continuing to think, at least in part, from within the perspective we presently occupy. Precisely because reflection is the response to a problem, it is always situated: only in the light of our existing views can we so much as identify the problem before us, and we cannot hope to handle it except by drawing upon the relevant information at our disposal. When we reflect by imagining what someone important to us would say, we make use (for example) of what we understand to be that person's characteristic habits of mind. So too, when we consider impersonally what we ought to think or do, we base our reasoning on the knowledge we have acquired, not only of the matter before us, but also, more broadly, of how belief should be proportioned to evidence or of how people are to be treated fairly. The impersonal point of view is not the view from nowhere. It always bears the mark of our time and place.

And yet, I must add, its claim to being impersonal does not thereby show itself to be a sham. Our access to reality as it is in itself is always mediated through the contingencies of history. This is not the place to enter into a discussion of epistemological questions, but the general position to which I am alluding is easily summarized.[5] Impersonal reasons, I have said, are reasons that stem solely from facts outside of us, uncolored by our own interests and attachments. Though reflecting on what impersonal reasons we have certainly entails appealing to our existing conception of those facts, our conclusions are still valid precisely to the extent that the beliefs on which we rely, for all their rootedness in the prior course of our experience, constitute knowledge of the matter at hand. To be sure, we may be wrong about the reliability of these beliefs. But that just means that our ideas concerning what impersonal reasons we have are always revisable, which is neither surprising nor ruinous. Impersonal reflection is, after all, an achievement, and, consequently, it is the subject of constant scrutiny for lingering traces of bias or distortion.

At this point, however, there arise some crucial questions. Does reflection, impersonal or not, really aim at truth? Is it an organ of knowledge, and if so, what can it provide knowledge *of*? These questions would appear to admit of a ready answer. We reflect in order to be better able to discern how we ought to think or act in the given circumstances, and that seems clearly to count as an object of knowledge. For it is something of which we begin by feeling ignorant and seek, by reflecting, to gain a correct grasp. What we ought to do is tantamount to what there is reason for us to do. So reflection, in essence, aims at knowledge of reasons for belief and action.

---

[5] For a closer discussion, see Charles Larmore, *The Autonomy of Morality* (Cambridge: Cambridge University Press, 2008), chapter 1, "History and Truth."

Such a conception results from taking literally the way we ordinarily talk about reflection, and in my view it ought to be no cause for alarm. But many disagree. In their eyes, it entails an untenable metaphysics and is, in any case, untrue to the nature of reflection. To suppose that reflection's relation to reasons is one of knowledge means not only attributing to the world a domain of irreducibly normative fact, but also imagining that knowledge by itself could ever move us to action as reflection manifestly does. Belief by itself is motivationally inert, and can lead us to act only in conjunction with some additional, conative element of the mind, such as a desire or a commitment. Reflection, it is therefore claimed, is a practical rather than a theoretical enterprise: when we reflect on what we have reason to do, our purpose is to settle how we want to live, not to discover some fact about the world. To this set of claims I now turn.

III. Reflection and Knowledge

Reasons for belief and action are essentially normative in character. What we have reason to do is what we *ought* to do, all else being equal. There is no explaining what is meant by reasons except by appeal to this or similar ways of speaking. Reasons cannot therefore be equated with any features of the natural world, physical or psychological, even though they certainly depend on the natural facts being as they are. That is why many philosophers balk at allowing that reasons can properly count as objects of knowledge. If knowledge is of what is the case independently of our coming to hold a view about it, then supposing that reasons figure among the things we can know entails that the world, as the totality of what is the case, must include normative facts about how we ought to think and act. Such a view runs counter to the naturalism that constitutes the reigning philosophical orthodoxy of our day. All that really exists, it is said, belongs to the domain of the natural sciences, the realm of physical fact or of psychological fact too, if the latter is not further reducible to the physical. As should be plain, I reject this sort of naturalism. But my main business here is to clarify the character of reasons and to explain why we should conceive of reflection as a way of acquiring knowledge about them.[6]

Consider then, first, why it is that a reason cannot consist in a physical state of affairs. We sometimes say that the rain, or the fact that it is raining, is a reason to take an umbrella when leaving the house. Strictly speaking, however, my reason to do so is not the rain itself, but rather a certain relation that the rain bears to my possibilities of action. After all, one might agree that it is raining, yet dispute that this fact gives me a reason to take an umbrella. Only insofar as the rain justifies or counts in

---

[6] A more detailed version of the following argument is presented in Larmore, *The Autonomy of Morality*, chapter 5, especially sections 7–8.

favor of carrying an umbrella does it take on the status of a reason, and this status—the relation of *counting in favor of*—is not a physical quality of the rain. It is a *normative* attribute. "The rain is a reason to take an umbrella" means the same as "Given the rain, I *ought* to take an umbrella." To be sure, other things may count in favor of not taking one, of wearing a hat instead, or of just getting wet. As a rule, reasons are in themselves *pro tanto*, as are the "ought"s to which they correspond. Only if they are not outweighed by contrary considerations do they indicate what we overall have reason or ought to do. The point is that, whether *pro tanto* or decisive, reasons are not identical with the physical facts that may give rise to them.

So too, the reason people have to believe this or do that is not the same as any psychological state in which they find themselves. In particular, it is not, contrary to a widespread view, a combination of belief and desire.[7] My reason to take an umbrella, some would say, consists in my belief that it is raining conjoined with my desire to keep dry. But that cannot be right. It may be true that I would not have such a reason unless I wanted to stay dry, so that in this respect the reason is indeed conditional, binding only insofar as I have that desire. (Though it can also make perfect sense to say that I ought to take an umbrella against the rain whether I want to keep dry or not.) Even so, the reason does not consist in the desire as such, but rather in the fact that the desire counts in favor of taking an umbrella. After all, I might have the desire and still have no reason to take one, if, for example, the rain—unbeknownst to me—has ceased. Moreover, what makes it true that the desire favors that action is not my belief that it is raining, as though the reason were constituted by that belief conjoined in some appropriate way with the desire. The reason to take an umbrella depends in no way on my believing that it is raining. It is the fact that it is raining that gives rise to the reason. If you learned that the weather had just improved, you would inform me that I really have no reason to fetch my umbrella, even though clearly I still believe it is raining. In short, a reason is the possible object of a belief and not itself a mental state.[8]

Recognizing that the reasons we *have* cannot consist in anything psychological, some have nonetheless supposed that the reasons that *move* us

[7] The classic statement of such a doctrine is Donald Davidson, "Actions, Reasons, and Causes" (1963), reprinted in Davidson, *Essays on Actions and Events* (Oxford: Oxford University Press, 1980), 3–19.

[8] "Internal" reasons, as Bernard Williams famously defined them, are reasons we would come to grasp, were we to deliberate soundly on the basis of our present beliefs and desires. See Williams, "Internal and External Reasons," in Williams, *Moral Luck* (Cambridge: Cambridge University Press, 1981), 101–13. Whether or not such reasons are, as he claimed, the only sorts of reasons we can rightly be said to have, they are not (contrary to what the term suggests) anything "in" the mind. When we conclude that our present convictions give us a reason to believe this or to do that, we do not think we have discovered a fact about our own psychology. For the reason does not derive from our having those convictions, but from what those convictions are about. What they are about, not the convictions in and of themselves, is after all the object of our deliberation.

must belong to the mind. How else could it be said that reasons cause us to act? Whence a common distinction between "normative" reasons, which serve to justify an action, and "motivating" reasons, which are invoked to explain it.[9] Yet there are not in reality two different kinds of reasons. Talking about reasons as though they were motivating states in the mind is a bit of shorthand. Strictly speaking, the reference is to our view of the reasons we have, since in such cases only this attitude of ours, not the actual existence of those reasons, is thought relevant to the sort of explanation being sought. But the reasons we believe there to be are the reasons that appear to us to justify what we do. So-called motivational reasons, understood as psychological states moving us to act, are no more than our conception of the normative reasons we have. Moreover, sometimes there actually being such reasons, and not just our thinking they exist, does play an explanatory role—as when it turns out that we did the right thing for in fact the right reason. In such cases, reasons themselves lead us to act, via our correct ideas of them.

It is, then, their essentially normative character that precludes identifying reasons with any physical or psychological facts. As a consequence, they can have no place in the world itself as naturalistically conceived. This, as I have said, is one main line of argument leading many philosophers to deny, either implicitly or as a matter of doctrine, that reflection about what we ought to think or do can rightly count as a mode of knowledge. Conclusions about the reasons we have are not, it is held, really descriptive in intent, but serve instead to embody or announce our commitments for dealing with the world around us. After all, and this is meant to be a corroborating argument, knowledge alone cannot move us to act, as reflection is geared to do. The judgments we make about what we ought to think or do are practical, not theoretical, in nature.

It is a sign of how thoroughly modern philosophy has absorbed the naturalistic worldview that the otherwise rival schools of Hume and of Kant, which occupy so much of the terrain, are each impelled to embrace this view of reflection. Expressivists in the Humean tradition construe normative judgments of the form "A ought to X," not as aiming to describe correctly the reasons A has, but as simply expressing our acceptance of a norm entailing that A conduct himself thus in the given circumstances.[10] Reflection is seen as charged with making clear to ourselves what norms we want in this sense to endorse, or what the norms we do endorse entail in a given situation. Kantians may differ from Humeans in their eagerness to deduce internal constraints governing the sorts of rules we can in this way coherently make our own—constraints that supposedly amount to the basic features of morality. But they agree that reasons cannot form

[9] See, for example, Michael Smith, *The Moral Problem* (Oxford: Blackwell, 1994), 94ff.
[10] Allan Gibbard, *Wise Choices, Apt Feelings* (Cambridge, MA: Harvard University Press, 1990).

part of reality itself. What we have reason to think or do is determined by principles of thought and action that we impose upon ourselves. Only through our own "autonomy," that is, self-legislation, can the value-neutral facts of experience acquire significance for our conduct. "The ethics of autonomy is the only one consistent with the metaphysics of the modern world."[11]

This widespread view of reasons and reflection is indeed driven by metaphysical assumptions. For naturalism, one should remember, is not a conclusion of the modern natural sciences themselves, which do not claim that they exhaust all that can count as real. Global assertions of that sort are the province of philosophy. Now I have no objection to metaphysics as such. But I do complain when metaphysical preconceptions contradict fundamental aspects of our everyday self-understanding. Such is the case here. The notion of reasons espoused by expressivists and Kantians alike can make no sense of what it is to reflect or even to reason.

Expressivists often focus on morality alone, even though their task is to explain the nature of normative judgment in general. It may seem plausible that moral judgments do no more than express a certain kind of approval or disapproval of their object, given the ease with which some people can persuade themselves that moral distinctions are ultimately of our own creation. But expressivism looks far less palatable when stated in its properly universal form. Can we really believe that the canons by which we judge whether a scientific theory is true—its fit with experimental data, its coherence with existing doctrine, its performance on severe tests—have only the authority we bestow on them? If we hold that there is good reason to adhere to such principles, are we only expressing our endorsement of a norm to the effect that everyone (ourselves included) ought to abide by them whether one happens to want to or not? Does our endorsing such a norm explain what it is to regard those principles as valid? If we were not constrained by an allegiance to naturalism, we would surely suppose that the order of explanation is the other way around. It is the perceived validity of the principles that accounts for why we think anyone ought to adhere to them and to endorse a norm to this effect.

Denying that we reflect in order to discover something we do not yet know—namely, what there is reason to think or do in the given circumstances—renders the process of reflection unrecognizable. In fact, the underlying refusal to countenance the reality of reasons distorts the very nature of reason, as we can observe if we look at the parallel

---

[11] So says Christine Korsgaard, one of the most important neo-Kantians of our day, in Korsgaard, *The Sources of Normativity* (Cambridge: Cambridge University Press, 1996), 5. For a more extensive version of the following critique of Korsgaard, see Larmore, *The Autonomy of Morality*, chapter 5, sections 6, 8. I find much to endorse in Derek Parfit's similar criticisms, as developed in his essay "Normativity," in *Oxford Studies in Metaethics*, vol. 1, ed. Russ Shafer-Landau (Oxford: Oxford University Press, 2006), 325–80.

Kantian notion of autonomy. Kantians think of reason as self-legislating, as giving itself principles of conduct, intellectual and practical, in the light of which alone facts in the world can acquire the status of being reasons to think and act in certain ways.[12] But reason, like any faculty of mind, is to be defined in terms of the activity that is its characteristic exercise. What then could be more obvious than that *reason* is the faculty of *reasoning*? And how else can the activity of reasoning be understood except in terms of its being responsive to *reasons*? The most straightforward account of the nature of reason presumes, therefore, that reasons are a reality we discover, not an artifact of our ways of thinking. To be sure, we do sometimes impose rules on ourselves whose authority is of our own making. But we do so precisely because there appear to be reasons that warrant this step. If I give myself a rule never to borrow, it is in virtue of both knowing how prone I am to borrow more than I can pay back and accepting the antecedent authority of the principle that debts are to be repaid. Autonomy makes no sense as a global account of reasons.

Yet what of the counterargument that figuring out what reasons we have cannot consist in discovering some further facts about the way things are? Beliefs purport to represent the facts as they are, but beliefs alone, so it is held, cannot move us to act, as the results of reflection typically do. Thus, when we conclude that we have reason to act in a particular way, we are not reporting a discovery but rather expressing our confidence that the conduct in question satisfies or promotes our existing needs, interests, or commitments: "the word 'reason' refers to a kind of reflective success."[13] Reasons, it is said, are the outcome of reflection when carried out well, not a reality to which reflection responds: what we have reason to think or do is what we can coherently endorse as we put our thinking in order.

This line of argument is a mainstay of both the Kantian and Humean traditions. Yet for all its popularity, it is rather poor. First, one might note that people (and other animals too) often act for reasons without reflecting. A more telling objection is that endorsing some option on the basis of our existing convictions depends on supposing that they justify this decision—that they indeed give us reason to endorse the option. Reasons cannot be simply the output of reflective success, since success in reflecting consists precisely in how well we respond to the reasons that there are.

---

[12] Such is the way Korsgaard defines her "procedural moral realism," in contrast to a "substantive" realism that regards reasons as a reality to which our reasoning responds (Korsgaard, *The Sources of Normativity*, 36). I caution that the sense of "autonomy" in question is the one for which Kant coined the term and which concerns our relation to the reasons for which we think and act. It is not the sense that has to do with our relation to other people, as when it is said that autonomous agents decide matters for themselves instead of being impelled by custom or coercion. Autonomy in this latter sense is not my concern here.

[13] Korsgaard, *The Sources of Normativity*, 93.

However, the underlying error lies deeper still. It is a flawed conception of belief. Conclusions about reasons certainly serve to guide our conduct. Yet this does not mean that they cannot have the character of beliefs. For belief by itself is not in fact motivationally inert. Consider what it is, in general, to believe this or that. A belief is not a feeling (say, the particular vivacity with which an idea stands before the mind), nor is it the act of assenting to some proposition. It is a disposition, and one intimately connected with both the presumed truth of what is believed (since to believe that p means to believe that p is true) and with the behavior of the person whose belief it is (since we attribute beliefs to people in order to explain what they do). To believe that p is to be disposed to think and act in accord with the presumed truth of p. A person who has said he believes that the cat is on the mat, yet walks across the mat as though nothing were there, will not normally be held to believe what he has said he believes. To be sure, the specific things a belief disposes someone to do depend on other elements in his outlook, just as it is true that one sometimes fails to heed a belief one has. So the person in question may have his reasons for ignoring the cat or may be tramping across the mat out of inadvertence. But if he believes the cat is there, then he will be moved, all other things being equal, to comport himself compatibly with what, in his view, the truth of that belief implies. Beliefs do not merely represent the way things are or consist in holding certain facts to be true. They are at once descriptive and prescriptive. Being disposed to draw appropriate inferences from what we believe is an inherent part of believing. In other words, beliefs are commitments in their own right, commitments to think and act in accord with the presumed truth of what is believed.

Thus, reflection can very well aim at discovering what we have reason to do at the same time as it serves to guide us in how to live. Its goal is to arrive at correct beliefs about the reasons we have, beliefs which themselves, like all beliefs, commit us to conducting ourselves accordingly. Reflection is inseparably both theoretical and practical.

IV. THE REALITY OF REASONS

So far, I have been arguing, negatively, against the idea that reflection cannot be an organ of knowledge. But I have yet to explain what sort of reality is constituted by the reasons for thought and action which are the objects of reflection. Here I must be brief.[14] If reasons belong to the fabric of reality, they are not, to be sure, some sort of independent entities, hovering alongside the more down-to-earth things we see and touch. As I have already suggested, reasons consist in a certain *relation*—the relation

---

[14] For more detail, see Larmore, *The Autonomy of Morality*, chapter 3 and chapter 5, sections 7–8.

of *counting in favor of*—that features of the natural world, the physical and psychological facts making it up, bear to our possibilities of thought and action. This is a normative relation, and thus reasons cannot be equated with anything in nature. Yet, being relational, they manifestly depend on the existence of what they relate, and that means they depend on the natural (physical and psychological) facts being as they are, as well as on our having possibilities of thought and action. In this sense, therefore, reasons exist only because we do too, and it would certainly be bizarre to think otherwise. It does not follow, however, that we are the authors of the reasons there are, that they amount to the significance we bestow upon those facts. That one thing counts in favor of another is a relation (a normative relation) that we discover, that we can be right or wrong about, not one we institute ourselves. Relations are in general no less real than the things they relate when they enjoy this sort of independence from our beliefs about their existence and nature. Thus, reasons, too, form part of the world, understood broadly as the totality of what exists.

This conception may rightly be called "Platonistic," since it holds that reasons, like Plato's Forms, constitute an intrinsically normative order of reality. But it is not an extravagant kind of Platonism. It does not suppose that reasons dwell in some Platonic heaven, unsullied by the contingencies of the world here below. On the contrary, this account follows closely our ordinary sense of what reasons are. When we suppose, as we ordinarily do, that how we ought to think and act is a matter of how the facts bear on the options before us, what we mean, in effect, is that reasons for belief and action are both relational and real. And when we conclude, in particular, that we have an impersonal reason to do something, what we mean is that the facts in and of themselves count in favor of that option, apart from our own interests and attachments. Theories that reduce reasons to an expression of our commitments have to devise formulas to mimic these ways of talking without taking them literally, and it is not surprising that the simulation never quite succeeds.[15]

Not only do reasons not exist independently of the natural world or of us in particular, they also do not exist independently of one another. Reasons bear various logical and evidential connections to one another. Sometimes the reason we have to do one thing is contingent on our having a reason to do another, as when, thinking we have reason to believe the noise

[15] According to Gibbard, for instance, to say that we have a reason to do X independently of our interests and attachments is to mean that we accept both a norm requiring us to do X and a (higher-order) norm requiring us to accept that norm whether we want to or not (Gibbard, *Wise Choices, Apt Feelings*, 155–70). Now, is our supposed acceptance of this higher-order norm a brute fact or mere decision, or is the norm instead one we ought or have reason to accept? Only the latter will allow this analysis to keep pace with what is meant by an impersonal reason to do X. And yet Gibbard must analyze this alternative, in turn, as our acceptance of a still higher-order norm requiring us to accept the first higher-order norm whether we want to or not. The Gibbardian theory is constantly chasing after the idea of impersonality without ever catching up.

behind the bushes is a wild boar, we conclude that we have reason to climb up a nearby tree. And sometimes the reason to do a certain thing is, in essence, the application to particular circumstances of a far broader and standing reason—in other words, a principle—governing how we ought, in general, to comport ourselves. Thus, the reason we have to save part of our income, perhaps to buy a second home or to retire in some comfort, depends on our having more generally reason to be prudent and think about our long-term good.

What, then, about the relation between moral reasons and the other sorts of considerations that move us to act? It has often been thought, both in everyday life and in moral philosophy, that acting morally needs to be shown to be ultimately in the agent's own best interest. The idea goes back to Glaucon's appeal to Socrates at the beginning of Book II of Plato's *Republic* (357b): "Prove to us that it is better in every way to be just rather than unjust." Only if the reason to concern ourselves with another's good can be derived from the presumably more basic reason we have to pursue our own good can morality really be authoritative for our conduct. The philosophical proofs have taken many different forms, depending on how both the agent's good and practical rationality have been conceived. Plato had Socrates respond to the challenge by arguing that "justice" or morality alone ensures the harmony of the soul to which we each ultimately aspire. The more common version in our own day has followed the lead of Thomas Hobbes, arguing that the adoption of principles of mutual restraint and cooperation is the most efficient means for each individual to satisfy his own interests over the long run, whatever they may be, given the essentials of the human condition.

This is not the place to evaluate in detail these various attempts to show how we may reason ourselves into the moral point of view from a standpoint located outside it and presumed to be more basic.[16] Let me observe here, not only that they all fail (for that is well known), but that they fail in two distinct ways. They do not succeed in explaining how the moral "ought" derives from the "ought" of individual prudence, duly enlightened. Even more importantly, the very understanding of morality on which they rely is typically defective, since it is slanted to fit the extra-moral starting point they invoke.

Consider the Hobbesian approach, as developed in our time by a great many writers. It conceives of morality as a set of rules for social cooperation, founded upon mutual advantage. The limits these rules place on the pursuit of our own ends are held to maximize our good in the long run through the interactions they permit with others, provided that others, too, comply with these restraints. Yet such a view

---

[16] See Larmore, *The Autonomy of Morality*, chapter 5, sections 1-6. There I examine, among other attempts, David Gauthier's version of the Hobbesian argument; a summary of my objections appears in the next two paragraphs.

excludes from the domain of moral concern two groups of people whom it is the business of morality to move us to treat better than we would otherwise be inclined to do: those unlikely to come into frequent contact with us and thus ever to contribute to our good, and those with neither the power nor the ability to enhance or jeopardize our interests in any way, however often we may cross their path. Morality conceived as a cooperative scheme for mutual benefit fails to embody so fundamental a norm as the respect we owe to *strangers* and to *the weak*. This is not, moreover, a failure to account for some marginal phenomena, to be remedied by further refining the theory. For surely it belongs to the very core of our moral thinking that we are to show equal respect to those who, through circumstance or misfortune, may never be in a position to benefit us in return. Indeed, we act toward the powerful and the useful in a moral and not merely prudent fashion, when we behave as we would even if they lacked those assets that make them of interest to our own endeavors. We aim then to treat them with the respect they deserve as human beings, not with the sort of circumspection we exercise in dealing with the various natural forces for good and ill in our environment.

The Hobbesian idea of morality reflects the notion of the rational agent, concerned to pursue his own interests as efficiently as possible, that Hobbesians take as their point of departure for showing how we can reason ourselves into morality. That is why this idea is so distorted. For if, as I have assumed from the outset (and will explain more thoroughly in the next section), the moral point of view consists in seeing in another's good, in and of itself, a reason for action on our part, then how could it ever come within reach of a person whose reasoning focuses essentially on satisfying his own interests? Let these interests be other-directed as well as self-directed; it does not matter. There is all the difference in the world between respecting or fostering another's good because one has among one's interests a particular attachment to that person, and doing so simply because that person's good is in question. It is the latter, the impersonally motivated act, that embodies the properly moral attitude. Every attempt to bring the moral point of view within the orbit of the rational pursuit of one's own concerns is bound to erase its most distinctive feature, which is the concern we conceive for another's good just because it is his or hers.

We cannot, then, reason ourselves into an appreciation of what it is to act morally, beginning from some location outside the moral point of view. Morality has to speak for itself. It constitutes a class of reasons for action that is *sui generis,* unintelligible in terms of any supposedly more primitive class of reasons. This fact ought not to be disturbing, though it does have an important philosophical consequence.

To understand why it does not make a mystery of moral thinking, consider the case of prudence—precisely the form of reasoning in which philosophers (and no doubt others too) feel a hankering to ground morality. How would we go about changing the mind of someone who perceives no reason to be prudent, no reason to take into account, in deciding what to do, the desires that he will predictably have later even if they are not his at the moment? We might have some luck by exposing the erroneous assumptions that keep him perhaps from recognizing the value of prudence (such as the notion that reasons for action can be but the expression of one's given desires). But if negative arguments of this sort do not work, what else can we do? There can be no prospect of reasoning him into an acceptance of prudential reasons by appealing to some deeper set of motivations he could be presumed to possess. What would such an argument look like? That it is in his interest to be prudent? That is hopelessly circular. The fact is that prudence is just like morality: it constitutes a class of *sui generis* reasons for action, underivable from any more basic sorts of considerations.

Herein lies an important philosophical lesson, not just about morality, but about reflection in general. If we are to move the person who has been stubbornly refusing to listen to the voice of prudence, we can only say something like: "Think about what you will surely want one year from now. Don't you see that you ought to act accordingly?" In the end, people just have to acknowledge that there exist reasons of prudence. There is no way they can be led to reason themselves from some external standpoint into a sense of the value of prudence. So, too, with morality. We simply have to see that another's good is, in itself, a reason for action on our part. Reflection does not always proceed, then, by inferring some reasons from others with which are already familiar. It also includes the power of acknowledging the force of reasons that speak for themselves. Such is the kind of reflection that deep shifts in our thinking typically require.

This conclusion may seem to contradict my earlier insistence (in Section II) that our capacity for reflection develops as we mature. But that is not so. When we are young, as I said, reflecting means taking up the standpoint (or what we imagine to be the standpoint) of those to whom we feel close, judging ourselves and our possibilities accordingly. As our horizons broaden and we encounter conflicts among our various loyalties, we are moved to work out less partisan standards of evaluation. Thus, we develop an ability to reflect impersonally on what we ought to believe and do. Yet though this process takes place step by step, it does not consist in grasping how our various interests and attachments, along with the desire to handle the tensions among them, point us to reasons for belief and action that are impersonal in character. The capacity of reflection is one thing; its objects are another. We learn to stand back from our individual commitments so as to view the world as it is in itself. But this achievement by itself leaves open what reasons, if any, we then discover about how we are to think and act. To see what reasons there are, we must actually reflect. After all, when we realize that our own good does not, absolutely speaking, matter more than the good of others, we might perhaps conclude that therefore neither theirs nor ours matter at all. Being impartial has been known more than once to produce indifference.

Some will urge that if we are not to remain indifferent, we must care about how people in general fare. This is true. Yet the ready appeal to feelings does little to illuminate the matter. For why would we care, if not that we see some reason to do so? The point at issue is precisely how we come to discern such a reason. It is not, I have argued, by determining what in the long run or in the deepest sense will serve our own good. If there is a reason to care about the good of others in and of itself, it has to be one that speaks for itself when we view the world impersonally. But it is also true that impersonal reflection must look in the right place. We need, in particular, to focus not on the fact that from the standpoint of the universe no one's good matters much at all, but on the fact that each person's good matters enormously from his own perspective.

V. The Moral Point of View

Such then are the basic features of reflection, its modalities and aims. We reflect in order to figure out what we ought to think or do in response to a problem that has disrupted our usual ways of dealing with the world. To find a solution, we stand back from how we have gone on before, looking at ourselves from the outside and appraising our options from a standpoint we consider authoritative for the problem before us. The explicit object now before our mind is what we have reason to think or do, and the reasons we seek to discover are by definition *universal:* if they are valid for us, then they are valid for all under similar circumstances. They are, in addition, *impersonal* if they are reasons we can grasp as binding on us independently of our own interests and attachments.

With this framework in place, it is time to return to the main theme. We are moral beings, I have said, because of the remarkable power of self-transcendence that reflection makes possible when it becomes impersonal. We can learn how to stand back from our own concerns so as to be able to see in another's good, in and of itself, a reason for action on our part. The preceding analysis has shown what is involved in reflection taking on an impersonal form. But much more needs to be said about the role that impersonal reflection plays in our moral thinking.

I have not, for instance, explained what sort of being this "other" is whose good appears from the moral point of view as an intrinsic object of concern. Is it any human being as such, or is it more broadly all living beings, animals and even plants included, that may be considered to possess a good? How widely does our moral responsibility extend? I have been assuming that it encompasses every human being, and that is the assumption in all that follows. But I do not suppose that our moral concern should stop at the boundaries of humanity. As to how far it should extend, I have no systematic answer, and I believe moreover that we should not be in a rush to devise one. Uncertainty about the scope of our moral responsibility seems to me in keeping with the present intellectual situation. For plainly those traditional answers will not do that equate the objects of moral concern with those who are themselves able to take up the moral point of view. Such is the approach adopted whenever one conceives of morality as a set of rules for social cooperation (as in the Hobbesian tradition) or as a system of reciprocal claims rational agents make upon one another (as in the Kantian tradition). And the approach fails because it cannot even attribute to all human beings a moral standing in their own right—not to infants, not to the mentally disabled, not to the doddering elderly, which with the advances of modern medicine we all have a good chance of becoming. At best, it can award such people only a derivative status, dependent on what is owed to their morally functioning trustees. Surely, then, the domain of moral concern must extend beyond the domain of moral agents, and how far it reaches is a question at the frontiers of moral thinking today.[17]

What I do want to discuss in some detail here is the relation itself between impersonal reflection and morality. On several different scores, one might in fact dispute whether so intimate a connection exists between the two as I have been asserting. Does the essence of the moral point of view really consist in recognizing that the good of another, purely by virtue of being a person's good, is of equal moment with our own?

It will help to review the position I have assumed. There is, in general, more than one basis on which we can see in another's good a reason for us to act in some way, to refrain from doing what might otherwise prove attractive or even to do what we can to help him to achieve his good. We may, for instance, hope that thereby the person, or others happening to witness our behavior, will treat us well in return. Or we may feel a special bond of affection for the person—a relative, friend, or coreligionist perhaps—and on this basis put his good at the center of our attention. Finally, however, we may act so as to respect or foster another's good without an eye to our own interests and attachments but simply because someone's well-being is at stake. The person may not be anyone we know or suppose we will ever meet again, or he may be an individual to whom we do have some particular tie but whose situation and needs we are considering apart from that bond. In either case, the reason we then recognize to care about the other's good is impersonal in character, and this sort of thinking—such has been my refrain—constitutes the heart of the moral point of view. It can become a matter of habit, and that is quite desirable. Yet not only do we acquire this sort of concern for others by

---

[17] Cf. Martha Nussbaum, *The Frontiers of Justice* (Cambridge, MA: Harvard University Press, 2006). I should note that I am talking here about our moral thinking, and not about political life, for which, unlike Nussbaum, I hold that a principle of respect for persons understood as being able to think and act for reasons should be determinative. (See, e.g., Larmore, *The Autonomy of Morality*, chapter 6.)

learning to reflect impersonally, but we need continually to reflect anew, exercising the same capacity of distancing ourselves from our own interests and attachments to survey the possibilities before us, if we are to monitor and refine our moral outlook on the world.

Now one might immediately object that this conception of morality is a highly contentious one. Does not its insistence on impersonality and the need to stand back from our own concerns signal an allegiance, for all my rejection of the idea of autonomy (in Section III), to the rigoristic distinction between duty and inclination typical of Kantian ethics? In large part, this objection is a misunderstanding. I have so far said little about moral feelings such as sympathy, but my aim has not been to deny their importance when we take an intrinsic interest in another person's good. Contrary to Kant, moral character does not show through most when one does what is right despite "being cold in temperament and indifferent to the sufferings of others," [18] since there is nothing much left for moral character to be, given that sort of insensibility. Our thinking about right and wrong takes shape through experience in the way I sketched earlier (in Section II). We handle the conflicts between our various allegiances by learning to consider others from a wider perspective, and this process involves a generalization of the ability to care about how another fares that we first acquire in our relations to those who are close to us. But it is crucial to understand rightly the role feelings play. To sympathize with the pain or joy of others, at least insofar as morality is concerned, is not to feel their pain or joy ourselves, as though by a sort of contagion; it is to feel sadness *at* their suffering, delight *at* their happiness, a second-order feeling in which we express our sense that they have *reason* to feel as they do. Sympathy consists in being moved by the good of others. It therefore remains narrower than it might otherwise be, so long as it is filtered through our own interests and attachments. Feelings come to have a moral role precisely to the extent that they take us out of ourselves, and in this way they become indeed impersonal.

Nothing, then, in the conception of morality on which I have been leaning appears peculiarly Kantian. In fact, if I had to cite a single source of inspiration, it would not be Kant, but rather Scripture—though I hasten to add that my agenda is strictly secular. In both the Hebrew Bible and the New Testament, we meet the precept, "Love thy neighbor as thyself." [19] It contains, I believe, a profound insight into the true character of moral thinking. All of us by nature love ourselves, caring immensely whether our desires are satisfied and whether our lives go as we would like.

---

[18] Immanuel Kant, *Grundlegung der Metaphysik der Sitten* (*Groundwork of the Metaphysics of Morals*) (1785), Akademie-Ausgabe (Berlin: Reimer, 1900-), vol. IV, 398–99.

[19] Leviticus 19:18; Matthew 19:19, 22:39; Mark 12:31. Note that this precept is quite different from the Golden Rule of doing unto others as we would have them do unto us (Matthew 7:12), at least when the latter is understood as a norm of reciprocity, for then it ties our treatment of others to what would be conducive to our own interests.

Obviously, this self-love often stands in the way of our caring about others as we should. Yet it also offers a paradigm of what a concern for others would be like if we were to look beyond our own sphere—beyond, that is, our individual interests as well as the interests of those who matter to us because of their special connection to ourselves. For the conspicuous feature of self-love is not so much its magnitude as its immediacy. The concern we feel for our own good is not channeled through other considerations: we do not care about how our own lives go because we are someone to whom we feel particularly close, or because we hope that we will secure from ourselves some benefit in return. Each of us cares quite simply because "it's me!" Suppose, then, that we care about another's good in the same direct, unmediated way, solely because it is his or her good. That would be, in the Biblical phrase, to "love thy neighbor as thyself," or, in the more analytic language I have used, to see in another's good, in and of itself, a reason for action on our part. Such, I claim, is the core of morality.

Two other features of this conception should also be noted, again to avoid misunderstanding. The first is that it does not assume that the demands of morality are supremely authoritative. To see in another's good a claim on our attention no less direct than the claim made by our own does involve regarding these claims as essentially equal—differing only in the importance and urgency of what is at stake, and not in our happening to be one of the persons involved. The moral point of view consists in seeing oneself as but one person among others. Yet it does not follow that the morally best action is always the one that, all things considered, we have most reason to do. We become moral beings by learning to recognize in another's good, in and of itself, a reason for action on our part. But that means that we must, in given situations, weigh such reasons against the other sorts of reasons we perceive, reasons that may favor our own interests or attachments. There is, I believe, no general principle that can plausibly inform us how to handle every such case, certainly none that can convince us that morality has to override all other concerns. Philosophers in the Kantian tradition have often tried to show that morality possesses supreme authority, but generally they have proceeded by supposing that reason must give itself its own principles of action, arguing then that the conditions under which it can coherently do so amount to the self-legislation of basic moral norms. If instead, as I have argued (in Section III), reason consists essentially in a responsiveness to reasons, then there can be no such *a priori* guarantee that the claims of morality must prove paramount. We have to consider the particularities of the situation at hand.

Thus, to invoke an example made famous by Bernard Williams, if we can rescue from imminent death only one of two people and one happens to be our spouse, it would appear to be "one thought too many" were we to rush toward our spouse, not solely out of love, but also with the idea that it is morally permissible in such a situation to favor the people we love, or even (as a utilitarian might hold) that devotion to loved ones is generally the best means for each individual to maximize the general good.[20] In cases such as this, requiring an impersonal justification for our response, of the sort provided by morality, is worse than superfluous. It casts considerable doubt on the genuineness of our love. Morality need not be our ultimate standpoint of evaluation. Sometimes other things rightly matter a lot more. Only the moralistic believe that being moral means always putting morality first.

A second misunderstanding would be to suppose that if the moral point of view consists in seeing everyone's good as of equal moment, acting morally must therefore amount to acting so as to bring about the most good overall. That is not so. Nothing inherently favors this sort of "consequentialist" position. On the contrary, the moral point of view is in itself mute about how exactly we are to advance the good of others and adjudicate the competing claims they make on our attention. Principles of moral reasoning have to be introduced to make the moral point of view operational.

One principle is aggregative: giving equal consideration to each person's good can be taken to mean that, in effect, we should consider each person impartially as we determine what will most increase the total good of all. That is precisely the consequentialist approach. But it is wrong to think, like many philosophers, that if we have a concern for other people's good, then wanting to bring about as much of it as possible is the only step that makes sense. We could instead resolve to respect each person's good as precious in its own right. Another principle is thus distributive: if each person's good is to be treated equally—at least in ways that protect and foster his very ability to have and pursue a conception of his good—then it ought not to be compromised or sacrificed even for the sake of ensuring a greater good for others. This is the underlying rationale of deontological theories, which define what we owe to a given person, the treatment we should (as in keeping a promise) and should never (as in doing violence) accord him, without regard to how we could otherwise act so as to benefit others or to what others might do in response to our action.

It is clear that these two ways of thinking are not the same and can lead to very different judgments about what to do. But it is also clear that sometimes the one and sometimes the other seems the natural approach to take. When a great number of people may be affected and their needs are particularly urgent, satisfying the needs of as many as possible—in other words, bringing about the most good overall—easily looks like the

---

[20] Bernard Williams, "Persons, Character, and Morality," in Williams, *Moral Luck* (Cambridge: Cambridge University Press, 1981), 17–19. In this essay, Williams was not as clear as he should have been that the problem is not with the conception of morality as impersonal, but rather with the belief that moral considerations are always supreme.

path to adopt. But when that is not the case, or when helping the many entails doing significant harm to some, respecting the integrity of the individual tends to square better with our conscience. Sometimes, of course, we find ourselves unsure about whether, in the given situation, the one or the other stance is more appropriate. I do not believe that we should try to settle, in a general way, which of these two basic principles of moral reasoning, consequentialist or deontological, defines the single correct theory of morality. Each of them is a plausible interpretation of what the moral point of view means in practice. That is why it can so often appear right, depending on the situation, to base our actions on the one instead of on the other. We do better, then, to recognize their common validity as well as their capacity to conflict.[21]

What ought not to be lost sight of, however, is that both the consequentialist and deontological principles have their basis in the impersonal perspective in which each person's good presents itself as constituting an equal reason for concern on our part. It is not that they can somehow be derived from that perspective or that their content can be explicated in terms of that perspective alone. But they presuppose it and are not fully intelligible without it. Stephen Darwall seems to me to miss this truth when he argues in his recent book, *The Second-Person Standpoint*, that moral reasons for action are founded in basic relations of mutual accountability in which we all stand to one another and thus that the moral point of view is "intersubjective" rather than "impersonal."[22] Here is his favorite example to illustrate the thesis. If someone steps on your foot, you might assert that he ought to get off for two different reasons—either because he is in a position to stop the pain you are undergoing, or because he has no business treating you in such a fashion. The one reason is impersonal or "agent-neutral," since a third party would have the same reason to remove that person's foot so as to end the pain if he were able to do so. The other reason is "second-personal" or "agent-relative," since it is one that the perpetrator alone can be said to have in this situation, a reason he has because of the relations of mutual accountability in which he stands with regard to you and others. Moral obligations, Darwall argues, rest essentially on reasons of this second, intersubjective sort.

Such reasons certainly exist. Moreover, in a strict sense (narrower than what has become common usage), the term "moral obligation" refers, not to the whole of what we ought morally to do, but solely to what we owe to others in virtue of the relation in which we stand to them, a relation that gives them a corresponding right to demand that we act in the

---

[21] In an earlier work, *The Patterns of Moral Complexity* (Cambridge: Cambridge University Press, 1987), chapter 6, I called this the "heterogeneity" of morality. The term now seems to me a bit misleading. The two principles are best understood as competing interpretations of the same root idea.

[22] Stephen Darwall, *The Second-Person Standpoint* (Cambridge, MA: Harvard University Press, 2006), 8, 60, 102.

appropriate way, such that if we fail to do so, we have not simply done wrong, but have wronged them.[23] A clear example is the obligation to keep our promises, in contrast, say, to the fact that we ought to give to charity, which is not something we owe to the poor or something they have a right to demand. Yet is it not then plain that part of morality, at least, has nothing to do with agent-relative reasons? For surely giving to the poor, like rescuing someone in danger or indeed relieving someone's pain, figures among the things we ought morally to do and constitutes, in an appropriately broad sense, a "moral obligation," even though such duties are ours for the same (agent-neutral) reason that anyone has to aid those who happen to be in distress. Imagine, for instance, that a person is in pain, not because of being treated negligently by someone else, but as a result of some natural disaster. People in a position to help ought morally to do so, despite the fact that the person has not been wronged by anyone. Darwall's theory offers no place for obligations of this sort.[24]

Furthermore, in the part of morality where agent-relative reasons do play an essential role, their validity depends on a deeper set of reasons that come into focus only within an impersonal point of view. Take again the case where someone steps on your foot. Only because it is an act that can cause pain, an ill which, as such, anyone has reason to put an end to, can you claim that that person owes it to you not to do such a thing and that you have a right to complain if he does. The agent-relative reason he has not to treat you in such a way rests on the agent-neutral consideration that pain is something to be prevented or stopped when it occurs. True, the person owes it to you to avoid stepping on your foot even if the act does not in fact cause you pain, since it expresses a lack of respect for your person. But it shows disrespect because it is an act that might well have caused pain, or that shows disregard for that possibility.

The same is true in the case of promising. Only because there is an impersonal reason to value the benefits that people derive from being able to trust one another, does the practice of promise-keeping acquire the authority it has and do we thus have the agent-relative reason to keep our

---

[23] For illuminating remarks on this strict sense of moral obligation, see H. L. A. Hart, "Are There Any Natural Rights?" *Philosophical Review* 64, no. 2 (April 1955): 175–91; and H. L. A. Hart, "Legal and Moral Obligation," in A. I. Melden, ed., *Essays in Moral Philosophy* (Seattle: University of Washington Press, 1958), 82–107.

[24] Darwall distinguishes between our "obligation to" someone having a correlative right and the idea of "obligation simpliciter" or "obligation period." (See Stephen Darwall, "Reply to Korsgaard, Wallace, and Watson," *Ethics* 118, no. 1 [October 2007]: 52–69, at 60–63.) But what he means by the latter notion is the authority belonging to members of the moral community in general (and not just to those whom we owe certain duties) to demand that we honor our rights-entailing obligations—an authority entitling them to claim, if we fail, that we have done wrong (simpliciter) even if we have not wronged them. Consequently, this point does nothing to acknowledge that there exist obligations based in agent-neutral reasons. Darwall also broaches the idea that an agent-neutral concern with the welfare of others might be housed within an agent-relative conception of morality, but without explaining how such a derivation would go (Darwall, *The Second-Person Standpoint*, 95, 130).

promises to those to whom they are made. After all, do we not conclude that we should break a promise to a person if keeping it would do him or others a far greater harm, judged impersonally, than our breach of trust would cause him or them? It may well be true that this harm must consist not merely in some lessening of their potential happiness, but in our failing to honor a weightier duty we have to them (say, to avoid telling them a wicked lie or causing them bodily pain), if it is to license our breaking the promise.[25] But how are we to determine that in the circumstances the other duty takes precedence, if not by considering impartially the good of all those involved?

In general, the kinds of respect we owe to one another depend on these relations of mutual accountability serving what is each person's good, considered impersonally. I do not mean that such practices have a claim on us because they tend to bring about the most good overall, for, again, the impersonal standpoint is not in itself consequentialist, any more than it is in itself deontological. The point is, rather, that only if each person's good is understood to be of equal moment does it become intelligible what is at stake in the kinds of respect we owe to others and why we owe such respect to anyone who happens to stand in certain basic relations to us. Darwall's account of mutual accountability is essentially a reconstruction of the deontological outlook.[26] All the more reason, it seems to me, to recognize that morality, even where it displays this "intersubjective" character, draws upon an underlying impersonal point of view.

VI. CONCLUSION

We are moral beings because we can stand back from our individual concerns and determine by reference to the world itself, peopled by others no less real than ourselves, what we have reason to think and do. It is not, to be sure, in morality alone that we exercise this power of impersonal reflection. We do so, too, whenever we set about to weigh the evidence for some belief without regard for what we would like to be true or for what common opinion would say. Yet nowhere does this self-transcendence show forth more vividly than when we turn our attention from our own happiness to that of another, taking the same direct interest in that person's good—just because it is his or hers—as we naturally harbor for our own good.

This ability to stand outside ourselves is our most distinctive trait as human beings. It sets us off from the other animals. It shapes our greatest and noblest achievements. Clearly, not everything that is valuable in our

[25] W. D. Ross, *The Right and the Good* (Oxford: Oxford University Press, 1930), 18.
[26] I should also observe that Darwall's account attributes an intrinsic moral standing only to those able to make moral claims of others, a view of the sort I criticized at the beginning of Section V. For Darwall's own reflections on this score, see *The Second-Person Standpoint*, 28–29.

lives originates from this standpoint. The love we feel for particular individuals does not derive from an impersonal consideration of their merits (as though we found them to be the most deserving of our affection). Its sources are instead the bonds of family, the transports of passion, the blossoming of chance encounters. Nonetheless, our love would not be a truly human love if it did not contain a sense of how small and fleeting an affair it is in the larger scheme of things. Our humanity consists in this mix of commitment and distance, the devotion to our own sphere combined with the realization that it makes up but one life among many in the world.

We cannot then understand the kind of beings we are except in terms of the capacity for self-transcendence to which our moral thinking so vividly attests. Some philosophers have held that morality is a poor guide to self-understanding since it generally disguises the narrower, more elementary motivations on which it actually draws, and never more so than when it presents itself as impersonal in character.[27] This mistrust is too hasty. Theories of the human condition, such as the one just mentioned, claim to base themselves on the facts, asking us to evaluate their truth by taking up toward our own person the same distanced attitude we assume toward the rest of mankind. That we can occupy an impersonal point of view ought not therefore to be in doubt, and the only question is whether, from such a vantage point, we can also see reason to care about another's good, simply because it is his or hers, in the same way that we see an immediate reason to care about our own. There can be no *a priori* way of answering this question, in fact no other way—as I emphasized earlier (in Section IV)—than to go ahead and reflect, to see what we find. In the end, only conscience can tell whether morality is what it claims to be.

Philosophy, Brown University

---

[27] The great champion of this view was, of course, Friedrich Nietzsche, followed more recently by Bernard Williams. See, in particular, Williams, "Nietzsche's Minimalist Moral Psychology," in his *Making Sense of Humanity* (Cambridge: Cambridge University Press, 1995), 65–76.

UNTYING A KNOT FROM THE INSIDE OUT: REFLECTIONS ON THE "PARADOX" OF SUPEREROGATION*

By Terry Horgan and Mark Timmons

I. Introduction

In his seminal essay, "Saints and Heroes" (1958), J. O. Urmson argued that the then-dominant tripartite deontic scheme of classifying actions—as exclusively either obligatory, or optional in the sense of being morally indifferent, or wrong—ought to be expanded to include the category of the supererogatory.[1] Colloquially, this category includes actions that are "beyond the call of duty" (beyond what is obligatory) and, hence, actions that one has no duty or obligation to perform. The title of Urmson's essay indicates (by reference to character types) some of the main types of action—saintly and heroic—that are supposed to belong in this category. But it is a controversial category. Anti-supererogationists either deny the coherence of the concept, or, granting its coherence, argue that the corresponding category is empty. Pro-supererogationists argue that the category is not empty, and that therefore the corresponding concept is coherent, although the pro-supererogationists often disagree about the conceptual contours of the category. The apparent conceptual tension regarding supererogation, sometimes referred to as the "paradox of supererogation," has been a main focus of philosophical discussions of the topic. Roughly speaking, the paradox is that, on the one hand, supererogatory actions are notable because they are morally good, indeed morally best, actions. But then, on the other hand, if they are morally best, why aren't they morally required, contrary to the assumption that they are morally optional? In short, how can an action that is morally best to perform fail to be what one is morally required to do?

* An earlier version of this paper was presented at the following venues: "The Varieties of Moral Experience: A Phenomenological Investigation," Durham University, August 27–28, 2008; the Brackenridge Philosophy Symposium, "The Ethical and Epistemic Dimensions of Robert Audi's Intuitionism," University of Texas, San Antonio, February 7–8, 2009; and the Department of Philosophy Colloquium Series, University of Nevada, Las Vegas. We wish to thank audiences at these conferences for very useful discussion of this paper. We also wish to thank Robert Audi, Matt Bedke, Paul Bloomfield, Michael Bukoski, Ginger Clausen, Josh Gert, Michael Gill, David Heyd, Uriah Kriegel, Victor Kumar, Ellen Frankel Paul, Stefan Sciaraffa, and especially Doug Portmore for very helpful comments on earlier versions of this paper.
[1] J. O. Urmson, "Saints and Heroes," in A. I. Melden, ed., *Essays in Moral Philosophy* (Seattle and London: University of Washington Press, 1958), 198–216.

The source of this alleged paradox has been dubbed the "good-ought tie-up."

In what follows, we plan to address this alleged paradox by first making a phenomenological case for the reality of instances of genuine supererogatory actions, and then reflecting on the relevant phenomenology, explaining why there is no genuine paradox. We set for ourselves four tasks. Because the issues regarding supererogation are complicated, our first task is to set up the rest of the essay by: (i) clarifying various elements that figure in the concept of supererogation, as well as (ii) clarifying the paradox just mentioned. This task is taken up in Sections II and III. Our second task, which we address in Section IV, is to motivate our phenomenological approach to the putative paradox—approaching it "from the inside," as it were. One reason for dwelling on the relevant phenomenology is that it can serve as a guide for making good theoretical sense of supererogation. Moreover, a good theory about such matters will accommodate the actual phenomenology and will treat it as appropriate rather than somehow erroneous. Our third task (addressed in Section V) is to examine some of the details of moral experience—its phenomenology—contrasting experiences of moral obligation with experiences of supererogation. Our fourth task is to address the paradox of supererogation, which we do in Sections VI and VII. In Section VI, we argue that one can make sense of supererogation by recognizing what we call a "merit-conferring" role that moral reasons can play. We describe this sort of role partly by contrasting it with two other roles that practical reasons can play: what Joshua Gert calls a "requiring" role and a "justifying" role.[2] If one recognizes the multiple roles that a moral reason can play (inspired by reflection on the phenomenology of supererogation), one has the conceptual resources to untie the good-ought knot and thereby make sense of supererogation—to untie a philosophical knot starting "from the inside." In Section VII, we briefly compare our view with two proposals that are like ours in recognizing that moral reasons can play more than one role. Section VIII is our conclusion.

II. Terminology

We begin with some remarks about how we understand various terms of moral evaluation (and the concepts they express) that play a role in discussions of supererogation.

---

[2] See the works by Gert cited in note 37 below. Practical reasons concern all sorts of considerations that (as reasons) bear on choice and actions, and thus include nonmoral as well as moral reasons. Gert introduces the requiring/justifying distinction with respect to roles bearing on the rationality of action, and hence with regard to practical reasons generally. Moral reasons too, as a species of practical reasons, may play either a requiring or a justifying role. In Sections VI and VII, we explain and illustrate the idea of roles that practical reasons in general, and moral reasons in particular, may play.

Supererogation. We will use 'supererogation' (and its cognates) in what we take to be the common-sense usage of the term, and thus as capturing the colloquial idea of actions whose performance is "beyond the call of duty." Being beyond the call of duty (moral obligation), supererogatory actions are not morally required (obligatory or one's duty). Nonetheless, such actions possess a kind of moral value in virtue of which their performance, when properly motivated, is morally meritorious. Since the concept of supererogation is a primary source of philosophical contention, let us list what we take to be its essential elements, involving both deontic and evaluative concepts, and related aspects having to do with reactive attitudes.[3]

Deontic elements: Supererogatory actions are

(D1)   neither all-things-considered (all-in, for short) morally required, nor prima facie morally required,[4]

(D2)   nor are they morally wrong, and in most cases not even prima facie wrong,[5]

(D3)   and so (given the standard interpretation of basic deontic concepts) such actions are morally optional. But they are not morally indifferent, because of their evaluative significance.

Evaluative elements: In addition, then, supererogatory actions are

(E1)   actions that realize, or are intended to realize, (more or less) moral value or goodness having to do with benefits to others (persons other than the agent), and are such that when performed because of the moral value or goodness in question, they are (more or less) morally meritorious,

(E2)   but their nonperformance is not demeritorious.

[3] Deontic concepts are used to morally evaluate actions and practices, and such concepts are expressed in English by such terms as 'duty', 'obligation', 'right', 'wrong', and 'optional'. Evaluative concepts used with moral significance are expressed by such English terms as 'good' and 'bad' and are applied not only to actions but to persons and states of affairs. Reactive attitudes (of moral significance) have to do with such responses as praise and blame, guilt and indignation—attitudes that are appropriate responses to morally significant actions, practices, and persons in light of whatever moral significance they possess.

[4] To say that an action is *prima facie* morally required is to say that there are reasons for performing the action which, if not outweighed by reasons favoring an alternative action, suffice to make the action in question all-things-considered (all-in) morally required.

[5] Arguably, there can be cases of supererogation in which one must violate a prima facie duty (either to others or to oneself) in order to perform the action. If I have agreed to meet you for an appointment, I have a prima facie duty to keep it. But if, on the way to the appointment, I stop to help someone whose car has run out of gas, my action can still qualify as supererogatory even though (in the circumstances) my fulfilling my prima facie duty to you implies that I have a prima facie duty not to stop. In what follows, we set such cases aside and focus on "pure" cases of supererogation, in which the supererogatory action is completely optional in the sense that it is neither prima facie required nor prima facie wrong.

Reactive attitudes: In light of these evaluative facts, supererogatory actions

(R1) are morally (more or less) praiseworthy,
(R2) but their nonperformance is not morally blameworthy.[6]

There are three general remarks we wish to make about our characterization. First, the types of actions that are generally recognized as paradigm instances of supererogatory actions include: (1) acts of heroism and saintliness;[7] (2) beneficence (including, e.g., acts of charity, generosity, and gift-giving); (3) favors; (4) volunteering; (5) forbearances (as when, out of compassion, one demands from another less than what one is due); and (6) forgiveness (including acts of mercy and pardons).[8] Obviously, the level of merit that is realized by actions of these various types can vary greatly: small favors and other commonly performed acts of supererogation are far less morally notable than the actions of saints and heroes (indicated in the above characterization by the "more or less" qualifiers).

Second, what we have just described is sometimes called "unqualified" or "strong" supererogation, in order to contrast it with "qualified" or "weak" supererogation. This latter notion differs from the former in denying that failures to supererogate are *completely* morally optional (that is, the latter notion allows that such failures require justification).[9] Therefore, what some call unqualified or strong supererogation, we call 'superero-

---

[6] We are not proposing these elements as a hard and fast definition. For instance, some authors deny that genuine altruistic motivation is a necessary component of the supererogatory. We focus on cases of supererogation that fit our description because they seem to be the sorts of cases that Urmson and others writing on the topic have tended to focus upon. For an excellent discussion of the contentious nature of this concept, see David Heyd, *Supererogation* (Cambridge: Cambridge University Press, 1982); and Heyd, "Supererogation," *The Stanford Encyclopedia of Philosophy,* 2006. See also Gregory Mellema, *Beyond the Call of Duty: Supererogation, Obligation, and Offense* (Albany: State University of New York Press, 1991), chap. 2.

[7] Andrew M. Flescher, *Heroes, Saints, and Ordinary Morality* (Washington, DC: Georgetown University Press, 2003), 172–91, characterizes heroes as those whose heroic actions are triggered by what he calls "reactive altruism," while saints, who make helping others a vocation, engage in what he calls "proactive altruism."

[8] We take our list from Heyd, *Supererogation,* chap. 7. Cf. Millard Schumaker, *Supererogation: An Analysis and Bibliography* (Edmonton: St. Stephen's College, 1977), chap. 2.

[9] Heyd introduced the unqualified/qualified terminology in his *Supererogation;* and Jonathan Dancy distinguishes strong from weak supererogation in "Supererogation and Moral Realism," in J. Dancy, J. Moravcsik, and C. C. W. Taylor, eds., *Human Agency—Language, Duty, and Value: Philosophical Essays in Honor of J. O. Urmson* (Stanford, CA: Stanford University Press, 1988); and Dancy, *Moral Reasons* (Oxford: Blackwell, 1993), 130–31. These pairs of terms (as they are used by those who have introduced them) are extensionally equivalent. According to unqualified/strong conceptions, (a) supererogatory actions have an intrinsic value, but (b) being "completely" or "purely" optional (in the sense that they are not even prima facie required, and hence failing to perform them is not prima facie wrong), they are not moral duties or obligations of any kind, nor are they requirements of rationality. Qualified/weak conceptions accept (a), reject (b), and then go on to claim that so-called supererogatory actions are either moral requirements which agents are excused from having to fulfill, or perhaps actions which, while being prima facie morally required, are not all-in morally required.

gation', and we prefer the term 'quasi-supererogation' for what others refer to by talk of 'qualified' or 'weak' supererogation.[10]

Third, our characterization above (in particular E1) is meant to capture what we may call *meritorious* supererogation, to be distinguished from *nonmeritorious* supererogation. The difference concerns an agent's primary reason for performing an action that goes beyond duty. Someone who risks his life to save someone in peril, but whose main motive is to make the evening news, does count (according to contemporary usage)[11] as doing something supererogatory. But the action is not morally praiseworthy, because it is not morally meritorious. By contrast, someone who, in going beyond the call of duty, risks her life from purely altruistic motives performs a meritorious act of supererogation worthy of praise. In the literature on supererogation, one often finds characterizations that build into the very definition of supererogation the idea that such actions are (owing to motive) morally meritorious.[12] Such characterizations are, strictly speaking, too narrow to capture the range of cases to which the concept is ordinarily applied. But these cases of supererogation are of particular interest to moral philosophers because of the special moral value they possess in virtue of being meritorious.[13] In what follows, then, we will focus exclusively on cases of meritorious supererogation.

---

[10] Mellema, *Beyond the Call of Duty*, chap. 5, uses the term 'quasi-supererogation' more narrowly than we do, to refer to nonobligatory actions whose performance is praiseworthy, but whose nonperformance is blameworthy. Our use of the term subsumes Mellema's.

[11] For instance, the *Oxford English Dictionary*, compact edition (Oxford: Oxford University Press, 1991), 3159, entry for 'supererogation' includes the following two senses: 1. "The performance of good works beyond that which God commands or requires, which are held to constitute a store of merit which the church may dispense to others to make up for their deficiencies," and 2. "Performance of more than duty or circumstances require; doing more than is needed." The first sense reflects the Roman Catholic doctrine of Indulgences (instituted during the Crusades, ca. 1080–1300), according to which (roughly) sinners could withdraw merit for a fee from what was called the Spiritual Treasury of the Church (that had been built up by the good works of Jesus and the Saints) and then could apply that merit toward their own salvation. Unlike the first sense, the second sense makes no mention of supererogatory actions being meritorious. Other dictionaries—including *The Cambridge Dictionary of Philosophy*, 2d ed., ed. Robert Audi (Cambridge: Cambridge University Press, 1999), 890; the *Merriam-Webster Online Dictionary*, http://www.merriam-webster.com/supererogation; and the *American Heritage College Dictionary*, 4th ed. (Boston and New York: Houghton Mifflin Co., 2002), 1384—feature definitions that are very similar to the second of the two senses just quoted. Heyd, *Supererogation*, chap. 6, defines 'supererogation' partly in terms of merit, thus preserving what he argues is an important element in the traditional Christian understanding of the term. Again, along with many other philosophers who write about supererogation, we are particularly interested in those instances of supererogatory actions that are praiseworthy because of how the agent was motivated. Hence, we focus on meritorious supererogation.

[12] See, for example, Heyd, *Supererogation*, chap. 6. In any case, with respect to nonmeritorious supererogation, the paradox arises because such actions are still good in virtue of what they bring about (or are intended to bring about), yet they are morally optional. So the solution to the paradox we propose in Section VI will apply to all cases of genuine supererogation—both meritorious and nonmeritorious.

[13] We thank Holly Smith, Tom Hurka, and Doug Portmore for prompting this particular clarification.

Obligation and duty. We propose to use the terms 'obligation' and 'duty' interchangeably[14] to indicate actions that one is morally required (either prima facie or all-in) to perform. We prefer talk of moral requirement, a term that perhaps carries less unwanted baggage than do the other two, though it is also convenient in some contexts to use the terms 'duty' and 'obligation' (for example, see the discussion of perfect and imperfect obligation later in this section).

Ought. The term 'ought' is used in various ways in contexts of moral evaluation, and some of these ways contribute to confusion, particularly in connection with supererogation. For instance, one should distinguish between (i) 'S (morally) ought to do A' and (ii) 'S has a moral obligation to do A', where the former is often used in a much broader way than the latter. When used broadly, it may be said that a supererogatory act is one an agent 'ought' to perform (because such an act is morally good and perhaps the morally best act open to an agent on some occasion), even though it is false that the agent has a moral obligation (even prima facie) to perform that action.[15] So, to avoid confusion, in what follows we avoid use of 'ought' as a term of moral evaluation. The same goes for 'should'.

Perfect/imperfect obligations. We distinguish 'perfect' or 'narrow' obligation from 'imperfect' or 'wide' obligation mainly in terms of the so-called latitude one is afforded in fulfilling obligations of these types, which in turn depends on the degree of specificity with respect to what one is required to do.[16] The distinction drawn in this way is complicated because there are the following dimensions along which an obligation may be more or less perfect:

> *Recipients:* Assuming we are discussing obligations to others, one may have an obligation to specified individuals (e.g., a debtor) or to unspecified individuals (e.g., some persons who are in need).

[14] Although there are some differences in the ordinary uses of the concepts of moral duty and moral obligation—the former having more to do with specific jobs, roles, and stations; the latter having more to do with agreements and benefactions—we will, following what is fairly standard usage in contemporary moral philosophy, use these terms interchangeably. However, for reasons noted in the next paragraph in the text, we depart from what we take to be common philosophical usage in not using these terms interchangeably with 'ought' (even in cases where 'ought' is used for moral evaluation). For a discussion of these concepts and their interrelations, see R. B. Brandt, "The Concepts of Obligation and Duty," *Mind* 73 (1964): 374–93.

[15] On this point, see Heyd, *Supererogation,* 171, who distinguishes the broader "commendatory" sense of 'ought', which may be properly applied to supererogatory actions, from what he calls the "prescriptive, personal" sense of the term, which may not be so used.

[16] There are other ways in which the perfect/imperfect obligation distinction is drawn, including one where the distinction hinges on whether, corresponding to an obligation to do or refrain from some action, others have corresponding rights that one perform or refrain from the action in question. See T. D. Campbell, "Perfect and Imperfect Obligations," *The Modern Schoolman* 52 (1975): 285–94, who finds five distinct contrasts that this pair of terms has been used to indicate. See also Millard Schumaker, *Sharing without Reckoning* (Waterloo, Canada: Wilfrid Laurier University Press, 1992), chap. 1, for further discussion.

Act type: An obligation may require the performance of a relatively specific act type (e.g., repaying a $20 loan in U.S. currency), but other obligations, such as helping the needy, may be fulfilled by a wide range of types of charitable action (e.g., donating money, volunteering one's skills, etc.).

Occasion: An obligation may require the performance of an action on some fairly specific occasion (e.g., to repay a debt tomorrow), or fulfillment of the obligation may be wide open as to the occasion (e.g., to perform some charitable action at some time or other).

Notice that the latitude afforded by each of these dimensions of obligation can vary independently of the others, so that some duties are narrow with respect to, say, recipients (e.g., the obligations of parents to care for their children), but wide with respect to many of the ways in which this obligation can be fulfilled.

The importance here of characterizing imperfect obligation is to distinguish this category from that of supererogation. These categories share two common features. First, part of the idea of imperfect obligation is that (in general) specific actions that fulfill such obligations on some occasion are not, qua acts of some specific type performed on that occasion, morally *required*. They are, taken as specific actions, strictly optional, even though in performing them, one contributes to one's fulfilling an obligation. And, of course, acts of supererogation are also morally optional. Second, one main type of imperfect duty is a duty of beneficence: a duty, with significant latitude, to help others. Actions one performs that fulfill this duty thus serve (if successful) to help others. Supererogatory acts are also actions that (if successful) serve to benefit others in some way.

Nonetheless, supererogatory actions can be distinguished from actions that merely fulfill an imperfect duty of beneficence. The duty of beneficence, properly understood, is the duty to perform, from time to time, actions (such as donating one's time or money) that benefit those in serious need of help, where one's doing so does not involve great self-sacrifice. Actions that in some way benefit those who are not in serious need of help (e.g., acts of small kindness), or actions that would require great self-sacrifice in order to benefit others (e.g., acts of heroism), are not actions that are called for by the duty of beneficence. And if they are not called for by the duty of beneficence, then in performing them one is not performing actions that fulfill this duty. Such actions may, however, be acts of meritorious supererogation.

Furthermore, it is possible to go beyond the mere fulfillment of an imperfect duty of beneficence. Clearly, one can do too little by way of fulfilling one's imperfect obligation of beneficence even if, once in a great while, one does something to benefit some of those who are in need. Granted, it is perhaps never clear how much in the way of helping others is enough to fulfill the imperfect duty of beneficence over the course of a certain period of time. But surely it is possible for one to do far more in the way of helping others in need than anyone could reasonably expect, and, in so doing, one would be going beyond the call of duty. Such beneficent actions are in excess of what it takes to fulfill one's imperfect obligation and thus are not properly described as merely fulfilling that obligation.

III. The Knot

The so-called paradox of supererogation involves a tension between the presumption that there are (or even could be) acts of supererogation, and a line of argument concerning the relation between deontic and evaluative concepts that leads to the conclusion that there *cannot* be such actions. Here the tension is conceptual, and we think it can be set forth as follows.

Begin with what we take to be a fairly widespread common-sense assumption:

(S) Some persons have (or could have) performed, or might perform, supererogatory actions,

which entails the following conceptual claim:

(Sc) The concept of supererogation (and thus the category of actions it picks out) is coherent.

This conceptual claim and thus (S) are threatened by the following line of argument (Argument A):

(1) A supererogatory action[17] is one whose performance is (or would be) morally good and meritorious, but whose performance is not all-in or prima facie morally required.
(2) If an action is (or would be) morally good and meritorious (and it is the only such action in the circumstances), then there are good moral reasons that favor performing it, reasons that are better than any competing moral reasons that favor doing something else (call these 'morally best reasons').
(3) If there are morally best reasons that favor performing an action that one is in a position to perform, then one is at least prima facie morally required to perform that action, and one is perhaps all-in required to perform that action.[18]

---

[17] Here, and throughout, we are referring to meritorious supererogation.
[18] If there are morally best reasons to perform some action A, why does it not follow automatically that one is all-in required, and not just prima facie *morally* required, to per-

Thus,

(4) In cases where one is in a position to perform a supererogatory action, one is at least prima facie morally required to perform that action, and one is perhaps all-in required to perform that action.

But the conclusion contradicts the very notion of (meritorious) supererogation that is expressed in premise (1). We are then driven to the conclusion that the very concept of supererogation is incoherent (~Sc), and thus that there never have been and could never be genuine acts of supererogation (~S)!

The connection in this argument among the various moral concepts it features is sometimes referred to as the "good-ought tie-up": moral goodness allegedly is conceptually connected via reasons (in the case of this particular version of the argument) to obligation, and thus moral goodness of action allegedly entails obligation.[19] But, of course, the very concept of supererogation requires a conceptual disconnect between moral goodness and obligation.

One kind of response to this alleged conceptual tension is to revise (replace?) the concept by admitting that the sorts of actions typically classified as supererogatory are not really deontically optional. Rather, they are at least presumptively morally required, but owing to various mitigating factors, one is justified in failing to perform them (or perhaps excused from performing them), and thus failure to perform them does not call for the sorts of negative reactive attitudes that are appropriate for unjustified or unexcused cases of wrongdoing. This revised concept is what we call 'quasi-supererogation'.

Clearly, this revisionist response to Argument A gives up on the idea that a morally meritorious action can be *beyond the call* of duty, and so gives up on the concept of supererogation (despite appropriating the corresponding term). We ourselves are preservationists, not revisionists, so we understand the challenge presented above as one of finding an error in Argument A. Our attempt to meet this challenge begins in the next section.

This completes our first task, that of articulating and clarifying the main conceptual contours of the concept of supererogation and explain-

---

form that action? It does not follow automatically because, as argued by Douglas W. Portmore, "Are Moral Reasons Morally Overriding?" *Ethical Theory and Moral Practice* 11 (2008): 369–88, the inference in question assumes that (i) nonmoral reasons are not relevant in determining the overall deontic status of an action, and (ii) moral reasons always override competing nonmoral reasons. Portmore argues that these assumptions, while often taken for granted by moral philosophers, are false. So the premise in question is stated in a manner that allows for the possibility that (i) and (ii) are false.

[19] A particularly clear presentation of the paradox in terms of reasons for action is to be found in Joseph Raz, "Permissions and Supererogation," *American Philosophical Quarterly* 12 (1975): 164.

ing the associated paradox. We now proceed to our second task, that of motivating our phenomenological approach.

IV. STRATEGY MATTERS

In his essay "Normative Guidance" (2006), Peter Railton usefully contrasts two strategies for doing moral philosophy. One approach proceeds, as it were, from the outside of agents in attempting to construct a system of ethics, while the other proceeds from the inside of agents in addressing this same constructive endeavor. Here is how Railton explains the contrast.

> I sometimes feel that those of us who hanker after system in ethics tend to opt unconsciously for the first [outside] approach, tracing the outlines of moral practice from outside and setting it into a coordinate system and unified perspective external to the agents themselves. We should probably try more often to work from the inside of agents, from their centers of mass as agents and moral beings. From such an approach, questions of normative guidance become questions about how normative guidance occurs within the agent, what gives norms their life, and how they enter into the shape and meaning of the agent's experience, thought, feeling, and action.[20]

Railton's recommendation that one work from the "inside" of agents in addressing questions of interest to moral philosophers is, we think, a good one and one that we plan to follow in connection with supererogation beginning in the next section. Specifically, we plan to focus on the first-person phenomenology characteristic of experiences of supererogation, and we will do so partly by contrasting such experiences with those of perfect as well as imperfect obligation. We have three related reasons for engaging in this sort of "phenomenology-first" approach.

First, since the very existence of supererogatory actions is put into question by the anti-supererogationists, it seems especially appropriate to describe cases of concrete moral experiences of (allegedly) supererogatory action in order to experientially anchor a prima facie case in favor of such actions. This will, we think, go some way toward placing the burden of proof on the backs of the anti-supererogationists. After all, a philosophical theory that accommodates a relevant range of people's moral experiences is (all else equal) more plausible than a competing theory that does not. We think it is fairly common that people sometimes experience what they do as (in effect) supererogatory, and we think that a philosoph-

[20] Peter Railton, "Normative Guidance," in R. Shafer-Landau, ed., *Oxford Studies in Metaethics*, vol. 1 (Oxford: Oxford University Press, 2006), 3.

ical theory that allows that such experiences are not illusory is, ceteris paribus, more plausible than one that does not.[21]

Second, since some anti-supererogationists argue that alleged cases of supererogation can be subsumed under the category of imperfect obligation, we spend some time in the next section describing experiences of both perfect and imperfect obligation that will help put into relief experiences as of supererogation.[22] This puts some pressure on moral theories that would attempt to absorb alleged cases of supererogation in this way.

Third, examining the phenomenology of supererogation and contrasting it with other types of moral experience will suggest *how* to accommodate such phenomenology and do so in a way that treats it as appropriate, rather than somehow the product of irrationality, confusion, or clouded emotions.

In implementing our phenomenology-first methodology, we plan to focus exclusively on mundane, everyday experiences of supererogation. Doing so is important for two reasons. First, as noted in Section II, there is a broad range of types of action that count as supererogatory (assuming that any actions so count), ranging from the remarkable deeds of saints and heroes to rather unremarkable, but nevertheless supererogatory, acts of kindness. It is the latter kinds of cases which, assuming there are acts of supererogation, are by far the most common such acts. And we think it is good philosophical methodology (at least for purposes of addressing an apparent paradox that threatens the very category in question) to pay close attention to ordinary cases. Furthermore (and this is our second point), cases of saints and heroes, at least those cases that have been documented and studied by social scientists and historians, raise the following well-known problem of interpretation which makes them particularly contentious. When interviewed, people who perform saintly or heroic acts consistently make claims much like the following, which is excerpted from an interview with

---

[21] Another articulation of the general methodological point being embraced here is what Michael Huemer, *Ethical Intuitionism* (New York: Palgrave Macmillan, 2005) calls the Principle of Phenomenal Conservatism, according to which "it is reasonable to assume that things are the way they appear" (99).

In committing ourselves to the claim that, in some cases, people nonerroneously experience what they do as being beyond the call of duty, we take no stand on metaphysical issues concerning whether there is some property, *being supererogatory*, of the sort that a moral realist would countenance. We ourselves favor a version of metaethical expressivism, which denies the metaphysical claims of the moral realist, but allows for the idea that moral judgments (including those about the supererogatory) are subject to being true or false.

[22] The expression 'experiences as of supererogation' is being used here (and elsewhere) instead of the expression 'experiences of supererogation' in order to remain neutral in our characterization of such experiences with respect to whether, on a particular occasion, there is a genuine act of supererogation that is the object of one's experience. Thus, to describe an experience being an experience as of supererogation allows that one's experience may not have as its object a genuine supererogatory action. That there are genuine instances of supererogatory actions is a claim we go on to defend against the anti-supererogationists. Similarly, the expression 'experience as of obligation' is used in contexts where it is important to remain neutral with respect to the question of whether the action being experienced is a genuine obligatory action.

one of the so-called righteous gentiles who, during the 1930s and 1940s, risked their lives to hide Jews from Nazis:

> I don't think I did anything that special. I think what I did is what everybody normally should be doing. We all should help one another. It's common sense and common caring for people.[23]

Many of the pro-supererogationists who want to hold up saintly and heroic actions as exemplars of supererogation must say one of two things (or both) about saints and heroes who offer such testimonies. First, they may say that some, if not all, of these people (perhaps because they misremember or because they are being overly modest) are misdescribing their experiences, which really were experiences as of supererogation. Or they may say that while some, if not all, of these people are accurately describing their experiences, their experiences as of being obligated are erroneous and the actions being described really are (or were) supererogatory.[24] By contrast, some anti-supererogationists attempt to make use of such testimonies in arguing against supererogation.[25]

Because of the controversy over the testimonies of saints and heroes (about which we remain officially neutral), it seems to us that the almost exclusive focus on saintly and heroic actions as primary cases of supererogation has been unfortunate, distracting attention from cases that are far less contentious (even if not wholly uncontentious). As we have been saying, then, in examining conceptual questions about supererogation, one is well advised to focus on the common and comparatively uncontentious examples of what are putative cases of supererogation.

Having completed our second task—that of presenting our reasons for delving into matters of moral phenomenology, and explaining why we shall focus in particular on ordinary, mundane cases of supererogation—let us turn now to our third task, which involves offering phenomenological descriptions of types of moral experience.

---

[23] This quotation is to be found in Kristin R. Monroe, *The Heart of Altruism* (Princeton, NJ: Princeton University Press, 1996), 104. This sort of reaction among righteous gentiles is robust. For instance, Philip Hallie, *Lest Innocent Blood Be Shed* (New York: Harper, 1979) relates part of an interview with Magda Trocmé, one of the righteous gentiles in the southern French village of Le Chambon who protected Jews from Nazis:

> Madame Trocmé was not the only citizen of Le Chambon who scoffed at words that express moral praise. In almost every interview I had with a Chambonnais or a Chambonnaise there came a moment when he or she pulled back from me but looked firmly into my eyes and said: "How can you call us 'good'? We were doing what had to be done. Who else could help them?" (20).

[24] Urmson, "Saints and Heroes," 103–4, is among the pro-supererogationists who take the first tack, while Jonathan Dancy, *Moral Reasons* (Oxford and Cambridge, MA: Blackwell, 1993), 141–42, is among those who take the second tack.

[25] See, for instance, S. C. Hale, "Against Supererogation," *American Philosophical Quarterly* 28 (1991): 273–85.

V. Moral Phenomenology

'Moral phenomenology' has two related uses. The term is often used to refer to one's concrete moral experiences. Those experiences are said to have a phenomenology—a what-it-is-like-ness—and so to talk about one's moral phenomenology is to talk about the what-it-is-like-ness of one's moral experiences. But 'moral phenomenology' is also used to refer to the largely descriptive first-person enterprise of observing one's own moral experiences with the aim of describing them and comparing them with first-person descriptions that others offer of their moral experiences. The latter usage has to do with a particular descriptive and comparative practice whose subject matter is indicated by the first usage. (There is also a third usage, which we do not discuss, that refers to doing moral philosophy in the phenomenological tradition initiated by Edmund Husserl and that characterizes the work in ethics of such philosophers as Max Scheler and Emmanuel Levinas.)[26]

In a series of recently published essays,[27] we have discussed the phenomenology of what Maurice Mandelbaum called "*direct* experiences of moral obligation," where one is presently confronting a situation in which one "feels" morally required to perform or refrain from performing some action. Mandelbaum, in his book *The Phenomenology of Moral Experience* (1955), contrasts cases of direct moral experience with what he calls "removed" moral experiences.[28] Removed moral experiences comprise two sorts of cases. First, there are those experiences in which one judges either of one's past self or of another person that a particular action performed (or not performed) by that individual was or is morally required. Second, there are those cases where one's experience includes a value judgment about

---

[26] For a helpful introductory discussion of this third usage and its relation to the discipline/subject-matter usages, see Uriah Kriegel, "Moral Phenomenology: Foundational Issues," *Phenomenology and the Cognitive Sciences* 7 (2008): 1–19. For a thorough treatment of the phenomenological tradition, see Herbert Spiegelberg, *The Phenomenological Movement: A Historical Introduction*, 2d ed., vols. 1 and 2 (The Hague: Martinus Nijhoff, 1969). See especially chap. 14 in vol. 2, "The Essentials of the Phenomenological Movement."

[27] See, for instance, Terry Horgan and Mark Timmons, "What Does Moral Phenomenology Tell Us about Moral Objectivity?" in Ellen Frankel Paul, Fred D. Miller, Jr., and Jeffrey Paul, eds., *Objectivism, Subjectivism, and Relativism in Ethics* (Cambridge: Cambridge University Press, 2008), 267–300; Horgan and Timmons, "Prolegomena to a Future Phenomenology of Morals," *Phenomenology and the Cognitive Sciences* 7 (2008): 115–31; Horgan and Timmons, "Morphological Rationalism: Making Room for Moral Principles," *Ethical Theory and Moral Practice* 10 (2007): 279–95; Horgan and Timmons, "Moorean Moral Phenomenology," in S. Nuccetelli and G. Seay, eds., *Moorean Themes in Epistemology and Ethics* (Oxford: Oxford University Press, 2007), 203–26; Horgan and Timmons, "Moral Phenomenology and Moral Theory," *Philosophical Issues* 15 (2005): 56–77; and Horgan and Timmons, "Mandelbaum on Moral Phenomenology and Moral Realism," in Ian Verstegen, ed., *Maurice Mandelbaum and American Critical Realism* (London: Routledge, 2010). See also Horgan and Timmons, "The Phenomenology of Virtue," in *Moral Twin Earth and Beyond* (Oxford and New York: Oxford University Press, forthcoming).

[28] Maurice Mandelbaum, *The Phenomenology of Moral Experience* (Glencoe, IL: The Free Press, 1955; reprinted, Baltimore, MD: The Johns Hopkins University Press, 1969), 127.

the overall goodness or badness of some individual (oneself or another) or of some individual character trait possessed by oneself or another. One of the essential differences (according to Mandelbaum) between direct and removed moral experiences is that judgments included in experiences of the former type are those of an *agent* confronting a personal moral decision, while those of the latter type are made from the perspective of a *spectator*.[29] Since our focus here is on the experience of an agent making a morally significant choice in circumstances that the agent is presently confronting, we shall restrict our attention to direct moral experiences.

Before proceeding, there are two preliminary remarks we wish to make. First, although we think Mandelbaum's characterization of direct moral experiences is roughly correct, we plan to modify what he says about this type of experience. Our modifications, which we will explain below, involve both expanding and enriching the category of direct moral experiences. In expanding the category, we will include cases of supererogation, thus not confining direct moral experiences to cases involving judgments of moral obligation. We will enrich the category by including in our phenomenological descriptions certain elements that we think are often part of such experiences but that Mandelbaum does not mention. In particular, Mandelbaum omits from his phenomenological descriptions an agent's often peripheral sense of the psychic cost of failing to perform whatever action he or she experiences as being morally demanded. We think this is an important oversight on Mandelbaum's part, and we shall be appealing to this aspect of moral experience in characterizing the difference between experiences of perfect and imperfect obligation.

Second, Mandelbaum's characterization of direct experiences of obligation features an agent experiencing a felt demand grounded in the agent's sense of an action either fitting or not fitting the circumstances he or she presently confronts. As we shall presently explain, all direct moral experiences, including those of obligation and supererogation, involve an agent's sense of a contemplated action fitting the situation he or she confronts. However, one of the main phenomenological differences between experiences of obligation (on the one hand) and experiences of supererogation (on the other) is that the former, but not the latter, involve an element of felt demand. Let us now proceed, then, to examine some of the phenomenological detail of direct moral experiences, beginning with experiences of obligation.

A. Direct experiences of obligation

Valerie's volunteering. In her local newspaper, Valerie reads about the city's need for volunteers to help south-side citizens (whose neighbor-

---

[29] For further differences between direct and removed moral experiences, see Horgan and Timmons, "Mandelbaum on Moral Phenomenology and Moral Realism."

hood has been ravaged by a tornado) do some neighborhood clearing and cleaning up. Valerie calls the contact number and agrees to help this coming Saturday morning. But when Saturday comes along, she is not in the mood to participate; she would much rather take it easy. She considers just not showing up, thinking that because of the many volunteers likely to be involved, her not showing would not make a noticeable dent in the clean-up effort. But she thinks, "Once I get out there, maybe I'll perk up and it won't be so bad, and besides, I did *say* I'd help, so I really *ought* to get ready and just go." With that thought, she looks for her gardening gloves, which she'll need for the job.

Don's donation. Ambitious and successful Don lives comfortably in his upscale Manhattan condo. One day he receives a letter in the mail requesting money on behalf of Doctors without Borders, an international humanitarian aid organization that he has heard of (from listening to National Public Radio), but whose mission he has never thought about. Typically, he automatically throws away such mail, along with grocery store flyers, credit card offers, coupons from Bed, Bath, and Beyond, and other such "junk." But for no particular reason, he opens the donation request letter and reads about the recent and not so recent tragic events from around the world that have left people in desperate need of medical aid. Moved by the reports contained in the letter, he decides to do a bit more exploring by going to the organization's Web site, where he listens to radio broadcasts, watches videos, and reads more about the needs of people across the globe. He hasn't made charitable donations in the past—it never seriously entered his mind—but now he is thinking about it. He thinks about his own well-being and reflects on the kind of good luck he's had throughout his life, compared to the bad luck of people living in hostile circumstances. As he mulls this over, he thinks, "Well, I don't *have* to give to this organization— and besides, don't I pay taxes, and doesn't some of that money go to foreign aid? But I really *should* give something to some organization some time or another. And why not do it now? So that's what I *will* do." Don clicks the "donate" button on the main menu of the Web site, then selects the "donate stock" option and makes a generous stock donation.

These stories include bare psychological sketches of the experiences of the characters they feature; they do not include descriptions of any feelings or other psychological phenomena that Valerie and Don may each experience as they consider whether or not to perform the actions they contemplate, and as they then come to make a choice. In particular, we have omitted mention of any aspects of their occurrent conscious experience that may accompany their moral ought/should judgments as they decide what to do—keep a promise in one case, donate in the other. But these sorts of elements are part of people's everyday moral experiences, and at least some of them are captured in Mandelbaum's nuanced treatment of cases of direct experiences of obligation. According to Mandelbaum, ordinary judgments of direct obligation can be properly described as involving two "layers" of introspective awareness. Let us take these up in order.[30]

First, the experience of moral obligation involves a felt demand that itself is experienced as a kind of vector force which, Mandelbaum claims, like all forces, can only be described by referring to its experienced origin and direction:

> It is my contention that the demands which we experience when we make a direct moral judgment are always experienced as emanating from "outside" us, and as being directed against us. They are demands which seem to be independent of us and to which we feel that we ought to respond.[31]

For Mandelbaum, the demand that is characteristic of direct moral judgments is "reflexive"—it is directed against the agent making the judgment—and its origin is experienced as independent of the agent. As he goes on to explain, this sense of "independence" is what gives direct moral experiences their "objective feel," in that the demand appears to come from features of the situation that one confronts and that are themselves independent of one's desires, preferences, and aversions.

So the first layer of phenomenal description of direct moral experiences is that they involve what the agent (in effect) takes to be objectively grounded reflexive demands. The second, more fundamental, layer concerns what one's experiences reveal (within their phenomenology) about the *basis* of the felt demand, which Mandelbaum identifies as the experientially-presented relational characteristic of *fittingness* (and its counterpart, *unfittingness*). Note that this relation of fittingness involves as relata: (i) an actual or possible action or attitude of the agent, and (ii) certain considerations which, in the circumstances in question, constitute reasons that favor the action or attitude in question. The fittingness relation, then, is a normative-reasons relationship in which some consideration favors, and thus constitutes a reason for, some action or attitude. In the case of unfittingness, the considerations in question disfavor the action or attitude.

In the case of experiences of obligation, one experiences a demand upon oneself to perform (or refrain from performing) some particular action (on that occasion), and one experiences this demand as itself based on what is presented to one as an objective relation of *fittingness* or *unfittingness* obtaining between such an action and the features of the situation one is confronting. More precisely, one experiences certain features of the environment or situation confronting one as "calling forth" or *requiring*

---

[30] The next two paragraphs are taken from our essay "Moral Phenomenology and Moral Theory."

[31] Mandelbaum, *The Phenomenology of Moral Experience*, 54.

some action on one's part. Expressed in the language of reasons, one experiences oneself as being confronted with reasons that have a requiring force to them, giving rise to a felt demand. To illustrate, let us return to our two examples.

In Valerie's case, the relevant situation she confronts comprises such facts as that she made a promise to help with the community project on Saturday, that this is the relevant Saturday, that she is able to keep the promise, and in general that there are no other pressing obligations that compete with the one in question. In contemplating her choice (to go or stay), it is reasonable to suppose (following Mandelbaum) that at one point in her thinking, she feels the pressure of having made a promise as she realizes that the time to keep it is upon her. The pressure is experienced as directed toward her, and coming from the external situation she faces—"external" in the sense that the felt demand to keep the promise is experienced as independent of her desires, inclinations, and preferences. Indeed, in her case she experiences the demand as contrary to what she prefers to do. She would prefer to stay home. At a more precise level of description, one can say that Valerie's feeling a certain pressure to perform a particular series of actions is grounded in her sense of a contemplated relation of fittingness between the series in question and her situation, together with her sense of the unfittingness that would obtain were she not to keep her promise. Again, expressed in the language of reasons, Valerie experiences a felt demand that is grounded in various considerations (reasons) that she experiences as requiring certain actions of her.

Don's case is similar in some respects to Valerie's, but not in all. He confronts the situation of being in a position to help aid distant people in need of medical attention, and he experiences the sort of pressure characteristic of a felt external demand that is presumably grounded in his recognition of the fittingness between his donating and people needing medical aid. However, in Don's case, his situation does not involve having made a promise, nor (arguably) is he under any sort of role obligation that one undertakes as a father, or an organization member, and so forth. Put in terms of traditional moral theory, Valerie has a "perfect" or "narrow" obligation—there is some fairly specific action she is to perform, on a fairly specific occasion, on behalf of a fairly specific group. Don, however, has no such *specific* obligations that bear on the imagined case, even if we assume he has what is called an "imperfect" or "wide" duty of charity. Don thinks that his donating (to this particular cause, on this particular occasion) is, morally speaking, "up to him" and not strictly required. And so we should expect that his overall moral phenomenology would differ somewhat from Valerie's.

Mandelbaum does not discuss whatever phenomenological differences might characterize experiences of imperfect obligation, compared to those of perfect obligation, and here is one place where we think Mandelbaum's view could benefit from enriching the descriptions of direct experiences of obligation. In cases where one construes a particular contemplated action as fulfilling a perfect duty, one senses that one would appropriately experience guilt and be appropriately subjected to blame were one to refrain from performing the action in question. If such thoughts are not at the forefront of one's conscious awareness (as they may be), then one's phenomenology may well include (however dimly) a "looming threat" of unpleasant feelings—guilt feelings—were one to not perform the action. By contrast, in cases where one experiences an obligation as imperfect (or in a way that reflects the imperfectness of the obligation), one senses (however dimly) that one would appropriately feel shame or perhaps some sort of mild self-directed disappointment—disappointment in oneself—for passing up the opportunity to fulfill an imperfect obligation. There are two thoughts here. First (and for our purposes, most important) is the observation that direct moral experiences of obligation, in addition to including a sense of fittingness, unfittingness, and a resulting felt demand, also involve (at least often enough) the sense that one would be subject to some sort of psychic discomfort as a result of failing to perform the contemplated obligation-fulfilling action.[32] As we have noted, this "sense" may vary in the degree to which it is "focal" in one's overall moral experience.[33]

The second thought, which we are very tentatively suggesting, is that in typical cases of direct experience involving perfect obligations, one's sense of the psychic cost of nonperformance has to do with being held accountable (by others and by oneself) for a particular wrongdoing. The manifestation of such accountability is in terms of reactive attitudes including guilt and blame. Arguably, in cases where one does not feel obligated

[32] Although experiences of both perfect and imperfect obligation involve a felt demand, in the case of imperfect obligations the felt demand attaches to rather unspecific act-types, in contrast with cases of perfect obligation, in which the felt demand attaches to a fairly specific act-type.

[33] Two comments are in order here. First, it is certainly very common to have one's everyday experiences "colored" by an overall mood (e.g., depression) or by some more particular emotion (e.g., fear of missing a deadline). Such occurrent psychological features of one's experience at a time need not be the focus of one's attention, at least in those persons who seem to function quite normally under such conditions, though such features are part of one's overall experience. Second, Mandelbaum treats such emotions as disgust, indignation, admiration, and the like as by-products of removed moral judgments—moral judgments made from a spectator's point of view. If one sticks to Mandelbaum's direct/removed distinction, then what we are proposing is that first-person experiences of being morally obligated typically involve, as a part of the overall experience, viewing one's moral choice from a detached, spectator perspective. This seems plausible in light of the prevalence of the role in direct moral experiences of thoughts associated with such questions as: "What sort of person would I be if I did/didn't do such and such?" and "How would I feel if someone did/didn't do such and such for me?" Viewed this way, it makes sense to characterize different phases of the moral experience of the sort featured in our scenarios as including (a) an initial phase in which one experiences a felt demand grounded in one's apprehension of fittingness or unfittingness, (b) a reflective phase in which one mulls over one's choice (a phase in which one may imaginatively adopt a spectator's perspective), and (c) a final phase in which one decides what to do. Of course, such "phases" need not be temporally separate, but might instead be experientially superimposed.

to perform some specific action, but where one is responding to a general open-ended felt demand, one's sense of the psychic cost does not have to do with being held responsible for performing some particular act, but rather with negative feelings about oneself.[34] In both cases, there is this underlying similarity: one is aware that certain considerations constitute reasons that *require* that one undertake either some fairly specific course of action (in the case of perfect obligation), or that one undertake some course of action at some time or other (in the case of imperfect obligation).

Having described the key elements of experiences of moral obligation, and having distinguished experiences of perfect obligation from those of imperfect obligation, let us now turn to cases of supererogation.

B. Direct experiences as of supererogation

Mandelbaum never discusses cases of supererogation. Urmson's paper, recall, came out three years after the 1955 publication of Mandelbaum's *Phenomenology.* We have mentioned a range of types of action that are taken (by pro-supererogationists) to be instances of supererogation, including spectacular cases of heroism and more mundane cases such as favors. As we explained in the previous section, cases of heroism are particularly contentious, owing partly to the testimonies of heroes. Thus, we begin with a mundane case in which the agent does not experience herself as being morally obligated to perform some action, but in which, nevertheless, she performs the action out of altruistic motives.

Olivia's offer. Olivia and her husband Stan have recently moved to St. Louis, each having accepted an academic appointment at one of the local universities. During their first week in their new home, Olivia attends a block party organized by one of their new neighbors where she meets a recently widowed woman, Mary, a neighbor who lives a few doors down from Olivia and Stan. In conversation, Olivia learns that Mary lost her husband to cancer after forty-eight years of marriage. She also learns that Mary is an avid baseball fan and that she and her husband used to regularly attend Cardinals games. But without anyone to go with, she doesn't go anymore. The next day, it occurs to Olivia that it would be a nice gesture to offer to go to a Cardinals game with Mary, although she herself has no particular interest in the game. But she thinks: "Here is a chance to do something nice for someone, and the fall semester doesn't begin for another couple of weeks. Why not?" She calls Mary, who is delighted by the invitation, and they end up going to a game.

In our little story, Olivia does not feel a demand of any sort to take Mary to a baseball game. Nor does she experience any sort of demand to

---

[34] Walter Sinnott-Armstrong, "You Ought to Be Ashamed of Yourself (When You Violate an Imperfect Obligation)," *Philosophical Issues* 15 (2005): 193–208, argues that violations of perfect duty call for guilt on the part of the agent, while violations of imperfect duty call for shame on the part of the agent.

do something nice for Mary or for neighbors generally. Olivia isn't callous; she would gladly do favors for others if *asked*. But in our story, she is simply moved by her neighbor's circumstances, together with the fact that there is something she can do that would be much appreciated by Mary. Taking Mary to the baseball game would be "beyond the call of duty" and, in effect, is experienced by Olivia as such. We say "in effect" because, of course, while the thought that her offer is beyond the call of duty need not enter Olivia's mind, her experience involves her sense that the offer is not something she is morally required to do, but something that it would be good to do, something the doing of which would be fitting. In contrast to cases of obligation, Olivia does not experience the reasons she has to initiate contact with Mary as requiring her to do so, although, of course, the reasons in question are experienced as *favoring* the initiation of contact. Such reasons, then, are experienced differently than are the reasons involved in experiences of obligation. This aspect of Olivia's experience of reasons (besides not seeming to require that she call up Mary) is reflected in the fact that Olivia experiences no sense (however dim) that guilt, shame, or blame would be an appropriate response were she to pass up the opportunity in question. She does not take herself to need an excuse for simply not extending the invitation.[35] She may, of course, feel in some sense good about herself for what she does, but her motive (so we stipulate) is purely altruistic.[36]

Let us now do some comparing and contrasting in order to highlight important similarities and differences among the types of direct moral experience we have just described. There are three points of similarity. All of the types of experience are "direct" in Mandelbaum's sense of being experiences in which an agent is presently confronting a situation in which she contemplates a choice to be made by her in that situation. Furthermore, the situations in question all involve an agent who contemplates performing an action of some moral significance. In addition, the action that the agent contemplates performing strikes him or her as fitting the situation. Alternatively, this third point can be expressed in terms of

[35] Hale, "Against Supererogation," refers to the alleged phenomenon that failure to perform supererogatory actions calls for an excuse, and appeals to this phenomenon as evidence that supposed cases of supererogation are really cases of imperfect duty. But Olivia does not take her nonperformance to call for an excuse. If asked by her husband why she didn't go ahead and call Mary (in a scenario where she does not perform this particular act of supererogation), Olivia may say that she just didn't feel like it. Her not feeling like it explains why she didn't call, but it is not put forth as an excuse. Nor, from a spectator's point of view or her own, does she need an excuse. Like many other writers on the topic, Hale seems to focus on contentious cases of saintly and heroic actions, and she seems to assume that if an action is good then it is prima facie required.

[36] For those with egoistic leanings who are skeptical of putative cases of pure altruism, we recommend the experimental work of social psychologist C. D. Batson as an antidote. See, for example, Batson, "How Social an Animal?" *American Psychologist* 45 (1990): 336–46; and Batson, *The Altruism Question: Toward a Social Psychological Answer* (Hillsdale, NJ: Lawrence Erlbaum, 1991).

reasons: the agent featured in each of our scenarios takes it that there is a good moral reason, given the situation he or she confronts, that favors performing a particular action.

The major point of contrast between the two cases of obligation (on the one hand) and the case of supererogation (on the other) is that in the former, but not the latter, the agent's experience includes that of there being a felt demand. In the case of Valerie, she experiences a *focused* felt demand to perform a particular action, while Don's experience involves more of an open-ended, less focused felt demand to perform actions of a certain type at some time or other. Moreover, they each have a looming sense of some sort of psychic cost that each would experience were they to refrain from performing the action each of them contemplates performing. By contrast, our characterization of Olivia's phenomenology did not include either of these elements. Although Olivia takes the fact that she could do something nice for Mary as a reason for extending the invitation to the baseball game, she does not experience this consideration (and the situation in which it is embedded) as imposing a demand on her. Nor does her experience include a looming sense of psychic cost when she considers not extending the invitation. These related points of difference can be described in terms of how the various moral reasons that favor the various actions featured in our scenarios are experienced by the agents. Valerie and Don experience moral reasons as not merely favoring some course of action, but as requiring and hence demanding something of each of them. By contrast, Olivia does not experience a felt demand to invite Mary to the baseball game, and this reflects the fact that she experiences a moral reason (doing something nice for Mary) as favoring a course of action, but she does not experience it as requiring the action in question. This difference in moral phenomenology between experiencing a moral reason as *requiring* and experiencing a moral reason as *favoring but not requiring* is, as we shall explain in the next section, a phenomenological reflection of an important distinction between requiring and nonrequiring moral reasons, a distinction which we claim is the key to resolving the apparent paradox of supererogation.

This completes our third task, the task of providing a phenomenological description of what we take to be basic forms of direct moral experiences involving cases of perfect and imperfect obligation as well as certain common, everyday cases of supererogation. We have enriched Mandelbaum's description of direct experiences of moral obligation by including elements having to do with anticipated responses to the contemplated options one faces in a moral choice situation, and we have enlarged this category by including experiences of supererogation. We have also drawn attention to important phenomenological differences between experiences of obligation and experiences of supererogation, at least of the kind represented by our case of Olivia. In doing all of this, we have stressed in particular the differences in the way moral reasons are experienced. Having completed our third task, we turn now to our fourth: addressing the paradox of supererogation.

VI. UNTYING THE KNOT

Return for a moment to Argument A, which we used (in Section III) to articulate the paradox of supererogation, and focus on premise 3:

> If there are morally best reasons that favor performing an action that one is in a position to perform, then one is at least prima facie morally required to perform that action, and one is perhaps all-in required to perform that action.

It is this tempting premise that we think ought to be questioned. In extending the invitation to Mary, Olivia acts for a good reason (to cheer her neighbor) and, being other-regarding, it is a moral reason. But (so we claim) had she not acted for this reason (or some similar reason) and just gone about her business, she would not to the slightest degree be morally accountable; the good moral reason in question does not (in the case under consideration) have *any* obligating force. What the case of Olivia suggests, then, is the idea that not all good moral reasons for an agent to perform some action, even reasons that are plausibly considered "best," are such as to require that she perform that action, even prima facie. Some moral considerations clearly do have a requiring force, but (we submit) others need not. And if this is correct, then premise 3 is false, and so Argument A can be resisted. In short, a more fine-grained understanding of moral reasons and how they bear on the actions they favor is needed to untie the so-called good-ought tie-up.

Thus, we offer our case of Olivia as providing phenomenological evidence that premise 3 of Argument A is false. Moreover, as we just noted, the case suggests how one might go about substantiating our claim that this premise is false. We are thus appealing to the facts of phenomenology as data for philosophical theorizing, and we are claiming that a philosophical view that treats the phenomenology in a non-debunking way is preferable to one that does not. But phenomenological evidence is, like most evidence, defeasible. After all, a critic might grant that, in our story, Olivia's experiences are as we have described them, but he might go on to claim that her experiences fail to register the requiring force of the reasons that favor doing something nice for Mary. In light of this sort of response to what we have done so far, we now wish to strengthen our case for rejecting premise 3 by defending the following series of related claims.

(A) What is called for in rejecting premise 3, as well as making sense of the case of Olivia and similar cases, is a defense of the idea that practical reasons generally, and moral reasons in particular, can play roles that are logically distinct from the sort of requiring role in which they are typically cast.

(B) In particular, we propose what we call a nonrequiring, "moral-merit-conferring" role that a moral reason can play and that makes sense of the very idea of supererogatory acts: acts that are completely morally optional, but good and morally meritorious to perform.

(C) Furthermore, there are considerations that provide reason to recognize a merit-conferring role that moral reasons can play without also playing a requiring or justifying role—considerations other than the fact that recognizing a merit-conferring role for moral reasons figures into a solution to the apparent paradox of supererogation.

Finally, in addition to defending these claims, we briefly compare our view to related views about supererogation—views that also recognize a variety of roles that a moral reason can play. (This comparison can be found in Section VII below.)

Having done all this, we will have done enough to justify the claim that our view represents a plausible solution to the paradox of supererogation. We now proceed to address claims (A) through (C), taking them in order in the following three subsections.

A. Practical reasons playing a nonrequiring role

In defending the claim that moral reasons can play a nonrequiring role, we appeal to some excellent work by Joshua Gert in which he argues for a conception of practical reason that features a contrast between two logically distinct normative roles that a practical reason can play: what he calls a "requiring role" and a "justifying role." [37] The significance of Gert's work for our project of addressing the alleged paradox of supererogation is that it will provide some independent reason to think that practical reasons generally, and moral reasons in particular, can play roles other than the requiring role. Moreover, Gert's view will provide useful background for the proposal we will make, since our proposal will be framed

---

[37] See Joshua Gert, *Brute Rationality* (Cambridge: Cambridge University Press, 2004); and Gert, "Normative Strength and the Balance of Reasons," *Philosophical Review* 116 (2007): 533–62. Patricia Greenspan also defends the idea that practical reasons can function in ways that do not require. See, for example, Greenspan, "Asymmetrical Reasons," in M. E. Reicher and J. C. Marek, eds., *Experience and Analysis: Proceedings of the Twenty-Seventh International Wittgenstein Symposium* (Vienna: OEBV and HPT, 2005), 387–94; Greenspan, "Practical Reasons and Moral 'Ought'," in R. Shafer-Landau, ed., *Oxford Studies in Metaethics*, vol. 2 (Oxford: Oxford University Press, 2007), 172–94; and Greenspan, "Making Room for Options: Moral Reasons, Imperfect Duties, and Choice," elsewhere in this volume.

in a way that exhibits certain important differences from Gert's own treatment of alternative roles for practical reasons.

Gert's view is concerned with practical rationality generally and not specifically with morality or moral reasons; however, he partly motivates his conception of practical rationality by calling attention to requiring and justifying roles for moral reasons in common-sense morality (as well as certain moral theories), and then he suggests that practical rationality is like morality in this regard.[38] Here, then, is how Gert distinguishes the two roles in question.

Central to Gert's view about these roles is that they need not covary. A consideration that counts in favor of some action can be a strong justifying reason but it need not have an equivalent requiring strength; indeed, it may completely lack requiring strength. According to Gert, one can describe the role of a practical reason in terms of how a reason in that role affects the overall rational assessment of actions—how it affects whether an action (or omission) is rationally required, optional (merely permissible), or irrational. The function of a requiring reason that favors some action or omission Φ is to overcome reasons for not Φ-ing. It is not irrational to eat bananas. But if one suddenly develops a strong allergic reaction to them, then the fact *that one will suffer harm* is a reason that makes eating a banana irrational—it requires that one refrain from eating one. By contrast, a practical reason plays a justifying role when it functions to make rationally permissible an action (or omission) Φ that would otherwise (owing to competing considerations) be irrational to perform (or omit). To use one of Gert's own illustrations: *that it is extremely dangerous* is a reason (one that has requiring force, on his view) to not rush into the flow of fast-moving traffic. But the fact *that there is a helpless child in the traffic who might be killed* is a reason that justifies (but does not require) one to rush into the traffic to save him: the act of rushing into the traffic is thus rationally permissible, but not rationally required. In general, then, a practical reason plays a *requiring* role when it serves to make an action that would otherwise be rationally permissible rationally impermissible (and thus make the omission of the act rationally required), as in the case of the banana. By contrast, a practical reason plays a *justifying* role when it makes rationally permissible the performance of an action that would otherwise be rationally impermissible, as in the case of the helpless child in traffic.

Here is one way to think about these roles. When it comes to questions about the practical rationality of an action, there are three basic categories into which it might fall: the rationally required; the rationally optional (permitted, but not required); and the rationally impermissible. What practical reasons do, according to Gert's picture, is to take an action (or omission) that would otherwise belong in one of these categories and

---

[38] See Gert, *Brute Rationality*, chap. 2.

move it to another category. Let us extend the term 'deontic', which is typically used in association with the moral categories of the obligatory, optional, and wrong (impermissible), and apply it to the analogous categories of rational evaluation pertaining to action. Then we can say that Gert's requiring/justifying distinction with regard to roles that practical reasons can play has to do with how reasons may operate—how they do the work they do—within the "space" of deontic evaluation.

Although Gert's work is concerned exclusively with reasons as they bear on the rationality of action, as we noted a few paragraphs back, he partly motivates the requiring/justifying role distinction by appealing to cases in which moral reasons seem to play a justifying role that is distinct from playing a requiring role. As an example, Gert points out that one is morally justified in harming or killing in self-defense, although one is arguably not morally required to do so. Therefore, considerations of self-defense may serve to justify and thus make morally permissible the performance of an action (intentionally harming someone) that would otherwise be morally wrong. So the requiring/justifying distinction applies to roles that can be occupied by moral reasons as well as by nonmoral practical reasons.[39]

Over the course of his 2004 book *Brute Rationality*, and in subsequent essays,[40] Gert does much to elaborate and defend his claim that practical reasons can play these logically distinct roles, so we refer our readers to Gert's work as a defense of our first claim: namely, that practical reasons in general, and moral reasons in particular, can play a role that is logically distinct from a requiring role. We turn now to our second major claim, which brings us to the heart of our proposal.

B. Merit-conferring moral reasons

What one needs in order to make sense of supererogation[41] is a role that a moral reason *can* play, but one that neither morally requires what would otherwise be morally wrong to omit doing, nor serves to morally justify what would otherwise be morally wrong to do. In seeking to identify such a role, we employ Gert's way of characterizing normative practical-reason roles in terms of how the occupiers of those roles affect the overall assessment of actions. But to identify the kind of role one needs, one must look to nondeontic forms of moral evaluation. It will not

---

[39] In the following subsection, we say more about how the requiring/justifying distinction relates to supererogation.

[40] In addition to the works mentioned in note 37, see also Joshua Gert, "Reply to Tenenbaum," *Canadian Journal of Philosophy* 37 (2007): 463–76.

[41] Here it is important to recall that our focus in this essay is on cases in which the supererogatory action in question is neither prima facie required nor prima facie forbidden. As explained above in Section II, cases in which a "supererogatory" action is prima facie morally required, but with respect to which there are competing reasons that make the action all-in morally optional, are what we call cases of "quasi-supererogation."

work to focus only on deontic evaluation and the roles that reasons play as they bear on the deontic status of actions. The moral reasons that figure in supererogation need not affect the deontic status of an action, as the case of Olivia illustrates. So the obvious move is to appeal to nondeontic moral assessments of actions—assessments having to do with whether an action has positive moral merit, negative moral merit (demerit), or no merit.

We thus introduce the idea of what we call a *moral-merit-conferring* role that a moral reason can play. We characterize this role in terms of the bearing that reasons playing this role have on the overall merit of an action. *A moral reason, M, plays a moral-merit-conferring role when performing an action for reason M confers some degree of moral merit on an action which, were it performed for some other reason, would either lack merit or enjoy less merit.*

Notice two features of this characterization. First, in mentioning the *degree* of moral merit an action may enjoy, the characterization implies that reasons occupying this role can vary in merit-conferring strength. What sorts of factors determine the merit-conferring strength of a moral reason? Certainly the degree of self-sacrifice involved in some action plays a role. The greater the degree of self-sacrifice, the greater the merit conferred by the reason in question will tend to be. Suppose, for instance, that before meeting Mary, Olivia had bought tickets to go to the baseball game, and finds herself with an extra ticket as game day approaches, so her going will not involve any self-sacrifice. When she decides to invite Mary along, less merit accrues to Olivia's action than in the original story. No doubt other factors affect the strength of merit-conferring reasons. Here is not the place to explore this issue of what factors affect the merit-conferring strength of moral reasons. We do note, however, that our characterization of a moral-merit-conferring role is specified so that it allows that acts of supererogation can be more or less meritorious.

A second feature of our characterization is that it allows that an action's being morally meritorious can be overdetermined. That is, there may be cases where even if the action is not performed for some particular moral-merit-conferring reason, M, there may be some other moral-merit-conferring reason, N, for which the agent acts and which thus confers moral merit on the action. In cases where there are, for example, two moral-merit-conferring reasons for performing an action A, and it is possible to perform A for both reasons, and the agent performs the action for those reasons, then one may expect the degree of moral merit conferred upon the action to be greater than the moral merit that would accrue were the agent to perform the action for only one of the reasons. If there were two neighbors, Mary and Nancy, who would benefit from going to a Cardinals baseball game, then if Olivia were to invite them both to the game, she would presumably be acting for two morally meritorious reasons, each affecting somewhat the degree of merit her course of action enjoys.

So far, then, we have introduced a role that a moral reason can play, one that is distinct in terms of how reasons that occupy this role bear on the moral evaluation of actions. Moreover, we propose that recognition of this sort of role is what is needed to adequately accommodate cases of meritorious supererogation exemplified by our character Olivia. So let us pause for a moment to see how much progress we have made in addressing the paradox of supererogation.

The idea of a merit-conferring role for a moral reason to play should not be too controversial. After all, most moral philosophers will agree that in some cases there can be moral reasons for performing an action which are such that if the agent performs the action for those reasons, what she does is morally meritorious. So we have called attention to, and partially characterized, a role for moral reasons in virtue of which occupiers of the role function to confer merit. But what we claim is that a moral reason can play a merit-conferring role without also playing either a requiring role or a justifying role.[42] We do not deny that a moral reason can, in a particular circumstance, play multiple roles. For instance, assuming that there are duties of self-preservation, seriously risking one's life by running out into the flow of busy traffic to save a child (for the child's sake) both morally justifies an action (running into traffic) that would otherwise be wrong *and* confers merit upon what one does. But our case of Olivia is supposed to be one in which her inviting Mary is completely morally optional. She is not prima facie required to perform the kind action, nor is her performance of it prima facie wrong and thus in need of justification.

We have already noted that our appeal to moral phenomenology featured in the Olivia case only provides defeasible evidence for the rejection of premise 3 and in favor of our positive proposal involving a moral-merit-conferring role that a moral reason can play. A critic may want to insist that the moral reason for which Olivia acts, although merit-conferring, also functions to require (at least prima facie) that she perform the act in question. This sort of critic will claim that even if our phenomenological description of Olivia is accurate, we have nevertheless described the moral experiences of someone who simply fails to respond properly to the moral reasons that favor her act of kindness. Such reasons, the critic will say, impose a prima facie moral requirement on Olivia; she morally ought to take Mary to the baseball game unless she has some reason of sufficient justifying strength that would permit her to do something else.

Responding to this challenge requires that we defend the third claim we announced at the outset of this section; it requires that we go beyond an appeal to phenomenology and explore the possibility of providing a further rationale for our idea that moral reasons can play a moral-merit-conferring role in some circumstances without having to play either a requiring or a justifying role. We claim that such a rationale is available

---

[42] That is, without playing the sort of role that Gert characterizes as the justifying role.

and provides support (in addition to the support provided by phenom-enology) for the claim that there are merit-conferring reasons that are not obligation-generating. The sort of rationale we have in mind appeals to normative moral considerations having to do with certain elements of life and experience that people normally take to have intrinsic value.

C. A moral-normative rationale

So why do moral reasons—in this case, other-regarding ones that favor helping or doing something for others—sometimes function not to require or "justify" (in Gert's sense) but merely to confer merit on the deed in question? This question asks about the significance of the category of moral merit, and raises questions that are similar to (if not identical with) questions about the sort of rationale that can be provided for the category of the supererogatory. In what immediately follows, we offer an answer to this question, making some use of ideas that David Heyd offers in his defense of supererogation.

Heyd usefully distinguishes between two types of rationale that one may offer in defense of supererogation: theoretical and normative. A theoretical rationale appeals to the category of supererogation in order to make sense of certain ethical intuitions and experiences.[43] Our appeal to the case of Olivia (and similar cases) can be viewed as offering a theo-retical rationale for recognizing the category of supererogation. The way in which Olivia experiences the reasons for inviting Mary to the baseball game, and the value that Olivia realizes through her action, fit best with a description of her action as completely morally optional, but morally meritorious and thereby praiseworthy. Of course, as Heyd points out,[44] anti-supererogationists will challenge the veridicality of Olivia's moral experience and will want to insist that her experience fails to register the fact that moral reasons, whatever else they may do, function to require the acts they favor.

Against this line of criticism, Heyd claims that the defender of super-erogation can usefully appeal to a moral-normative rationale that attempts to explain the overall moral significance of acts of supererogation. He fur-ther claims that this sort of rationale has both a negative and a positive com-ponent. The negative component stresses the value to the individual of being morally free to pursue individual projects without having to worry about the promotion of the general good, without needing an excuse or a justi-fication for not performing actions that pro-supererogationists take to be beyond the call of duty. Expressed in the language of rights, this negative rationale focuses on the fact that individual autonomy is not only of pos-

---

[43] An example of this kind of rationale would be to argue (as Urmson does in "Saints and Heroes") that a morality that does not put limits on what duty requires, and thus does not make room for supererogation, would not be livable given typical human psychology.

[44] Heyd, *Supererogation*, 165.

itive value, but is the ground of a moral right to pursue one's projects and interests without being subject to a duty to act for the benefit of others, at least in a large range of cases—cases where, intuitively, one needs no excuse or justification for pursuing one's own interests.

The positive component of the moral-normative rationale focuses on the sort of value that is realized by a supererogatory action. Heyd's basic claim is that the exercise of one's autonomy with respect to actions that are entirely morally optional but done for the good of others allows for the expression of certain valuable attitudes and traits that would otherwise not be possible. Here is the crucial passage in which he makes this point:

> Being purely optional, the supererogatory act is spontaneous and based on the agent's own initiative. Not being universally required (of everyone in a similar situation), supererogatory action breaks out of the impersonal and egalitarian framework of the morality of duty— both by displaying individual preferences and virtues, and by allowing for some forms of favoritism, partial and unilateral treatment of someone to whom the agent wishes to show special concern. This may result in friendship and in an attempt to return a supererogatory service (thus creating a higher type of reciprocity than that required by the system of mutual rights and duties). These characteristics of supererogatory behavior can be realized only under conditions of complete freedom and would be stifled under a moral totalitarian concept of duty. Supererogation is necessary as providing an opportunity to exercise certain virtues.[45]

This sort of positive moral-normative rationale offered by Heyd requires further development in order to be fully convincing, far more development than we are able to provide here. However, we do wish to add something that we think complements Heyd's remarks about the positive value of supererogation. Specifically, we propose to focus, if only briefly, on the phenomenology of care. In doing so, we call attention to the moral value of such forms of life as friendship and love and associated experiences of such forms of life. We also call attention to the fact that such forms of life and associated experiences seem to require that moral reasons can, in some circumstances, play the role of conferring moral merit on an action performed for those reasons without also having to play either a requiring or a justifying role vis-à-vis that action.

---

[45] Ibid., 175. In defending supererogation against the paradox, Heyd claims that "the model of reasons is inadequate to the explanation of supererogation" (ibid., 170). However, his claim is apparently based on the assumption that reasons for action can only play a requiring role in how they favor an action. Nevertheless, it seems to us that the sorts of considerations that Heyd brings forth in defense of supererogation could be cast in terms of the language of reasons if, as we are suggesting, one recognizes a moral-merit-conferring role that moral reasons can play.

What we have in mind concerns the sorts of experiences associated with acts of caring that are performed in contexts of love and friendship. In this connection, the experiences of both the agent and the recipient are worth considering. From the perspective of the *agent* performing the action, there is the experience of responding to the needs and preferences of a lover or a friend, which involves a feeling of deep connectedness or special union with the other person. We submit that not only is this sort of feeling of intrinsic value and worth desiring for its own sake, but it reflects the sort of "special concern" directed toward a particular individual (mentioned by Heyd in the quoted passage) which, as a constellation of benevolent dispositions, has intrinsic value.

But there is something it is like to be the *recipient* of what one interprets as an act of "pure" caring—caring that is not guided by a sense of duty, but rather done out of love or friendship.[46] Being the beneficiary of an act of genuine caring (and experiencing it as such) may trigger certain feelings of comfort (in being cared for) and feelings of being "in union with" or deeply connected to another person—aspects of one's experience that are intrinsically valuable.

Of course, in the case of Olivia, her offer to Mary does not involve the kind of phenomenology involved in cases of love and friendship. But Mary's experiencing Olivia's offer as one of pure kindness (assuming she does) has a significance that would be absent were Mary to think that Olivia's offer is prompted by an *impersonal* imperfect duty of beneficence. Acting on the basis of merit-conferring reasons (that do not, in the circumstances, also either require or justify) allows for such actions to have the sort of personal significance that may be registered in the qualitative feel of one's experiences. And of course, there is more than just a certain sort of qualitative feel. There is here a form of human interaction that is not possible without it being possible to do something for another that is morally meritorious without being morally required. Such relationships are intrinsically valuable in a morally significant way, and their value depends partly on the fact that the actions in question are not morally required.

Consider now the question of the conditions of the possibility of such forms of caring as we have briefly described. These forms seem to have the particular significance they do because they involve responding to others for reasons that, in the circumstances, do not involve the sort of demand on one's behavior that issues from either a perfect or an imperfect obligation. This thought can perhaps be reinforced by imagining a

---

[46] We distinguish between actions guided by a sense of duty and those *guarded* by a sense of duty. Actions guided by duty include those performed because the agent believes them to be required (perfect duties), and those performed because they are believed to fulfill an imperfect duty. By contrast, actions are guarded by duty when the agent is careful about not doing something that violates duty. Actions guarded by duty in this way may nevertheless be done for reasons that serve to confer merit.

community of creatures whose interactions are guided exclusively by a sense of duty toward others. In some cases, they act out of a sense that the action in question must be performed, and in other cases out of a sense that the action in question fulfills an imperfect duty. It is far from clear (and we think very unlikely) that such creatures would have the sorts of caring and being-cared-for experiences that we have been highlighting. In particular, there would be certain kinds of interpersonal relationships that they would not be able to enter into, relationships that we humans consider intrinsically very valuable. If this speculation is correct, then surely these creatures lack forms of life and associated experiences that are of great value.

We offer these reflections on the value and possibility of certain morally significant forms of care to bolster the presumptive case we made in the previous subsection for the recognition of a role that moral reasons can play without also having to play either a requiring role or a justifying role. If there is good reason (as we think we have shown) to recognize a moral-merit-conferring role for reasons to play, then we have hopefully provided sufficient reason to reject premise 3 of Argument A (the anti-supererogation argument), and in the process we have been able to make sense of the category of supererogation. Indeed, the case we have been making for merit-conferring reasons by appealing to the phenomenology of supererogation, and by appealing to the sorts of intrinsically valuable forms of relationship that we have just been discussing, puts a substantial burden on the backs of anti-supererogationists. It looks as if they would need to argue that people are not only mistaken in their phenomenology but also deeply mistaken or confused in valuing the kinds of interpersonal relations that humans clearly do have and value very highly.

We now proceed to consider a pair of related views that we think help bolster our case for the recognition of the sort of merit-conferring role that a moral reason can play on some occasions without also having to play a requiring or a justifying role.

VII. Related Views: Dreier and Portmore

We have argued that the only way to accommodate cases in which a supererogatory action is completely optional, is to reject the claim that moral reasons can play only one sort of role; they must be able to play a nonrequiring role as well. Douglas Portmore[47] and Jamie Dreier[48] have each made proposals for understanding supererogation that employ the

---

[47] Douglas Portmore, "Are Moral Reasons Morally Overriding?" *Ethical Theory and Moral Practice* 11 (2008): 369–88; and Portmore, *Commonsense Consequentialism: Wherein Morality Meets Rationality* (work in progress).

[48] James Dreier, "Why Ethical Satisficing Makes Sense and Rational Satisficing Doesn't," in Michael Byron, ed., *Satisficing and Maximizing* (Cambridge: Cambridge University Press, 2004), 131–54.

idea that moral reasons can do something other than require. Before we conclude, it will be useful to compare the view we have been defending with these related views.

Dreier's proposal for avoiding the paradox of supererogation embraces the idea that not all moral reasons serve to require; some moral reasons are nonrequiring. His suggestion (which he puts forth tentatively) is that there are two moral points of view. The point of view of justice involves reasons that have strong moral requiring strength. By contrast, the point of view of beneficence involves reasons that lack moral requiring strength. Thus, in cases of supererogation where reasons of beneficence favor performing an altruistic act that we normally think of as supererogatory (and where reasons of justice do not apply), the reasons of beneficence do not function to make the act in question morally required. Hence, the action favored by the best moral reasons in the circumstances is not at all thereby morally required.

What exactly reasons of beneficence do (what role they play) is not developed by Dreier. But in any case, the important point of contrast between Dreier's proposal and the view we have been defending is that Dreier's requiring/nonrequiring distinction is applied to types of moral reasons rather than to types of roles that moral reasons can play. And the resulting problem (pointed out by Portmore)[49] is that it is implausible to suppose that reasons of beneficence never function to require (even prima facie) the actions they favor. That I can easily help someone in desperate need, and can do so at almost no cost or inconvenience, seems to be a reason that requires that I help. So Dreier's proposal has the right idea (moral reasons need not require) but does not properly locate the bearers of the requiring/nonrequiring distinction. Perhaps if one were to narrow the scope of reasons of beneficence so that only a proper subset of such reasons are the ones that favor (without requiring) the supererogatory action, then Dreier's view and our own would converge. In any case, it is better, we think, to draw the distinction between reasons that require and those that do not in terms of roles that reasons can play.

Portmore addresses the question of how a moral theory can accommodate so-called agent-centered options, understood as morally permissible options that one sometimes has in certain circumstances of either pursuing one's own interests and projects, or sacrificing those interests and projects in order to benefit others—the latter option being an act of supererogation. In doing so, Portmore makes use of Gert's requiring/justifying distinction applied to roles that moral reasons can play. Thus, in determining an action's deontic status, reasons can play a moral requiring role and they can play a moral justifying role. And so, associated with each of these roles, moral reasons can enjoy two distinct dimensions of strength: morally requiring and morally justifying strength, respectively. Accord-

[49] Portmore, "Are Moral Reasons Morally Overriding?" 381.

ing to Portmore's characterization, (i) supererogatory actions are actions that are morally optional (they are neither all-in morally required nor all-in morally forbidden), but (ii) they are actions that one has "most moral reason" to perform. Of course, these two claims are in apparent tension; they reflect the paradox of supererogation. And Portmore agrees with us that a resolution of the alleged paradox requires denying the idea that moral reasons only play a requiring role. But he also claims that in denying this assumption there are two ways of explaining the possibility of supererogation: the non-moral-reasons (NMR) explanation, and the insufficient-moral-requiring-strength (IMRS) explanation.

The first of these explanations involves the following three claims. First, reasons of self-interest, despite being *nonmoral* reasons, are nevertheless morally relevant in that they can figure in the determination of the overall deontic status of actions. Second, nonmoral reasons can prevent moral reasons from generating an all-in moral requirement to perform the action favored by the moral reason. Nonmoral reasons in such cases thus play the role of moral justifiers in that they invoke considerations of self-interest in order to make morally permissible what would otherwise be a morally impermissible action. Third, nonmoral reasons lack moral requiring strength (otherwise, the nonmoral reasons in question would generate a moral requirement to act out of self-interest, and thereby turn the putative act of supererogation into a morally impermissible act).

Given these three claims (which Portmore does much to defend), one is able to explain the possibility of supererogation because Portmore's view allows for the possibility of cases in which one has nonmoral reasons of sufficient strength to prevent the moral reasons that *favor* the act of supererogation from morally *requiring* that act. And yet, since such nonmoral reasons do not themselves have moral requiring strength, they do not generate a moral obligation to promote one's self-interest and thus an obligation to refrain, in such circumstances, from doing something supererogatory.

Note that this explanation fits those cases in which the moral reasons that favor performing the supererogatory act are playing a requiring role, and it is thanks to nonmoral reasons of sufficient justifying strength that acts of supererogation do not end up being all-in morally required. But this means that the non-moral-reasons explanation is meant to address what we have been calling cases of quasi-supererogation. Consequently, this particular explanation cannot account for such cases as Olivia's offer to Mary. If one agrees that there are or can be cases like Olivia's offer, then appealing to the distinction between requiring and justifying roles that moral reasons may play (together with Portmore's additional three claims) will not be enough to accommodate genuine supererogation. It is because the requiring/justifying distinction with regard to reasons operates exclusively within the space of the deontic, shifting actions from one deontic category to another, that the distinction will prove inadequate for handling cases of supererogation. This is why one needs to recognize a role for moral reasons to play that does not function to move an action from one deontic category to another.

As we noted above, however, Portmore does allow that there is another way one might try to avoid the alleged paradox of supererogation. This second way is to embrace the so-called insufficient-moral-requiring-strength explanation, according to which (roughly) moral reasons that favor the supererogatory action lack requiring strength. This is how Dreier tries to explain supererogation, and it is the kind of explanation we have offered in terms of the claim that moral reasons are capable of playing a merit-conferring role (without also playing a requiring role). What Portmore argues is that not all cases of "supererogation" admit of this kind of explanation—there are cases in which the reasons that favor the super-erogatory option do have moral requiring force, and thus the only way to make sense of them is by appeal to the NMR explanation. Now we can happily grant this claim since, as we have noted, the cases that seem to require the NMR explanation are what we have been calling cases of quasi-supererogation. What we claim is that not all cases of supereroga-tion (using the term broadly now to include both quasi and non-quasi cases) admit of the NMR explanation.[50]

VIII. Conclusion

Much of the philosophical controversy over supererogation involves the alleged paradox of supererogation, whose source is the supposedly tight connection between the evaluative and deontic concepts involved in the very notion of supererogation—the "good-ought tie-up." Our central aim has been to dissolve the seeming paradox, guided by facts about experiences of supererogation—their phenomenology. We set for our-selves four tasks. The first was to clarify the concept of supererogation and explain the paradox. The second task was to motivate our phenom-enological approach to the topic. The third was a task of phenomenolog-ical description: describing the phenomenologies of moral requirement, both perfect and imperfect, and contrasting them with each other and with a prototypical case of experiencing an action as of supererogation—considering the phenomenon from the inside. Our fourth task was to address the paradox of supererogation in light of moral phenomenology. With respect to the good-ought tie-up that generates the alleged paradox, we argued that the source of the tie-up is the assumption that the only way in which a moral reason can favor an action is by tending to require that action. So to undo the good-ought tie-up—to untie the knot and thus dissolve the apparent paradox—we identified and characterized a non-requiring role that moral reasons may play in making sense of supererero-gation. We called it a moral-merit-conferring role. If a moral reason can

[50] Portmore does not deny this claim.

play this merit-conferring role without also playing the role of requiring whatever action the reason favors, then it is possible for an action to be deontically optional yet morally meritorious. And this is what is central to the notion of meritorious supererogation that has been our focus. In defending our proposal, we offered a moral-normative rationale in defense of the claim that moral reasons can play a merit-conferring role (without also functioning to require). Finally, we briefly compared our account of supererogation with related accounts.

Philosophy, University of Arizona

SUBJECTIVE RIGHTNESS*

By Holly M. Smith

I. Background

In the early part of the twentieth century, writers on moral philosophy—prominently Bertrand Russell, C. D. Broad, H. A. Prichard, and W. David Ross—noted that there are many situations in which an agent's misapprehension of his circumstances results in an evaluator's feeling pulled to evaluate the agent's actions as *both* morally right and morally wrong.[1] Consider, for example, the following case:

Twin Towers I: Following the crash of an airplane into a skyscraper, security guard Tom, believing that the elevators will cease working, tells office workers to evacuate the building via the stairwell rather than the elevators. In this case, using the stairs takes too long and all the office workers are killed when the building collapses, whereas the elevators remain operational long enough for the employees to have used them to evacuate safely.

* I am grateful for discussion on these topics to participants in my graduate seminar during the spring of 2008, and in particular to Preston Greene, who convinced me that principles of objective rightness might include reference to the agent's beliefs. I am also grateful to the other contributors to this volume (especially Mark Timmons) for helpful discussion, as well as to the participants (especially Evan Williams and Ruth Chang) in the Rutgers University Value Theory discussion group, the participants in Elizabeth Harman's 2009 ethics seminar, the participants in the 2009 Felician Ethics Conference (especially Melinda Roberts), the participants in the 2009 Dartmouth workshop on *Making Morality Work* (Julia Driver, Walter Sinnott-Armstrong, Mark Timmons, and Michael Zimmerman), and to Nancy Gamburd, Alvin Goldman, Preston Greene, and Andrew Sepielli for comments on earlier versions of this essay. Ellen Frankel Paul provided welcome encouragement to clarify a number of key points.

[1] Bertrand Russell, "The Elements of Ethics" (originally published in 1910; reprinted from Russell, *Philosophical Essays*), in *Readings in Ethical Theory,* ed. Wilfrid Sellars and John Hospers, 2d ed. (New York: Appleton-Century-Crofts, 1970), 10–15; C. D. Broad, *Ethics,* ed. C. Lewy (Dordrecht: Martinus Nijhoff, 1985), chapter 3 (from lectures given in 1952–53); H. A. Prichard, "Duty and Ignorance of Fact" (1932), in H. A. Prichard, *Moral Obligation and Duty and Interest* (Oxford: Oxford University Press, 1968), 18–39; W. D. Ross, *Foundations of Ethics* (Oxford: Clarendon Press, 1939), chapter 7. G. E. Moore has an early discussion of the "paradox" in question, but eventually concludes that we should say the action with the best consequences is right, although the person who does it, believing that it will have bad consequences, is to blame for his choice. See G. E. Moore, *Ethics* (1912; New York: Oxford University Press, 1965), 80–83. Henry Sidgwick uses the terms "subjective rightness" and "objective rightness," but uses the first term to refer to the agent's belief that an action is right (a status now often labeled "putatively right"), and the second term to refer to the fact that the action is the agent's duty in the actual circumstances. See Henry Sidgwick, *The Methods of Ethics* (1874; Chicago: The University of Chicago Press, 1907), 206–8.

When we focus on the actual outcome of Tom's action of telling the employees to use the stairwell, we want to say that it is wrong—indeed tragic, since it results in the avoidable deaths of scores of office workers. But if we focus on what Tom reasonably believes about the employees' options at the time he advises them, we want to say that he did the right thing. Consider also the following case:

> *Twin Towers II:* Following the crash of an airplane into a skyscraper, security guard Joan, believing that the elevators will cease working, but nursing a grudge against her ex-husband who works for High Tower Investments, tells the High Tower employees to evacuate the building via the elevators rather than the stairwell. The employees comply, and reach safety, whereas if they had taken the stairwell the building would have collapsed and killed them.

Here, when we focus on the actual outcome of Joan's action, we want to say that it is right—that she saved the employees' lives. But if we focus on her giving them advice that she thought would result in their death or injury, we want to say that what she did was very wrong.

To resolve the apparent paradox of such actions being judged both right and wrong, moral theorists in the first half of the twentieth century argued that we must recognize several different senses of such moral terms as "right," "wrong," "obligatory," and "permissible." In one sense of "morally right," they argued, we mean something like "the morally best action in the actual circumstances"; while in another sense of "right," we mean something like "the action that is morally most appropriate in light of the agent's beliefs about those circumstances, even if the beliefs are mistaken."[2] Granting that there are different senses of these terms dissolves the paradox arising from our judgment that each security guard's action is both morally right and morally wrong, since the act can be right in one sense but wrong in the other. Moreover, for those theorists disconcerted by the idea that an act might be an agent's duty even though the agent (through ignorance or mistakes about factual matters) doesn't know the act to be his duty, the concept of an act that is best relative to the agent's beliefs identifies a type of duty to which the agent would always have epistemic access, and thus could fairly be held to blame for violating.[3]

---

[2] These locutions are somewhat misleading, since a morally *right* action is not necessarily the unique morally best action available to the agent, but may be one of several equally good options. However, for simplicity of exposition, I shall often use "right" when "ought to be done" or "obligatory" would be more accurate. I shall also frequently use "objective rightness" or "subjective rightness" to stand in for the objective or subjective moral status of an action more generally speaking. Note that here and throughout this essay, I am speaking only of *all-things-considered* moral status, not *prima facie* or *pro tanto* moral status. Many of the same issues arise for these latter concepts, and much of my discussion can be applied to them.

[3] Prichard forcefully articulates this worry in "Duty and Ignorance of Fact."

Many writers have come to see the importance of making such a distinction. The terms used for expressing these different senses of "right" and "wrong" have varied, but contemporary usage has coalesced around the term "objectively right" for the first sense, and "subjectively right" for the second. The use of these terms to express this distinction is now widely, although not universally, accepted among moral philosophers.[4]

The gap between what is best in light of the actual circumstances of an action, and what is best in light of the agent's beliefs about the circumstances, arises most visibly in the context of consequentialist theories in which the long-term consequences of an action—not readily knowable by its agent—determine its moral status. But this gap can easily arise for deontological or nonconsequentialist theories as well, since the relevant *circumstances* or *nature* of an action (apart from its consequences) may also be difficult for the agent to ascertain accurately.[5] Deontological theories

---

[4] See, for example, the following discussions: Tim Mulgan, *The Demands of Consequentialism* (Oxford: Clarendon Press, 2001) (discussing versions of consequentialism): "The objectively right action is always what would have produced the best consequences. . . . The subjectively right action is what seems to the agent to have the greatest expected value" (42); David Sosa, "Consequences of Consequentialism," *Mind*, New Series 102, no. 405 (January 1993): "[T]hey can agree that what he did was, say, 'subjective-right' and 'objective-wrong'" (109); Graham Oddie and Peter Menzies, "An Objectivist's Guide to Subjective Value," *Ethics* 102, no. 3 (April 1992): "The subjectivist claims that the primary notion for moral theory is given by what is best by the agent's lights . . . regardless of what is actually the best. The objectivist claims that the primary notion for moral theory is given by what is best regardless of how things seem to the agent" (512); and James L. Hudson, "Subjectivization in Ethics," *American Philosophical Quarterly* 26, no. 3 (July 1989): "In moral philosophy there is an important distinction between *objective* theories and *subjective* ones. An objective theory lays down conditions for right action which an agent may often be unable to use in determining her own behavior. In contrast, the conditions for right action laid down by a subjective theory guarantee the agent's ability to use them to guide her actions" (221; italics in the original).

Some contemporary theorists use the term "rational" to refer to what I am calling "subjectively right." However, since what it would be rational for an agent to do, or what an agent has reason to do, may be ambiguous in just the same way that what it would be right for an agent to do may be ambiguous, I shall not adopt this terminology. Note, though, that the distinction between subjective and objective rightness arises not just in morality but also in other practical fields, such as law, prudence, etiquette, etc. My discussion will be confined to ethics, but much that is said here can be carried over into these other domains.

Some theorists have introduced the distinction between objective and subjective rightness (or something closely similar), not for the reasons I describe, but to serve other argumentative purposes, such as to address the criticism of utilitarianism that it requires agents to constantly calculate the utilities of their actions and thus diverts them from direct attention to the kinds of pursuits and relationships that make life worthwhile. See, for example, Peter Railton, "Alienation, Consequentialism, and the Demands of Morality," *Philosophy and Public Affairs* 13 (Spring 1984): 134–171.

[5] Philip Pettit, in his essay "Consequentialism," in Stephen Darwall, ed., *Consequentialism* (Malden, MA: Blackwell Publishing, 2003), points out that many nonconsequentialists assume that the properties of actions they find morally relevant are ones such that the agent will always be able to know whether or not an option will have one of those properties. In Pettit's view, this is not generally so. Hence, according to Pettit, "the non-consequentialist strategy will often be undefined" (ibid., 99). In "Absolutist Moral Theories and Uncertainty," *The Journal of Philosophy* 103, no. 6 (June 2006): 267–83, Frank Jackson and Michael Smith argue that absolutist nonconsequentialist moral theorists cannot define a workable account of what it would be subjectively best to do in light of uncertainty.

may forbid killing the innocent, lying, committing adultery, convicting innocent defendants, stealing, failing to compensate those whom one has unjustifiably harmed, and so forth. But any given agent may be mistaken as to whether a possible killing victim is innocent, whether the statement he makes is untrue, whether the person with whom he has sexual relations is married, whether the defendant is guilty of the crime, whether an item of property belongs to him or to someone else, or whether a given level of compensation covers the loss. Thus, the pressure to recognize two senses of "right" and "wrong" arises equally for both consequentialist and nonconsequentialist moral theories.

The argument for distinguishing objective from subjective rightness may have originally arisen to deal with the fact that in certain circumstances we are pulled to evaluate an agent's action as paradoxically both right and wrong. However, it quickly became clear that another need is served by this distinction as well. It is commonly held that a—or the— main function of moral theories is to guide agents in making decisions about what to do.[6] Suppose the security guards in our cases have moral codes that tell them to save the lives of people in the building.[7] Tom, in *Twin Towers I*, can use his moral code to guide his decision, since, in light of his belief that using the stairwell is the only safe evacuation route, he can infer from his moral code that he ought to direct the employees to use the stairwell. His code can guide his decision even though he is mistaken about the facts, and thus chooses, on the basis of his theory, an act that the theory condemns. But consider the following case:

Twin Towers III: Following the crash of an airplane into a skyscraper, security guard Pete must advise the office workers how best to evac-

---

[6] For a selection of examples, see Eugene Bales, "Act-Utilitarianism: Account of Right-Making Characteristics or Decision-Making Procedure?" *American Philosophical Quarterly* 7 (July 1971): 256–65; Stephen Darwall, *Impartial Reason* (Ithaca, NY: Cornell University Press, 1983), 30–31; Hudson, "Subjectivization in Ethics"; Allan Gibbard, *Wise Choices, Apt Feelings* (Cambridge, MA: Harvard University Press, 1990), 43; Frank Jackson, "Decision-Theoretic Consequentialism and the Nearest and Dearest Objection," *Ethics* 101, no. 3 (April 1991): 461–82; Christine Korsgaard, *The Sources of Normativity* (Cambridge: Cambridge University Press, 1996), 8; Ron Milo, *Immorality* (Princeton, NJ: Princeton University Press: 1984), 22 ("Our primary purpose in passing judgments on our actions is to enable us to guide our choices about how to act"); Jan Narveson, *Morality and Utility* (Baltimore, MD: The Johns Hopkins Press, 1967), 12; J. J. C. Smart, "An Outline of a System of Utilitarian Ethics," in J. J. C. Smart and Bernard Williams, *Utilitarianism: For and Against* (Cambridge: Cambridge University Press, 1973), 44, 46; Michael Stocker, *Plural and Conflicting Values* (Oxford: Clarendon Press, 1990), 10; Mark Timmons, *Moral Theory: An Introduction* (Lanham, MD: Rowman and Littlefield, 2002), 3; and Bernard Williams, "A Critique of Utilitarianism," in Smart and Williams, *Utilitarianism: For and Against*, 124.

[7] Throughout this essay, I will talk about "theories," "principles," and "codes" of objective and subjective rightness. A particularist would reject such generalized statements of what makes actions right or wrong. Nonetheless, the particularist, too, will have to deal with problems arising from agents' mistakes and uncertainties, so he will need to attend to the issues addressed in this essay—something that appears to have been little discussed among particularists.

uate. Pete believes there is an 80 percent chance that the elevators will become inoperative before they reach the ground floor, and also believes there is a 50 percent chance that people evacuating via the stairwell will not escape the building before it collapses. Pete directs the employees to use the stairwell, but descending takes too long and all the employees are killed when the building collapses. The elevators, however, remain operational long enough for the employees to have used them to evacuate safely.

In this case, Pete cannot use his moral code to make a decision, because it simply tells him to save the lives of people in the building; it tells him nothing about what to do when the probability of saving their lives is less than 100 percent. However, since advising the employees to use the stairwell has a 50 percent chance of saving their lives, whereas advising them to use the elevators has only a 20 percent chance of saving their lives, there is a clear sense in which Pete's advising them to use the stairwell is the better action. Unfortunately, there is an equally clear sense in which this action is the worse action, since it leads to the employees' death, whereas advising them to use the elevators would have saved their lives. *Twin Towers III* demonstrates that the concept of "subjective rightness" can usefully serve a second function: it can be used to pick out the action that it would be wise to perform even though the agent cannot derive guidance directly from his moral code. For Pete, telling the employees to use the stairs is the subjectively right action, while telling them to use the elevators is subjectively wrong; he can decide what to do by choosing the action that has the superior subjective status. Consideration of cases such as this led theorists to recognize that the original distinction between objective and subjective rightness could be leveraged: the concept of subjective rightness can be utilized to provide the moral guidance needed by agents who are *uncertain* (as opposed to *mistaken*) about the circumstances or consequences of their actions, and who therefore need some standard beyond objective rightness in deciding what to do. The frequent uncertainty that agents have about the objective moral status of their prospective actions means that many agents are unable to use their moral code directly to make decisions about what to do. Ideally, the concept of subjective moral rightness dissolves this problem: for every agent who is capable of making a moral decision, on each occasion for decision-making there will be some act identifiable by the agent as one that is subjectively right for her to perform. If she looks to morality for guidance, she can choose the subjectively right act even when she cannot identify which act is objectively right.[8]

---

[8] Occasionally people respond to *Twin Towers III* by saying, "Of course Pete can use his moral code to make his decision, since it tells him to save the lives of the people in the building, or to choose the method that has the greatest chance of saving their lives." But

Of course, the concepts of moral rightness and wrongness are heavily linked to the concept of moral blameworthiness.[9] Once the distinction between objective and subjective rightness/wrongness is recognized, it becomes natural to say something like, "An action is blameworthy only if it is subjectively wrong." An action can be *objectively wrong* but still not blameworthy, as *Twin Towers I* and *III* show: security guards Tom and Pete are not blameworthy for directing the employees to use the stairwell, even though their actions are objectively wrong. One promising way to explain why these actions are not blameworthy is to invoke the concept of subjective rightness, and say that the actions are subjectively right, and hence not blameworthy, even though they are objectively wrong.

Thus, it appears as though the distinction between objective and subjective rightness is an extremely valuable contribution to moral theory. However, it might be claimed that we do not really need this distinction—that we can do all the work we want to do with a more limited set of moral concepts that includes objective rightness/wrongness and blameworthiness/praiseworthiness, but not subjective rightness/wrongness. Thus, it might be claimed that we can say all we need to about *Twin Towers I* and *II* by saying that Tom's act is objectively wrong but not blameworthy (because he believed his act to be objectively right, and had the excuse of ignorance), while Joan's act is objectively right but still blameworthy (because she believed her act to be objectively wrong, but nonetheless chose it). But we cannot say all we need to about *Twin Towers III* by using just these concepts, since we need some way to articulate the moral appropriateness of Pete's act of advising the employees to use the stairwell rather than the elevators (even though this leads to their deaths). It is true that Pete's act is objectively wrong, and that he is not blameworthy for this act. But we cannot explain why he is not blameworthy by saying that Pete believes his act to be objectively right (as we explain Tom's not being blameworthy). By hypothesis, Pete's moral code does not evaluate his act as objectively right, and Pete himself does not believe that it is objectively right, since he is uncertain which act would satisfy his duty to save lives. Thus, it appears we need the distinction between objective and subjective rightness to articulate the moral status of the choice-worthy action in cases where the agent is uncertain which action would be objectively best. Once we have accepted the need for the distinction in

---

Pete's moral code says only that he is to actually save their lives; advice about what he should do when it is uncertain which escape route would have the greatest chance of saving their lives is part of the job of principles of subjective rightness, and shows why we need them. We are so used to thinking in this fashion that we often do not notice we have switched from a judgment about objective rightness to a judgment about subjective rightness. But see also the remarks about "Remodeling" theorists in the text below.

[9] They are also linked heavily to the concept of an excuse, and in particular to the fact that we excuse (not justify) people for their acts done in ignorance, but I will not try to spell out the ramifications of this in the present essay.

these cases, we can accept its usefulness in cases such as *Twin Towers I* and *II* as well.

   While some theorists might have hoped we could make do with just the standard concepts of objective rightness/wrongness and blameworthiness/ praiseworthiness, other theorists (let us call them "Remodeling" theo- rists)[10] have tried to simplify our moral toolbox by abandoning the *traditional* concept of objective rightness/wrongness, and elevating the concept of subjective rightness/wrongness to take its place. On this view, an action can have only one type of rightness or wrongness, but this fundamental status is determined, not by the action's actual circum- stances and consequences, but rather by the content of the agent's beliefs about its circumstances and consequences. A Remodeling theorist would say that the only "right or wrong" judgment we need to make about Tom's action in *Twin Towers I* is that it is right because it is the action most appropriate to the agent's beliefs about its circumstances and consequenc- es.[11] According to such theorists, there is no need to go beyond this by evaluating the action in light of its actual circumstances. Theorists who take this stance are often moved by what they take to be the chief function of moral theories, namely, to guide agents' decision-making. They argue that because agents are frequently mistaken or uncertain about the cir- cumstances and consequences of their actions, it is better to eliminate any evaluation that rests on facts that are unknown to them, and focus solely on evaluations that rest on the decision-maker's beliefs about his circum- stances, beliefs which are more accessible to him. For example, many utilitarians have proposed that act or rule utilitarianism be formulated in terms of the *expected* rather than *actual* consequences of the act or rule. According to such Remodeling theorists, Tom's act is right in this funda- mental sense of "right"; it can guide him in making his decision. There is no need to introduce any additional concept of rightness. The concept of blameworthiness is then tied fairly directly to the "fundamental" wrong- ness of the action.[12]

---

[10] This is a term I employ in *Making Morality Work* (manuscript in progress), and repre- sents a change from the terminology I employed in "Two-Tier Moral Codes," *Social Philos- ophy and Policy* 7, no. 1 (1989): 112–32.

[11] Common variants of this view would stipulate that the action must be most appropriate to the beliefs that a reasonable person would have in the agent's circumstances, or some similar constraint.

[12] Both Prichard, "Duty and Ignorance of Fact," and Ross, *Foundations of Ethics*, are Remod- eling theorists. Recent discussions and defenses of Remodeling theories include Hudson, "Subjectivization in Ethics," 221–29; William H. Shaw, *Contemporary Ethics: Taking Account of Utilitarianism* (Malden, MA: Blackwell Publishers, 1999): 27–31; Brad Hooker, *Ideal Code, Real World* (Oxford: Clarendon Press, 2000); Michael Zimmerman, "Is Moral Obligation Objective or Subjective?" *Utilitas* 18, no. 4 (December 2006): 329–61; and Jackson, "Decision-Theoretic Consequentialism." In *Living with Uncertainty* (Cambridge: Cambridge University Press, 2008), Michael Zimmerman provides the most developed contemporary version and defense of this type of theory. Fred Feldman argues, in "Actual Utility, the Objection from Imprac- ticality, and the Move to Expected Utility," *Philosophical Studies* 129 (2006): 49–79, that the

I believe that such Remodeling theorists are mistaken, and that we need both the concepts of objective and subjective moral status. It is not the purpose of this essay to argue for this view. However, before we can seriously assess the view of these theorists, we need a firm grasp on the concept of subjective rightness/wrongness, so that we can accurately determine whether it is sensible to elevate this concept in the manner that Remodeling theorists recommend. The aim of this essay is to propose a novel definition for the concept of subjective moral status. I shall review the definitions available in the literature, and argue that the general approach embodied in these definitions is wrongly conceived and must be abandoned in favor of a more fruitful strategy. A successful definition will help us understand the distinction between objective and subjective moral status, will create an important foundation for evaluating proposed substantive principles of subjective rightness, and will provide groundwork for assessing the claims of the Remodeling theorists.

One final clarification: agents can be mistaken or uncertain about normative matters, as well as about matters of non-normative fact. The difficulties facing such agents, and what to say about them, are deep problems.[13] However, in this essay I will focus only on the difficulties arising from agents' mistakes and uncertainty about matters of non-normative fact, and, where necessary, I will assume the agent has the requisite beliefs about normative matters.

II. Defining "Subjective Rightness" and "Subjective Wrongness"

Despite the fact that theorists have converged on the terms "objective" and "subjective" rightness/wrongness to draw the distinction I have described, the definitions proposed for the terms "subjective rightness" and "subjective wrongness" have varied significantly. Clearly, we need to establish acceptable definitions for these crucial concepts.

The terms "subjective rightness" and "subjective wrongness" were introduced to fill gaps in the existing common and philosophical vocabulary. Hence, assessing the adequacy of any proposed definition will not be a matter of simply determining how accurately it reflects common usage, but rather determining whether it fills the perceived gaps in the desired ways. Reflection on the discussion so far suggests certain criteria that any acceptable definition must meet. One complexity we must acknowledge

---

Remodeling version of act-utilitarianism using expected utility cannot achieve all the goals its advocates have hoped for.

[13] For initial investigations of these problems, see Ted Lockhart, *Moral Uncertainty and Its Consequences* (New York: Oxford University Press, 2000); Jacob Ross, "Rejecting Ethical Deflationism," *Ethics* 116 (July 2006): 742–68; and Andrew Sepielli, "What to Do When You Don't Know What to Do," in Russ Shafer-Landau, ed., *Oxford Studies in Metaethics* IV (Oxford: Oxford University Press, 2009).

is that (a) dissolving the paradoxical tension created by evaluating an agent's action as both right and wrong (for example, in the *Twin Towers I* and *II* cases) may have slightly different requirements from (b) providing an uncertain agent with guidance (for example, in the *Twin Towers III* case). In stating the criteria for an acceptable definition of "subjective rightness," I will give pride of place to the need to provide guidance for a decision-making agent. Thus, the first-person perspective—that of the agent deciding what to do—will predominate.

A. Criteria of adequacy

I shall work with the following set of criteria of adequacy for a definition of "subjective rightness." These are somewhat rough, but are usable for our purposes.

> *Criterion 1. Normative Adequacy:* A definition of subjective rightness should enable us to identify principles of subjective rightness that will accurately assess (given appropriate background information) the subjective moral status of actions, where an action's subjective moral status will often contrast, in an acceptable manner, with its objective moral status. The principles of subjective rightness should classify actions as subjectively right that strike us as ones it would be reasonable or wise for the agent to choose, given the agent's (possibly faulty) grasp of the situation.

> *Criterion 2. Domain Adequacy:* The definition of subjective rightness should enable us to identify principles of subjective moral status that assign subjective status to every action that has objective moral status.[14]

> *Criterion 3. Guidance Adequacy:* The definition of subjective rightness should endorse a system of principles of subjective rightness from which agents can derive moral guidance in every situation in which they find themselves, even though an agent may be uncertain or mistaken about which actions have the features that would make them objectively right in that situation.[15]

---

[14] See Holly M. Smith, "Making Moral Decisions," *Noûs* 22 (1988): 89–93, for a detailed discussion of the concepts of "theoretical" and "practical" domains of a moral principle. The statement of Criterion 2 is fairly rough. Moreover, given the possibility discussed in the text below that a non-possible action is subjectively right, we want the domain of principles of subjective rightness to extend *beyond* the domain of principles of objective rightness. In addition, Criterion 2 is too strong, since an agent may be totally unaware that a certain action (under any description) is available to him (for example, he may not believe he can touch his nose with the tip of his tongue, never having tried or even thought about trying to do this); thus, that action might have objective moral status without having any subjective moral status.

[15] As I shall understand the concept of "moral guidance," it includes *permissions* for agents to act in certain ways, as well as demands that they act in certain ways. Almost every

Criterion 4. Relation to Blameworthiness: The action classifications arising from the definition of subjective rightness should bear appropriate relationships to assessments of whether the agent is blameworthy
or praiseworthy for her act.

Criterion 5. Normative Compatibility: The definition of subjective rightness should be compatible with the full range of plausible theories of
objective moral rightness, so that it is possible to identify acts that are
subjectively right relative to each such theory.[16]

Criterion 6. Explanatory Adequacy: The definition of subjective rightness should provide illumination about why subjectively right acts
are reasonable or wise to perform, why agents should guide their
conduct by reference to such acts, and why these acts are linked to
accountability.

I shall use these criteria as guides in assessing proposed definitions of
"subjective rightness." However, the Guidance Adequacy Criterion requires
further comment. What is it to use a normative principle—such as a
principle of subjective rightness—to guide one's decision? Consider John,
who wants to follow the principle "Always stop at red traffic lights, and
always proceed at green traffic lights." He believes that he sees a red light,
and forms the desire to stop his car. But things don't go according to plan:
perhaps he stops, but the light was actually green, and what he saw was
a red beer advertisement; or perhaps the traffic light was red, but his
brakes fail and the car doesn't stop. In both these cases, there is an obvious sense in which he has *not* regulated his behavior in accordance with
his principle—but there is another obvious sense in which his decision
clearly *has* been guided by it. Reflecting on this case, we may draw the
following distinction: an agent is able to use a principle as an *internal
guide* for deciding what to do just in case the agent would directly derive
a prescription for action from the principle if he wanted to, while an agent
is able to use a principle as an *external guide* for deciding what to do just
in case the agent would directly derive a prescription for action from the
principle if he wanted to, and the act whose prescription he would derive
in fact conforms to the principle.[17]

---

situation is one in which there are several equally morally good options, even though there
may be many morally bad options that must be avoided.
[16] Note that there may be limits on this. Some otherwise plausible theories of objective
rightness may not be compatible with *any* theory of subjective rightness. This is arguably a
fault of these theories of objective rightness, not a deficiency in the definition of subjective
rightness. See Frank Jackson and Michael Smith, "Absolutist Moral Theories and Uncertainty," for an argument that absolutist nonconsequentialist theories suffer this failing.
[17] See Holly M. Smith, "Making Moral Decisions," 91–92, for discussion of this distinction.
The definitions given in the text are overly simple; the definition of being able to use a principle as an internal guide is further refined by Definition (8) in Section V of the current essay.

Clearly, it would be ideal if every normative principle, whether it be a principle of objective or subjective rightness, could be used by each agent as an external guide for decision-making. But we have already seen that principles of objective rightness fall short of this ideal, and we must be prepared to discover that principles of subjective rightness may fall short of it as well. However, it seems realistic to insist that principles of subjective rightness—which, after all, are designed to guide agents in making decisions when they are mistaken or uncertain about what the governing principle of objective rightness requires of them—should at least be capable of being used as *internal* decision guides. An agent who cannot find any way to translate his moral values into his *choice* of what to do is an agent who cannot find a way to govern his decision by the considerations he deems most relevant. His decision does not express his moral values, and so in an important way undermines his autonomy.[18] Thus, we want principles of subjective rightness to be capable of being used as internal guides to action, even if they cannot successfully be used as external guides to action. I shall interpret the Guidance Adequacy Criterion as requiring that principles of subjective rightness jointly be usable as internal decision-guides in every situation in which an agent must make a decision.

There are, of course, possible principles of subjective rightness which are not usable as internal guides by a given agent here and now, precisely when the agent must make her decision—but would be usable if she had more information, or had more time to reflect on her circumstances, or had the mental acuity to notice that her beliefs entail, via some complex chain of reasoning, that a certain act is the one prescribed by the principle. By the same token, however, a principle of *objective rightness* that may not be usable as an internal guide by a given agent here and now, when she must make her decision, would be so usable if only the agent had more information, or more time to reflect, or greater mental acuity. We need principles of subjective rightness precisely because agents must often make decisions despite their lack of information or time or ability to deliberate further. Principles of subjective rightness are needed precisely to assist agents in deciding what to do in these circumstances. Hence, when we ask whether a given principle of subjective rightness satisfies the Guidance Adequacy Criterion, we should understand the question to be whether agents are able to use that principle of subjective rightness *at the time they are making a decision, with just the intellectual and informational resources they have at hand*—not whether they would be able to use it if they had more time or some idealized set of resources. Of course, an agent may be blameworthy for not having better resources—perhaps she should have researched her decision more thoroughly before having to make it.

---

[18] For further discussion of this claim, see Holly M. Smith, "Making Moral Decisions," section V. Pekka Väyrynen has picked up and pursued this idea in "Ethical Theories and Moral Guidance," *Utilitas* 18, no. 3 (September 2006): 291–309.

But we and she want to know what is best for her to decide, given her actual information, however culpably impoverished it may be.

B. Approaches to defining "subjective rightness"

In the literature, there have been four prominent approaches to defining "subjective rightness." Although details vary, these four approaches can be stated as follows:

(1) Act A is subjectively right just in case A is the act most likely to be objectively right; and
A is subjectively wrong just in case A is not the act most likely to be objectively right.[19]
(2) Act A is subjectively right just in case A is the act that has the highest expected value; and
A is subjectively wrong just in case there is some alternative to A that has a higher expected value than A.[20]
(3) Act A is subjectively right just in case A would be objectively right if the facts were as the agent believed them to be; and
A is subjectively wrong just in case A would be objectively wrong if the facts were as the agent believed them to be.[21]

[19] See Russell, "The Elements of Ethics," 12 (". . . the [act] which will probably be the most fortunate . . . I shall define . . . as the *wisest* act"); Smart, "An Outline of a System of Utilitarian Ethics," 46–47 (". . . the 'rational' . . . action . . . is, on the evidence available to the agent, *likely* to produce the best results . . ."); C. I. Lewis, *Values and Imperatives* (Stanford, CA: Stanford University Press, 1969), 35–38 (". . . right if it probably would have the best consequences"), as quoted in Marcus C. Singer, "Actual Consequence Utilitarianism," in Philip Pettit, ed., *Consequentialism* (Aldershot, England: Dartmouth Publishing Company Limited, 1993), 299; Ross, *Foundations of Ethics*, 157; John Hospers, *Human Conduct* (New York: Harcourt, Brace, and World, 1961), 217 (". . . our subjective duty, namely the act which, in those circumstances, was the most likely to produce the maximum good").
[20] See Derek Parfit, *Reasons and Persons* (Oxford: Clarendon Press, 1984), 24–25; William H. Shaw, *Contemporary Ethics*, 27–31 (as a theory of objective rightness); and Timmons, *Moral Theory*, 124.
[21] See Richard Brandt, "Towards a Credible Form of Utilitarianism," in Hector-Neri Castaneda and George Nakhnikian, eds., *Morality and the Language of Conduct* (Detroit: Wayne State University, 1965), 112–14; Richard Brandt, *Ethical Theory* (Englewood Cliffs, NJ: Prentice-Hall, 1959), 365 (". . . 'did his duty' in [the subjective] sense means 'did what would have been his duty in the objective sense, if the facts of the particular situation had been as he thought they were, except for corrections he would have made if he had explored the situation as thoroughly as a man of good character would have done in the circumstances'"); Peter Graham, "'Ought' Does *Not* Imply 'Can'," unpublished manuscript, 2007: 3–4, http://people.umass.edu/pgraham/Home.html; Fred Feldman, *Doing the Best We Can* (Dordrecht: D. Reidel, 1986), 46; Broad, *Ethics*, 141 (". . . we must say that he is under a formal obligation to set himself to discharge what he knows *would* be his material obligation *if* the situation were as he mistakenly believes it to be"); Milo, *Immorality*, 18 ("If the agent is mistaken about a matter of fact, and, if, had the facts been as he supposed, his act would be wrong, then, unless there are excusing conditions, his act is blameworthy and immoral"); and Judith Jarvis Thomson, "Imposing Risks," in William Parent, ed., *Rights, Restitution, and Risk* (Cambridge, MA: Harvard University Press, 1986), 179 (". . . presumably 'He (subjectively) ought' means 'If all his beliefs of fact were true, then it would be the case that he

(4) Act A is subjectively right just in case A is best in light of the agent's beliefs at the time he performs A; and
A is subjectively wrong just in case A is not the best act in light of the agent's beliefs at the time he performs A.[22]

I have phrased several of these definitions in terms of what the agent actually believes. But one popular family of variant definitions involves defining "subjective rightness" in terms of what the agent ought to have believed, what a reasonable person in the agent's position would have believed, what the agent would have believed if she had exercised due diligence, what she would have been justified in believing, etc.[23] Thus, Definition (1) might alternatively read: "Act A is subjectively right just in case A is the act that a reasonable agent would believe to be objectively right." For brevity, I will discuss these popular "reasonable belief" variants only in footnotes until Section VI. Each of these definitions, except (4), assumes a background understanding of the concept of "objectively" right/wrong. For the purposes of this essay, I will assume the informal characterization given in Section I: namely, that an action is objectively right just in case the action is the best one in the actual circumstances. However, subsequent discussion will shed some light on this characterization.

C. Definition (1)

Definition (1) states that *an act A is subjectively right just in case A is the act most likely to be objectively right; and A is subjectively wrong just in case A is not the act most likely to be objectively right.* This definition, like Definition

---

(objectively) ought'"; although note that Thomson doubts there is any subjective sense of "ought"). Note that the American Law Institute's Model Penal Code, Section 2.04(2) provides that the defense of ignorance of fact "is not available if the defendant would be guilty of another offense had the situation been as he supposed. . . ." Cited in Douglas Husak and Andrew Von Hirsh, "Culpability and Mistake of Law," in Stephen Shute, John Gardner, and Jeremy Horder, *Action and Value in Criminal Law* (Oxford: Clarendon Press, 1993), 161.

[22] See Gibbard, *Wise Choices, Apt Feelings*, 42 ("Thus an act is . . . wrong in the subjective sense if it is wrong in light of what the agent had good reason to believe"; note that Gibbard uses the "good reason to believe" formulation of this definition); Prichard, "Duty and Ignorance of Fact," 25 (". . . the obligation depends on our being in a certain attitude of mind towards the situation in respect of knowledge, thought, or opinion"); Ross, *Foundations of Ethics*, 146–47 (". . . when we call an act right we sometimes mean that . . . it suits the subjective features [of the situation]. . . . The subjective element consists of the agent's thoughts about the situation"; see also ibid., 150, 161, 164); Graham Oddie and Peter Menzies, "An Objectivist's Guide to Subjective Value," *Ethics* 102 (April 1992): 512–33, at 512 (". . . is the morally right action the one which is best in the light of the agent's beliefs?"); and Jackson and Smith, "Absolutist Moral Theories and Uncertainty," 270 (". . . we are in fact talking about what a subject ought to do given their epistemic situation.").

[23] For example, Gibbard, *Wise Choices, Apt Feelings*, 42; Brandt, *Ethical Theory*, 365; and Hospers, *Human Conduct*, 217.

(2), but unlike Definitions (3) and (4), contains a *substantive rule* for determining an action's subjective status.[24]

As a number of writers (but not all) have noticed, Definition (1) must be rejected, because it often delivers an unacceptable appraisal of an act as subjectively right. Consider the following case (a variant of one much discussed in the literature):[25]

> *Strong Medicine:* Patient Ron consults his physician, Sue, about a moderately serious ailment. Sue can treat Ron with either of two drugs. She believes that giving him no treatment would render his ailment permanent; that drug X would cure Ron partially; and that there is an 80 percent chance that drug Y will cure Ron completely, but a 20 percent chance that Y will kill him.

Suppose Sue's moral code tells her to maximize the welfare of her patients. Her choice, then, appears to be as follows, if we supply some reasonable figures as estimates of the welfare of the patient. "Situation S" is the situation in which *if* Ron takes drug Y he will be completely cured, while "Situation S*" is the situation in which *if* Ron takes drug Y he will be killed. Of course, the outcome for Ron if he receives no treatment, or if he takes drug X, is the same whether Situation S or Situation S* obtains.

TABLE 1. *Possible outcomes in* Strong Medicine

Action	Situation S (probability = .80)	Situation S* (probability = .20)
No treatment	Ron continues ill (value = −500)	Ron continues ill (value = −500)
Give drug X	Ron partially cured (value = 100)	Ron partially cured (value = 100)
Give drug Y	Ron is cured (value = 1,000)	Ron dies (value = −25,000)

According to Definition (1), the subjectively right act for Sue is to prescribe drug Y, since it is most likely to be objectively right. Prescribing drug Y has a .80 probability of maximizing Ron's welfare (and so being objectively right), since there is a .80 probability that Situation S will obtain and Ron will be cured—the best possible outcome. Prescribing drug X has only a .20 probability of maximizing his welfare (and so being objectively right), since there is a .20 probability that Situation S* will

[24] Some authors offer Definitions (1) and (2) as definitions of the concepts of subjective rightness/wrongness, while other authors seem to assume (without stating them) some more general definitions of these concepts, and offer (1) and (2) as substantive rules for determining which acts are subjectively right or wrong. My discussion will focus on (1) and (2) as proposed definitions.

[25] Zimmerman, "Is Moral Obligation Objective or Subjective?" 334; Zimmerman takes the example from Jackson, "Decision-Theoretic Consequentialism," 462–63.

obtain, in which case prescribing drug Y would kill Ron (whereas prescribing drug X would partially cure him), and giving him no treatment
would also have a worse outcome than prescribing drug X. Giving him no
treatment has a zero probability of maximizing his welfare (and so being
objectively right).

But clearly this is incorrect: Sue should not run a 20 percent risk of
killing Ron in order to possibly achieve a full cure in this case; it would
be wiser of her to prescribe drug X, which will not achieve a full cure, but
runs no risk of killing him. Definition (1) gives Sue the wrong advice
about what choice to make because it fails to take into account *how* bad (or
good) the possible outcomes of her actions are, apart from the bare comparative fact that one outcome is better or worse than another. Hence, it
is insensitive to the fact that when prescribing drug Y to Ron does not
produce the best outcome, it produces an outcome far worse than anything that might be produced by any of the other options. Definition (1)
fails the Normative Adequacy Criterion.[26]

D. Definition (2)

Definition (2) states that *an act A is subjectively right just in case A is
the act that has the highest expected value; and A is subjectively wrong just
in case there is some alternative to A that has a higher expected value than A.*
Definition (2) is explicitly formulated to overcome the problem just
seen for Definition (1), since it is formulated to take into consideration,
not just the probabilities of the various outcomes of an agent's actions,
but also how good or bad those options are, beyond the bare comparative fact that they are better or worse than the outcomes that would
be produced by another of the agent's alternatives. The "expected value"
of an act is the sum of the expected values of each of its possible
upshots, where the expected value of an upshot is the value of that
upshot, weighted by the probability of the upshot's occurring. Thus,
the expected values of Sue's acts in the *Strong Medicine* case would be
as follows:

---

[26] Note that it would not help Definition (1) to rephrase it along "Reasonable Belief" lines
as "Act A is subjectively right just in case A is the act which it would be reasonable for the
agent to believe to be most likely to be objectively right, and A is subjectively wrong just in
case A is not the act which it would be reasonable for the agent to believe to be most likely
to be objectively right." Adverting to what it is reasonable (etc.) for the agent to believe does
not enable Definition (1) to escape the problem just discussed.
    As several writers have noted, there are cases in which an act that is certain to be
objectively wrong is nonetheless one of those that would be subjectively right: see Donald
Regan, *Utilitarianism and Co-operation* (Oxford: Oxford University Press, 1980), 264–65; and
Jackson, "Decision-Theoretic Consequentialism," 462–63. We can see such a case if we add
drug Z to *Strong Medicine,* and in Situation S*, drug Z would completely cure the patient, but
in Situation S, drug Z would kill the patient (the opposite of drug Y in these situations).
Then giving drug X is certain to be objectively wrong, because in Situation S, drug Y would
be better, whereas in Situation S*, drug Z would be better.

TABLE 2. *Expected values in* Strong Medicine

Action	Situation S (probability = .80)	Situation S* (probability = .20)	Overall expected value
No treatment	Ron continues ill (value = −500)	Ron continues ill (value = −500)	−500
Give drug X	Ron partially cured (value = 100)	Ron partially cured (value = 100)	100
Give drug Y	Ron is cured (value = 1,000)	Ron dies (value = −25,000)	−4,200

According to Definition (2), Sue's prescribing drug X to Ron would be the subjectively right act, because it has the highest expected value (100). Prescribing drug Y would be subjectively wrong, because its expected value (−4,200) is less than the expected value of prescribing drug X. This recommendation to prescribe drug X has vastly more intuitive appeal than the recommendation derived from Definition (1). Because of the intuitive appeal of such recommendations, as well as other reasons, Definition (2) has a long history of support from moral philosophers and decision theorists.

However, even though Definition (2) offers an account of subjective rightness that accords well with our intuitive understanding of what makes some acts better choices than others when the agent is uncertain about the actual facts of his situation (and thus satisfies the Normative Adequacy Criterion), it fails to satisfy the Guidance Adequacy Criterion. The Guidance Adequacy Criterion requires that a definition of subjective rightness endorse principles of subjective rightness that provide guidance to an agent who cannot decide what to do because he is uncertain about the facts of his situation. The principle of subjective rightness endorsed by Definition (2) is simply: "An act is subjectively right if it would maximize expected value, and subjectively wrong otherwise." To apply this principle in making a decision, an agent such as Sue need not have certainty about her circumstances; she need not, for example, feel certain that drug Y would cure Ron. But she *does* need to have probability estimates—not mere "possibility" judgments—about the relevant circumstances. Sue, for example, must be able to assign probabilities to drug Y's curing Ron and to drug Y's killing Ron. Moreover, she must have beliefs about the expected values of her various alternatives, which would normally require her to have calculated these values.[27] In a simple case such as *Strong Medicine,* many (although not all) agents could do this. But many of the decisions that agents must make would necessitate their assigning values and probabilities to events

[27] Of course, it is possible that some advisor might simply inform Sue what the expected values of her options are, relieving her of the need to make these calculations. Regrettably, such advisors are thin on the ground for agents making complex decisions.

about which they have very little notion what their likelihood is, and would involve the agents' making enormously complex calculations to arrive at each action's expected value. It is completely implausible that every agent has beliefs about the required value assignments and probability estimates, or has the time or ability to make these calculations, or, more generally, has the belief about some action that it would maximize expected value, before a decision must be made.[28] We must conclude that Definition (2), although it directly endorses what is often the correct principle to use in selecting an action, nonetheless violates the Guidance Adequacy Criterion, because this principle cannot be used as a guide by many agents who lack the necessary beliefs or ability or time to apply it.[29]

[28] For a graphic description of these problems, see Feldman, "Actual Utility," 49–79. Note that these problems arise whether the definition or principle of subjective rightness is phrased in terms of objective probabilities or subjective probabilities. Even if it is always possible for an agent to elicit his own subjective assignments of probability, he may not have time to do this before a decision must be made. (Of course, an agent might believe that some act would maximize expected value without having made any calculations.)

To be sure, decision theorists have proven that any decision-maker whose decisions conform to certain rationality postulates governing his subjective probability assignments and his choices over uncertain prospects will necessarily choose the action that maximizes his own expected value. For a classic presentation, see R. Duncan Luce and Howard Raiffa, *Games and Decisions* (New York: John Wiley and Sons, 1957), chapter 2. But these subjective values and probability estimates are latent dispositions to make choices in certain situations; the agent himself cannot know what these values and estimates are without a good deal of work. Prior to doing that work, he does not have the information necessary to consciously apply the principle advising him to maximize expected value. Moreover, there is no guarantee that his subjective values (revealed by an array of choices) are actually identical to the moral value that he consciously seeks to maximize in making the present decision. In any event, we are interested in providing a decision-maker with *normative advice* on how to proceed in choosing his action. To be told that he will, if rational, inevitably select the action that maximizes his expected value provides him with no moral guidance.

[29] I argue elsewhere that Definition (2) also fails as a general definition of subjective rightness because it is incompatible with moral theories having certain structures (see my *Making Morality Work*, manuscript).

Note that it would not help Definition (2) to be restated in the form of a Reasonable Belief definition as "Act A is subjectively right just in case A is the act that it would be reasonable for the agent to believe has the highest expected value, and A is subjectively wrong just in case there is some alternative to A that it would be reasonable for the agent to believe has a higher expected value than A." Here, too, adverting to what it might be reasonable (justified, etc.) for the agent to believe does not enable Definition (2) to escape the problem just discussed. There may indeed be cases in which the agent's evidence is sufficiently comprehensive that it would be possible to say that the agent (based on that evidence) would be justified in believing that a given act would have the highest expected value. However, there will be many other cases in which the agent's evidence (or the evidence available to him) is not sufficiently comprehensive to justify a belief about which act has the highest expected value. Moreover, at the time a decision must be made, the agent may not believe that he is justified in having any belief about which action would maximize expected value, or may not be able to identify which such belief would be justified (even though he may be so justified). For this reason, too, the agent could not use a principle of subjective rightness endorsed by this version of Definition (2) in order to make his decision.

E. Definition (3)

Definition (3) states that *an act A is subjectively right just in case A would be objectively right if the facts were as the agent believed them to be; and A is subjectively wrong just in case A would be objectively wrong if the facts were as the agent believed them to be*. Definition (3) works well in cases such as *Twin Towers I*. In that case, in light of security guard Tom's beliefs about the elevators and the stairs, he also believes that he will save the lives of people in the building by directing the employees to evacuate by the stairs rather than the elevators. Were the facts as Tom believed them to be, his act of directing the employees to use the stairs would be objectively right, so this act counts as subjectively right according to Definition (3). This prescription satisfies the Normative Adequacy Criterion in this case, since we feel that this act is the wisest act for Tom to perform (despite the fact that it results in avoidable tragedy). It also satisfies the Guidance Adequacy Criterion, since Tom can use it to decide which act to perform.

Unfortunately, Definition (3) does not meet these criteria in every case. Consider how to apply it to *Twin Towers III*, in which security guard Pete's relevant beliefs are *probabilistic* ones: he believes that there is an 80 percent *chance* that the elevators will become inoperative before they reach the ground floor, and he believes there is a 50 percent *chance* that people evacuating via the stairs will not get out of the building before it collapses. He further believes that directing the employees to the stairs has the greatest *chance* of saving the employees' lives. To apply Definition (3) to Pete's decision requires us to determine what act would have been objectively right if the facts were as Pete believed them to be. This was easy enough in *Twin Towers I*, since we only needed to ask which act would have been objectively right if the facts were as Tom believed them to be (i.e., if he were correct in believing that he would save the employees' lives by directing them to use the stairs). In a case such as *Twin Towers III*, however, it is much less easy to see how to apply Definition (3). What would the "facts" be if they were as Pete believed them to be? We might try to identify a probabilistic "objective fact" corresponding to Pete's belief that directing the employees to the stairs offers the greatest chance of saving their lives. On some views about probability, there are no "objective" probabilistic "facts" such as a probabilistic fact that directing the employees to the stairs has the greatest chance of saving their lives.[30] On these views, we are blocked from applying Definition (3) to Pete's decision, since we cannot determine which act would be objectively right if the "facts" were as Pete believed them to be—there are no such "facts." In this circumstance, Definition (3) fails to satisfy the Nor-

---

[30] That is, there are no probabilistic facts other than ones in which the probabilities are 1 or 0. But Pete's beliefs cannot be translated into facts such as these.

mative Adequacy Criterion, the Domain Adequacy Criterion, and the Guidance Adequacy Criterion, since it cannot identify any act as the subjectively right act.

On other views about probability, there might be a sense of objective probability according to which directing the employees to the stairs offers the greatest objective chance of saving their lives. On these views, we would apply definition (3) by asking what act would be objectively right if directing the employees to the stairs offers the greatest objective chance of saving their lives. But Pete's moral code, like most moral codes, ascribes objective moral status to an action in virtue of its *non-probabilistic* features: his moral code says that an action is objectively right if it *will actually* save the employees' lives. His moral code says nothing about the objective status of an action that has the *greatest objective chance* of saving their lives. In the context of his moral code, this probabilistic characteristic of the action is morally irrelevant. Hence, his moral code does not provide an assessment of the objective moral status of any of Pete's options as he understands them. Once again, we are blocked from applying Definition (3) to Pete's decision, since it cannot evaluate actions as subjectively right or wrong in the context of a theory of objective moral rightness that does not ascribe moral relevance to probabilistic features of those actions.[31] Definition (3) must be rejected as violating the Normative Adequacy Criterion, the Domain Adequacy Criterion, and the Guidance Adequacy Criterion in the many cases in which agents have probabilistic beliefs about their options.[32]

III. "Best in Light of the Agent's Beliefs"

We have now seen that Definitions (1), (2), and (3) fail to satisfy all the criteria we introduced for evaluating proposed definitions of the concept of subjective rightness/wrongness.

This leaves us with Definition (4), which states that *an act A is subjectively right just in case A is best in light of the agent's beliefs at the time he performs A; and A is subjectively wrong just in case A is not the best act in light of the agent's beliefs at the time he performs A.* Although worrisomely vague, Definition (4) looks promising. Since it states that an act is evaluated for

---

[31] Similar conclusions hold if we interpret "probability" as "epistemic probability." Thus, Pete's belief might be interpreted as "My credence level is .8 that the elevators will become inoperative." But there is no way to get from the truth of this belief to a conclusion about what would be objectively right for Pete to do, given that his objective moral code simply tells him to save the lives of the people in the building.

[32] Note that it would not help Definition (3) to be restated in the form of a Reasonable Belief theory such as "Act A is subjectively right just in case A would be objectively right if the facts had been as the agent had reason to believe them to be; and A is subjectively wrong just in case A would be objectively wrong if the facts had been as the agent had reason to believe them to be." What the agent has reason to believe, in many cases, will be probabilistic (as in Pete's case), and so will run into the same problems as the original Definition (3).

subjective rightness in light of the agent's beliefs, it is at least consistent with the appropriate evaluations of the agents' choices in *Twin Towers I, II,* and *III,* and in *Strong Medicine,* and thus seems likely to satisfy the Normative Adequacy Criterion. Moreover, since agents normally have access to the contents of their beliefs, it appears that agents can ascertain which action is subjectively right, and hence can apply this concept, as characterized by Definition (4), in their decision-making—which enables it to meet the Guidance Adequacy Criterion. Since blameworthiness is clearly a function (at least in part) of what the agent believes about the circumstances of her choice, Definition (4) appears likely to satisfy the Relation to Blameworthiness Criterion. And, since it appears compatible with any plausible theory of objective rightness, it appears likely to meet the Normative Compatibility Criterion as well.

Nonetheless, there are difficulties with Definition (4). Let us examine them.

A. The accessibility of beliefs

Definition (4) states that whether or not an action is subjectively right (or wrong) is a function of the agent's beliefs. For example, in *Twin Towers I,* it suggests that even if Tom's action of directing the employees to use the stairs is objectively wrong, nonetheless this act is subjectively right, because Tom believes that the employees' lives would be saved by their taking the stairs rather than the elevators. For a principle of subjective rightness, built on Definition (4), to meet the Guidance Adequacy Criterion—to guide any agent in making a moral decision—it must be the case that agents *always* have access to their own beliefs. Thus, it must be the case that even though security guard Pete in *Twin Towers III* does not know (or believe) which escape route would actually be best, he does have access to his belief that directing the employees to the stairs has the greatest chance of saving their lives. If what it is subjectively right for him to do is a function of this belief, and he is aware that he has this belief, then he can make a choice based on a principle of subjective rightness that tells him what to do in light of his beliefs. But if Pete is *unaware* or *uncertain* what his relevant beliefs are, then he cannot apply any principle of subjective rightness that meets Definition (4) in deciding what to do. If agents can be uncertain about the existence and content of their relevant beliefs, then any principle of subjective rightness meeting Definition (4) would fail to satisfy the Guidance Adequacy Criterion in those cases.

Or suppose it is possible for an agent to feel certain what his relevant beliefs are, but to be mistaken about this. Imagine that Pete feels certain he believes that directing the employees to the elevator has the greatest chance of saving their lives, even though he actually believes just the reverse. In such a case, it appears that Definition (4) implies that Pete's subjectively right act is to direct the employees to use the stairs, but he would *believe* that his subjectively right act is to direct the employees to use the elevators. This possibility would open up a gap between what is actually subjectively right for the agent and what the agent may conclude is subjectively right: a gap somewhat parallel to the original gap between what is objectively right for the agent to do and what is subjectively right for him to do. It would undermine one of the original attractions of the concept of subjective rightness, which is that it could be used to identify a type of duty to which the agent has infallible access in his decision-making, even though he may be mistaken or uncertain about which act is objectively right.[33]

But *can* agents be uncertain or mistaken about the content and existence of their own beliefs in the way I just proposed? Of course, in many cases, people do have accurate access to their own beliefs. Some philosophers have argued that this is always the case. However, most philosophers and psychologists now hold that a person's own beliefs are not necessarily accessible to that person (or at least accessible in the time available for making a quick decision). Agents may be unaware of, mistaken, or uncertain regarding the existence or content of their beliefs, just as they can be unaware of, mistaken, or uncertain about the consequences of their actions. Many of our beliefs are "tacit" or stored at an unconscious level—many people believe, for example, that their house has a roof, but that belief is not one of which they are typically conscious or aware in the course of their day-to-day activities. Sometimes we are simply mistaken: a person may, without reflection, assume she has a certain belief, but under the right revelatory circumstances discover she does not have the belief at all. For example, a churchgoer brought up in a conventional religious family may believe that she believes in God, but be mistaken about this, as she discovers when challenged about the content and foundation for this belief. Some beliefs are, and often remain, unconscious because we are motivated not to acknowledge them. Someone raised in a racist community may believe that he personally no longer harbors racist beliefs, but he may be mistaken about this. Or, alternatively, he may have become convinced (through attendance at too many diversity workshops) that he *does* harbor racist beliefs, when actually he does not. Our beliefs, in other words, are not "luminous." (A belief is luminous just in case it is true that if we have that belief, we believe that we have that belief.) Nor are we

---

[33] It might be urged at this point that Definition (4) should be interpreted as identifying the subjectively right act in light of *all* the agent's beliefs—both his beliefs about his alternative actions, and his beliefs about his own beliefs. But this inclusive set of beliefs would seem to generate two inconsistent answers to what action is subjectively right for him (one arising from the content of his beliefs about the circumstances, and one arising from the content of his beliefs about his own beliefs), so this strategy seems likely to fail. Noting this, however, does call our attention to the fact that we may need to restrict the scope of the agent's beliefs that affect which actions are subjectively right and wrong for him. And, of course, an agent's beliefs about his beliefs about his beliefs about his actions can also be mistaken or uncertain.

infallible with respect to our beliefs. (We are infallible with respect to belief B just in case it is true that if we believe we have belief B, then we do have belief B.)[34]

To see the implications of this for Definition (4), consider the following case:

> *Learning Disability I:* Allison has overwhelming evidence, and in her heart of hearts she recognizes, that her daughter has a significant learning disability. However, she cannot bring herself to consciously face this fact. If asked, she would truthfully say that she believes that she does not believe her daughter to have any disability. She also believes that having her daughter tested would subject her daughter to peer teasing and undermine her self-confidence, but would maximize her happiness if the test were positive and resulted in remedial action. When given the option to have her daughter tested for the disability, Allison declines.[35]

Let us say that the governing principle of objective rightness tells Allison that an act is objectively right just in case it will maximize her daughter's lifetime happiness, and the governing principle of subjective rightness tells Allison that an act is subjectively right just in case she believes the chance of the act's maximizing her daughter's lifetime happiness is no lower than the chance of any alternative act's maximizing her daughter's happiness.[36] Let us assume that on this theory Allison's declining to have her daughter tested is objectively wrong and—according to Definition (4) and the governing principle of subjective rightness—is also subjectively wrong, since in her heart of hearts Allison believes that her daughter has a learning disability and that having her tested will maximize her lifetime happiness. However, since Allison does not recognize all her own beliefs, she does not regard declining to have her daughter tested as either objec-

---

[34] For a recent influential philosophical discussion of this issue, see Timothy Williamson, *Knowledge and Its Limits* (Oxford: Oxford University Press, 2000), chapter 4. Williamson introduced the term "luminous," which he applies to cases in which we *are in a position to know something.* For a seminal discussion of the different types of (possible) "privileged access," see William Alston, "Varieties of Privileged Access," *American Philosophical Quarterly* 8 (1971): 223–41. Although most philosophers (and almost all psychologists) would agree with my statements in the text, there has long been philosophical controversy over this point.

Note that the debate about whether the content of mental states, and in particular beliefs, is "broad" or "narrow" is relevant here as well. If the content of a belief (say, the belief that water quenches thirst) partly depends on matters *external* to the believer (e.g., whether the common liquid substance is H_2O or XYZ), then clearly an agent can be mistaken or uncertain about these external matters, and thus mistaken or uncertain about the content of the beliefs he holds.

[35] This case is based on one described in Ian Deweese-Boyd, "Self-Deception," *Stanford Encyclopedia of Philosophy* (October 17, 2006), section 3.0, http://plato.stanford.edu/entries/self-deception/.

[36] Of course, we have already seen that such a principle is normatively faulty, but for reasons of simplicity I will use it in this example.

tively or subjectively wrong—instead, she holds that this action is both objectively and subjectively right.

Allison's psychology might be somewhat different, as described in the following version of the case.

> *Learning Disability II:* Allison has substantial evidence, and in her heart of hearts she recognizes, that her daughter has a significant learning disability. However, she cannot bring herself to consciously face this fact, even though from time to time it strikes her that her daughter is not learning as fast as other children. When push comes to shove, Allison is uncertain what degree of belief she has that her daughter has a disability, or what degree of belief she has that her daughter's learning ability is within the normal range. She believes (and knows she believes) that having her daughter tested would subject her daughter to peer teasing and undermine her self-confidence, but would maximize her happiness if the test were positive and resulted in remedial action. When given the option to have her daughter tested for a disability, Allison is uncertain about what to do.

Allison's declining to have her daughter tested would be objectively wrong and—according to Definition (4) and the governing principle of subjective rightness—would also be subjectively wrong, since in her heart of hearts Allison believes that her daughter has a learning disability and that having her tested would maximize her daughter's lifetime happiness. However, if Allison accepts Definition (4) and the governing principle of subjective rightness, she is uncertain about whether declining to have her daughter tested is subjectively right or wrong, since she knows that subjective wrongness depends on what probabilities she ascribes to the various relevant facts, but she is uncertain about what she believes on this score.

Thus, if Definition (4) is correct in stating that the subjective moral status of an act depends on the agent's beliefs, there can be cases in which an agent (unaware of or mistaken about her beliefs) can be mistaken about an action's subjective status; and there can also be cases in which an agent (uncertain about her beliefs) can be uncertain about an action's subjective status. The fact that agents can be unaware, mistaken, or uncertain about their own beliefs means that Definition (4) fails the Guidance Adequacy Criterion: there are cases in which the agent can derive no moral guidance from the principles of subjective rightness that the definition endorses, even though some of the actions available to her are subjectively right.[37]

---

[37] Note one complication here. I have described this case, and Allison's beliefs and uncertainties, relative to a particular principle of subjective rightness. But there may be additional

B. The moral significance of beliefs

The discussion up to this point has assumed that the moral significance of beliefs arises only because an agent may be mistaken or uncertain about the features of his possible actions that are relevant to their objective moral status—what we may call the "objective right-making" or "objective wrong-making" features of his acts. As we have seen, because of agents' frequent errors and uncertainties regarding objective right- and wrong-making features of actions, it is useful to define a secondary type of moral status that an action may have in virtue of an agent's beliefs. This secondary status—subjective rightness or wrongness—can be used to pick out the action that it would be best for the agent to choose in light of what he believes, even when his beliefs about the action's objective right- and wrong-making characteristics are faulty.

What we must realize, however, is that there are moral views according to which an action's *objective* moral status may be partly or wholly a function of the agent's beliefs.[38] In other words, an action's objective right- or wrong-making features may include the agent's beliefs. For example, on many moral views, *lying* is wrong, where "lying" is defined (roughly) as asserting what the agent believes to be a falsehood with the intention of deceiving his audience.[39] To perform an act of lying requires

---

principles of subjective rightness that ascribe subjective moral status to actions in light of *different* beliefs, and Allison might be certain what her beliefs about those matters are, even though she is not certain about the beliefs relevant to the principle in the text. Thus, she could be certain about what this second principle tells her it would be subjectively right to do even though she is not certain about what the original principle tells her. In such a case, her uncertainty about some of her beliefs does not stand in the way of her assigning subjective rightness to one of her actions, because she has certainty about other relevant beliefs. As I will argue later in the text, and have argued elsewhere (Smith, "Making Moral Decisions," 98–99), each principle of objective rightness needs to be supplemented by a variety of principles of subjective rightness, since agents often need to make a decision even though they may not have all the beliefs required to apply the favored principle of subjective rightness to their circumstances. Thus, an agent would have to be uncertain (or mistaken) about a great many of her beliefs to be in a position in which she could not ascribe any subjective moral status to her potential actions.

It would be possible to define a Reasonable Belief version of Definition (4), along the following lines: "An act A is subjectively right just in case A is best in light of the beliefs it would be reasonable for the agent to have at the time she performs A; and A is subjectively wrong just in case A is not the best act in light of the beliefs it would be reasonable for the agent to have at the time she performs A." However, this version of Definition (4) also violates the Guidance Adequacy Criterion—indeed, more pervasively than does the original Definition (4)—since agents are often unaware, mistaken, or uncertain about which beliefs it would be reasonable for them to have.

Note finally that the problem for Definition (4) discussed in this section also arises for Definition (3), and for Definition (2) when the agent must assess her own probability and value assignments.

[38] This is denied by Jackson and Smith, "Absolutist Moral Theories and Uncertainty," 269.

[39] How precisely to define "to lie" is a complex and controversial issue. For a survey treatment, see James Edwin Mahon, "The Definition of Lying and Deception," *Stanford Encyclopedia of Philosophy* (published February 21, 2008), http://plato.stanford.edu/entries/lying-definition/.

the agent to have two beliefs: the belief that his assertion is false, and the belief that his assertion will deceive his audience.[40] Other types of acts commonly held to be wrong also involve attitudinal states that, on analysis, turn out to involve the agent's beliefs.[41] Examples include *stealing* (taking possession of property one believes to belong to another) and *committing murder* (acting in a way that one believes and intends will result in the death of another person). The canonical statement of the Doctrine of Double Effect specifies (among other things) that it would be wrong for an agent to intend a bad effect that he believes will bring about a disproportionately larger good effect.[42] We regard certain kinds of *"attempts"*—such as attempting to murder someone—as objectively wrong, and in such cases, too, the agent must have certain beliefs about the possible upshot of his bodily motions for his act to count as an attempt. Similarly, we think that an agent's *risking* certain grave harms is an objectively wrongful act in itself, even if the harms fail to materialize.[43] Finally, some moral codes prescribe or proscribe certain purely mental acts or attitudes that include beliefs: for example, the Ten Commandments tell us to *honor our parents* (which includes believing one's parents are worthy of respect), but not to *covet our neighbor's house* or *wife* (which includes believing that the house or wife belongs to one's neighbor); and Christianity tells us to *have faith* (which involves believing in God).[44]

[40] For a recent discussion of the assumption that intending to do A always involves believing that one will do A, and references to the literature, see Kieran Setiya, "Cognitivism about Instrumental Reason," *Ethics* 117, no. 4 (July 2007): 649–73. On some views, intending only requires the weaker belief that doing X is *likely* to result in one's doing A.

[41] Of course, criminal and tort law typically define disallowed conduct as including a belief element (e.g., in the definitions of fraud and murder).

[42] For a recent defense of the "intentional" version of the Doctrine of Double Effect, see Michael S. Moore, "Patrolling the Borders of Consequentialist Justifications," *Law and Philosophy* 27 no. 1 (January 2008): 35–96, as cited in John Oberdiek, "Culpability and the Definition of Deontological Constraints," *Law and Philosophy* 27 (March 2008): 105–22. Of course, the full Doctrine of Double Effect also refers to the side-effects of the agent's action, and to the means to his goal.

[43] In this case, to risk something involves believing there is a chance it will occur.

[44] Of course, the Biblical command to honor one's parents includes a command to *act* toward them in certain ways (such as obeying them), but it also seems to involve a command to hold a certain attitude toward one's parents. My comments focus on this latter aspect of the commandment.

There are major issues, of course, about whether such mental activities are appropriate objects for moral duties, since it is unclear to what extent an individual can perform (or avoid performing) the activity voluntarily. The requirement that any duty be one that the agent has the ability to perform "on command" is a common but controversial one; this is not the occasion to discuss it further. See Robert Adams, "Involuntary Sins," *The Philosophical Review* 94, no. 1 (January 1985): 3–32; Richard Feldman, "The Ethics of Belief," *Philosophy and Phenomenological Research* 60, no. 3 (May 2000): 667–95; and Pamela Hieronymi, "Responsibility for Believing," *Synthese* 161, no. 3 (April 2008): 357–73, for defenses of the idea that there can be duties or responsibilities to have certain mental states. Of course, some purely mental "activities" do seem to be ones over which we have the same kind of control that we do over bodily actions: on command, one can search one's memory, do mental arithmetic, review the considerations that favor a certain course of action, etc. In matters of belief, one's

It could be cogently argued (and I am sympathetic with this argument) that in the case of each of these types of performance (except those that involve purely mental activities, such as believing in God), it is only the underlying non-mental activity that is objectively wrong. On this view, when we evaluate as "right" or "wrong" the more complex act (such as lying or stealing)—an act that involves bodily motions, the surrounding circumstances, *and* the agent's beliefs and desires—we are using a kind of time-saving (but misleading) shortcut that merges together considerations of objective moral status, subjective moral status, and blameworthiness. Thus, in the case of lying, it could be argued that what is genuinely *objectively* wrong is making an assertion that misleads the person who hears it; what is *subjectively* wrong is making an assertion in the belief that it is false and will mislead; and what is *blameworthy* is performing an act that one believes to be subjectively wrong. Similar analyses, identifying an objectively wrong bodily movement (and set of circumstances) at the core of each of these acts, could be offered for stealing, committing murder, and harming someone in order to bring about a good effect.

However, successfully carrying out this program of eliminating reference to any mental aspects when defining objectively wrong actions may not be easy. For example, philosophers who have worked on precise definitions of "lying" have concluded that one can only lie to one's *intended* audience, not to an eavesdropper who happens to overhear and be misled by one's statement.[45] But if we agree that lying must involve misleading an intended audience, we have re-imported into the morally relevant definition of the act a reference to the agent's beliefs about his audience that would be difficult to eliminate. It would also be difficult to provide an eliminative account of "attempting" and "risking" harms.[46] And even if the "elimination" program were successful, it would undeniably fly in the face of the stated content of many commonly accepted moral codes, which incorporate, in the list of activities that are objectively wrong, activities whose definitions undeniably refer to the agent's beliefs. And, of course, such a program could not touch activities, such as coveting one's neighbor's wife or believing in God, which are purely mental and involve beliefs. Finally, if we ask a deeper question about what kinds of human conduct are properly subject to moral evaluation, the answer must include human *acts* as contrasted with mere human *behavior* such as sneezing. But acts are human behaviors that the agent intends to perform (or which are generated by more basic acts that the agent intends to

---

mental inquiry or search may be controlled, but not one's mental response to the result of the inquiry.

[45] See Mahon, "The Definition of Lying and Deception," for discussion. Clearly, this condition would be deemed to be relevant to the lie's *moral* status; eavesdroppers have no right that they not be misled.

[46] Wrongful acts such as *attempting to harm someone* seem to depend on one's beliefs about what one is doing, not (for example) on the objective probability of one's acting in a way that will harm the person. I thank Preston Greene for pointing this out.

perform). To intend to perform an act, in most cases, involves having certain beliefs, such as the belief that one's moving one's finger will pull the trigger and fire the gun. Thus, the performance of even an unintentional and unforeseen act (such as accidentally killing Jones) requires the agent to have certain beliefs (say, the belief that moving his finger will pull the trigger, fire the gun, and kill the deer that the agent mistakenly believes he sees).

It appears, then, that many activities are commonly deemed to be objectively right or wrong in whole or in part because of the agent's beliefs—in short, that the agent's beliefs are, in some cases, objective right- or wrong-making features of an act. Definition (4), however, defines an act A as subjectively right just in case A is best in light of the agent's beliefs at the time he performs A; and it defines A as subjectively wrong just in case A is not the best act in light of the agent's beliefs at the time he performs A. A deontological moral code that prohibits lying (as it is usually understood) implies that an act of lying is wrong *at least partly in light of an agent's beliefs*. According to Definition (4), it appears as though such a moral code could be interpreted as saying that lying is *subjectively* wrong, whereas the aim of the code is to prohibit lying as *objectively* wrong. The point of an objective code prohibiting lying is not to offer an agent guidance about what it is wisest to do when the agent's grasp of his circumstances is faulty or inaccurate; that is the aim of principles of subjective, not objective, rightness. Exactly how Definition (4), would handle "mixed" acts—ones whose right- and wrong-making features include the agent's bodily movements, surrounding circumstances, *and* the agent's beliefs—is somewhat unclear.[47] However, if a moral code prescribes or prohibits certain beliefs in themselves, such as the belief in God, it seems clear that it would be classified by Definition (4) as a code of subjective rightness. And this seems to be a mistake, since the point of the principle prescribing belief in God is to tell an agent what it is simply best for him to believe—not to tell him what it is best for him to believe in light of the fact that he is mistaken or uncertain about what he believes.

What we are seeing here is that an agent's beliefs might be relevant to the *objective* moral status of an activity, not just to the subjective moral status of that activity. Whether or not an agent believes P is, of course, an "objective" fact, just as whether or not her act would cause pain to someone else is an "objective" fact. Clearly, a moral theory can cogently entail that an agent's beliefs affect the objective moral status of her actions in the

---

[47] Note that subjectively right/wrong acts themselves are typically understood to have "objective" features in addition to what the agent believes of them: they must be acts that are potentially performable by the agent, not just figments of the agent's imagination. There may be temporal factors as well, linking the time of the action and the time of the agent's beliefs. If this is correct, then Definition (5) (discussed below in Section IV) must apply to acts having mixed "objective" and "subjective" features. But for discussion of this assumption, see the fifth point in my discussion of Definition (5) below.

same way that the consequences of the action affect its objective moral status, or in the same way that the fact that the action would break a promise affects its objective moral status.[48] Whether and how the agent's beliefs affect the objective status of her actions is an entirely separate question from the question of whether and how the agent's beliefs affect what we are calling the "subjective" status of her actions. One can hold that lying is objectively wrong, and that lying necessarily involves making a statement one believes to be false, without addressing our initial question of how to reconcile apparently conflicting evaluations of an agent who acts from false beliefs about the nature of her act, or our initial question of how a moral code can provide guidance to an agent even though she may be mistaken or uncertain about the nature of her action.

Moreover, it is clear that a moral code that deems an agent's beliefs to be relevant to the objective moral status of her actions needs the distinction between objective and subjective rightness, just as does a moral code that deems only non-mental states to be relevant to the objective moral status of an action. Suppose one accepts that an agent's beliefs affect the objective moral status of her activities (one accepts, for example, that lying is wrong, and that in order to lie one must believe one's statement to be false; or one accepts that faith in God is morally required). As we saw in Section III.A, agents may be unaware of, mistaken, or uncertain regarding the existence or content of their beliefs, just as they can be mistaken or uncertain about the consequences of their actions. The churchgoer brought up in a conventional religious family believes that she has faith in God, but she may be mistaken about this. The person raised in the racist community believes that he no longer harbors racist beliefs, but he may be mistaken about this. Allison is mistaken or uncertain about what she believes regarding her daughter's learning abilities. Thus, a moral code that assesses the objective moral status of actions partly or wholly in terms of the agent's beliefs must confront situations in which what the agent actually believes diverges from what she believes (or is certain) her beliefs are. These are the very kinds of situations that the concept of subjective rightness was invented to handle.

What this means is that we cannot tell, merely by noting that an isolated moral principle ascribes moral status to an action in virtue of the agent's beliefs, whether that principle is a principle of objective or subjective rightness. The schema "An act is morally right if it has features F, G, and H," where at least one of these features involves the agent's beliefs, could be either a principle of objective rightness or a principle of subjective rightness. Content alone will not tell us this, because the agent's beliefs might be right-making for a principle of objective rightness, or right-making for principle of subjective rightness. What we must recognize is that the concept of subjective moral status always implicitly

---

[48] I am grateful to Preston Greene, who persuaded me of this point.

imports a paired concept of objective rightness, relative to which it must be understood.[49] A principle of subjective rightness has to be defined in relation to a foundational principle of objective rightness, and the principle of subjective rightness can only be understood and assessed as appropriate relative to the principle of objective rightness.

IV. Proposed Solution to Defining "Subjective Rightness"

We need to find a definition of subjective rightness that satisfies the six criteria set out in Section II.A and avoids the problems we have noted for the preceding four definitions. I believe the best way to do this is to approach the question somewhat differently. Up until now, we have focused on proposed definitions of an *act's* being subjectively right/wrong. What we need to do instead is to focus first on characterizing what makes a normative *principle* a principle of subjective rightness/wrongness, and then use this definition to characterize when an act is subjectively right/ wrong. What makes a normative principle a principle of *subjective* rightness is not its content per se, but rather its relation to some governing principle of objective rightness. The principle of subjective rightness lays out the evaluative status of actions, relative to the principle of objective rightness, for agents who are mistaken or uncertain about whether those actions have the right-making features specified by the principle of objective rightness. Our definition must capture this essential fact.

Our definition of a principle's being subjectively right/wrong also needs to accommodate the fact that a given principle of objective rightness may need to be supplemented by *several* substantive principles of subjective rightness, since a principle of subjective rightness that one agent may be able to apply in one set of circumstances may not be usable by other agents (or by the same agent in a different set of circumstances) when those agents have less rich sets of beliefs about their options. For example, an agent who does not have a rich enough set of beliefs to use a principle prescribing the maximization of expected value might still have a sufficiently rich set of beliefs to use a satisficing principle, or the maximin principle. These principles of subjective rightness can be understood as forming a rough hierarchy. If the agent has a set of beliefs that would enable him to use a more highly ranked principle in this hierarchy, then what is subjectively right for him will be the act prescribed by the more highly ranked principle.[50] Clearly, a normative standard is needed for

[49] This point is further enforced by the fact that many Remodeling theorists have advocated, as principles of *objective* rightness, principles with exactly the same content as principles advocated by others as principles of *subjective* rightness (e.g., "One ought to maximize expected utility"). Examination of the right-making feature identified by this principle does not tell us whether it is a principle of objective or subjective rightness.

[50] I have argued for the necessity of a hierarchy of principles of subjective rightness in my essays "Making Moral Decisions," and "Deciding How to Decide: Is There a Regress Prob-

determining what makes one principle "higher" than another, but developing such a standard must be the work of another occasion.

Given these ideas, we can characterize a principle of subjective status (rightness or wrongness) as follows:

Definition (5):
If Q is a principle of objective moral status, and Q stipulates that F is a right-making[51] feature of actions and that G is a wrong-making feature of actions, *then*

(1) A normative principle P is a principle of *subjective rightness* relative to principle Q just in case, for any agent S, either of the following is true:

    (A) *if* agent S believes (correctly or incorrectly) of some act A that A is possible for him to perform and that A has feature F, *then* principle P prescribes A, relative to principle Q and relative to S's non-normative beliefs about A; or

    (B) *if* (i) agent S believes (correctly or incorrectly) of some act A that A may be possible for him to perform, *and if* (ii) S is uncertain whether any act available to him has feature F, and if so, which act does have F, *then* principle P prescribes A relative to principle Q and relative to S's non-normative beliefs about A; and

(2) A normative principle P is a principle of *subjective wrongness* relative to principle Q just in case, for any agent S, either of the following is true:

    (A) *if* agent S believes (correctly or incorrectly) of some act A that A is possible for him to perform and that A has feature G, *then* principle P prohibits A, relative to principle Q and relative to S's non-normative beliefs about A; or

    (B) *if* (i) agent S believes (correctly or incorrectly) of some act A that A may be possible for him to perform, *and if* (ii) S is uncertain whether any act available to him has feature G, and if so, which act does have G, *then* principle P prohibits

---

lem?" in Michael Bacharach and Susan Hurley, eds., *Essays in the Foundations of Decision Theory* (Oxford: Basil Blackwell, 1991), 194–219. For decision theorists' discussions of the need for multiple decision-guides, see Clyde C. Coombs, Robyn M. Dawes, and Amos Tversky, *Mathematical Psychology* (Englewood Cliffs, NJ: Prentice-Hall, 1970), chapter 5; and Michael Resnik, *Choices* (Minneapolis: University of Minnesota Press, 1987), 40.

[51] "Right-making" is here construed as "all-things-considered right-making." A parallel version of Definition (5) could be stated for "prima facie right-making" (and similarly for "wrong-making").

A relative to principle Q and relative to S's non-normative beliefs about A.[52]

Definition (5) is intended to capture several ideas: (i) that we need to focus first on a definition of what makes a moral principle a *principle* of subjective moral status (rather than objective status) before moving on to say what makes a given *act* subjectively right; (ii) that a principle of subjective status has that standing *relative to* some principle of objective status, not simply taken in isolation; (iii) that when an agent believes that some act has a right-making (or wrong-making) feature identified by the principle of objective status, then an agent can use the principle of objective status internally to make a decision, so that it can serve as a principle of subjective status; and (iv) that provision must be made for the fact that in cases of uncertainty, there may be more than one principle of subjective status available to decision-making agents.

Thus, for example, suppose Q is a principle of objective status stating that an action is wrong if it involves killing an innocent person. One possible subordinate principle P states that when an agent is uncertain about whether act A would involve killing an innocent person, it would be wrong (relative to Q, and to the agent's non-normative beliefs) for her to perform act A if she believes that the action has a probability greater than .001 of killing an innocent person. Principle P qualifies as a principle of subjective wrongness relative to Q. To say that principle P qualifies as a principle of subjective wrongness relative to Q is not, of course, to say that it is an acceptable principle of this sort, or that, if acceptable, it ranks high in the hierarchy of appropriate principles of subjective wrongness relative to Q. It is only to say that principle P *should be understood and evaluated* as a candidate principle of subjective wrongness relative to Q.

What does Definition (5), together with principle Q, imply for a case in which the agent believes that act A would definitely involve killing an innocent person? In such a case, Q can serve as a principle of subjective wrongness relative to itself, prescribing the wrongness of A, given that the agent believes of A that it has a wrong-making feature stipulated by Q. Thus, Q can be a principle of subjective wrongness relative to itself when the agent has sufficiently rich non-normative beliefs to apply Q itself, whether his beliefs are correct or incorrect.[53]

[52] Note that there may be cases in which an agent has "mixed" types of beliefs. For example, the agent might believe that he has several options (e.g., A, B, and C), and might be certain that A has a wrong-making feature according to Q, but uncertain whether B or C has right-making or wrong-making features. Definition (5) needs to be revised to accommodate such cases more cleanly.

[53] Strictly speaking, it is not principle Q itself ("A is right if and only if A has F") that serves as the principle of subjective rightness, but a version of this principle stated in terms of "if" rather than "if and only if." This change is necessary to accommodate the fact that there may be more than one principle of subjective rightness. Note that Definition (5) leaves open whether the most appropriate principle of subjective rightness for an agent who has

Let us consider some of the implications of Definition (5). First, it implies, as I have argued it must, that one cannot simply examine the right-making features identified by a normative principle in order to ascertain that it is a principle of subjective rather than objective rightness. (Henceforward, for simplicity of exposition, I shall focus on principles of subjective *rightness,* and let the reader infer parallel statements about subjective wrongness.) One has to know whether the principle is part of a larger moral theory in which it plays the role of prescribing choices for agents who are mistaken or uncertain about which act the governing principle of objective rightness prescribes.[54]

Second, like Definition (4), it identifies the agent's beliefs as the basis (along with the governing principle of objective rightness) for the action's subjective evaluative status.[55] Definition (5) specifies that the beliefs in

---

sufficiently rich beliefs to apply Q itself is principle Q itself (e.g., "A is right if A has F") or a "subjectivized" version of Q that includes overt reference to the agent's beliefs (e.g., "A is right if the agent believes that A has F"). This means that Definition (5)'s clause "relative to principle Q and relative to the agent's non-normative beliefs" can be satisfied in either of two ways: the agent's beliefs can figure as part of the subjectively right-making features of the action stipulated by the principle (as is true in the subjectivized version of Q), or the agent's beliefs can figure as part of the conditions that make it appropriate to evaluate an action by a principle that specifies subjectively right-making characteristics that themselves involve no reference to the agent's beliefs. By virtue of this clause in Definition (5), every acceptable principle of subjective rightness will evaluate actions relative to the agent's beliefs.

[54] I have argued above that one cannot determine that a normative principle is a principle of subjective rightness just by ascertaining that the right-making features it identifies refer to the agent's beliefs (since some principles of objective rightness also identify right-making features that refer to the agent's beliefs). In parallel, we can now note that it is not possible to infer that a principle of subjective rightness *must* identify right-making features that refer to the agent's beliefs. If a principle of objective rightness Q can serve as a principle of subjective rightness relative to itself in a case in which the agent believes of some act that it has the right-making feature identified by Q (and this feature does not refer to the agent's beliefs), then Q, in its guise as a principle of subjective rightness, does not identify right-making features that refer to beliefs. (See the previous note.) We also know this from theorists who argue that the best principles of subjective rightness for act-utilitarianism may be the rules of common-sense morality, which have no reference to the agent's beliefs. See the discussion below under the third implication of Definition (5).

Note also that a given normative principle might have unique features that make it an appropriate principle of subjective rightness for a single principle of objective rightness. Other normative principles may be appropriate for many principles of objective rightness.

[55] Since, according to Definition (5), a principle of subjective rightness P prescribes actions relative to Q and relative to the agent's non-normative beliefs, the agent's beliefs form part of the *basis* for the subjective moral status of the agent's actions. This is true whether or not the principle of subjective rightness overtly stipulates that the agent's beliefs are part of the subjective-rightness-making features of the actions.

There is a question whether we should make subjective rightness rest on the agent's beliefs, or on all the agent's doxastic states, or on the agent's doxastic states together with relevant sub-doxastic states. We should certainly include the agent's *credences*—his degrees of belief in something. (Note that the line between "believing P" and "having credence C (very high, but less than 1.0) in P" is not a clean one, and, hence, the line between what it is best to choose in light of one's mistaken beliefs, and what it is best to do in light of one's uncertainties, may not be clean either.) We should probably include the agent's suspension of belief about some issues. But what about his unconscious or merely latent "stored" beliefs? I suspect these should not be included, since the agent may have no access to them,

question are the agent's *non-normative* beliefs. This enables us to deal correctly with cases in which the agent has beliefs about the objective or subjective rightness of his action, but these normative beliefs do not relate appropriately to his non-normative beliefs. For example, suppose an agent Ralph believes that his pulling the trigger has a probability of .25 of killing an innocent person—and also believes that his pulling the trigger is subjectively right. According to the principle P just described, Ralph's act is subjectively wrong relative to principle Q, even though he believes it to be subjectively right.[56] Once we note that the action an agent believes to be subjectively right may be different from the action that is actually subjectively right, the question arises which of these actions is the one most relevant for *blameworthiness*. Is Ralph blameworthy for doing what he believes to be subjectively right? In the normal case, it appears to me that agents' blameworthiness depends on what they *believe* to be subjectively right or wrong, not on what is *actually* subjectively right or wrong for them. On this view, Ralph is not to blame for pulling the trigger.[57]

---

and by hypothesis is not aware of them at the time of decision. Thus, the agent is not in a position to consciously guide his decision in light of these unconscious beliefs. However, further work on this issue is needed. If such unconscious stored beliefs play a causal role in agents' decision-making, it is less plausible to deny them a role in what is subjectively right for the agent. (For example, the agent may not have a conscious belief that the floor under his feet is solid, but this unconscious belief may play a causal role in his decision to step forward.)

It would be natural to think that Definition (5) should be phrased in terms of the agent's non-normative beliefs *about her action*. However, some facts that are taken by many moral codes to be relevant to an action's moral status may not be conceptualized by agents as facts about the action, so it seems best not to restrict the content of the agent's non-normative beliefs any further.

[56] What should be said about a case such as the following? Suppose the best principle of subjective rightness prescribes the act that, according to the agent's beliefs, would maximize expected value. Let us stipulate that Sue, in *Strong Medicine* (described in Section II.C-D), believes the facts described in the middle two columns of table 2, but lacks any beliefs about the facts stated in the right-most column (which describes the expected values of her options). So Sue has no belief of any action that it would maximize expected value, although the fact that giving Ron drug X would maximize expected value is entailed by her other non-normative beliefs.

I believe adherence to the Guidance Adequacy Criterion implies that we should interpret Definition (5) *not* to imply in such a case that Sue's giving Ron drug X would be subjectively right—since Sue herself does not believe of this act that it would maximize expected value. Although the contents of Sue's beliefs may entail that giving Ron drug X would maximize expected value, nonetheless she herself does not see this, since she has not derived the logical implications of her own beliefs. Perhaps in the next moment she will derive these implications. Definition (5) implies that it would *then* be subjectively right for her to give Ron drug X. The situation at the earlier time is a case in which the logical link between the contents of beliefs Sue does have and the content of the belief that would enable her to apply a given principle of subjective rightness is short and direct, so one may balk at refusing to say that giving Ron drug X would be subjectively right for Sue. However, there are other cases in which the link—although just as tight—is distant and obscure, and we are hardly surprised that the agent does not observe this link. In both cases, since we are focusing on what it is subjectively right for the agent to choose at t_i, we need to focus on what her actual beliefs at t_i would support.

[57] However, this matter is complicated. In certain pathological cases, where the agent adheres to an erroneous ethical theory, his action in accord with the absolutely subjective

Thus, there is a connection between subjective rightness and blameworthiness, but it is less direct than we might have supposed.

Third, Definition (5) allows room for principles of subjective rightness whose right-making features do not "match" the right-making features of the underlying principle of objective rightness. For example, the principles of subjective rightness may evaluate actions in terms of their probabilistic features, even though the governing principle of objective rightness evaluates actions in terms of their nonprobabilistic features. On some views, the lack of match could be even more extreme: for example, some act-utilitarians hold that a principle such as "It is wrong to kill an innocent person" is an appropriate principle of subjective wrongness relative to act-utilitarianism, since people are more likely to have beliefs, and indeed true beliefs, about whether their proposed action would involve killing an innocent person than they are to have beliefs about whether their action would maximize utility.[58] It is sometimes held that what makes a principle of subjective rightness appropriate to an underlying principle of objective rightness is the actual pattern of actions that agents would (or would likely) perform if they tried to follow the principle of subjective rightness.[59] This view about what justifies principles of subjective rightness implies that, so long as agents are sometimes mistaken about what objective right-making features actions have, there will be nonmatching objective and subjective right-making features.

Fourth, Definition (5) includes a clause specifying that the action is prescribed as relative to the agent's non-normative beliefs, *including her beliefs about which acts are possible for her.* This feature allows for cases in which the agent is physically unable to perform some act, but because she is unaware of this, her non-normative beliefs entail that this act would be best among all her alternatives. Thus, an agent Rachel might believe it

---

right-making characteristics may be blameless, even though he himself views his action as wrong and blameworthy. See Jonathan Bennett, "The Conscience of Huckleberry Finn," *Philosophy* 49, no. 188 (April 1974): 123–34. Moreover, since an agent can be criticized for performing an action that he believes to be subjectively right, but performs for the "wrong reason" (e.g., not because it is subjectively right but because it will harm his enemy), the tie cannot be as close as the text suggests. Note also, as Preston Greene points out, that the luminosity-of-beliefs problem also crops up in connection with such a definition of blameworthiness.

[58] See, for example, John Stuart Mill, *Utilitarianism,* chapter II; Sidgwick, *The Methods of Ethics,* chapters III, IV, and V; Smart, "An Outline of a System of Utilitarian Ethics," section 7; R. M. Hare, *Moral Thinking: Its Levels, Method, and Point* (Oxford: Clarendon Press, 1981), esp. section I.3 ("The Archangel and the Prole"); Shaw, *Contemporary Ethics,* 145–50; and perhaps Peter Railton, "Alienation, Consequentialism, and the Demands of Morality," in Peter Railton, ed., *Facts, Values, and Norms* (Cambridge: Cambridge University Press, 2003): 165–68. For relevant contemporary discussion in psychology, see Gerd Gigerenzer, Peter M. Todd, and the ABC Research Group, *Simple Heuristics That Make Us Smart* (New York: Oxford University Press, 1999).

[59] This is a common (but not the only) account of what makes a principle of subjective rightness appropriate to an underlying principle of objective rightness.

would be best for her to turn the car ignition key, only to discover after she tries that she has suffered a stroke and cannot move her arm. In terms of her beliefs at the time of choice, turning the ignition key would be prescribed, and we want to recognize this fact, and give her credit (if there is any blame in question) for making the best choice, even though it turns out that this act was not possible for her.[60] This feature also allows for cases in which the agent does not believe of some action that it is physically possible for her, although in fact it is possible. Such an action might be objectively right (or wrong) according to Q, but it will have no subjective moral status.

Fifth, Definition (5) does not provide a *substantive account* of the content of principles of subjective rightness. It does not tell us, for example, that an agent who is uncertain which action would maximize utility would be subjectively right to choose the act that he believes would maximize the expectation of utility. But it is not the job of a *definition* of subjective rightness to provide such a substantive account (despite the fact that some of the definitions we examined earlier attempt to do this). The job of the definition is to provide an understanding of the concept of subjective moral status. Once we have that understanding, including a grip on the six criteria advanced in Section II.A of this essay for evaluating proposed definitions, we can proceed to find and evaluate substantive principles that will serve this role.

Sixth, it appears that Definition (5) satisfies our six criteria, or comes as close as possible. Because it bases subjective rightness on the agent's beliefs, principles that accord with it can recommend actions that strike us as reasonable or wise for the agent to choose, given his (possibly faulty) grasp of the situation. Thus, it satisfies the Normative Adequacy Criterion. Because the definition permits multiple principles of subjective rightness to augment any governing principle of objective rightness, each principle of objective rightness can be supplemented with a broad array of principles of subjective rightness designed to assess the status of every action assigned objective moral status—and, indeed, because principles satisfying Definition (5) assess the status of actions that are not possible for the agent to perform, it may ascribe subjective status to actions that cannot have any objective status. Thus, Definition (5) satisfies the Domain Adequacy Criterion.[61] However, the fact that an agent may be mistaken

---

[60] This will be relevant to discussions of free will and moral responsibility when the agent could do no other than what she does, as in "Frankfurt-style" cases, originally described by Harry Frankfurt in "Alternate Possibilities and Moral Responsibility," *Journal of Philosophy* 66, no. 23 (December 4, 1969): 829–33.

See Graham, "'Ought' Does *Not* Imply 'Can'," 4, for discussion of the fact that an act may be subjectively right even though the agent cannot perform it (although Graham dismisses the need for a concept of subjective rightness).

[61] Possibly there will be agents whose belief sets, or mental capacities, are so impoverished that *no* principle of subjective rightness can assess which action would be best for them. This, however, is a not a problem reflecting any inadequacy in Definition (5).

or uncertain about what her (relevant) beliefs are raises the question whether there will be cases in which an agent (such as Allison in *Learning Disability I* or *II*) cannot derive any guidance from an appropriate principle of subjective rightness. If such cases exist, then we would have to conclude that Definition (5) fails to fully satisfy the Guidance Adequacy Criterion. Since we cannot answer this question until we have seen how the notion of "the subjectively right act" should be defined, I will place this question temporarily on hold. The Relation to Blameworthiness Criterion seems to be satisfied by Definition (5), since it is reasonable to say that (in most cases) agents ought to guide their decisions by reference to what they believe to be objectively right, or in the case of cognitive impediments, by reference to what they believe to be subjectively right as characterized by Definition (5). An agent who decides to do what he believes to be either objectively or subjectively right is normally not blameworthy for his choice. Furthermore, given its generous breadth, Definition (5) appears to be compatible with the full range of plausible theories of objective moral status, and thus appears to satisfy the Normative Compatibility Criterion. Finally, Definition (5) provides some illumination about why subjectively right acts are reasonable or wise for agents to perform. Given their mistakes or uncertainty about the facts directly relevant to their principle of objective rightness, their need to make a decision, the importance of their being able to exercise moral autonomy through their decisions, and the dependence of blameworthiness on an agent's psychological states, these agents' best recourse is to guide their actions by principles that recommend actions in light of the agents' actual beliefs. The hierarchy of principles of subjective rightness provides normatively appropriate guidance. Thus, Definition (5) appears to satisfy the Explanatory Adequacy Criterion. Unlike the previous contenders we have surveyed, Definition (5) appears to be a successful characterization of what makes a normative principle a principle of subjective rightness.[62] However, the extent to which it satisfies the Guidance Adequacy Criterion remains to be determined.

---

[62] Definition (5), like some of the others we have reviewed, opens the question whether "subjective rightness" should be restricted, as most discussions have restricted it, to the moral status of an action relative to the *agent's* beliefs at the time of choice. Advisors and onlookers may also have beliefs in virtue of which they appraise the agent's action (or prospective action). The agent himself may have different beliefs at different times (both before and after the action) relative to which the action can be appraised. The agent may gradually gain more information in the run-up to the action, in virtue of which its "subjective" status changes; and he may gain more information after having acted, in virtue of which the action's "subjective" status may change and he may regret having chosen it. Given the importance of these additional assessments, it would be both possible and perhaps useful to broaden the definition of "subjective rightness" so that it is relative to any given set of beliefs-at-a-time. However, for purposes of this essay I will leave subjective status as defined in terms of the agent's beliefs (implicitly) at the time of choice.

V. The Subjectively Right Act

Given Definition (5), which defines when a normative *principle* is a principle of subjective rightness/wrongness, we can now provide a definition of an *act's* being subjectively right/wrong:

Definition (6):
(1) Act A (which would be performed at time t_j) is *subjectively right* at t_i relative to principle of objective status Q just in case A is an act prescribed by the highest principle of subjective rightness relative to Q that the agent is able to use as an internal guide at t_i; and
(2) Act A (which would be performed at time t_j) is *subjectively wrong* at t_i relative to principle of objective status Q just in case A is an act proscribed by the highest principle of subjective wrongness relative to Q that the agent is able to use as an internal guide at t_i.[63]

Definition (6) only states what makes an act count as subjectively right or wrong relative to some principle of objective status or other. However, we may want to know whether the act is subjectively right or wrong relative to the *correct* principle of objective status. To capture this idea, we can define the concept of *absolutely* subjectively right/wrong actions:

Definition (7):
(1) Act A (which would be performed at time t_j) is *absolutely subjectively right* at t_i just in case A is an act prescribed by the highest principle of subjective rightness (relative to the correct principle of objective rightness) that the agent is able to use as an internal guide at t_i; and
(2) Act A (which would be performed at time t_j) is *absolutely subjectively wrong* at t_i just in case A is an act proscribed by the highest principle of subjective wrongness (relative to the correct principle of objective wrongness) that the agent is able to use as an internal guide at t_i.

Both Definitions (6) and (7) utilize the concept of an agent's being "able to use" a given principle of subjective status as an internal guide. The basic idea, articulated in Section II.A of this essay, is that the agent can derive a prescription or proscription for an action from the principle. But in an obvious sense an agent often "can derive" a prescription from a

[63] Note that an act may be subjectively right at t_i (because it is prescribed by the highest principle of subjective rightness the agent can use at t_i) even though the agent does not ask himself at t_i the question of whether to perform the action, or whether it would be subjectively right to perform the action.
    Definition (6) would have to be further developed to handle cases (such as the Regan-type case, described in note 26) in which the agent has *mixed* information about his various possible options—for example, having beliefs about what the expected value of some acts would be, but not having any beliefs about the expected value of other acts.

principle, even if the agent cannot derive the prescription for any action under what Eugene Bales calls "an immediately helpful description."[64] Some descriptions may accurately pick out an action, but not in a manner that enables the agent to identify it in such a way as to perform it if he wants to. Such descriptions are "unhelpful." Thus, someone who has no idea what the consequences would be of his various alternatives can still derive a "prescription" from act-utilitarianism—he can derive the prescription "Perform the act that would maximize utility." The description "act that would maximize utility" picks out a unique act, but this is no help if he cannot identify which act this is in terms that would enable him to perform it in the way that describing the act as "Tell the employees to use the stairwell" enables one of the security guards to perform this act. To get around this problem, we need a somewhat complicated definition, as follows (here, again, I shall focus just on prescriptive principles):[65]

Definition (8):
An agent S is able at t_i to use normative principle X as an internal guide to decide at t_i what to do at t_j just in case (1) there is some (perhaps complex) feature F such that X prescribes actions that have feature F, in virtue of their having F; (2) S believes at t_i of some act-type A that S could perform A (in the epistemic sense) at t_j;[66] (3) S believes at t_i that if she performed A at t_j, her action would have feature F; and (4) if S wanted at t_i to derive a prescription from

---

[64] Bales, "Act-Utilitarianism," 261.

[65] There is a highly developed literature on rule-following that focuses on questions somewhat distinct from those at issue in this essay. See, for example, Peter Railton, "Normative Guidance," in Russ Shafer-Landau, ed., *Oxford Studies in Metaethics*, vol. 1 (Oxford: Oxford University Press, 2006), 3–34.

[66] That is, slightly revising Alvin Goldman's definition of "ability to perform an act" in the epistemic sense, S believes (doubtless expressed in her own concepts) that

(1) There is an act-type A* which S truly believes at t_i to be a basic act-type for her at t_j;
(2) S truly believes that she is (or will be) in standard conditions with respect to A* at t_j; and
(3) either
  (a) S truly believes that A* = A, or
  (b) S truly believes that there is a set of conditions C* obtaining at t_j such that her doing A* would generate her doing A at t_j.

See Alvin I. Goldman, *A Theory of Human Action* (Englewood Cliffs, NJ: Prentice-Hall, 1970), 203. Roughly speaking, a person is in standard conditions with respect to an act property just in case (a) there are no external physical constraints making it physically impossible for the person to exemplify the property, and (b) if the property involves a change into some state Z, then the person is not already in Z. See ibid., 64–65. Note that on Definition (8) the agent believes that she truly believes there is a basic act-type for her, etc., but she may be wrong about what she believes and whether her belief is true.

Further complications would have to be introduced to deal with cases in which the agent is uncertain whether some act is one she can actually perform, and to deal with deviant causal chain cases.

principle X at t_i for an act performable at t_j, S would derive a prescription for A in virtue of her belief that it has feature F.[67]

For example, Rachel (the unwitting stroke victim) is able to use the
normative principle "Maximize utility" to make a choice, since (i) this
principle prescribes actions having the feature that they will maximize
utility; (ii) Rachel believes that she can turn the ignition key; (iii) she
believes that turning the ignition key would maximize utility; and (iv) if
she wanted to derive a prescription from the principle "Maximize utility,"
she would derive a prescription to turn the ignition key in virtue of its
being the act that would maximize utility.

Note several implications of Definition (8). First, while S believes she
can perform A, it may not be true that she can. Second, while S believes
that if she performed A, her action would have feature F, in reality her
performing A may not have F. Third, the time at which the choice would
take place is not necessarily identical with the time at which the act would
take place; one can choose now to perform an act later on (although
typically one has to reaffirm this choice when the time for action comes).
Fourth, S may believe that there are several acts performable at t_j that
have feature F; for S to be able to use X to make a choice, all that is
necessary is that S would derive a prescription for *one* of these acts.

Definitions (6) and (7) also utilize the notion of a principle of subjective
rightness being "the highest" principle of subjective rightness relative to
some principle of objective rightness. As I have noted above, to accommodate the great variation in the kinds of beliefs agents have when they
must make moral decisions, we need a rough hierarchy of principles of subjective rightness that are appropriate for a given principle of objective rightness. Thus, agent S's beliefs might make it possible for her either to use
principle P_1 (advising her to maximize expected utility) or to use principle
P_2 (advising her to minimize the maximum loss of utility). Both of these
principles may have a place in the hierarchy of principles of subjective rightness appropriate for the act-utilitarian principle of objective rightness. But
if S is able to use either one, P_1 is arguably higher in the hierarchy than P_2,
and the act prescribed by P_1 is subjectively right relative to act-utilitarianism.

Using these new tools, let us now ask whether or not Definition (5)
licenses principles of subjective rightness that satisfy the Guidance Adequacy Criterion, which requires that a definition of subjective rightness
should endorse principles of subjective rightness that agents are able to
use as an internal guide for decision in every situation in which they find
themselves, even though an agent may be mistaken or uncertain about
which actions have the features that would make them objectively right
in that situation.

---

[67] One would want variants on this for actions that are forbidden, but since our main
focus is on an agent's deciding what to do (not just what not to do), in the interests of shorter
exposition I will omit these variants.

Since Definition (5) identifies a principle as a principle of subjective rightness, relative to some governing principle of objective rightness, based on the beliefs of the agent, and since agents are typically better informed about their beliefs than they are about the circumstances and consequences of their actions, it appears that Definition (5) should have little problem meeting the Guidance Adequacy Criterion. But we have seen that agents are sometimes mistaken or uncertain about their beliefs. How does Definition (5) deal with these situations?

To see this, let us consider the following moral theory (MT-1) and its implications in a case in which the agent is mistaken about her own non-normative beliefs. MT-1 is comprehensive, in the sense that it includes not only a principle of objective rightness, but also principles of subjective rightness, a rank-ordering of these principles, and a statement of when it deems an action to be subjectively right.

MT-1

Principle of objective rightness:
Q: An act X is objectively obligatory if and only if X maximizes value.

Principles of subjective rightness:
P: An act Y is a candidate for being subjectively obligatory if Y would maximize value.[68]
R: An act Z is a candidate for being subjectively obligatory if Z would maximize the minimum value.

The subjectively right act:
(a) Principle P is higher than principle R; and
(b) An act W is subjectively obligatory if and only if W is pre-scribed by the highest principle of subjective rightness listed above that the agent is able to use as an internal guide.

Consider how MT-1 applies in the following (abstract) case in which the agent (S) is mistaken about her own beliefs:

CASE 1

(a) Agent S believes MT-1 is the correct moral theory.
(b) S believes of act A that it would maximize value.

---

[68] Note that the principles of subjective rightness are phrased as sufficient conditions (". . . if . . .") rather than as necessary and sufficient conditions (". . . if and only if . . ."). This phrasing is needed to accommodate the fact that there may be many principles of subjective rightness, so each can only offer a sufficient (but not necessary) condition for an act's being a candidate for being subjectively right.

(c) S does not believe that she believes of any act that it would maximize value (this is S's mistake about her beliefs).
(d) S believes of act B that it would maximize minimum value.
(e) S believes that she believes of act B that it would maximize minimum value.
(f) Act A would maximize value.
(g) Act B would maximize minimum value.

Taking MT-1, the facts in Case 1, and our definitions of what it is for a principle to be internally usable (Definition [8]) and of what it is for an act to be subjectively right relative to a principle of objective rightness (Definition [6]), we can infer the following:

(1) According to Definition (8), on the straightforward version of the psychology in this case, principle P is *not* usable by S, because it is false that if S wanted to derive a prescription from P, she would do so. (She would fail to derive a prescription from P because she does not believe that she believes of any act that it would maximize value.)
(2) S would believe that P is not usable by her.
(3) According to Definition (8), principle R *is* usable by S, since she believes of act B that it would maximize the minimum value, and it is true that if she wanted to derive a prescription from R, she would do so.
(4) Thus, R is the highest usable principle of subjective rightness for S.
(5) In light of her information, S is in a position to conclude that R is the highest usable principle of subjective rightness for her.
(6) Hence, S is in a position to conclude that act B is subjectively right, since she is in a position to conclude that B is prescribed by the highest usable principle of subjective rightness relative to principle Q.
(7) Act A is not subjectively right, because even though it is prescribed by principle P (the highest principle of subjective rightness relative to Q), principle P is not usable by S.
(8) Act B is in fact the subjectively right act for S relative to principle Q, since it is prescribed by the highest usable principle of subjective rightness relative to Q.[69]

[69] In point (1) of this list of eight points, we construed the case as one in which principle P is not usable by S, since she does not believe that she believes of any act that it would maximize value. But, alternatively, the psychology of the case could be such that P *is* usable by S, since, given that S actually does believe of act A that it would maximize value, she might (to her surprise) derive a prescription for A from P. On this construal, the case would turn out as follows:

Thus, MT-1, founded on Definition (5), provides an internally usable decision guide for this agent, even though she is mistaken about her relevant beliefs.[70] Case 1 serves to reassure us that an agent's mistakes *about her beliefs* will not prevent her from using principles of subjective rightness as internal decision guides.

Suppose that in Case 1, S is mistaken in believing that act B would maximize minimum value; in fact, some third act C has this characteristic. Then act B would not actually be subjectively right for S; instead, act C would. This case shows us that principles of subjective rightness, even when they are usable as *internal* decision guides, are not necessarily usable as *external* decision guides. We suspected from the beginning that even principles of subjective rightness would not succeed as external decision guides, and this case confirms this suspicion. Just as there can be a gap between what is objectively right for an agent and what she believes is objectively right, there can be a gap between what is subjectively right and what she believes is subjectively right. Invoking the concept of subjective rightness does not ensure that agents are infallible when they seek to perform the wisest action. In our case, this feature does not depend on the agent's mistakes about her own beliefs. It could crop up in any case in which the agent is mistaken in believing that an action has a subjective-right-making feature that it lacks.

The analysis of MT-1's usability can be duplicated for cases in which an agent is *uncertain* about her own beliefs—for example, the agent actually believes that act A would maximize value, but is uncertain whether she believes that A would maximize value. In these cases, too, the agent is able to derive internal guidance for what to do.[71] Thus, it appears that mistakes

---

(1') Principle P is usable by S, since she believes of act A that it would maximize value, and if she wanted to derive a prescription from P she would do so, in virtue of this belief.

(2') Thus, Principle P is the highest usable principle of subjective rightness for S.

(3') In light of her information, S is in a position to conclude that P is the highest principle of subjective rightness usable by her.

(4') Hence, S is in a position to conclude that act A is subjectively right, since she is in a position to conclude that A is prescribed by the highest usable principle of subjective rightness relative to Q.

(5') Act A is prescribed by the highest usable principle of subjective rightness, and so is subjectively right.

On this alternative construal of this case, S is also able to use one of the principles of subjective rightness for Q as an internal decision guide.

Note that if 3' ("S is in a position to conclude that P is the highest principle of subjective rightness usable by her") is false, then S would mistakenly conclude that A is not subjectively right.

[70] Note that S could have mistaken normative beliefs (she might not believe MT-1 contains the correct principle of objective rightness, or she might mistakenly believe that principle of subjective rightness R is higher than principle P, or she might not be able to grasp any or some of these principles). These cognitive errors, too, may lead her astray in various ways. These are complications I explore in *Making Morality Work*.

[71] Similarly, the analysis can be duplicated for moral theories that are subjectivized, i.e., ones in which principles such as P explicitly refer to the agent's beliefs as grounds for the

or uncertainty about her non-normative beliefs do not stand in the way of an agent's finding an internally usable guide for her decision-making, appropriate to a principle of objective rightness Q, so long as Q is supplemented by a rich enough set of principles of subjective rightness (and the agent is familiar with these). Although normative ignorance or mistake may stand in her way, non-normative ignorance or mistake, even about her own beliefs, will not. Definition (5), when combined with Definitions (6) and (8), appears to license moral theories whose subordinate principles of subjective rightness will jointly meet the Guidance Adequacy Criterion.

VI. Reasonable Beliefs as the Ground for Subjective Rightness

As I have noted, many theorists hold that "subjective rightness" should be defined in terms of what it would be reasonable for the agent to believe (or what an agent would be justified in believing, etc.), rather than in terms of what the agent actually believes. Given the tools we have developed, let us consider this suggestion more fully. In light of our earlier rejection of this approach based on Definitions (1) through (4), the natural strategy for a proponent of this approach would be to offer a revised version of Definition (5) that incorporates reference to reasonable beliefs in place of (5)'s reference to actual beliefs. A version of such a definition (here stated for rightness only, in the interests of brevity) could be stated as follows:

Definition (5)*:
If Q is a principle of objective moral status, and Q stipulates that F is a right-making feature of actions and that G is a wrong-making feature of actions, *then*

(1) A normative principle P is a principle of *subjective rightness* relative to principle Q just in case, for any agent S, either of the following is true:

> (A) *if* it would be reasonable for agent S to believe of some act A that A is possible for him to perform and that A has feature F, *then* principle P prescribes A, relative to principle Q and relative to the non-normative beliefs that it would be reasonable for S to have about A; or
> (B) *if* (i) it would be reasonable for agent S to believe of some act A that A may be possible for him to perform, *and if* (ii) it would be reasonable for S to be uncertain whether any act

---

subjective status of the action, as in "An act Y is a candidate for being subjectively obligatory if the agent *believes that* Y would maximize value." See note 53 for discussion of "subjectivizing" a moral principle.

available to him has feature F, and if so, which act does have F, *then* principle P prescribes A relative to principle Q and relative to the non-normative beliefs it would be reasonable for S to have about A.[72]

The standard principles of subjective rightness licensed by Definition (5)* would refer to the beliefs it would be reasonable for an agent to have. For example, such a principle might state that an act would be subjectively right just in case it would be reasonable for the agent to believe that it would maximize expected value. Unfortunately for this approach, it is clear that agents frequently have no beliefs about what it would be reasonable for them to believe, or are uncertain or mistaken about what it would be reasonable for them to believe. Hard-pressed decision-making agents typically do not ask themselves what it would be reasonable for them to believe. And even an agent who does ask herself this, and realizes that she should have investigated further (or deliberated more carefully or longer) before making a decision, and who therefore believes that her present beliefs may not be reasonable, may have little idea what beliefs about the facts she *would* have had if she had investigated or deliberated further.

What does this imply about the acceptability of Definition (5)*? To see this, consider the following moral theory (MT-1*) and its implications. MT-1* is modeled on MT-1, but substitutes "it would be reasonable for the agent to believe" for "the agent believes."

MT-1*

Principle of objective rightness:
  Q: An act X is objectively obligatory if and only if X maximizes value.

Principles of subjective rightness:
  P*: An act Y is a candidate for being subjectively obligatory if it would be reasonable for the agent to believe that Y would maximize value.
  R*: An act Z is a candidate for being subjectively obligatory if it would be reasonable for the agent to believe that Z would maximize the minimum value.

The subjectively right act:
  (a) Principle P* is higher than principle R*; and
  (b) An act W is subjectively obligatory if and only if W is prescribed by the highest principle of subjective rightness listed above that the agent is able to use as an internal guide.

---

[72] Note that a version of Definition (5) phrased in terms of the beliefs S actually has that *are reasonable* would not be tenable, since many agents would have no reasonable beliefs relevant to the choice they must make, and yet still need guidance in making that choice.

Now consider a case in which the agent does not have the relevant beliefs about what it would be reasonable for her to believe.

CASE 2

(a) Agent S believes that MT-1* is the correct moral theory.
(b) It would be reasonable for S to believe of act A that it would maximize value, and reasonable to believe of act B that it would maximize minimum value.
(c) S does not believe that it would be reasonable for her to believe of any act that it would maximize value, or would maximize minimum value.
(d) Neither principle P* nor principle R* is usable by S, because it is false that if S wanted to derive a prescription from P* or from R*, she would do so. (She would fail to derive a prescription from either of these principles because she does not believe of any act that it would be reasonable for her to believe of that act that it would maximize value, or maximize minimum value.)
(e) Since neither P* nor R* is usable by S, there is no act which is subjectively right for S to perform.
(f) S would not conclude about any act that it is subjectively right for her to perform it.

Thus, application of MT-1* to Case 2, in which S does not believe that it would be reasonable for her to believe of any act that it either maximizes value or maximizes minimum value, indicates that there is no act that is subjectively right for S, and MT-1* provides S with no usable internal decision guide.

Of course, MT-1* is a highly impoverished theory, and could be expanded by adding more principles of subjective rightness. This might help the usefulness of MT-1*, since the expanded version might include some lower-level principle of subjective rightness which would be usable even if higher-level principles are not. For example, if the expanded MT-1* includes principle T* ("An act W is a candidate for being subjectively right if it would be reasonable for the agent to believe that W might produce some positive value"), and S believes it would be reasonable to believe of act A that it might produce positive value, then T* would be usable by S as an internal guide for making decisions according to MT-1*.

But even though the lower-level principles of subjective rightness for the expanded MT-1* (such as principle T*) would not place heavy demands on the agent's beliefs about what it would be reasonable for her to believe, nonetheless there will be many cases in which the agent must decide here and now what to do, and in which—because she hasn't asked herself the question—she has no beliefs about what it would be reasonable for her to believe. In such cases, even an expanded MT-1* would not provide any decision guide for the agent—even though the agent may well have beliefs about various features her actions have, and so would be able to use MT-1 to guide her decision.[73]

Thus, since agents often lack beliefs about what it would be reasonable for them to believe about their various options, Definition (5)* licenses moral theories that are usable in a significantly smaller range of cases than the moral theories that are licensed by Definition (5). Adoption of Definition (5)*, as opposed to Definition (5), would result in numbers of agents who lack any usable principle of subjective rightness at all. I conclude that we should reject Definition (5)* on the grounds that it cannot provide sufficiently widely usable decision guides.[74] Even an agent who has given no thought to what it would be reasonable for her to believe, or has no idea which belief would be reasonable, still has to make a decision, and her moral theory should enable her to do so.

[73] For every moral theory, there may be a "bottom-level" principle of subjective rightness—the lowest principle in the hierarchy, to be used when the agent completely lacks any relevant information about his prospective acts. It is plausible that, for MT-1* (or any moral theory), the bottom-level principle should designate as morally permissible any act the agent can perform, since, by hypothesis, the agent has no way to rule out any act as inconsistent with the values of the principle of objective rightness. Thus, the bottom-level principle of subjective rightness for MT-1* would be "An act W is a candidate for being subjectively permissible if W is an act that it would be reasonable for the agent to believe he can perform." Such a principle makes very limited cognitive demands on an agent. Nonetheless, it makes more demands than the parallel principle for MT-1 ("An act W is a candidate for being subjectively permissible if W is an act that the agent believes he can perform"), since it still requires that the agent have beliefs about what it is reasonable for him to believe—and many agents may not have such beliefs, either because they are not thinking about what it is reasonable for them to believe, or because they are uncertain what it is reasonable for them to believe. Thus, even when it is augmented by such bottom-level principles, MT-1* is less widely usable than MT-1.

[74] One of the major arguments in favor of defining subjective rightness in terms of beliefs that it would be reasonable to have, rather than in terms of actual beliefs, is that "reasonable beliefs" rather than "actual beliefs" are arguably the beliefs most relevant to the agent's blameworthiness. This position on blameworthiness is itself controversial. I would argue that it is incorrect: while it is true that an agent may be blameworthy for not making the inquiries she could and should have made (or for not drawing the correct conclusions from her evidence), it does not follow from this that she is blameworthy for making the choice that appears best in light of the directly relevant beliefs she actually has at the time of decision. The role of principles of subjective rightness is to provide her with the guidance she needs and can use at the time she must make her decision, not the guidance that a better agent could use. For further discussion, see my "Culpable Ignorance," *The Philosophical Review* 92, no. 4 (October 1983): 543–71. But even a theorist who holds that the blameworthiness of an agent depends on the beliefs it would be reasonable for her to have (as opposed to those she actually has) should still accept the original Definition (5) of subjective rightness, since it—but not Definition (5)*—provides autonomy to agents seeking to guide their decisions by reference to their potential acts' moral value. This theorist can then define "blameworthiness" in terms, not directly of the agent's performing what she believes to be the objectively or subjectively right act, but rather in terms of the agent's performing what a reasonable agent would have believed to be the objectively or subjectively right act. This conception needs further refinement, however, since surely an agent may blamelessly choose an act while mistakenly (but perhaps reasonably) believing it to be what a reasonable person would have believed to be subjectively wrong.

VII. Conclusion

The concept of subjective rightness was originally introduced to enable us to deal with two issues: (1) the paradoxical tension between (a) what is best for an agent to do in light of the actual circumstances in which she acts and (b) what is wisest for her to do in light of her mistaken or uncertain beliefs about her circumstances; and (2) the need to provide moral guidance to an agent who may be uncertain about the circumstances in which she acts, and hence is unable to use her principle of objective rightness directly in deciding what to do. Surprisingly, there have been relatively few attempts to provide a clear and detailed analysis of the concept of subjective rightness. In this essay, I have described criteria of adequacy for any successful definition of subjective rightness, canvassed the major existing strategies for defining this notion, and rejected each of them as inadequate. I then argued we must take a different approach to the problem, focusing on defining *principles* of subjective rightness rather than subjectively right *acts*. I proposed Definition (5), which captures the crucial insight that a normative principle can be characterized as a principle of subjective rightness only relative to a governing principle of objective rightness. Along the route, I have argued that the concept of subjective rightness should be defined by reference to the agent's actual beliefs, rather than by reference to the beliefs it would be reasonable for an agent in her position to have. Definition (5) provides a solid framework for addressing our two issues: it enables us to dissolve the tension of issue (1) by distinguishing what an agent ought objectively to do from what she ought subjectively to do, and it enables us to address issue (2) by using principles of subjective rightness to provide moral guidance to agents who are uncertain about the circumstances or consequences of their actions. Armed with Definition (5), we can recognize that each moral theory must include a multiplicity of principles of subjective rightness to address the epistemic situations of the full range of moral decision-makers. Definition (5) places us in a position to evaluate and rank-order substantive principles of subjective rightness, to explore more adequately the links between subjective rightness and blameworthiness, and to assess the Remodeling proposal that principles of subjective rightness be elevated to the status of principles of objective rightness. There is much work to be done, but the groundwork has been laid.

Philosophy, Rutgers University

UNDERIVATIVE DUTY:
PRICHARD ON MORAL OBLIGATION

By Thomas Hurka

I. Introduction

H. A. Prichard is known as the author of a paper with one of the best titles in the history of philosophy, "Does Moral Philosophy Rest on a Mistake?" (1912)[1]—and, alongside G. E. Moore, W. D. Ross, and others, as one of the non-naturalists[2] whose views dominated metaethics in the early twentieth century. But this common picture of Prichard underestimates his place in the history of ethics, which I believe is central. This is not because he defended completely distinctive ideas; his most important views were shared by other philosophers of his period, from Henry Sidgwick to A. C. Ewing. But it was often Prichard who stated those views most forcefully and defended them best.

These views can be summarized in a slogan Prichard himself did not use: "Duty is underivative." But this slogan can be applied at three different levels. The first concerns the normative realm as a whole; here it expresses the non-naturalist view that normative truths are *sui generis,* neither reducible to nor derivable from non-normative truths such as those of science. Duty is underivative in the sense that truths about how we ought to act, in the broadest sense of "ought," are self-standing. The second level focuses more narrowly on moral judgments, as one kind of normative judgment. Here the claim is that truths about how we ought morally to act are also underivative, not only from non-normative truths but also from any other normative truths; there are no nonmoral "oughts" or values from which moral "oughts" derive. The final level is that of specific deontological duties such as duties to keep promises, not harm others, and so on. For Prichard, these duties do not derive from a more general consequentialist duty to promote good consequences. The main reason we ought to keep our promises or not harm others is just that we ought to; those duties, like the normative realm as a whole and moral duty in general, are self-standing.

Prichard accepted all three of these claims, though he did not distinguish the first two from each other, as many present-day philosophers do.

---

[1] H. A. Prichard, *Moral Writings,* ed. Jim MacAdam (Oxford: Clarendon Press, 2002), 7–20.
[2] Non-naturalism holds that normative judgments, including in particular moral judgments, (1) can be objectively true, but (2) are neither reducible to nor derivable from non-normative judgments such as those of science. There are normative truths, but they are distinct from all other truths.

My main interest is in his defense of the second claim, about moral duty in general; this defense appears in his famous argument that it is a mistake to ask "Why ought I to do what I morally ought to do?" because the only possible answer is "Because you morally ought to." But I will begin by examining his defense of the third claim, about deontological duties, because it sheds light on his methodology in discussing the other two. This is the subject of Section II; later sections will address claims one and two.

II. Deontological Duty Is Underivative

The substantive moral view in "Does Moral Philosophy Rest on a Mistake?" (hereafter "Mistake") is close to that later defended by Ross, who probably took it over from Prichard. On this view, there is not just one basic moral duty, as consequentialism and also Kant say, but several— some (perhaps) to bring about certain consequences, but others largely independent of consequences, such as duties to keep promises, not harm others, and so on, where the latter duties make the view deontological. The various duties can conflict, but when they do there are no rules for deciding between them: we can only make a direct intuitive judgment about which duty is stronger. In expounding this pluralist view, Prichard did not use the language Ross would introduce of "prima facie duties," though Prichard at one point suggested the equivalent term "claim."[3] But the two philosophers' views were close: there is a plurality of (sometimes) deontological duties, with no single unifying ground for them.

Prichard's defense of this view, and especially his critique of consequentialism, emphasized one of two distinct arguments a deontologist can make. Sixty years after "Mistake," Robert Nozick said that utilitarian attempts "to derive (approximations of) usual precepts of justice . . . do not yield the particular result desired, and they produce the wrong reasons for the sort of result they try to get."[4] Prichard sometimes made the first of these objections to consequentialism, saying, for example, that it can favor outcomes that are unjust and therefore wrong to produce.[5] But his more common objection was the second one, about explanation: that even when consequentialism yields the right conclusion about how we ought to act, it gives the wrong reason for it. In "Mistake," Prichard wrote:

> Suppose we ask ourselves whether our sense that we ought to pay our debts or to tell the truth arises from our recognition that in doing so we should be originating something good, e.g. material comfort in

[3] Prichard, *Moral Writings*, 79.
[4] Robert Nozick, *Anarchy, State, and Utopia* (New York: Basic Books, 1974), 202.
[5] Prichard, *Moral Writings*, 2.

A or true belief in *B*, i.e. suppose we ask ourselves whether it is this aspect of the action which leads to our recognition that we ought to do it. We at once and without hesitation answer "No."[6]

According to Prichard, we ought to pay our debt because we incurred it, and not because (or only because) of any good that will result. He made a similar objection to Kant's attempt to unify the moral duties under the first formulation of his categorical imperative:

> No one could suppose that the reason why an act ought to be done consists in the fact that everyone could do it. Even Kant could not have supposed this. The difficulty escaped him because it didn't occur to him that his criterion of moral rules must express what, on his view, is their reason.[7]

Or, as the same point has recently been put, even if Kant's universal law formulas do flag actions from certain motives or maxims as wrong, they "do not adequately explain *why* acting on those maxims is wrong. What is wrong with slavery, for example, is not adequately explained by saying that it is impossible for everyone to act [on] the maxim of a would-be slave-owner."[8]

Prichard's interest in the explanation of particular duties was shared by many other philosophers of the late nineteenth and early twentieth centuries. The British Idealists allowed that utilitarianism mostly yields correct verdicts about which acts are right, but insisted that the reason why those acts are right is not that they promote pleasure; it is that they promote perfectionist goods.[9] In *Principia Ethica*, Moore said that we ought most of the time to obey those rules obedience to which will best preserve society, and that these rules will be the same given any plausible theory of what is good. But he still called the question of what is in fact good the "primary ethical question," because it concerns the reason why those

---

[6] Ibid., 10.

[7] Ibid., 59. This passage confuses Kant's test for an act's being permissible with a test for its being required, but Prichard's objection does not depend on that confusion; it is likewise implausible to say that the explanation of why an act is permitted is that everyone could do it. Prichard also objected that Kant's universalization test yields the wrong results (ibid., 60).

[8] Thomas E. Hill, Jr., "Kantian Normative Ethics," in David Copp, ed., *The Oxford Handbook of Ethical Theory* (New York: Oxford University Press, 2006), 488; emphasis in the original.

[9] F. H. Bradley wrote, "What we hold to against every possible modification of Hedonism is that the standard and test is in higher and lower function, not in more or less pleasure." See Bradley, "Mr. Sidgwick's Hedonism," in Bradley, *Collected Essays*, vol. 1 (Oxford: Clarendon Press, 1935), 97. For a similar view, see T. H. Green, *Prolegomena to Ethics*, ed. A. C. Bradley (Oxford: Clarendon Press, 1883), sections 332, 356.

rules are best.[10] And Prichard's emphasis on explaining particular duties
was very much shared by Ross. Ross too sometimes argued that consequentialism yields the wrong conclusions,[11] but he titled his defense of
deontology "What Makes Right Acts Right?" and argued that even when
consequentialism is right about which acts are right, it is wrong about
why they are right. If we think we ought to keep a promise, he insisted,
the reason is not that this will have good consequences; it is simply that
we promised.[12]

Prichard's emphasis on explanation also fits a moral epistemology he
shared with Ross and C. D. Broad. Unlike Sidgwick, Prichard did not
believe we can come to know abstract moral principles by reflecting on
them just as abstract principles; moral intuitions are elicited only in particular situations. But what we intuit in a particular situation is that an
act's having some nonmoral property tends to make it right or wrong—
for example, that its being the return of a favor tends to make it right: "We
recognize that this performance of a service to X, who has done us a
service, just in virtue of its being the performance of a service to one who
has rendered a service to the would-be agent, ought to be done by us."[13]
Though prompted by a particular situation, the intuition is implicitly
general, since it implies, as Prichard emphasized, that any act of returning
a favor is, other things equal, right. And this implication, while not equivalent to the principle that we ought, other things equal, to return favors,
is sufficiently close to it that our grasp of the principle follows by a small
step.[14]

This epistemology contradicts the not uncommon view of Prichard as
a moral particularist, who denied the truth of general principles and held
that moral knowledge concerns only particular acts as particular. On the
contrary, he often emphasized the importance of moral principles, applaud-
ing Kant, for example, for recognizing that "any particular right action
involves a principle binding on every one always."[15] Prichard's epistemology also connects with his main line of objection to consequentialism,
since it makes the primary moral intuition one about explanation: that an
act's having a nonmoral property like being the return of a favor explains
why it is, other things equal, right. But if our primary intuitions are

[10] G. E. Moore, *Principia Ethica* (Cambridge: Cambridge University Press, 1903), 158.
Similar remarks about the "primary ethical question" are on pp. 27, 77, 90–91, 138, 140, 184,
189, and 222.
[11] See, e.g., W. D. Ross, *The Right and the Good* (Oxford: Clarendon Press, 1930), 34.
[12] Ibid., 17; see also 19, 24, 36–39, and W. D. Ross, *Foundations of Ethics* (Oxford: Clarendon
Press, 1939), 65, 68–69, 113, 187.
[13] Prichard, *Moral Writings*, 13; see also 4–5, 77. Ross's presentation of this view is in
Foundations of Ethics, 168–71.
[14] Ross, borrowing from Aristotle in the *Posterior Analytics*, called this step one of "intuitive induction"; see Ross, *Foundations of Ethics*, 170, 320. For the same view in similar
language, see C. D. Broad, *Five Types of Ethical Theory* (London: Routledge and Kegan Paul,
1930), 145–46, 177–78, 271–72.
[15] Prichard, *Moral Writings*, 63; see also 4–5, 77.

explanatory, then to assess a moral theory for its claims about explanation is to assess it against the most secure moral knowledge we have.

Prichard's epistemology also widened the range of intuitions a successful moral theory must accommodate. Sidgwick is often taken to have argued that utilitarianism fits not only our intuitions about abstract principles but also our judgments about particular cases.[16] But, for him, these judgments tended to concern only what is in fact good or right, so it does not matter if utilitarianism gives instrumental explanations for the goodness of things that common sense thinks are good in themselves. Moore criticized Sidgwick sharply on this score, saying that even if hedonism yields the right conclusions about which pleasures are best, by considering their effects on future pleasures, it does not capture our convictions about why they are best, which concern what they are pleasures in now.[17] Prichard similarly expanded the judgments to be captured by a theory of the right when he included, and in fact made central, judgments about why right acts are right rather than just those about which acts they are.

Prichard expressed his objection to consequentialism in a radical way. He thought the proper description of a moral duty must always mention its explanatory ground: if the reason we ought to perform some act is that it has property F, then our duty in the situation is really to perform the act that has F.[18] But then, in trying to derive the duty to keep promises from a duty to promote the good, consequentialism turns the duty to keep promises into a quite different duty to promote value—if that is what explains the duty, that is what the duty is.[19] And this means that consequentialism turns the duty to keep promises into something it is not, and thereby distorts the moral phenomena: in trying to explain the duty to keep promises, consequentialism destroys it.

This idea of distorting the moral phenomena was central to Prichard's argument that moral duty in general is underivative, and, in particular, the ideal was central to the third and most distinctive of three stages in that argument. Before we address that, however, there is a question about how far-reaching his critique of consequentialism was.

Ross thought consequentialism is at least partly right, since for him one important duty is to promote good consequences, and whenever there is a duty to promote some state X, it is in part because X is good. When Prichard in "Mistake" set himself "in opposition to the view that what is

[16] See, e.g., J. B. Schneewind, *Sidgwick's Ethics and Victorian Moral Philosophy* (Oxford: Clarendon Press, 1977). For a contrary reading, see Peter Singer, "Sidgwick and Reflective Equilibrium," *The Monist* 52 (1974): 490–517; and Anthony Skelton, "Henry Sidgwick's Moral Epistemology," *Journal of the History of Philosophy* (forthcoming).

[17] Moore, *Principia Ethica*, 94–95.

[18] Prichard, *Moral Writings*, 5, 27–28, 121–23.

[19] Prichard here assumes what Philip Stratton-Lake has called the "eliminative" view of derivative moral duties; see Philip Stratton-Lake, "Eliminativism about Derivative Prima Facie Duties," in Thomas Hurka, ed., *Underivative Duty: British Moral Philosophers from Sidgwick to Ewing* (Oxford: Clarendon Press, forthcoming).

right is derived from what is good,"[20] was he agreeing with the view
Ross would later defend, or did he mean to reject consequentialism in
some more comprehensive way?

We can distinguish three views about the duty to promote a state of
affairs X: (1) The duty to promote X is entirely underivative, and in
particular does not depend on any claim that X is good. (2) The duty to
promote X depends partly on the claim that X is good and partly on the
independent claim that we have a duty to promote whatever is good; X's
goodness supplies some but not all of the ground of the duty. (This was
Ross's view.) (3) The duty to promote X is grounded wholly in the claim
that X is good, because claims about the good directly entail claims about
what we ought to do. (This was, notoriously, Moore's view in *Principia
Ethica*.) Prichard clearly rejected view (3), but was his target in "Mistake"
just (3), or did he mean also to reject (2)? Jonathan Dancy has recently
defended the second reading, arguing that while for Prichard there may
be acts whose rightness depends on their consequences (for example, on
the fact that they promote pleasure), their rightness never depends on
those consequences' being good.[21]

But this reading is hard to square with the text of "Mistake." First,
Prichard's target in that paper was the view that "what is right is derived
from what is good," and that is not the view of (2), which treats the duty
to promote whatever is good as underivative. Only view (3) derives the
right from the good. Second, many of Prichard's arguments were relevant
only to (3). He insisted that "[a]n 'ought' . . . can only be derived from
another 'ought',"[22] but (2) agrees with him on this point if it treats the
duty to promote whatever is good as underived. More specifically, he
argued that deriving the right from the good requires that the good be
understood as what "ought to be,"[23] and this is again not true of (2),
which can understand "good" in whatever way it likes so long as it adds
an independent duty to promote value as so understood. It is only view
(3)'s attempt to derive the right entirely from the good, combined with the
principle that an "ought" can only follow from another "ought," that
requires an "ought" within the meaning of "good." Finally, Prichard located
his target in "Mistake" in a passage from Hastings Rashdall's *Theory of
Good and Evil* that argued, just as Moore had, that "right" means "productive of the most good."[24] And that is view (3), not (2).[25]

[20] Prichard, *Moral Writings*, 14.
[21] Jonathan Dancy, "Has Anyone Ever Been a Non-Intuitionist?" in Hurka, ed., *Underivative Duty*.
[22] Prichard, *Moral Writings*, 9.
[23] Ibid.
[24] The passage is in Hastings Rashdall, *The Theory of Good and Evil* (London: Oxford
University Press, 1907), vol. 1, 135–36.
[25] At one point, Prichard says that we do not come to appreciate a moral duty by an
argument of which "a premiss" is the appreciation of something's goodness (*Moral Writings*,
13–14); this suggests that a claim about goodness is not even part of the ground of duty. But

Thus, Prichard's anticonsequentialist argument in "Mistake" was consistent with recognizing a duty to promote the good, as Ross did. Nonetheless, Prichard's substantive view, especially later in his career, was in two respects further removed from consequentialism than Ross's.

First, in his early writings, Prichard held that it is a necessary condition of an act's being right that it produce something good: "unless the effect of an action were in some way good, there would be no obligation to produce it."[26] And this view was shared by Ross and E. F. Carritt.[27] Of course, none of these philosophers were consequentialists; they did not think right acts always maximize the good. But that is because they thought we can stand in certain relations to another person, such as having promised him something or caused him some harm, that make it right for us to produce less good for him rather than more good for someone else: the relation shifts the target of our good-promoting activity from one person to another. But it is still necessary, for an act to be right, that it have some good effect.

Carritt and Ross seem to have retained this view, but Prichard implicitly abandoned it. Whereas his early papers recognized a plurality of goods, including pleasure and knowledge,[28] a 1928 letter from him to Ross said there is only one intrinsic good: virtuous disposition. Pleasure and knowledge are not good, as Ross thought, nor is the active exercise of virtue better than its mere possession; the only good is being virtuously disposed.[29] But if Prichard believed this after 1928 and still affirmed duties to promote pleasure and knowledge, as he seems to have done, he could not ground these duties even partly in the claim that the states in question are good; the duties would have to be entirely underivative, as on view (1). Nor would it be true for him, as for Ross, that whenever there is a duty to promote X, X must be good.

Second, Ross thought that for states that are good in the strict sense, such as virtue and knowledge, there is a single undifferentiated duty to promote them in all people everywhere; the relations that help ground deontological duties are irrelevant. But in an early paper Prichard wrote that *any* moral principle must mention two things: "(*a*) a good thing which the action will produce, (*b*) a definite relation in which the agent

---

he goes on immediately after to deny that our sense of duty is "a conclusion" from the goodness of anything, thereby again denying only that a claim about goodness is sufficient to ground duty.

[26] Prichard, *Moral Writings*, 2; see also 4, 10.

[27] W. D. Ross, "The Nature of Morally Good Action," *Proceedings of the Aristotelian Society* 29 (1928–29): 267; and Ross, *The Right and the Good*, 162. See also E. F. Carritt, *The Theory of Morals* (London: Oxford University Press, 1928), 41–42; Carritt actually said that every right act must produce some satisfaction, and on that basis questioned whether there is any duty to keep promises to the dead.

[28] Prichard, *Moral Writings*, 10, 10 n. 4.

[29] H. A. Prichard, "Letter to W. D. Ross of Dec. 20, 1928," Bodleian Library, University of Oxford, Ms. Eng. Lett. D. 116 fols. 77–82. There is a brief published expression of this view in Prichard, *Moral Writings*, 173.

stands either to another or to himself."[30] And the same view appeared in his much later paper "Moral Obligation" (published posthumously in 1949). Prichard was there challenging the consequentialist idea that what makes an act right is just its causing something good, and taking as his example of something "indubitably good" an increase in someone's patience, as fit his later view that only virtue is good. He objected that the consequentialist idea ignores the difference between increasing one's own patience and increasing another person's, where the different relations in which we stand to the person whose patience is at issue make these different duties: "We shall be thinking of the acts as duties of different sorts just because the one will be making *ourselves* better and the other making *someone else* better."[31] Prichard therefore extended the grounding role Ross thought relations play only for deontological duties to all duties whatever, and on that basis Prichard held that our duties to produce the same good in different people can differ in strength. Ross thought that if we ought to spend more time promoting our own virtue than other people's, this is only because we can do so more effectively.[32] But Prichard held that, effectiveness aside, we have a stronger duty to promote our own virtue because it is ours, and may also have a stronger duty to promote our children's virtue.[33] Even when a duty is just to promote some good, it matters to the character of the duty whose good it is.

If this was Prichard's view, however, it should be read into his deontological critique of consequentialism. Even when consequentialism yields the right verdict about which act is right, he held, it oversimplifies the explanation of the act's rightness by omitting the crucial fact of relationship: the fact that the person we are acting toward stands in a specified relation to us, even that of being a stranger or being ourself. That he stands in this relation is a vital part of our intuitive understanding of what makes the act right, and in ignoring it consequentialism distorts the moral phenomena. A similar charge about distortion figured in Prichard's argument that moral duty in general is underivative, and in particular in the third stage of a three-stage argument he gave for that claim, as we will see in Section V.

III. Conceptual Minimalism

Prichard's second claim, that moral duty in general is underivative, can be combined with any view about what the content of that duty is. It says that the basic moral duties, whatever they are, are not grounded in any more fundamental considerations, either normative or non-normative. A

---

[30] Prichard, *Moral Writings*, 4.
[31] Ibid., 217.
[32] Ross, *The Right and the Good*, 26.
[33] Prichard, *Moral Writings*, 2, 217.

deontologist like Prichard can say that the duty to keep promises is underivative, but a consequentialist can say the same about his preferred fundamental duty. Asked why we ought to promote the good, a consequentialist can say there is no other answer than that we morally ought to. And that is what the leading consequentialists of Prichard's day— Sidgwick, Rashdall, and Moore—did say. Though differing from Prichard about what the basic moral duties were, they agreed that they were self-standing.

As I said at the start of this essay, Prichard did not distinguish the second claim, about specifically moral duty, from the claim that normative considerations in general are underivative. This is because he held that there are no "oughts" other than the moral "ought," so there are no normative considerations other than moral ones from which a moral duty could derive. This was an aspect of a conceptual minimalism that he again shared with other philosophers of his period and that grounded a first stage in his argument for underivative duty.

These philosophers thought that all normative claims could be expressed using just a few basic concepts. For some, there was only one basic normative concept: for Sidgwick, that of what one "ought" to do; for Moore in *Principia Ethica,* that of what is "good"; and for Broad and the middle Ewing, that of what is "fitting." Others such as Prichard, the later Moore, and Ross recognized two basic concepts, often "good" and "ought." But they all denied that there were more than a very few irreducible normative concepts.

Faced with a proposed additional normative concept, a minimalist of this kind can respond in either of two ways: by reductively analyzing the concept in question using one of his favored basic ones, or by denying that it is really normative. Both approaches were used by Prichard and his contemporaries. Thus, many of them held that "moral goodness" is just ordinary intrinsic goodness when had by a specific type of object (for example, an attitude to an object with some other moral property such as rightness or goodness). This illustrates the reductive option. Sidgwick, Rashdall, and Moore took a similar line about the concept of "my good," which they understood as that portion of what is good (however "good" is understood) that is located in my life, or is a state of me. But Prichard used the alternative approach for the related concept of what is a "good to" a person, or, in present-day language, what is "good for" her or a constituent of her "welfare." This, he claimed, is not a normative concept at all but makes only the descriptive claim that something will satisfy a person's desires or, more accurately, give her pleasure; something's being a "good to" a person, therefore, does not give her or anyone else reason to promote it.[34] Finally, the same two options present themselves for any proposed nonmoral "ought," such as the instrumental "ought" repre-

---

[34] Ibid., 173–76.

sented by Kant's hypothetical imperative. One possibility is to analyze this as a categorical imperative with a distinctive content, as on what is now called the "wide scope" reading of the hypothetical imperative. This treats this imperative as a command to make a certain conditional true, namely, to make it the case that if you desire or intend a certain end, you take (what you believe are) the means necessary to achieve it; this reading is suggested at least once by Sidgwick.[35] The other option is to deny that the instrumental "ought" is normative, and this was again the view of Prichard and Ross. Prichard argued that Kant's hypothetical imperative is not really an imperative at all, since it makes only the descriptive claim that a certain action is necessary for the achievement of a given goal. When we use "ought" instrumentally, "what we really mean . . . has to be expressed by the hypothetical statement: 'If I do not do so and so, my purpose will not be realized'."[36] For Ross, the hypothetical imperative says only "that a man who desires certain ends can hope to get them only if he adopts certain means."[37] This is why, for Prichard and Ross, there are no nonmoral "oughts." The only genuine "oughts" are categorical, and since (following Kant) all categorical "oughts" are moral, there are only moral "oughts" or moral requirements.

This conceptual minimalism contrasts starkly with the approach of much present-day moral philosophy, which operates with a larger number of irreducible normative concepts: the "good for" a person alongside what is simply "good," as well as prudential, aesthetic, and other "oughts" alongside the moral one. But in my view the minimalism of Prichard and his contemporaries is a far sounder view. Consider the conflict Sidgwick wrestled with, between a principle saying we ought to promote only our own pleasure and one telling us to promote the pleasure of all. If these principles are genuinely to conflict, they must use or at least entail claims using a common concept of "ought"; otherwise, they will talk past each other. But then resolving their conflict is a substantive matter, which involves deciding which of two claims using the common "ought" is stronger. If we like, we can label the first claim "prudential" or "rational" and the second "moral," but this will not alter the core issue, which is between two substantive claims about what we ought (in the common sense) to do. And the labeling only invites confusion, by suggesting that the issue turns somehow on conceptual questions about what "prudence"

[35] Patricia S. Greenspan, "Conditional Oughts and Hypothetical Imperatives," *Journal of Philosophy* 72 (1975): 259–76; John Broome, "Normative Requirements," in Jonathan Dancy, ed., *Normativity* (Oxford: Blackwell, 2000), 78–99; Henry Sidgwick, *The Methods of Ethics*, 7th ed. (London: Macmillan, 1907), 37. Sidgwick is not consistent in this reading, sometimes making remarks that suggest the "narrow scope" view; see, e.g., Sidgwick, *The Methods of Ethics*, 6–7.

[36] Prichard, *Moral Writings*, 166; see also 9, 34, 54–55, 126–28, 135, 143–44, 188.

[37] Ross, *Foundations of Ethics*, 48. Ross argued similarly that attributive uses of "good," as in "good knife" and "good liar," are purely descriptive; see Ross, *The Right and the Good*, 65–67, and Ross, *Foundations of Ethics*, 255–57.

or "rationality" and "morality" in the abstract involve. The great virtue of minimalism is that it avoids this confusion by presenting all normative issues as what they really are, namely, substantive issues about which claims using a common concept are true.

It may be objected that this common "ought" need not be labeled "moral"; it could instead be a generic practical "ought," with moral uses distinguished by, say, their subject matter, such as a reference to others' good. But if this objection grants that there is a single "ought," it raises only a verbal issue about what that "ought" should be called, and nothing substantive can turn on that. Moreover, I have suggested two arguments Prichard could give for calling this "ought" moral: it treats substantive questions as clearly substantive, and it fits a Kantian tradition whereby all categorical imperatives are moral. Whether or not these arguments are persuasive, it was certainly Prichard's view that the only "ought" is moral.

Given this view, his minimalism combined with his non-naturalism to yield a first stage in his argument that moral duty is underivative, or that it is a "mistake" to ask why we ought to do what we morally ought to do. If there is no "ought" other than the moral one, then there is no "ought" in terms of which this question can be framed; if moral truths are underivative from non-normative ones, as non-naturalism claims, they are completely underivative.

This again was a common view in Prichard's time. Moore said that the question "Why should I do my duty?" is "puzzling," because it reduces to "'Why is duty duty?' or 'Why is good good?'," while Carritt wrote, "If any one ask us, 'Why ought I to do these acts you call my duty?' the only answer is, 'Because they *are* your *duty*.'" [38] They too assumed, with Prichard, that the only normative concepts are moral. Sidgwick may seem an exception to this consensus, since he said that we ask "Why should I do what I see to be right?" when we do not ask "Why should I believe what I see to be true?" But his explanation was that we are torn between competing substantive views about what is right, and we express our uncertainty by asking the question; this implies that if it were settled what is right, there would be nothing to ask.[39] Thus, all these philosophers agreed with Prichard that the question "Why ought I to do what I morally ought?" does not arise, because the first "ought" cannot differ from the second. And that follows from one aspect of their shared conceptual minimalism.

IV. The Epistemological Argument

Prichard's minimalism, therefore, gave him an initial argument for the underivativeness of moral duty, but, on its own, this argument could not

[38] G. E. Moore, *The Elements of Ethics*, ed. Tom Regan (Philadelphia, PA: Temple University Press, 1991), 17–18; Carritt, *The Theory of Morals*, 29; emphasis in the original.
[39] Sidgwick, *The Methods of Ethics*, 5–6.

establish any substantive conclusions. It showed that whatever normative considerations are overriding should be called "moral," but Prichard wanted to do more. He wanted to show that the duties in his specific deontological view are underivative, and a consequentialist will want to show that the duty to promote the good is underivative. No mere conceptual claim about "ought" can show that; from conceptual premises only conceptual conclusions follow.

To see this, imagine how an instrumentalist in the style of Thomas Hobbes might respond to Prichard's minimalism. The instrumentalist may initially have said that a supreme principle of rationality tells us to do whatever will most satisfy our desires, and that moral "oughts" about keeping promises or promoting others' pleasure have normative force only when acting on them will be rational in this sense. If the instrumentalist accepts minimalism, he can no longer speak of a rational "ought," but that only requires him to reformulate his view. He can now say that the supreme *moral* principle tells us to do whatever will most satisfy our desires, and that more specific "oughts" about promises or promoting pleasure have force only when acting on them will satisfy this principle. His position will be substantively unchanged, and he will still deny that the duties Prichard and the consequentialist want to affirm have force.

Prichard implicitly recognized this possibility, and the second and third stages of his argument were directed against it. The second stage was an epistemological argument that addressed skeptical challenges to the conventional moral duties and paralleled Moore's well-known reply to skepticism about the external world. Moore held that we start out assuming we have direct awareness and therefore knowledge of external objects. A skeptic like David Hume may then propose a theory of knowledge according to which this assumption is false: we are directly aware only of our experiences, and we form our beliefs about external objects by inference from these experiences. But since all such inferences are unwarranted—premises about experiences license only conclusions about further experiences—our beliefs about external objects are unjustified and therefore not knowledge. Moore replied that, whatever theory of knowledge underwrites a skeptical argument like Hume's, we cannot have as much reason to believe it as we do to retain our initial belief that we know external objects. That common-sense belief is the foundation from which philosophy starts, and far from being refuted by a theory like Hume's, it shows that theory to be false.[40]

The second stage of Prichard's argument took a similar line. We start out believing we have an obligation to, say, keep promises. A skeptic like Glaucon in Plato's *Republic* may ask whether we really do have such an obligation, given that fulfilling it will often work against our interests.

---

[40] G. E. Moore, *Some Main Problems of Philosophy* (London: George Allen and Unwin, 1953), chap. 6.

The skeptic assumes something like Hobbes's instrumental principle: we have reason to do something only when it will further our desire-satisfaction, and we therefore have no reason to keep a promise when it will not. Prichard replied that we have less reason to believe the instrumental principle than to retain our initial conviction about the duty to keep promises, because that conviction involves direct apprehension of a self-evident truth and therefore is knowledge. That we have the specific duty is the better-grounded conviction, and its being so shows the instrumental principle to be false.

Prichard himself drew the parallel with the epistemological case. There, he said, we start out believing we have knowledge of, say, mathematics. A skeptic like Descartes can make us doubt whether this is so, but the correct response is to reflect on our original mathematical convictions and see that they were in fact knowledge, so that whatever theory generated Descartes's skepticism must be false.[41] The stage of being moved by such skepticism is not pointless; it is an essential part of philosophical reflection. But its end-result should be a return to our original convictions, and so it is with moral duty. Skeptics demand a proof that we have a duty to keep promises, but on Prichard's view this involves

> the mistake of supposing the possibility of proving what can only be apprehended directly by an act of moral thinking. Nevertheless the demand, though illegitimate, is inevitable until we have carried through the process of reflection far enough to apprehend the self-evidence of our obligations, i.e. the immediacy of our apprehension of them.[42]

Of course, not all philosophers are persuaded by Moore's reply to external-world skepticism, and not all will be persuaded by Prichard on moral duty. This is especially so since Prichard's response turns on an appeal to intuition: specifically, an intuition of the reality of a duty such as the duty to keep promises. But his argument is strengthened by his conceptual minimalism. Proponents of the instrumental view often call it a view about "rationality," implying that it has priority over merely "moral" claims about promise-keeping or promoting others' pleasure. But if the instrumental "ought" is the same as the moral "ought," the instrumentalist's claim is conceptually on a par with those other claims and must be weighed substantively against them—it has no epistemic advantage. Consider a case where a person's overriding desire is to become rich and he knows that the most effective way to do so is to kill his cousin and acquire her inheritance. Which is the true "ought" statement applying to him: that he ought simply to kill his cousin, as the instrumental view implies, or

[41] Prichard, *Moral Writings*, 18–19.
[42] Ibid., 19–20.

that he ought simply not to kill her, as Prichard believed? Surely most people will say the latter, and it is easier for them to do so if both statements use the same "ought." It likewise strengthens Prichard's reply if we distinguish the skeptic's reading of the instrumental or hypothetical imperative from ones that do not conflict with moral duty and therefore cannot undermine it, such as Prichard's non-normative reading and the wide-scope reading described above.[43] That the principle is true on one of these other readings does not imply that it is true on the skeptic's reading, which does conflict with duty. And once this distinction is made, the instrumentalist principle read in the skeptic's way looks decidedly unattractive. Surely most people faced with the foregoing example will find it more compelling that the person ought not to kill his cousin than that the supreme normative principle tells us to do whatever will satisfy our desires.

It may be objected that the instrumental view Prichard opposed is not the only one that allows us to ask, "Why ought I to do what I morally ought?" The instrumental view proposes a substantive criterion of rationality and says that moral "oughts" are binding only when they satisfy this criterion. But a different view allows that moral "oughts" have independent force, while holding that they must be weighed against other self-standing "oughts" such as prudential or aesthetic ones, to determine what a person ought to do all things considered. "Why ought I to do what I morally ought?" then becomes the question whether, in a particular case or generally, what I morally ought to do is the same as what I ought to do all things considered. And given the plurality of competing "oughts," proponents of this view think the answer is sometimes no.

To illustrate this objection, imagine that a person can produce either 9 units of pleasure for herself or slightly more, say, 10 units, for other people. Utilitarians will say she must produce the 10 units, but many will disagree. They will say that if she had a choice between 9 units of pleasure for herself and 1,000 for others, she would have a duty all things considered to produce the 1,000. But when the difference is smaller, as between 9 and 10 units, she does not have that duty but is permitted to prefer her own lesser pleasure. She may also be permitted to prefer the 10 units for others, but the point is that she is not required to do so. And this, the objector says, shows that the moral "ought" does not always uniquely determine the all-things-considered "ought." The moral "ought" has to be weighed against a prudential "ought" concerning a person's own pleasure, and in that conflict will sometimes lose.

As it happens, Prichard rejected a key premise of this objection. He believed, as Ross also did, that while we have a moral duty to promote

---

[43] Since the wide-scope reading requires one either to abandon an end or to take the most effective means to it, it does not imply that the person ought simply to kill his cousin. On the contrary, when combined with a moral "ought" forbidding killing, it requires him to abandon his desire above all to become rich.

other people's pleasure, we have no duty of any kind to promote our own: "we do not think it a *duty* to aim at—i.e. to act from the desire of—our happiness; nor do we even in fact think that it is a duty to do . . . those acts which we think will lead to our happiness."[44] If the basic normative considerations are all duties, this view implies that in the example above the person is not permitted to produce the 9 units of pleasure for herself; she must produce the 10 units for others. The view therefore underwrites a quick reply to the objection, but it does so at a heavy price. As Ewing and Michael Stocker have pointed out, it implies that the person ought also to prefer 9 units of pleasure for others to 10 for herself, and even 9 units for others to 1,000 for herself. In the latter case, she has some duty to produce the 9 but no duty to produce the 1,000, so she must prefer the lesser pleasure of others to a vastly greater pleasure of her own. And that is absurd.[45]

But Prichard need not have taken this line. Instead, he could have agreed that a person is permitted to prefer 9 units of her own pleasure to 10 units for others, but he could have generated that permission within morality itself, as a moral permission. More specifically, he could have supplemented the underivative moral duties in his and Ross's substantive view with an equally underivative moral permission to pursue one's own pleasure, a permission that, like the duties, is only prima facie and must be weighed against other considerations to determine what one is, all things considered, permitted or required to do. Prichard, Ross, and their contemporaries did not think much about underivative permissions; they tended to assume that the basic moral elements are all duties. But it is entirely consistent with their general approach to recognize such permissions, and if Prichard did, he could say that when a person has a choice between her own lesser pleasure and the vastly greater pleasure of others (say, 9 for herself and 1,000 for others), her other-regarding duty outweighs her self-regarding permission and she ought, all things considered, to produce the greater pleasure. But when the gap between the pleasures is smaller, as in the 9 versus 10 case, her permission outweighs her duty and she may prefer her lesser pleasure. The objection's claim about the 9 versus 10 case is therefore correct, but it does not show that a moral duty can be outweighed by something nonmoral; it only shows that it can be outweighed by a moral permission.

This alternative response to the objection has several merits. It explains why, while a person may prefer her own 9 units of pleasure to 10 units for

[44] Prichard, *Moral Writings*, 135; see also 10 n. 4, 171, 204. For Ross's version of this claim, see Ross, *The Right and the Good*, 21, 24–26, 151; and Ross, *Foundations of Ethics*, 72–75, 129–30, 272–74.

[45] A. C. Ewing, "A Suggested Non-Naturalistic Analysis of Good," *Mind* 48 (1939): 20; Michael Stocker, "Agent and Other: Against Ethical Universalism," *Australasian Journal of Philosophy* 54 (1976): 208. Ewing's and Stocker's objections are directed at Ross's version of the claim.

others, she may also prefer the others' 10 units. What she has concerning her own pleasure is only a permission, and if she declines to exercise that permission she does nothing wrong.[46] The response also yields a version of Prichard's and Ross's view that we have no duty to pursue our own pleasure; if we do not do so, we are again merely not exercising a permission. Finally, the response retains the central virtue of Prichard's minimalism. The issue raised by the 9 versus 10 case is how normative considerations concerning one's own pleasure weigh against considerations concerning the pleasure of others. But if the two sets of considerations are to conflict, their claims about "ought" and "may" must operate in the same field, and if they do, the issue between them is substantive rather than conceptual. Calling both sets of considerations "moral" recognizes this fact, while labeling one "prudential" and the other "moral" suggests falsely that the issue turns somehow on conceptual questions. Making the permission to prefer one's own lesser pleasure a moral permission rightly treats a substantive question as substantive, and similar treatments of aesthetic and other supposed nonmoral "oughts" will do the same.[47] At the same time, adopting the response would only slightly modify Prichard's epistemological argument. That argument supplements his conceptual claim that the only "oughts" are moral with the substantive claim that certain specific "oughts," such as those in his deontological view, are better grounded than any contrary principle a skeptic may appeal to. And that claim still stands if, alongside the moral "oughts," there are some moral permissions.

The history of twentieth-century British philosophy has usually been told in a Cambridge-centered way: there was a late nineteenth-century Idealist movement centered in Oxford that was exploded around the start of the new century by the Cambridge realism of Moore and Bertrand Russell. But there was a simultaneous realist movement in Oxford, initiated by John Cook Wilson and with Prichard and Ross as leading members. Prichard's writings are shot through with what Russell called a "robust sense of reality," as when Prichard said the ground of a duty to perform an action X cannot be properties X would have if it were performed, because nothing that does not exist can have properties.[48] It should be no surprise that part of his defense of moral duty mirrors a well-known realist response to skepticism about the external world, insisting that our knowledge of duty is more secure than our belief in any theory that could call that knowledge into question.

[46] The response also explains why she is permitted to prefer others' 9 units of pleasure to her own 10, that is, to prefer others' lesser pleasure to her own greater pleasure. This would not follow so readily if what she had were a duty or positive reason to promote her own pleasure, as the initial objection suggested.
[47] For a more recent argument for making the permission to pursue one's own lesser good moral, rather than seeing it as coming from outside morality, see Samuel Scheffler, *Human Morality* (New York: Oxford University Press, 1992), chap. 2.
[48] Prichard, *Moral Writings*, 99–100.

V. DISTORTING MORAL DUTY

The second, epistemological stage of Prichard's argument was directed mainly against a skeptical view that proposes a substantive criterion for a duty's having force and then says moral duties do not satisfy it. But this stage also challenged anti-skeptical views that say moral duties do satisfy some such criterion and therefore do have force; such a demonstration, it argued, is unnecessary. And Prichard had a further argument against these views: in trying to justify moral duties on some independent ground, they distort the moral phenomena. This was the third stage in his argument for underivativeness, and it echoed his critique of consequentialism.

Prichard's main target here was, again, an instrumentalist view that assumes moral duties ground genuine "oughts" only when fulfilling them will further the agent's interests, say, by maximizing his pleasure. Prichard sometimes argued that this view's key empirical claim is false: it is not true that fulfilling our moral duties always maximizes our pleasure.[49] But his more common argument was that, even if this empirical claim is true, the view gives the wrong explanation of our moral duties and thereby turns them into something they are not. The version of this argument in "Mistake" was very brief:

> The [instrumentalist] answer is, of course, not an answer, for it fails to convince us that we ought to keep our engagements; even if successful on its own lines, it only makes us *want* to keep them. And Kant was really only pointing out this fact when he distinguished hypothetical and categorical imperatives.[50]

But Prichard developed the argument more fully in later writings such as "Duty and Interest" (1929). There he argued that if what gives a moral duty normative force is the fact that fulfilling it promotes the agent's advantage, then the duty is really one to promote the agent's advantage: as in the critique of consequentialism, what explains the duty also gives its content. But this, he claimed, distorts the moral phenomena, since what we believe is that we have duties to keep promises, relieve others' pain, and so on just as such, or with promise-keeping and pain-relieving as their content. So the attempt to justify the duties instrumentally in fact destroys them.[51] More generally, Prichard argued that the instrumental justification of moral duties resolves the moral "ought" into the nonmoral one, in effect denying that there is a moral "ought" at all. It "covertly resolve[s] moral obligation into something else which is not moral obligation"; in response, the "apparent tautology 'moral obligation is moral

---

[49] Ibid., 26, 32, 180.
[50] Ibid., 9; emphasis in the original.
[51] Ibid., 26–30; see also 122–23.

obligation'" reminds us that "moral obligation ... is *sui generis*."[52] Or, what the instrumental justification is doing

> is denying by implication that there really are such things as right actions and wrong actions at all in the moral sense of these terms, and maintaining that all that exists instead is right actions and wrong actions in the purely non-moral sense of actions which are, and of actions which are not, conducive to our purpose.[53]

Given Prichard's conceptual minimalism, the distortion here is radical. If the nonmoral "ought" is not an "ought" at all, but makes only the non-normative claim that an act will promote the agent's interest, then the instrumental view does not replace one normative concept with another; it denies normativity altogether. In attempting to justify the moral "ought," it in effect denies that "oughts" exist.

Prichard's presentation of this argument assumed his radical view that a proper description of a moral duty must mention its explanatory ground, but the argument can be separated from that view. Then it says only that the instrumental view gives the wrong explanation of our moral duties. It says that we ought to keep our promises or promote others' pleasure because this will promote our own pleasure, and even if this does not destroy the duties, it is not the right explanation of them. We ought to do these things just as such.

However it is stated, Prichard's explanatory objection to instrumentalism, like his objection to consequentialism, turns on an intuition: in this case, it is the intuition that we have some moral duties, whether to keep promises or just to promote the good, that are binding on us as such and apart from any connection to our pleasure. And while an objector may deny this intuition, Prichard again seems to be on strong ground. Surely most of us think there are some things we ought to do, all things considered, even though they will not maximize our own pleasure. And the contrary instrumentalist view, if it is indeed normative, likewise appeals to an intuition, and thus has no epistemic advantage.

Alternatively, an objector may say that Prichard's argument tells only against an implausible instrumental justification of moral duty and does not generalize to all such justifications. This brings us to one of Prichard's distinguishing characteristics as a philosopher: that alongside his profundity he had a strong streak of perversity. This showed itself partly in the issues he discussed; he could worry at great length about a point that seems not to merit the attention, such as whether a not-yet-performed act can have properties. But it is especially evident in his interpretations of other philosophers, which could border on the absurd. He often assumed

---

[52] Ibid., 116.
[53] Ibid., 143; see also 43, 144–45, 150, 169, 183, 188–93, 237, 241.

that there were just two possible views on a topic, his own and some very implausible alternative, and then ascribed the alternative to anyone who rejected his view.

This occurs often in his moral philosophy, where he thought the main alternative to his non-naturalist deontology was a view combining the instrumental principle, read as non-normative, with psychological egoism, the claim that everyone desires only his own good or, more specifically, pleasure. Given these assumptions, the justification of moral duty has to be that fulfilling it will maximize the agent's pleasure. Prichard ascribed this view to some philosophers who did indeed hold it, such as Hobbes, as well as to some who at times suggested it, such as John Stuart Mill and T. H. Green. But he also ascribed it to philosophers for whom it is at least an uncharitable reading, such as Plato and Aristotle, and to some for whom it is ridiculous. He argued that Sidgwick's defense of his axiom of Rational Benevolence claims that acting on the axiom will maximize the agent's satisfaction,[54] and even interpreted Joseph Butler (Butler!) as a psychological egoist.[55] These misinterpretations can tempt one to reject Prichard's critiques of the best-known justifications of moral duty as simply missing their target, and that reaction has been common. But in my view it is a mistake, because the core of Prichard's critique still applies to these justifications when they are more charitably understood. Let me illustrate by examining his critique of ancient ethics, and especially of Aristotle.

VI. Prichard on Aristotle

Prichard's view of Aristotle may have changed over time. In "Mistake," Prichard noted "the extreme sense of dissatisfaction produced by a close reading of Aristotle's *Ethics*,"[56] and in so doing, he upset J. O. Urmson, who complained in his introduction to the 1968 edition of Prichard's *Moral Obligation* how "imperceptive" this remark was about what he thought the greatest ethics book ever written.[57] But Urmson had not bothered to read the next paragraph! For there Prichard explained that his remark was not intended to *criticize* Aristotle. Our dissatisfaction with the latter's *Ethics* arises from the fact that it does not do what we want it to, namely, explain why we ought to do what we think we morally ought to do. And Prichard's main point, as he then repeated,[58] was that this demand is illegitimate. If anything, "Mistake" praises Aristotle for correctly seeing that duty is underivative.

---

[54] Ibid., 147–49, 206–8.
[55] Ibid., 34–35.
[56] Ibid., 17.
[57] Ibid., xiii.
[58] Ibid., 17–18.

But this was not at all Prichard's later view. His notorious essay "The Meaning of *Agathon* in the *Ethics* of Aristotle"[59] ascribed to Aristotle the familiar combination of a merely instrumental "ought" and psychological egoism, and did so by arguing that when Aristotle talked of "good" (*agathon*) he always meant "conducive to the agent's pleasure." On this reading, Aristotle's argument that virtue is good was really the argument that virtuous action is pleasurable for the virtuous agent,[60] which Prichard said distorts the moral phenomena just as Hobbes's argument does. Prichard considered, as an alternative, that by *agathon* Aristotle meant (simply) "good," but perhaps assuming with Moore that "good" is necessarily agent-neutral, Prichard said this would commit Aristotle to holding that each person desires other people's virtue as much as his own, which Prichard said he did not: Aristotle thought each person cared only about his own virtue.[61] So Aristotle was another philosopher who reduced the moral to the nonmoral "ought."[62]

This was, to say the least, an uncharitable reading, and most scholars think it was decisively refuted by J. L. Austin.[63] They therefore reject Prichard's critique of Aristotle as based on a gross misinterpretation. But the criticism can be separated from the interpretation and, when it is, remains powerful.

Consider the following, more standard interpretation of Aristotle's *Ethics*. By "good" or *agathon* Aristotle meant what is "good for" a person, in the sense of contributing to his *eudaimonia*, well-being, or living a good life. This is not Moore's concept of the (simply) good, nor Prichard's non-normative concept of what will give a person pleasure. It is a normative concept but an independent one, and it grounds reasons that are only agent-relative, so that a thing's being "good for" a person gives only him ultimate reason to pursue it. Thus, when Aristotle said that virtue is "good," he meant that it is a constituent of the life that is best for a person, and his explanation of why we ought to perform the acts conventionally regarded as duties is that, if done from the right motives, they will express virtue on our part, which is an essential constituent of the good for us.

This interpretation does not involve psychological hedonism and need not be conceptually minimalist: it can ground moral duties in claims about *eudaimonia* that are normative but not moral. Even so, the view it ascribes to Aristotle is open to the Prichard-style objection that it distorts the moral phenomena. Consider a paradigmatically other-regarding

---

[59] Ibid., 102–13.

[60] Ibid., 109–13.

[61] Ibid., 109.

[62] A more moderate version of Prichard's view, arguing that Aristotle alternated between two meanings of *agathon*, is given by E. F. Carritt in "An Ambiguity of the Word 'Good'," *Proceedings of the British Academy* 23 (1937): 51–80.

[63] J. L. Austin, "*Agathon* and *Eudaimonia* in the *Ethics* of Aristotle," in J. M. E. Moravcsik, *Aristotle: A Collection of Critical Essays* (London: Macmillan, 1968), 261–96.

duty such as the duty to relieve another's pain. What, Prichard would ask, is the ultimate explanation of why we ought to fulfill this duty? Is it that doing so will make our own lives better, so that the duty is at bottom self-regarding? Or is it that doing so will make the other person's life better? On the standard reading, Aristotle's answer is that it will make our own lives better, by contributing, given the right motives, to our own *eudaimonia*. But that, the objection says, is not the right explanation. The right explanation is that relieving the other's pain will make *her* life better, so the duty is not just superficially but fundamentally other-regarding. The view standardly ascribed to Aristotle therefore gives the wrong explanation for the duty to relieve the other's pain, turning what we know intuitively is an other-regarding duty into a self-regarding one. The view is not as crudely egoistic as a hedonistic one, since it does not equate the agent's good with his pleasure. But it is egoistic at a deeper level, because it relates all his reasons for action to his own *eudaimonia*, which, whatever its content, must be a state of him. It is *his* good, not anyone else's, that is his ultimate goal, and any view that makes that true violates our intuitive sense that the ultimate point of other-regarding acts is to benefit others.

The philosophers of Prichard's period, though familiar with ancient ethics, thought its approach to moral questions was fundamentally misguided because it involved confusions about the basic normative concepts. Sidgwick identified the key issue when he said that the ancient philosophers did not distinguish between the questions "What ought I to do, all things considered?" and "What will make my life go best?"—or assumed without argument that the answer to these questions must always be the same.[64] This forced them into implausible claims: for example, that if it is, all things considered, right for me to sacrifice my life in battle, the value that courageous act will contribute to my life must be greater than the value of the hundreds of other virtuous acts I could perform if I lived, so my act involves no real sacrifice on my part.[65] But the ancient philosophers' approach also gave their theories a disturbingly egoistic cast, not only at the explanatory level Prichard emphasized but also in their more specific claims. Sidgwick said that Aristotle did not have the concept of benevolence, since the virtue on his list closest to it, liberality, is shown just as much in tasteful expenditure on a fine house for oneself as in spending on other people.[66] Others were repelled by Aristotle's account of the *megalopsychos* or "proud" man, who enjoys being more virtuous than other people—he is competitive about virtue—and will not give others small benefits, since that is beneath his dignity; only when great

[64] Sidgwick, *The Methods of Ethics*, 404–5.
[65] For this criticism, see A. C. Ewing, *Ethics* (London: English Universities Press, 1953), 28–29.
[66] Henry Sidgwick, *Outlines of the History of Ethics*, 5th ed. (London: Macmillan, 1902), 62, 122.

things are at stake will he deign to act. Rashdall noted "Aristotle's revolting picture of the high-souled man (*megalopsychos*)," adding "[o]f course I am aware of the explanations by which all superior people are accustomed to defend the Aristotelian ideal." [67] And Ross generalized the criticism when he said that Aristotle's description of the *megalopsychos* "betrays somewhat nakedly the self-absorption which is the bad side of Aristotle's ethics." [68]

There are, in fact, many points where Aristotle's ideal agent seems unattractively self-concerned. Aristotle held that a virtuous agent takes pleasure in his virtuous acts; he may also have thought that virtuous acts have their full value only when their goal is successfully achieved, as when an attempt to relieve another's pain does relieve it. So his virtuous agent may take pleasure in objects that include, as an effect of his act, some benefit or good for another. [69] But surely a virtuous person will be equally or almost equally pleased when another's pain is relieved independently of his own action, as when someone else like a doctor relieves the pain or it goes away by itself. Yet nowhere in his main discussion of virtue in Books II through IV of the *Nicomachean Ethics* did Aristotle say this; he did not suggest that a virtuous person takes pleasure in states of others that are unconnected to his own acts. [70] And it is hard to see how he could say this, when only a person's own acts and their effects are appropriately connected to his *eudaimonia* and can therefore from his point of view be good.

Or consider Aristotle's claim that a virtuous person will sacrifice for a friend and even let the friend perform noble acts rather than do so himself. These acts sound altruistic, but look at Aristotle's justification for them. When a virtuous person gives his friend wealth, he himself "achieves nobility" and therefore assigns "the greater good to himself." He may let his friend rescue a person from drowning, but the reason is that "it may be nobler to become the cause of his friend's acting than to act himself," so he still assigns "to himself the greater share in what

---

[67] Rashdall, *The Theory of Good and Evil*, vol. 1, 205; see also Carritt's remark about "the egoistic self-righteousness of Aristotle's *philautos*," in Carritt, "An Ambiguity of the Word 'Good'," 69. For a more recent criticism of Aristotle of this kind, see Bernard Williams, *Ethics and the Limits of Philosophy* (London: Fontana, 1985), 35.

[68] W. D. Ross, *Aristotle* (London: Methuen, 1923), 208.

[69] For this reading, see Jennifer Whiting, "Eudaimonia, External Result, and Choosing Virtuous Actions for Themselves," *Philosophy and Phenomenological Research* 45 (2002): 270–90.

[70] There are suggestions to this effect in Books VIII and IX of the *Nicomachean Ethics* about friendship; see Aristotle, *Nicomachean Ethics*, trans. W. D. Ross (Oxford: Oxford University Press, 1980), 1155b31–1156a5 and 1166b30–1167a20 about "goodwill." But, first, these suggestions come outside Aristotle's main discussion of virtue in Books II through IV and are not tied to his central theses about virtue, such as the doctrine of the mean. Second, he thinks that when it is not felt toward a friend, goodwill is too superficial to issue in any action (1167a1–2, a7–9), yet when it is felt toward a friend, it is felt toward "another self" (1166a31), one whose activities are an extension of one's own. Aristotle just does not have the idea that a virtuous person will have strong desires for states of other people just as states of them (and apart from any special relations they stand in to him).

is noble." However much his acts benefit others, the reason why he ought to perform them, and even his motive for doing so, is that they will increase his own *eudaimonia*. It follows that if two friends understand their situation, they will engage in an unseemly competition to act more virtuously. After all, if it is nobler for A to let B save the drowning person, it is also nobler for B to let A do the saving. So we can imagine an Alphonse-and-Gaston routine in which each tries to let the other do the saving—"You do it," "No, you do it," "No, you do it"—so *he* can have "the greater share in what is noble."[71] Egoism like this again seems inevitable in a view that grounds all normative demands in an agent's own *eudaimonia*; and that that is the wrong grounding was most emphasized by Prichard.

Again, however, some may argue that Prichard's objection applies only to *eudaimonist* theories and not to others that try to justify moral duties on some deeper ground. But in fact the objection is more widely applicable. Though I cannot argue the point here, many of the most influential recent attempts to justify moral duties—R. M. Hare's universalization argument for utilitarianism, John Rawls's veil-of-ignorance argument for his principles of justice, and Christine Korsgaard's appeal to "practical identities"—start with a picture of the moral agent as essentially self-concerned. The agent cares about the fulfillment of *his* preferences because they are his, or is concerned that social institutions allow him to promote *his* conception of the good whether or not it is true, or cares about acting from *his* practical identity. And no justification of moral duty with that kind of starting-point can do other than distort the moral phenomena. The objection must in each case be tailored to the details of the proposed justification, but its core goes back to Prichard.

VII. CONCLUSION

Many philosophers in the history of ethics and today have wanted to justify moral duties by deriving them from something other than moral duty, either from non-normative facts or from a normative consideration that is not itself moral. A sequence of British philosophers of the late nineteenth and early twentieth centuries rejected this program, holding both that normative truths in general are underivative from non-normative ones, and that more narrowly moral duties are also underivative. This is an important position in the history of the subject and a challenge to some influential projects in philosophical ethics today. But the philosopher who

[71] Aristotle, *Nicomachean Ethics*, 1169a18–1169b2. Alternatively, if A says that letting B save the drowning person is nobler than doing the saving himself, B can say that his letting A let B save the person is even nobler; A that his letting B let A let B save is nobler still; and so on to infinity. Again, each friend's concern with his own nobility leads to a priggish competition to be more virtuous.

defended the position most fully was Prichard, with his three-stage argument, and he was in particular most explicit in arguing that the attempt to justify moral duties on some other ground not only fails to yield the desired results but distorts the moral phenomena. That makes him, on this issue, a central figure in the history of the subject.

Philosophy, University of Toronto

"BUT IT WOULD BE WRONG"*

By Stephen Darwall

I. Introduction

At a critical juncture in the Senate Watergate hearings in 1973, H. R. Haldeman testified about a taped conversation he had heard between President Richard Nixon and the White House lawyer, John Dean. Nixon and Dean were discussing the possibility of raising hush money to meet the demands of one of the Watergate burglars, E. Howard Hunt, so that Hunt wouldn't spill the beans about the break-in at the Democratic National Committee headquarters. The president asked how much money would be required, and Dean answered, "Probably a million dollars—but the problem is that it is hard to raise." Nixon replied, "There is no problem in raising a million dollars, we can do that." Then, according to Haldeman, Nixon added the following, soon to be famous, phrase: "But it would be wrong."[1] We now know that Nixon did not actually say this, but it seems clear what Haldeman's intention was in saying he did.[2] Haldeman wished to portray Nixon as implying that if paying off Hunt would be wrong, then there was good reason, decisive reason in fact, not to pursue that course of action, and that it should therefore not be considered further.

Here arises a recently discussed philosophical problem.[3] Does the fact that an act would be wrong provide any reason *itself*, let alone a decisive

---

* For helpful comments, I am very much indebted to the other contributors to this volume, and to audiences at Brown University, the Western Canadian Philosophical Association meetings at the University of Alberta, the Scots Philosophical Club meetings at the University of Stirling, the University of Maryland, the University of Leiden, Washington University, the University of Oslo, Bielefeld University, the Moral Philosophy Working Group at Yale University, and the Middle Atlantic Reading Group in Ethics. I am also indebted to Ellen Frankel Paul for editorial advice.

[1] "Counterattack and Counterpoint," *Time* (August 13, 1973).

[2] Here is what the transcript of the March 21, 1973, tape says: "PRESIDENT: How much money do you need? DEAN: I would say these people are going to cost, uh, a million dollars over the next, uh,—two years. (Pause) PRESIDENT: We could get that. DEAN: Uh, huh. PRESIDENT: You, on the money, if you need the money, I mean, uh, you could get the money. Let's say— DEAN: Well, I think that we're going— PRESIDENT: What I mean is, you could, you could get a million dollars. And you could get it in cash. I, I know where it could be gotten. DEAN: Uh, huh." (Watergate Trial Conversations, Nixon Presidential Library and Museum, http://nixon.archives.gov/forresearchers/find/tapes/watergate/trial/transcripts.php.)

[3] See T. M. Scanlon, *What We Owe to Each Other* (Cambridge, MA: Harvard University Press, 1998), 11; Jonathan Dancy, "Should We Pass the Buck?" in *Philosophy, the Good, the True, and the Beautiful*, ed. Anthony O'Hear, supp. vol. 47 (Cambridge: Cambridge University Press, 2000): 159–73; Philip Stratton-Lake, "Scanlon's Contractualism and the Redundancy Objection," *Analysis* 63, no. 1 (2003): 70–76; Michael J. Zimmerman, "The Good and the Right," *Utilitas* 19, no. 3 (2007): 326–53; and T. M. Scanlon, "Wrongness and Reasons: A

reason, not to perform it? The question is not whether there is adequate reason to avoid wrongdoing. Recent discussion has tended to take it for granted that there is. The question, rather, is whether the fact that an action would be wrong is itself a reason of any kind, whether especially strong or conclusive or of any strength whatsoever. Various considerations have led some philosophers to think that it is not.[4] Briefly, these considerations include the following.

An action is wrong only if there are reasons that make it wrong—*wrong-making features* of performing the action or *"grounds"* of its wrongness.[5] It seems, then, that it should be these features of the action, the features that make it wrong, that are the reasons not to perform the wrongful act, not the fact that the action would be wrong itself. Such a further reason would seem superfluous, and might indeed be thought to involve a kind of double counting.

Moreover, it is sometimes pointed out that a morally good person is moved directly by wrong-making features of the wrongful act, rather than by the fact that the act would be wrong; the former and not the latter are *the good person's reasons* for acting as she does.[6] Someone who is moved primarily by overall moral verdicts, such as an action's being wrong, rather than by the grounds of the verdict, has been said to have a kind of "moral fetish," rather than being truly morally good.[7] Thus, even Haldeman's fantasy endowed Nixon with something less than moral goodness. It was as if the fact, say, that paying Hunt off would subvert justice left Nixon entirely unmoved until he realized that that made the act morally wrong.

Of course, from the fact that a morally good person is typically moved to act by the morally relevant features of an action, rather than by the moral status these features bestow upon an action, it hardly follows that

Re-examination," *Oxford Studies in Metaethics,* vol. 2 (Oxford: Oxford University Press, 2007), 5–20.

[4] These include Dancy, Stratton-Lake, and Zimmerman (see previous note).

[5] The latter term derives from Dancy, "Should We Pass the Buck?" When I speak of "good-making" or "right-" or "wrong-making" properties in what follows, I will have this sense in mind, namely, *grounds* or *normative reasons* for something's value, rightness, or wrongness. We might call this a *normative* sense, as opposed to a *metaphysical* sense of good-making or right- or wrong-making features (i.e., the features in which something's being good, right, or wrong consists metaphysically). I shall be arguing that an act's wrong-making features in the normative sense (i.e., the grounds of or normative reasons for something's being wrong) do not exhaust the reasons not to perform the wrongful act—that the fact that the act is wrong is itself a reason not to perform it. I should not be understood as claiming that if there is some complex fact or facts in which this latter fact consists metaphysically, the fact that an act is wrong is a reason that is additional to *these* facts, since, on the hypothesis in question, that is what the fact of an act's being wrong would itself consist in. I have been helped here by discussion with, among others, Janice Dowell and Peter Schulte.

[6] Cf. Michael Smith on the *de dicto* desire to avoid wrongdoing as opposed to *de re* desires to avoid actions of wrong-making kinds: Michael Smith, *The Moral Problem* (Oxford: Blackwell, 1994), 75–76.

[7] Ibid.

moral wrongness is not itself a reason for acting. Even if it is not a reason for a morally good person, it might still be a reason for those who are no better than morally mediocre. Or it might be a reason even for the morally good, though not a reason they typically act on.

Yet a further line of thought in favor of holding that moral wrongness is not itself a reason comes by analogy with T. M. Scanlon's "buck-passing" theory of value.[8] According to Scanlon, being good or having value is not itself a reason to have any attitude or take any action with respect to the valuable thing. Rather, value "passes the buck" to the good-making or value-making features of the valuable thing, and it is these features that provide reasons for the relevant (valuing) attitudes and actions toward it.[9] That the thing is valuable or good does not provide a further reason for the relevant attitudes or actions. If a buck-passing account is plausible for evaluative (good-making) properties, however, then why would it not be plausible for deontic (right- or wrong-making) properties also? Why not think that, as with goodness or value, moral wrongness passes the buck to wrong-making features, and it is (only) those features that provide reasons for the relevant attitudes and actions, including not performing the wrongful act?[10]

This has not, however, been Scanlon's view of wrongness. He has taken the position that being wrong is indeed a reason not to do what is wrong.[11] In what follows, I shall argue that Scanlon is right; taking a buck-passing approach to normative concepts in general, and to the concepts of moral obligation, right, and wrong, in particular, does not entail that an act's wrongness is not a reason not to perform it. To the contrary, I shall argue, the most plausible buck-passing theory of the concepts of moral obligation and wrong entails that an act's being wrong is a reason not to perform the act that is additional to the act's wrong-making features (in the normative sense of features that *ground* or are normative reasons for its wrongness).[12] I will argue this in three stages. First, in Section II, I will argue that although a buck-passing theory of a normative concept (or similarly, a "warranted-attitude" or "fitting-attitude" theory of the concept) entails that the fact that something instantiates the concept (say, is good, right, or wrong) is not a further reason for the specific attitudes that are conceptually tied to the normative concept, the theory may not entail that that fact is not a reason for some relevant choice, intention, or *action*, since the conceptually implicated attitude may not entail any relevant

---

[8] I take this to be a more pointed version of the first line of thought mentioned above.

[9] Scanlon, *What We Owe to Each Other*, 95–100.

[10] That is, why not think that moral wrongness passes the buck to features that are wrong-making in the sense of providing normative grounds of an act's wrongness? This differs from any features that might be wrong-making in the sense of being what an action's being wrong consists in metaphysically.

[11] See, e.g., ibid., 11; and T. M. Scanlon, "Wrongness and Reasons: A Re-examination," *Oxford Studies in Metaethics*, vol. 2 (Oxford: Oxford University Press, 2007), 5–20.

[12] See note 5 above.

action attitude (like intention or choice). Second, in Section III, I will present a buck-passing theory of the concepts of moral obligation, right, and wrong, according to which the fact that something instantiates one of these concepts is normative, at least in the first instance, not for intention or action, but for attitudes through which we hold people responsible for their actions and blame them (what P. F. Strawson called "reactive attitudes").[13] Third, in Section IV, I will argue that this theory entails that the fact that an act is wrong is indeed a further reason not to perform the action, and that the theory tells us what this further reason consists in. It consists in the fact that refraining from the act is something we legitimately *demand* of ourselves and of one another. Finally, in Section V, I will discuss some light the theory sheds on whether there is (always) overriding or conclusive reason to act as we are morally obligated to act (all things considered) and not do moral wrong.

II. Normative Concepts, Attitudes, and Action

Although it is possible to hold a buck-passing theory of value on other grounds, one natural line of thought that leads to it is a *warranted-attitude theory of normative concepts* in general.[14] It is plausible to suppose that what normative concepts all have in common is—as Allan Gibbard says, using a phrase of Wilfrid Sellars's—that they are "fraught with ought."[15] The basic idea derives from A. C. Ewing and ultimately from Henry Sidgwick.[16] Sidgwick said that all "ethical judgments" include "the fundamental notion represented by the word 'ought'."[17] "Ought" here has a "flavorless" sense, to use Gibbard's term, of thin justification or warrant— distinct, for example, from more thickly qualified senses like "morally ought" or "prudentially ought."[18] According to warranted-attitude theories, every normative concept is tied conceptually to some specific atti-

---

[13] P. F. Strawson, "Freedom and Resentment," in Strawson, *Studies in the Philosophy of Thought and Action* (London: Oxford University Press, 1968). I defend this analysis in greater detail in *The Second-Person Standpoint: Morality, Respect, and Accountability* (Cambridge, MA: Harvard University Press, 2006).

[14] In my view, the warranted-attitude theory (or, more specifically, the fitting-attitude theory, which I shall discuss presently) is the most plausible approach to analyzing normative concepts. It is not necessary to the argument of this essay, however, that it actually succeeds. We shall simply assume that it does succeed as the most plausible line of thought leading to the view that wrongness is not itself a reason for acting. My point will be that accepting a fitting-attitude theory of wrongness would not commit us to this. To the contrary, on the fitting-attitude theory of wrongness that I shall propose, wrongness is indeed itself a practical reason.

[15] Allan Gibbard, "Knowing What to Do, Seeing What to Do," in *Ethical Intuitionism: Re-evaluations*, ed. Philip Stratton-Lake (Oxford: Oxford University Press, 2003), 212.

[16] A. C. Ewing, "Suggested Non-Naturalistic Analysis of Good," *Mind* 48 (1939): 1–22; Henry Sidgwick, *The Methods of Ethics*, 7th ed. (London: Macmillan, 1967).

[17] Sidgwick, *The Methods of Ethics*, 25.

[18] Allan Gibbard, *Wise Choices, Apt Feelings* (Cambridge, MA: Harvard University Press, 1990), 7. See also Owen McLeod, "Just Plain 'Ought'," *The Journal of Ethics* 5 (2001): 269–91.

tude or set of attitudes; each is the concept of being a warranted object of its distinctive attitude or attitudes.

For example, the concept of the *desirable* is that of being a justified object of desire, of being such as there is normative reason to desire. The concept of the *estimable* is that of what is warrantedly esteemed. The concept of *dignity* is that of what warrants respect. And so on. Every normative concept can be represented in terms of its distinctive attitude or attitudes and the fundamental normative notion of warrant, justification, ought, or (normative) reason.

There is, however, a crucial qualification. As recent discussion of the "wrong kind of reasons" problem makes clear, not just any reason for having some attitude is a reason of the "right kind" to justify or warrant an attitude in the terms that are distinctively relevant to the normative concept that is conceptually tied to it.[19] For example, instrumental or strategic reasons for having some attitude—say, a desire or an intention to drink a toxin if one will be rewarded for having either attitude, as in Gregory Kavka's famous "toxin puzzle"—are reasons of the wrong kind to establish that drinking the toxin would itself be either desirable or choiceworthy.[20] Reasons of the right kind are "fittingness" reasons; they show that the attitude "fits" or is a fitting response to the object.[21]

On what we might better call *fitting-attitude theories* of normative concepts, therefore, every normative concept can be analyzed in terms of "fittingness" (that is, support by warrant or reasons of the right kind) and the attitude or set of attitudes that is distinctive of the concept. Thus, the concept of the *desirable* is that of being a fitting object of desire; the *estimable*, that of being a fitting object of esteem; *dignity*, that of being a fitting object of respect; and so on for every normative concept.

Now for fitting-attitude theories to be plausible, there must be some way of distinguishing reasons of the right kind from those of the wrong kind that does not itself depend upon the relevant normative concept. If the only way of distinguishing the right kind from the wrong kind of reasons to desire, say, is that the former bear on an object's desirability, then any attempt to analyze the concept of desirability in terms of the right kind of reasons to desire will be circular.

In my view, various promising suggestions have been made. Wlodek Rabinowicz and Toni Ronnøw–Rasmussen have proposed that reasons of

[19] Justin D'Arms and Daniel Jacobson, "The Moralistic Fallacy: On the 'Appropriateness' of Emotions," *Philosophy and Phenomenological Research* 61 (2000): 65–90; Justin D'Arms and Daniel Jacobson, "Sentiment and Value," *Ethics* 110 (2000): 722–48; Wlodek Rabinowicz and Toni Ronnøw-Rasmussen, "The Strike of the Demon: On Fitting Pro-Attitudes and Value," *Ethics* 114 (2004): 391–423.
[20] The "toxin puzzle" refers to a situation Kavka described in which there is an instrumental reason to form an intention to drink a toxin (e.g., that one would be rewarded if one did), but in which this apparently gives one no reason to act on the intention. See Gregory S. Kavka, "The Toxin Puzzle," *Analysis* 43 (1983): 33–36.
[21] D'Arms and Jacobson, "Sentiment and Value."

the right kind appear also in the object or content of the attitude they purport to support. In other words, what the reason is strictly for is not just some specific attitude, but a specific-attitude-toward-something-on-account-of-the-reason.[22] Pamela Hieronymi has argued that every attitude has its distinctive deliberative question and that reasons of the right kind are those that bear on that question.[23] And I have proposed that the right kind of reasons for an attitude are those that are capable of being *the subject's reason* for the attitude, that is, those *on account of which* someone can directly form the attitude.[24] Thus, it is not psychically possible for *an agent's own reason* for intending or desiring intrinsically to drink a toxin to be that she will win a reward if she intends or forms an intrinsic desire to drink it. She can desire to have an intrinsic desire to drink the toxin for this reason, but she cannot desire intrinsically to drink the toxin for this reason. Likewise, if she were offered a reward were she to believe that the U.S. war in Iraq was an unqualified success in every respect, she could *desire*, for that reason, to believe that proposition, but that reason could not be her reason for having the belief itself. It would be psychically impossible to form the belief *for that reason*. One cannot reason: "I will get a reward if I believe *p;* therefore, *p,*" as one would have to do if one were to believe *p* for the reason that one will get a reward.

Perhaps none of these proposals is fully satisfactory, but we need not worry about that. Since the most powerful line of thought leading to buck-passing is a fitting-attitude approach to normative concepts of some kind, we can simply assume that a solution to the "wrong kind of reasons" problem can be found. What we want to know is whether *if* a fitting attitude account of wrongness were true, this would show that wrongness is not itself a reason for acting—that is, whether it would support being a buck-passer about wrongness with respect to reasons for acting.

This brings us to Scanlon's buck-passing theory of value. As I said, the "letter" of the buck-passing theory—that being good or valuable is not itself a reason to hold any relevant attitude toward the valuable thing or to promote it—does not require a warranted- or fitting-attitude theory of normative concepts. Some things Scanlon says, however, suggest such a theory. For example, he says that "to claim that something is valu*able* (or that it is 'of value') is to claim that [one and] others have reason to value it."[25] This suggests a warranted- or fitting-attitude account of the valuable (in terms of warrant for some valuing attitude or other). So under-

---

[22] For example, it might be a reason not just for a desire to eat an apple, but for a desire to eat an apple on account of its taste. (Rabinowicz and Rønnøw-Rasmussen, "The Strike of the Demon," 414.) This is related to a suggestion of W. D. Falk's in "Fact, Value, and Nonnatural Predication," in W. D. Falk, *Ought, Reasons, and Morality* (Ithaca, NY: Cornell University Press, 1986), 117.

[23] Pamela Hieronymi, "The Wrong Kind of Reason," *The Journal of Philosophy* 102, no. 9 (2005): 437–57.

[24] Darwall, *The Second-Person Standpoint*, 66.

[25] Scanlon, *What We Owe to Each Other*, 95.

stood, value would be a generic evaluative concept, related conceptually to a set of valuing attitudes. Being desirable, estimable, having dignity, and so on, would then be distinct species of value.[26]

A buck-passing theory about value, at least with respect to the relevant valuing attitudes—that being valuable or good is not itself a reason to have the (valuing) attitude toward that thing—would then follow straight-away. If being valuable *just is* there being reason to have one or another valuing attitude toward something, and if how valuable that thing is depends on the weight and character of the reasons for valuing it, then the fact that something is valuable cannot be a further reason to value it. By creating a further reason, the exact value of something (say, A) would thereby make the thing more valuable ($A + B$, where B is the increased value owing to the additional reason created by the thing's having value A).[27] But that would seem to be absurd.[28]

Clearly, the reason why a fitting-attitude theory of value apparently entails buck-passing about value is that the attitudes that are implicated in the concept of value, and the attitudes with respect to which the question arises whether value does or does not provide a reason, *are the very same attitudes.* If the concept of the desirable is the concept of what there is reason (of the right kind) to desire, then the fact that something is desirable cannot provide a (further) reason to desire it. According to a fitting-attitude theory, something is exactly as desirable as the (right kind of) reasons for desiring make it. Its being desirable does not make it more desirable yet.

Does that mean, however, that being valuable cannot itself provide a reason for *action?* Presently, I will argue that there are kinds of value that do indeed provide reasons for action, namely, where the relevant valuing attitude does not itself conceptually implicate choice, action, or some other agential disposition. With respect to the desirable, however, there does seem to be a fairly tight conceptual connection. Some disposition to bring the desired state about seems to be part of the very concept of desire. But if that is so, then a buck-passing theory of the desirable would arguably entail not just buck-passing about reasons for desire, but also about reasons to bring about desire's object.

---

[26] For a defense of such a view, see Elizabeth Anderson, *Value in Ethics and Economics* (Cambridge, MA: Harvard University Press, 1990).

[27] See Zimmerman, "The Good and the Right," for a parallel argument against holding that wrongness creates an additional reason.

[28] For our purposes, we do not strictly need to suppose that a fitting-attitude theory actually does entail buck-passing about value. The argument of this essay is that even if it were to support buck-passing about the relevant valuing attitudes in this way, a fitting-attitude account of wrongness of the sort I will propose would not entail buck-passing about wrongness with respect to reasons for action. Here again, then, we can just assume that a fitting-attitude theory of value of the sort Scanlon gestures to entails buck-passing about value with respect to the relevant valuing attitudes. I am indebted here to discussion with Ruth Chang.

Whether a fitting-attitude theory of moral wrongness will entail buck-passing about reasons not to perform wrongful acts, therefore, will depend on precisely which attitude or attitudes are conceptually implicated in the concept of moral wrong. We must therefore ask: If the concept of moral wrong is a normative concept, what attitude or attitudes is it normative for?

The proposal whose implications we shall consider is one I have defended at greater length elsewhere, namely, that the concepts of moral obligation and moral wrong are irreducibly second-personal concepts, since they conceptually implicate attitudes through which we implicitly address agents and hold them accountable.[29] What is new in the present essay are the implications I draw from this analysis of moral obligation for the question of whether an action's wrongness is in itself a reason not to perform the action. The proposal I discuss is a version of John Stuart Mill's idea, taken up more recently by P. F. Strawson, Richard Brandt, Allan Gibbard, and others, that the concept of moral wrong is the concept of what would be *blameworthy*—that is, a warranted object of Strawsonian reactive attitudes including blame—if an agent were to perform the act without some adequate excuse.[30] I follow what I take to be the thrust of Strawson's point by analyzing reactive attitudes as invariably involving *demands* that are implicitly *addressed* to their attitudes' objects second-personally, if only in imagination. Mill said that "we do not call anything wrong, unless we mean to imply that a person ought to be punished in some way or other for doing it; if not by law, by the opinion of his fellow creatures; if not by opinion, by the reproaches of his own conscience."[31] As I interpret Mill through Strawsonian lenses, "punishment" in this passage should be taken in the broad sense of holding someone responsible with a reactive attitude like indignation, blame, or guilt.[32] *Holding* someone accountable, in this way, is implicitly a second-personal relation, since it involves the (imagined, at least) address of a demand to its object. The connection between the concepts of moral obligation and wrong (on

[29] See Darwall, *The Second-Person Standpoint*, 91–118. There I define a set of second-personal concepts, which conceptually involve the idea of claims and demands that can be *addressed* (to an addressee, second-personally), and I argue that these include the concepts of moral obligation, wrong, rights, the dignity of persons, and the very concept of a moral person (as a subject of obligations).

[30] Strawson, "Freedom and Resentment." Strawson uses the term "reactive attitude" to refer to a set of attitudes (which include indignation, resentment, guilt, and moral blame) that implicitly hold their objects responsible and thus regard them in a distinctively interpersonal (as I put it, "second-personal") way. For ease of expression, I will sometimes speak of actions, and not agents, as blameworthy; strictly speaking, however, it is the agent who is appropriately blamed for performing a "blameworthy action" (speaking loosely).

[31] John Stuart Mill, *Utilitarianism*, chap. V, sec. 14.

[32] I use "blame" throughout this essay to refer to an attitude rather than to any specific activity or speech act. It is thus possible to blame someone without ever saying anything to him or to anyone. Blame in this sense also differs from a belief or judgment that someone is blameworthy. One might say, for example: "I know that she still blames me for what I did twenty-five years ago, though we haven't talked in many years."

the one hand) and the reactive attitude of blame (on the other) is then this: What is morally wrong is what is blameworthy—that is, what is warrantedly blamed, if the action is done without adequate excuse.

If this is so, then the attitudes for which the concepts of moral obligation and moral wrong are conceptually normative are attitudes other than intention, choice, or any agential disposition like desire. The object of a reactive attitude is, in the first instance anyway, a person, and not some action or outcome as this might appear from an agent's deliberative standpoint. Consequently, if the concepts of moral obligation and moral wrong are normative for reactive attitudes, then the reasons for being a buck-passer about evaluative concepts like the desirable will not simply transfer directly to being a buck-passer about moral wrong with respect to reasons *for action*, specifically, for avoiding moral wrong. To be sure, if what is wrong is what is warrantedly blamed if done without adequate excuse, then, on the assumption that someone lacks such an excuse, the fact that he acted wrongly cannot provide a reason for holding him responsible through reactive attitudes and blaming him that is additional to those reasons provided by the act's wrong-making features.[33] On the proposal we shall consider, the latter reasons (the wrong-making features) consist in whatever reasons (of the right kind) there are for the reactive attitudes through which one holds someone responsible for performing an act of that kind. By analogy with our earlier point about the desirable, something does not become more blameworthy than its wrong-making features make it by virtue of being morally wrong; its being wrong just *is* its being blameworthy (if done without excuse) to whatever degree its wrong-making features make it. Anyone who accepts the fitting-attitude account of moral obligation and wrongness I will propose should therefore be a buck-passer with respect to reasons for blaming and holding morally responsible. But that would not entail being a buck-passer with respect to reasons for *action*, specifically, for avoiding moral wrong. The fact that an action is wrong might still itself be, and I shall argue actually is, a reason, indeed a decisive reason, not to perform the act or to intend or choose to do so.

Before I sketch this proposal in more detail, I would like to note briefly some other normative concepts where buck-passing about the relevant reasons for action is not very plausible. The explanation for this is that the attitudes that are conceptually implicated in the normative concept are attitudes other than intention and choice. (I will be arguing that this is also the case with moral wrong.)

Consider, for example, the concepts of the estimable and its contrary, the contemptible. To be estimable is to be worthy of esteem, and if some-

---

[33] That is, it cannot provide such a reason on the assumption we have been making, namely, that a fitting-attitude theory of a normative concept entails buck-passing with respect to reasons for the attitudes that the concept conceptually involves.

thing is estimable, that will be on account of its estimable-making features.[34] These features are all, and only, whatever reasons of the right kind there are for esteeming it. For now-familiar reasons, something's being estimable cannot be a further reason for esteeming it. And the same is true, mutatis mutandis, for the contemptible. The features that make something contemptible are all, and only, reasons of the right kind that exist for having contempt for it. But the rationale for being a buck-passer about reasons for esteeming (or having contempt) does not directly transfer to being a buck-passer about reasons for *acting* in some way or other with respect to the estimable or the contemptible. Even if esteeming some trait generally gives rise, say, to some desire to acquire the trait, the desire does not seem to be *conceptually* implicated in the former. We might imagine beings who admire some trait while lacking any desire whatsoever to act in any particular way with respect to it. Whatever relation exists between esteem and the desire to acquire or emulate seems different from the conceptual connection between a desire for some outcome and a disposition to bring that outcome about.

Thus, whatever rationale may exist for being a buck-passer about reasons for esteem and contempt, it could still be the case, and arguably is the case, that the fact that something is estimable is itself a reason to *act* in various ways regarding it—say, to promote the estimable trait or to realize it in one's own life. Thus, when Aristotle advances the view that virtuous activity (chosen for its own sake as noble or estimable) is the final good for us human beings and is therefore what we have most reason to seek, he is not simply mouthing an empty truth, such as that what we have reason to seek is what we have reason to seek (or an "almost empty" truth, such as that what we have reason to desire is what we have reason to bring about). He is making a substantive normative claim.

Or consider the concept of welfare or well-being. Most philosophers believe that this too is a normative concept. But if it is, the question arises, for what attitude or attitudes is it normative? It seems clear that, unlike the concept of the choiceworthy, the concept of well-being is not simply that of what a person herself has reason to choose, intend, or do, since whether or not we do, in fact, have reason to do anything other than promote our own welfare, it seems clear that no incoherence or conceptual confusion is involved in thinking we do (for example, in thinking that *others'* well-being, or moral considerations, or a whole host of other considerations give us reasons to act that are additional to those that concern our own well-being). But if that is so, then the concept of welfare cannot possibly be identical with the concept of what the person herself

---

[34] Again, such features are "estimable-making" in the sense of being normative *grounds* of something's being estimable, not in the sense of being facts in which the thing's being estimable consists metaphysically.

has reason to do. Nor can welfare simply be the concept of the desirable, for similar reasons. We often think that things that have nothing to do with us or our own well-being are desirable—such as the survival of the planet long after we ourselves are dead, the flourishing of our children in the future, or whatever. And whether or not any of these thoughts are true, there is no doubt that they are coherent.

I have argued elsewhere that the most plausible account of well-being as a normative concept holds that it is what is desirable for someone *for that person's sake;* that is, well-being is what there is reason to desire for someone out of care or sympathetic concern *for her.*[35] A *rational care theory of welfare* understands the normativity of welfare to be for desires for someone (or for some being) for her (or its) sake, that is, from the perspective of care or concern for her (or it). In other words, this concept of welfare is the one we need and make use of when, in caring for someone, we face the normative question of what to want (what we should want) for her. In yet other words, a person's welfare is what there is reason to desire for someone, conditional on there being reason to care for her.

If some account in this general direction is correct, then the warranted attitude that is conceptually involved in welfare or well-being is actually quite complex and does not itself conceptually involve intention or choice. Granted, if one cares for someone and is thereby disposed to have desires (and thereby to act) for her sake, then any reasons why something would be good for her—welfare-making features—will automatically become reasons to bring that thing about. But so far as the concept of welfare goes, this does not entail that, if something, X, is a welfare-making feature for Y (i.e., X would contribute intrinsically to Y's welfare), then there is reason for anyone, whether Y or anyone else, to bring X about. It is conceptually coherent to hold that something would contribute intrinsically to someone's welfare (by realizing some welfare-making feature), but nonetheless hold that there is no reason whatsoever to bring that thing about. Y herself might coherently judge this. Y might not care for herself or think she is worth caring for, and might think therefore that considerations of her own welfare provide no reasons for acting, either for her or for anyone else. What is conceptually incoherent is caring for Y, or thinking one should care for her (for reasons of the right kind), and not taking welfare-making features as reasons to desire that these features be realized in Y's life for Y's sake.

I take it as evidence that something in this general neighborhood is correct that there is no attraction whatsoever to holding a buck-passing theory of welfare with respect to reasons for action. No philosopher I am aware of seems tempted to deny that the fact that something will promote an agent's welfare or well-being is itself a reason for her to realize or

[35] Stephen Darwall, *Welfare and Rational Care* (Princeton, NJ: Princeton University Press, 2002).

promote it. To the contrary, it is hard to think of a more widely held view in the history of ethics. If a fitting-attitude approach to welfare is correct, something's being for someone's welfare must consist in there being reasons for some attitude or other toward that thing. And this would naturally lead to a buck-passing view *for that attitude or attitudes.* But a rational care theory of welfare illustrates the possibility of a fitting-attitude theory of welfare that does not entail buck-passing for welfare with respect to reasons for action.

III. Moral Obligation, Moral Responsibility, and the Second-Person Standpoint

Even if a fitting-attitude theory of a normative concept entails buck-passing with respect to reasons for the attitudes that the concept analytically implicates, therefore, the theory may nonetheless not support buck-passing with respect to reasons for action. What, then, about the concept of moral wrong? As with other normative concepts, whether a fitting-attitude theory of wrongness supports buck-passing about reasons for acting will depend on the attitude or attitudes that are distinctive of the concept.

In *The Second-Person Standpoint,* I argue that the concepts of moral obligation and moral wrong are irreducibly second-personal in the sense that they conceptually involve *addressable* (and so second-personal) authoritative demands. When we violate moral obligations, we violate legitimate expectations and demands that we have and can make, in principle anyway, of one another and ourselves as representative persons or members of the moral community.[36] When we think that an action is wrong, as Richard Nixon might or might not have thought about subverting the Watergate investigation by paying hush money to Hunt, we are committed to thinking that not performing that action is something we therefore warrantedly demand of ourselves and one another. My claim here is that, so understood, the fact that an act is wrong gives us a reason not so to act that is additional to reasons consisting of the act's wrong-making features — and that this reason is a *second-personal reason* owing to its conceptual connection to (second-personally) addressable demands.

The thesis that the ideas of moral obligation and moral wrong conceptually involve the notion of (second-personally) addressable legitimate demands is rooted in two further ideas. The first is the one I mentioned before, namely, Mill's and Strawson's idea that moral obligation and wrong are conceptually related to warranted reactive attitudes. What is morally wrong is what one is warrantedly held accountable and blamed for (with

[36] By the "moral community," I mean no actual community, but a regulative ideal like Kant's "kingdom of ends." We could as well say that the authority is one we have *as representative persons.* I am indebted to David Velleman and Samuel Scheffler for discussion on this point.

reactive attitudes) if one so acts without adequate excuse. The second idea is that holding someone responsible with a reactive attitude has an implicitly second-personal character (which is why Strawson contrasts its role in interpersonal relationships with taking an "objective" or third-personal view toward someone).[37] Holding someone responsible involves the putatively authoritative address of a demand, if only in imagination.

To prepare the way for considering this thesis and its implications, we need first to focus more precisely on the concepts of moral obligation and moral wrong in order to notice how they differ from other concepts with which they might be conflated. I take it as obvious, first, that "wrong" in the sense we are interested in refers to a narrower notion than the broader sense that is involved in just any kind of mistake, failure, or incorrectness. If, in doing a math problem, I make a mistake and get the wrong answer, I do no wrong in the sense with which we are concerned; I violate no moral obligation.

Neither is the idea of moral wrong in the current sense the same as that of acting against the balance of reasons, or even, indeed, against the balance of moral reasons. This is shown by the fact that supererogation, an act's being morally recommended but not morally obligatory or required, is a conceptually coherent possibility. That does not mean that theories that deny supererogation—like act-consequentialism, which holds that it is always wrong to do anything other than the morally best, optimific act—are mistaken. It just means that whether they are mistaken or not— whether there is such a thing as supererogation—is a substantive normative question that is not settled by the concept of moral obligation itself. And if that is so, moral obligation must be a different concept than that of being most morally choiceworthy.[38]

---

[37] See Strawson, "Freedom and Resentment," 81: "What I want to contrast is the attitude (or range of attitudes) of involvement or participation in a human relationship, on the one hand, and what might be called the objective attitude (or range of attitudes) to another human being, on the other. . . . To adopt the objective attitude to another human being is to see him, perhaps, as an object of social policy; as a subject for what, in a wide range of sense, might be called treatment; as something certainly to be taken account, perhaps precautionary account, of; to be managed or handled or cured or trained; perhaps simply to be avoided, though this gerundive is not peculiar to cases of objectivity of attitude. The objective attitude may be emotionally toned in many ways, but not in all ways: it may include repulsion or fear, it may include pity or even love, though not all kinds of love. But it cannot include the range of reactive feelings and attitudes which belong to involvement or participation with others in inter-personal human relationships; it cannot include resentment, gratitude, forgiveness, anger, or the sort of love which two adults can sometimes be said to feel reciprocally, for each other. If your attitude towards someone is wholly objective, then though you may fight him, you cannot quarrel with him, and though you may talk to him, even negotiate with him, you cannot reason with him. You can at most pretend to quarrel, or to reason, with him."

[38] But might the concepts of moral obligation and moral wrong be analyzed in terms of morally *conclusive* reasons—a moral obligation being something there is conclusive moral reason to do, and being wrong being something there is conclusive moral reason not to do? But what is it for reasons to be morally conclusive? On the one hand, if we give this an epistemic sense, such that reasons are conclusive if they conclusively establish that a certain

This should already make us suspicious of taking a buck-passing view of moral wrongness in relation to reasons for acting. If the concept of moral obligation were simply that of an action that is best supported by moral reasons, or best supported by reasons period, then being wrong could not be an additional moral reason, or reason period, not to perform the act. Being morally wrong would already involve being supported by all the reasons, or all the moral reasons, there are for acting. But that is not the way we normally think of it. Anyone who takes seriously the debate about whether views like act-consequentialism "demand too much," for example, must already take for granted that the ideas of moral obligation and moral wrong involve a notion of requirement or demand that differs conceptually from that of the balance of moral reasons.

But how are we to understand this notion? What is it for morality to demand something? Plainly, the idea of demand or requirement extends more widely than the moral. We speak, for example, of the requirements of reason: say, the demand not to have contradictory beliefs or plans. Unlike demands of reason or logic, however, talk of moral demands is conceptually linked to *accountability*.[39] What we are morally obligated to do is, as a conceptual matter, what we are morally answerable for doing.

There is thus an important difference between moral obligations and, for example, requirements that are imposed by logic. Moral obligation is tied to a distinctive kind of responsibility—accountability—*conceptually*. If I fail to act as I am morally required (without adequate excuse), it simply follows straightaway that reactive attitudes like blame and guilt are thereby warranted.[40] In contrast, responses like these seem appropriate to logical blunders only in certain contexts, and even here, what seems to be in question is a moral error of some kind (as when I have a special responsibility for reasoning properly).[41] Moreover, although a connection to accountability is intrinsic to the concept of moral obligation, it is obvi-

---

act is what morality most recommends, then this really adds nothing to the possibility just canvassed. On the other hand, if reasons are morally conclusive when they warrant a moral *requirement* or demand, then this possibility amounts to the one I go on to consider presently. In order for there to be some other possibility, we would have to have a notion of morally conclusive reason that we understand independently of the idea of moral requirement or demand, which we could then use to understand this latter idea. I doubt that this is so. I am indebted to Samuel Scheffler for discussion on these points.

[39] For this reason, I argue in *The Second-Person Standpoint* that the normativity of moral obligation is not adequately captured by the Kantian idea that moral demands are demands of reason. Of course, it could still be the case that what is morally demanded is also demanded by reason. I argue that the most promising line of argument supporting this, indeed, proceeds from a second-personal account of moral obligation's normativity.

[40] Indeed, the very idea of an "excuse" is not internal to the rules of logic; it must be understood in relation to a broader context that includes other norms.

[41] I do not mean, of course, that logical errors are not subject to criticism, or that we do not sometimes use words like "blame," as when a teacher says that he does not blame his student for a given error on a first try.

ously no part whatsoever of the idea of a logical requirement or demand of reason.

Mill seems on safe ground, then, in saying that our concept of wrongdoing is essentially related to accountability. Even if it is natural to think that a person falls short of full virtue if she does only what can be required of her in the sense of what she can be warrantedly *held to* through reactive attitudes like blame and guilt, she nonetheless does no wrong. We do not impute wrongdoing unless we take ourselves to be in the range of the culpable, that is, unless the action is such that the agent is not just morally criticizable in some way or other, but aptly *blamed* or the object of some other form of accountability-seeking reactive attitude if she lacks an adequate excuse.

This aspect of the concept of moral wrong has been stressed by a number of contemporary writers. John Skorupski says that calling an act "morally wrong . . . amounts to blaming the agent" and that the idea of moral wrong cannot be understood independently of that of blameworthiness.[42] Allan Gibbard quite explicitly follows Mill's lead in proposing that "what a person does is *morally wrong* if and only if it is rational for him to feel guilty for having done it, and for others to be angry at him for having done it."[43] And we can find versions of this Millian idea in other writers also.[44] It is consistent with these views, of course, that there remains a distinction between the wrongness of acts and the blameworthiness of agents. Someone is not to blame for wrongdoing if he has an excuse.

This gives us half of what underlies my thesis that the ideas of moral obligation and moral wrong conceptually involve (second-personally) addressable legitimate demands. The other half concerns the second-personal character of the distinctive attitudes—Strawsonian reactive attitudes—whose warrant is conceptually implicated in the idea of moral wrong. Reactive attitudes invariably involve a kind of "demand," as Strawson himself says, that is imaginatively addressed to its object and that must, therefore, presuppose the authority to address that object.[45]

Consider indignation, for example. Indignation is an instance of what Strawson calls an *impersonal* reactive attitude, since it is felt from an observer's perspective rather than from that of anyone involved in the situation to which one is responding. To feel indignation toward someone

---

[42] John Skorupski, *Ethical Explorations* (Oxford: Oxford University Press, 1999), 29, 142. This claim is, however, too strong, since one may not blame someone for acting wrongly if the person has some adequate excuse for doing so.

[43] Gibbard, *Wise Choices, Apt Feelings*, 42 (emphasis in the original).

[44] See, e.g., Kurt Baier, "Moral Obligation," *American Philosophical Quarterly* 3 (1966): 210–26; Richard Brandt, *A Theory of the Good and the Right* (Oxford: Oxford University Press, 1979); and Russ Shafer-Landau, *Moral Realism: A Defence* (New York: Oxford University Press, 2003).

[45] Strawson, "Freedom and Resentment," 92–93.

is to feel that he is to blame for some conduct and is therefore appropriately held accountable for it, if only by being subject to reactive attitudes
from himself (guilt) and others (blame or indignation). It is essential to
Strawson's argument in his classic essay "Freedom and Resentment" that
indignation differs from its seeming to one that some sanction would be
desirable or even that the sanction would make for a more valuable or
fitting whole (that it would realize something like poetic justice). The
feeling of indignation invariably includes a sense of legitimate or authoritative demand that may be absent from the thought that some sanction
would be either desirable or fitting. We feel indignation only when we
feel we can reasonably *expect* or demand of others that they act in certain
ways. Indeed, Strawson says, "the making of the demand *is* the proneness
to such attitudes."[46]

Similar points hold for *personal* reactive attitudes, which are felt, unlike
indignation or moral blame, not as if from the perspective of a disinterested third party, but as if from the victim's point of view or that of
someone identified with her.[47] We resent what we take to be violations
against ourselves or those with whom we identify. If you resent someone's treading on your foot, for example (or, even more, his rejecting your
request or demand that he stop doing so), you feel as if he has violated
your valid claim or demand and as if some claim-exacting or responsibility-
seeking response by you, or on your behalf, is justified.

Strawson contrasts "the attitude (or range of attitudes) of involvement
or participation in a human relationship" (taking a second-person stance,
in my terms), on the one hand, with "the objective attitudes (or range of
attitudes) to another human being, on the other."[48] We take an "objective" attitude toward those we see as unfit for "ordinary adult human
relationships," such as very young children and those with "deep-rooted
psychological abnormality," and we regard them as appropriately subject
to "treatment" or "management," rather than to reactive attitudes and
forms of interpersonal address that involve them.[49] What is distinctive
about reactive attitudes, then—whether they are *impersonal* attitudes like
indignation or blame, or *personal* attitudes like resentment—is that they
are felt as if in second-personal relation with another: they involve an
imagined *address* of a claim or demand *to* their object that holds their
object answerable for compliance.[50]

---

[46] Ibid. (emphasis in the original).
[47] In addition to negative personal reactive attitudes, Strawson also mentions gratitude,
which he regards as a (positive) personal reactive attitude—an attitude which, in this case,
is felt as if from the perspective of a beneficiary.
[48] Ibid., 79.
[49] Ibid., 81.
[50] Thus, an attitude can be second-personal in the requisite sense and be third-party or
"impersonal" in Strawson's sense. And the phenomenon of guilt shows that it is possible to
take a second-personal attitude toward oneself. What makes an attitude second-personal is
its having an implicit *addressee*.

IV. Moral Wrongness: A Second-Personal Reason to Act

I shall take it, therefore, that the fact that a certain action (say, stepping unbidden on someone's foot or subverting a criminal investigation) would be wrong amounts to the fact that it violates a legitimate demand we make of ourselves and one another as representative persons. My claim, then, is that this latter fact, the fact that an act violates such a demand, itself provides a reason not to perform the act that is additional to the act's wrong-making features. Because the notion of an *addressable* demand is itself part of this further reason, I call it a *second-personal reason*. Since it is impossible to make a demand of someone without addressing her in some way, the idea of second-personal address is built into the very ideas of moral obligation and moral wrong. Consequently, if the fact that an action would be wrong is a reason not to perform the act, it is a second-personal reason.

Wrong-making features, such as that an action would cause harm or subvert a criminal investigation, themselves entail nothing about legitimate demands and thus are not second-personal reasons.[51] My claim, however, is that in believing that such features *are indeed wrong making*, we are committed to thinking that these features nonetheless ground a legitimate demand not so to act and that this fact—the fact that the act would violate a legitimate moral demand and so be wrong—gives us a further reason not to perform the act.

One way to appreciate this is to consider the relation between the concepts of moral *rights* and moral wrong.[52] So far as I know, no one denies that the fact that an action would violate someone's rights is a reason not to perform the action. Since violating a right is itself a wrong-making feature, however, that may not seem to count against a buck-passing theory of moral wrong with respect to reasons for action. But there is an important difference between moral rights and most other wrong-making features. That violating someone's right is wrong (at least other things being equal) is not just a substantive normative truth; it is a conceptual truth.[53] As we shall see presently, something does not count as a violation of someone's right, unless it is something we legitimately demand that people not do to that person. So the fact that an act would violate someone's right is not itself independent of the fact that it would be wrong, at least other things being equal.

Suppose that I intentionally tromp on your foot to gain an advantage in getting to the table with designer underwear on sale when I could easily

---

[51] Again, by wrong-making features, I mean features that provide *grounds* or normative reasons for something's being wrong, not the features, if there are any, in which something's being wrong might consist metaphysically.

[52] For convenience, I shall shorten "moral right" to "right."

[53] I take it that it would be incoherent to assert that one has a right to something but that someone would do no wrong, not even other things being equal, if she were to deprive one of it.

have gone around and risked doing without a pair of Calvin Kleins. Here I clearly violate your right. But in what does this fact consist? What is it to have a right? A right of this sort is a "claim right" in Wesley Hohfeld's sense.[54] I follow Joel Feinberg in holding that it is "claiming that gives [such] rights their distinctive moral significance."[55] Claiming is, in its nature, second-personal; we make claims on others by addressing them second-personally. "I'm sorry, but that's my foot you're stepping on," you might say to me as I'm on my way to the Calvin Kleins, implying that I am where I have no right to be and where you have every right to demand I vacate, apologize, and so on.

Such a demand would not be a *mere* demand, however: it would not simply be an imposition of your will on mine. It would be addressed as a legitimate demand, one you have the authority to make of me—an authority it would be unreasonable of me not to recognize. It seems obvious, moreover, that the authoritative demand in which your right consists gives me a reason not to step on your foot that is additional to the fact that I would be causing you pain, suffering, inconvenience, and so on. Before the concept of human rights became established, people recognized the latter reasons of pain, suffering, and so on, but not yet the former reason consisting in a right not to be gratuitously caused these things. However, when we accept that we have rights we can legitimately claim of one another (that we all are, in John Rawls's phrase, "self-originating source[s] of valid claims"), we recognize an additional reason not to cause pain and suffering: namely, that this is something we legitimately claim from one another as our right.[56]

As Hohfeld points out, the concept of a claim right is conceptually related to that of a moral duty or *obligation to the rightholder*.[57] Your right against me analytically entails that I have a moral duty or obligation *to you*. An obligation *to* someone is a "directed" or "bipolar" obligation.[58] If I violate such a duty to you, I *wrong you*. In so doing, I violate an authority *you* have, as an individual person, to demand that others not tread on *you*. Our moral rights are what we have the authority to demand of one another *as individuals*. You have a right against me only if you have (1) the individual authority to demand that I not act in some way toward *you* and (2) a standing others do not have to hold me answerable, as is shown

[54] Wesley Newcomb Hohfeld, *Fundamental Legal Conceptions*, ed. Walter Wheeler Cook (New Haven, CT: Yale University Press, 1923).

[55] Joel Feinberg, "The Nature and Value of Rights," in Feinberg, *Rights, Justice, and the Bounds of Liberty* (Princeton, NJ: Princeton University Press, 1980), 151.

[56] John Rawls, "Kantian Constructivism in Moral Theory," *The Journal of Philosophy* 77 (1980): 546.

[57] Hohfeld, *Fundamental Legal Conceptions*, 65–75.

[58] For directed obligation, see Margaret Gilbert, *A Theory of Political Obligation* (Oxford: Oxford University Press, 2006), 40; and for bipolar obligation, see Michael Thompson, "What Is It to Wrong Someone? A Puzzle about Justice," in *Reason and Value: Themes from the Moral Philosophy of Joseph Raz*, ed. R. Jay Wallace et al. (New York: Oxford University Press, 2006).

by the fact that were I to violate the right, you would have a distinctive authority to forgive me at your discretion. It is a reflection of this individual authority that you can consent to my acting in ways that would otherwise violate your right, that it is up to you whether to seek compensation (as is recognized in the law of torts), and so on.

When I step on your foot unbidden, I fail to respect, and thus violate, this authority you have as an individual person, and thus I violate and fail to respect *you*. In so doing, moreover, I fail to appreciate a reason not to step on your foot that is additional to the fact that I am causing avoidable harm: namely, that it violates your right (that is, on the current analysis, your legitimate demand of me as an individual person).

As I have said, it is relatively uncontroversial that the fact that an action would violate someone's right, and thus wrong that person, is a reason not to do it. What is in question is whether the fact that something would be wrong *period* is a reason that supplements the wrong-making features of a wrongful action, including, perhaps, that it would violate someone's rights and thus wrong that person. On the second-personal analysis we are considering, however, wrongs and moral obligations *period* are no less conceptually connected to legitimate demands—and hence to the idea of a second-personal reason—than are wrongings and bipolar moral obligations *to* someone.

Moral obligations simpliciter are what we have the authority to demand of one another, not as individuals, but as representative persons—as representatives, as we might say, of the moral community.[59] So wrongdoing also always involves a failure to respect legitimate demands and the authority to make them that is additional to the individual authorities that are involved in violations of rights and wrongings. Wrongdoing violates our authority as representative persons to demand that people not act in that way. This means that it also involves a failure of respect (of this *representative authority*) and thus a failure to appreciate a further reason not to perform the act that is additional to the act's wrong-making features, including, indeed, even the fact that it might violate someone's right (her *individual authority* to demand that one not so treat *her*) and so wrong her.

You have an individual authority to make claims and demands of me regarding my treatment of you that others do not have. You have the authority to allow or forbid actions involving you and your body that others don't, and you also have a distinctive standing to object, to demand apology, to seek compensation, to forgive, and so on. If you want not to "make a scene" by objecting if I step on your foot, then others have a strong reason to respect your wishes. And it is up to you and not others whether, for example, to forgive my brutish treatment. It is a reflection of

---

[59] Again, "the moral community" refers here not to any actual social collectivity but to a regulative ideal like Kant's "kingdom of ends."

all this, that violations of rights (wrongs *to* someone) are, as Strawson points out, the object of warranted *personal* reactive attitudes like resentment.[60] A stranger cannot warrantedly, or even intelligibly, feel resentment when I step on your foot, although you (and others personally related to you) can.

Nonetheless, your individual authority is not the only relevant standing in the case, not even the only relevant standing you have. Although it is up to you in the first instance whether or not to object or complain about my action, it is not distinctively up to you whether or not to feel indignation or blame. The latter is an *impersonal* reactive attitude and thus is felt not as if from the victim's point of view, but as if from a disinterested or impartial perspective that abstracts from personal involvement.[61] Impersonal attitudes are the ones to which the concepts of moral obligation and moral wrong *period* are conceptually related. Something is wrong if it is blameworthy, lacking adequate excuse. But whether to blame someone, whether that person is *to blame*, is not distinctively a victim's question. It is a question we face as representative persons, not as someone personally involved.[62]

This difference between our individual authority to claim our rights, on the one hand, and our representative standing to hold one another and ourselves accountable through blame, on the other, is reflected in the difference between the civil and the criminal law. Whether or not to seek compensation in bringing a tort action is up to the victim. The state legitimately does not proceed on its own to rectify wrongings; rather, the law of torts gives individuals standing to bring cases on their own behalf. But it is not, or at least not always, up to the victim whether to prosecute a crime. That is a question for the people and their representatives. In this way, legal guilt is like moral guilt. Whether to blame someone, whether she is to blame, is a question we face as representative persons. This is reflected also in John Locke's distinction between the authority everyone has in the state of nature to punish transgressions of the law of nature, on the one hand, and the authority that individuals have, "to seek reparations" for violations of their individual rights, on the other.[63]

Because it would violate your right, I have a reason not to step unbidden on your foot that is additional to the fact that doing so will cause

[60] Strawson, "Freedom and Resentment," 72.

[61] Ibid., 84–85.

[62] Thus, if it is a conceptual truth that violations of rights (wrongings) are also, other things being equal, wrongs period—that violations of "bipolar" obligations *to* someone are also, other things being equal, violations of moral obligations period—then it follows that a personal reactive attitude, such as resentment, can be warranted only if an impersonal reactive attitude would be (at least, other things being equal). I believe this conceptual thesis is true, but notice that the claim that the fact that an action is wrong is a reason not to perform it (consisting in the fact that the act violates a legitimate demand we make of one another as representative persons) does not strictly depend on this conceptual thesis. I am indebted here to discussion with Verity Harte and Jules Coleman.

[63] John Locke, *Second Treatise of Government*, sections 7–11.

pain, suffering, and other things that are bad for you. Stepping on your foot does not simply harm you, it also disrespects your rights, and therefore disrespects you, as someone with the individual authority to demand that I not do that to you. And this gives me an additional reason not to step on your foot.

But if the fact that it would violate your right gives me reason not to step on your foot, so also does the fact that stepping on your foot would be wrong *period*. A wrongful act violates another authority in addition, not one you have as an individual, but one we all have as representative persons. In being blameworthy (unless excused), the wrongfulness of my act consists in its being a violation of some obligation that representative persons legitimately demand of me—that anyone can, at least in principle, demand (including me of myself) through reactive attitudes like blame (and the self-reactive attitude of guilt). Thus, all wrongs involve a kind of disrespect that is additional to disrespect of any individual's authority. Any wrong violates the legitimate demands of those to whom we are morally responsible, namely, one another as representative persons; thus, any wrong involves a failure adequately to respect this authority. Because this is so, an act's wrongness provides an additional reason not to perform it: namely, that the act would violate a legitimate demand and thus fail to respect our authority as representative persons. Since this reason is conceptually tied to an authority to address demands, an act's wrongness is therefore a second-personal reason not to do it.

Another way of seeing that wrongness creates an additional reason is to see the way in which being wrong interacts with the idea of reasonable demand. Since avoiding your foot puts no unreasonable burden on me, it is something we can demand of one another both as individuals and as representative persons. But what if stepping on your foot is the only way I can avoid significant injury to myself? In such a case, it seems arguable that we (and you) cannot reasonably demand that I not step on your foot, and so it is neither wrong nor a violation of your right for me to do so.[64] There seems to be a continuum of cases, holding fixed the harm to the victim, from ones where the burden to the agent is very great, and so his action not wrong, to ones where the burden is very small, and so his action clearly wrong. Let us suppose there are two different cases, A and B, between which there exists some just noticeable difference in the burdens to the agent, such that in case A the burden is insufficient to make the act of stepping on someone's foot not wrong (so in case A, the agent's stepping on the other's foot would be wrong), whereas in case B, with a somewhat greater cost to the agent, the same act would not be wrong. If

---

[64] Or, alternatively, though it violates your right and *would* be wrong (period) if I lacked this further justification, it is not wrong because the justification exists. What violates someone's rights would be wrong to do lacking some justification, just as what is wrong would be blameworthy if done without adequate excuse. It follows that what violates someone's rights would be blameworthy if it were done without *either* a justification or an excuse.

we consider just the wrong-making features of the act—the relative cost to agent and victim—these will, of course, create different and differently weighted reasons. That an agent could avoid stepping on someone else's foot at lesser cost in case A than he could in case B no doubt creates greater reason for the agent to absorb that cost in case A than in case B. But whatever reason the wrong-making features themselves create in these two cases seems not fully to capture the reasons that result from the further fact these features ground, namely, that we can legitimately demand that an agent absorb the cost involved in case A, but not in case B—in other words, that not absorbing the cost in case A amounts to wronging someone and thereby doing moral wrong (assuming there is no further justification).

V. A Conclusion Concerning Conclusive Reasons

Finally, it is an often-noted feature of the concepts of moral obligation and moral wrong that they purport to entail that an agent has not just *some* reason to act, but conclusive reason (or at least, as Scanlon says, reason that is "normally conclusive").[65] Obviously, this is no part whatsoever of the concepts involved in obligation-making or wrong-making features themselves: for example, that stepping on your foot in the case we initially imagined would impose a considerable cost on you at little cost to me. That does not rule out a buck-passing theory of wrongness with respect to reasons for acting by itself, however, since it might be that the concept of wrongness just is that of there being conclusive moral reasons (or reasons period) for doing something, with the reasons being provided entirely by wrong-making features. But we have already effectively excluded these possibilities. If action supported by conclusive moral reasons (or reasons period) just means action recommended by the weightiest moral reasons (or reasons period), we have already seen that this is a different concept from that of morally obligatory or demanded conduct. So far as our concepts go, an act may be thus supported or recommended without being morally required or obligatory. It follows, therefore, that if being morally obligatory purports to entail the existence of conclusive or normally conclusive reasons, then that must be because the facts of moral obligation and wrongness purport to provide some reasons that can guarantee overriding weight *themselves.*

In conclusion, I would like to indicate how the second-personal analysis of moral obligation and wrongness I have been discussing can explain the conclusive-reason-providing purport of moral obligation and moral wrong. The root of the explanation is moral obligation's conceptual tie to accountability and warranted blame. As Bernard Williams and others have noted, when we blame someone we imply that there was conclusive reason for her not to have done what we blame her for having done.[66] It makes no sense to blame someone for doing something and then add that she had, nonetheless, sufficient reason to do it, all things considered. Blame implies not just that the person shouldn't have done what she did "morally speaking," but that she shouldn't have done it period. A person who in one moment "admits" her guilt, but in the next asserts that she had, nonetheless, good and sufficient reasons for doing what she did, can hardly be said to have accepted responsibility for her action. Or to put the point the other way around, if someone can establish that she had sufficient reason to do what she did, then she will have accounted for herself, justified her conduct, and shown thereby that blame is unwarranted. The point is not that the fact that one blames someone entails the existence of conclusive reason. Rather, in blaming someone one implies that such reason exists.

When we think that an act is morally wrong, and therefore blameworthy if unexcused, we think that, lacking excuse, blame is the fitting attitude for anyone to take toward someone performing the act. When an agent takes such an attitude toward herself, and addresses a demand to herself through a self-reactive attitude like guilt (whether retrospectively or prospectively), she feels as though there is conclusive reason not to perform the act.[67] But if the facts that *make* an act morally wrong, in the sense of grounding or providing normative reasons for its wrongness, do not purport to be conclusive reasons themselves, and if the fact that an act is wrong is not *just* the fact that such conclusive reasons exist, then what we must be thinking when we take such an attitude toward one another and ourselves is that the fact that an act is morally wrong provides a reason itself not to perform the act, and that this guarantees conclusive reason not to do so. I have tried to say in this essay what this additional reason consists in: that the act is something we legitimately demand that people not do.[68] If this is right, trying to do without this thought will leave us with one thought too few.

Philosophy, Yale University

---

[66] See Bernard Williams, "Internal Reasons and the Obscurity of Blame," in Williams, *Making Sense of Humanity* (Cambridge: Cambridge University Press, 1995), 40–44; Gibbard, *Wise Choices, Apt Feelings*, 299–300; Skorupski, *Ethical Explorations*, 42–43; and Shafer-Landau, *Moral Realism: A Defence*, 181–83.

[67] For valuable insights about the relevance of prospective guilt, I am indebted to the work of Howard Nye.

[68] It should be clear that I am not saying that this is a wrong-making feature, in the sense of a ground or of normative reason for an act's wrongness. I am saying that this is what being wrong consists in, and that this fact provides a reason not to perform the wrongful act that is additional to the act's wrong-making features (grounds of or normative reasons for its being wrong).

MORAL OBLIGATION, BLAME, AND SELF-GOVERNANCE

By John Skorupski

I. Introduction

Moral judgment—the moral assessment of actions and people—is woven inextricably into personal and social life. "Beyond morality" is empty fantasy. A picture of our personal and social world that fails to exhibit this is misleading. How then to make an adequate picture? The moral emotions, their place in social relations, and their potential for both function and dysfunction will have to feature largely. Notions like self-determination, integrity, a common moral sense, and reconciliation with oneself and others will appear. Drawing the picture calls more on the skills of eloquence and hermeneutics than of conceptual analysis. Nonetheless, the latter has a structuring role to play; at any rate, it will be the main concern of this essay.

Two deep features of moral judgment will guide my discussion: the first is that moral judgment is rooted in the rationality of the feelings; the second is that moral agency is self-governing agency.

There are reasons for feelings as well as for beliefs and actions. There can be good or bad reasons for admiration, desire, gratitude, pride; for contempt, anger, resentment, fear. Furthermore, such reasons, which determine the rationality of feelings, are not reducible to epistemic reasons (reasons to believe something) or practical reasons (reasons to do something). I shall call them *evaluative* reasons. Moral propositions are propositions about evaluative reasons: specifically, about reasons for the sentiment of blame. Understanding the moral thus requires that we describe this sentiment without circularity and in sufficient depth.

This can be done because blame, like other sentiments, has characteristic objects and characteristic actions to which it disposes. We can identify the sentiment by describing them. In this essay, however, my focus will be almost entirely on object rather than action. I shall only sketchily describe the action to which moral blame disposes—*withdrawal of recognition*. The significance of this action is a subject that requires full treatment in its own right.[1]

---

[1] Some further discussion can be found in John Skorupski, *Ethical Explorations* (Oxford: Oxford University Press, 1999), part III; and Skorupski, "Blame, Respect, and Recognition: A Reply to Theo van Willigenburg," *Utilitas* 17 (2005): 333–47.

158 © 2010 Social Philosophy & Policy Foundation. Printed in the USA.

My first aim is to show how moral wrongness is definable in terms of evaluative reasons to blame, and how these reasons connect to practical reasons. This will require us to take account of the second deep feature of the moral: that moral agency is, by its very nature, a species of self-governing agency.

Self-governing actors can act from reasons. To do so, they must be able to think about what reasons they have. They must be able to audit those reasons reflectively, in order to assess whether they have sufficient reason to believe, or feel, or act—or whether they must investigate further before they have sufficient reason. And they must be able to act on their conclusions.

Beyond these indisputable points, however, we shall see that self-governance can be understood in weaker and stronger ways. Moral agents require at least the capacity for *self-determination*. This is a two-fold capacity: (i) the power to think about their reasons and determine whether they are sufficient or whether further inquiry is needed; and (ii) the power to act on their conclusions. I am self-determining if I determine myself by propositions about reasons which I myself accept—whatever the source of my acceptance. But self-governance is often understood to include not just self-determination but also *autonomy*. The idea of autonomy, understood in a broadly Kantian way, is stronger than that of self-determination; it is self-determination grounded in personal normative insight into truths about reasons: the ability to recognize such truths by one's own lights, in a first-person way. My second aim is to consider whether moral agency presupposes the weaker notion of self-determination or the stronger notion of autonomy. Modern ideals of morality place great weight on the idea that every moral agent is equally autonomous; but we shall see that moral agency requires only the capacity of self-determination, and that the idea that all moral agents are equally autonomous is hard to sustain.

In Section II, I define some concepts we shall need and summarize some structural theses about reasons. Sections III and IV examine the connections between moral wrongness, blame, and reasons. Sections V and VI discuss self-determination and autonomy. Section VII summarizes my conclusions.

II. Reasons and Self-Governance

We start, then, from the fact that there are three kinds of reasons: evaluative, epistemic, and practical. They have a largely common logical structure; in all cases, reasons are relations between facts, persons, and "responses" (feelings, beliefs, actions). Furthermore, in all these cases, three distinct reason-relations fall under the concept of a reason:

(i) One can say that some particular facts are a reason, weaker or stronger, for some person at some time to ψ (where ψ ranges over beliefs, feelings, and actions). I call such facts *specific* reasons (R): facts π_i are at time t a reason of degree of strength d for x to $\psi - R(\pi_i, t, d, x, \psi)$.

(ii) One can say that taking all the facts that count for and against into account, there is more or less strong reason *overall* for some person at some time to ψ. Such facts constitute an *overall* reason (R_o): facts π_i are at time t overall reason of degree of strength d for x to $\psi - R_o(\pi_i, t, d, x, \psi)$.

(iii) One can say that some facts give some person at some time *sufficient* reason to ψ. So we also have sufficient reasons (S): facts π_i are at time t a sufficient reason for x to $\psi - S(\pi_i, t, x, \psi)$.

When there is sufficient reason for x to ψ, we can say that x should* ψ. (I give this "should" an asterisk because while this is certainly one way we use "should," it has plenty of other uses.)

However, there is also an important difference between epistemic reasons and practical and evaluative ones. The facts that give you reason to believe must be facts that you know or could know, whereas that restriction does not apply to facts that give you reason to feel something or do something. If the building is about to explode, that is a reason for you to leave, whether or not you know it or could know it. Likewise, if a benefactor is anonymously helping you, that is a reason for you to be grateful to that person, even though you cannot find out who it is. But now suppose that a hurricane will strike London next year. Is that a reason for you to believe that a hurricane will strike London next year? No. Reasons to believe that proposition, now, must consist of evidence, or more generally, of facts that you could now come to know, whether or not you actually know them. Think of these facts as your *epistemic field;* your epistemic reasons (R, R_0, S) are relative to your epistemic field. Spelled out in full, therefore, these reasons have your epistemic field as one of their relata, whereas your evaluative and practical reasons do not.

We come now to a distinction that is critical for our purposes. Self-governance requires that one should be able to tell what reasons one has. You have to be able to reflect on your specific reasons, estimate how strong they are overall, and determine whether they are sufficient. Thus, in an example given by Allan Gibbard,[2] the way out of the forest that you *should** take is the one that is in fact the quickest: that is what there is sufficient reason for you to do. But you are lost; you don't know the quickest way, and there is no one to tell you. So what you actually have reason to do is, say, pick an arbitrary straight line and follow it.

As this example illustrates, we talk about reasons in two ways (among others), depending on whether or not we are thinking of them as *self-*

---

[2] Allan Gibbard, *Wise Choices, Apt Feelings* (Oxford: Oxford University Press, 1990), 18–19.

MORAL OBLIGATION, BLAME, AND SELF-GOVERNANCE   161

accessible. A way to mark this contrast, as I have just done, is to distinguish between

(i) the reasons there *are* for a person to ψ

and

(ii) the reasons a person *has* to ψ.

On this way of speaking, the reasons there *are* for a person are not in general self-accessible. He may need to investigate his epistemic field to discover them, or they may lie outside his epistemic field. In contrast, the reasons a person *has* are self-accessible: if he has them, he can know—recognize, tell—that he has them, solely by means of reflection and self-examination, including attention to the way things seem to him. (The levels of normative insight, cognitive competence, and self-scrutiny needed may require time and capacities that he does not have; the point is that nothing *else* is required.)

However, we also talk about "the reasons a person has" in other ways. Quite often, for example, we are not referring to a person's warranted reasons but to the reasons he *takes* himself to have. Or we may be referring to the reasons there would be for him if his factual beliefs were true. To avoid ambiguity, then, I shall talk about a person's self-accessible reasons as *warranted* reasons. And I shall call a warranted *sufficient* reason a warrant. When I refer to a person's reasons simpliciter, I am referring to the reasons there are for that person, not to the warranted reasons he has.

When we talk about the reasons a person has to ψ at a given time—in the sense of his warranted reasons—we are referring to what there is sufficient reason for him to believe are the reasons for him to ψ, on the sole basis of facts knowable by self-scrutiny at that time. (He may or may not actually form those beliefs, or come to know those facts.) These facts are a subset of his epistemic field: call them his *epistemic state.* Warranted reasons are then definable in terms of reasons: a person's warranted reasons to ψ are the reasons to ψ that there is sufficient reason for him to believe obtain, relative to his epistemic state. Thus, there is warrant for x to ψ at t if and only if, relative to x's epistemic *state,* x should* believe that x should* ψ at t.

Now if I can have knowledge of my reasons, it must be possible for me to tell, just by normative reflection—pure reflection about reason relations—that some facts would constitute a reason to ψ. Suppose one can tell solely by such reflection that were π_i to obtain, it would be the case that $R(\pi_i, x, \psi)$. Then we can say that if these facts obtained, they would be a *complete* specific reason for x to ψ. (Likewise for overall and sufficient reasons.)

In putting it this way, I am not assuming a particular meta-normative view about the epistemology and ontology of reasons. One can be a cognitivist or a noncognitivist with respect to claims about complete reasons (i.e., hold that they assert true or false propositions, or hold that they express affective attitudes) while accepting that agency requires that agents must be able to recognize, accept, or endorse complete reasons by pure reflection rather than empirical enquiry, if they are able to assess what warranted reasons they have at all.

These complete reasons may be very detailed or particularistic. For example, the fact that the house is about to explode may be a reason for you to leave it or a reason for you to enter it. It depends on whether you are a bomb-disposal expert. And if you are, then it also depends on other things, such as whether you are there in your official capacity, whether you are non-exploitatively employed, whether it is possible for a trained professional to go in without excessive risk, whether you are sufficiently trained, and so on. Any of these facts could be cited as a reason in an appropriate conversational context. But there must be a total set of facts in virtue of which the cited fact, whatever it is, can be said to be a reason. In general, there must be sets of facts that constitute complete reasons if there are reasons at all.

Self-governance, even as self-determination, presupposes the ability to recognize complete reasons (though not necessarily to state them). A Kantian argument from *autonomy* goes even further. It presupposes that complete reasons take the form of pure normative truths, and that self-governing agents have *a priori*, first-person insight into these truths. We shall come back to this.

III. Wrongness and Blameworthiness

But let us now turn to moral obligation. Saying that x has a moral obligation to α is clearly not identical in meaning to saying either that x should* α or that x has a warrant to α. It can be true that you should* α, true that you have a warrant to α, but false that you have a moral obligation to α. The converse is less plain: can it be true that you have a moral obligation to α but false that you should* α or that you have a warrant to α? We shall answer that question.

To say that you have a moral obligation to α is to say that it would be morally wrong for you not to α. There is then a connection between moral wrongness and blameworthiness. However, this connection is not straightforward. I take it to be as follows:

(1) It is morally wrong for x to α if and only if, were x to α from the beliefs that are warranted in x's epistemic state, then either x would be blameworthy for α-ing or extenuating circumstances would apply to x's α-ing.

Obviously, this requires explanation. Extenuating circumstances remove or diminish blame that would otherwise have been appropriate. The reference to action from the actor's actually warranted beliefs arises from the self-governing character of moral agency and will be explained and defended in the next section. But first let us consider what 'blameworthy' means.

There is a causal meaning of 'blame' in which one can blame the dud calculator-batteries for a mistake in the bill, blame the weather for the train delay, etc. Saying that they are to blame is just saying that they are the proximate cause of the unfortunate result. It is not this causal sense of 'blame' that is in play in thesis (1). There is also a moral sense. One can say, for example, both that Mary was to blame for the misunderstanding, and that she should not actually be *blamed*—she was justifiably attending to something else that was happening. She was to blame in the causal sense, but not in the moral sense. Blame in (1) is to be understood in the moral sense.

Now when we talk of blaming someone in this sense, we are normally referring to a judgment, or an action that is the expression of that judgment. The judgment is a judgment about the appropriateness of a sentiment—the feeling or sentiment of blame. To judge that someone is morally blameworthy is to judge that the blame-feeling toward them is reason-supported, that there is sufficient reason for it, whether or not one actually feels it. The act of blaming is the act of expressing that judgment. For convenience, however, I am going to use the term 'blame' to refer directly to the feeling, not to the judgment or the act. Thus, in (1), 'blameworthy' means 'blame-feeling-worthy': there is sufficient reason for the sentiment of blame.

It may happen, for a variety of reasons, that though the blame-feeling is reason-supported and the judgment that it is is warranted, it should not be expressed. It may be counterproductive to do so, for example, in getting someone to change their ways. It is thus important to keep clear the distinction between the sentiment and the act of blame. It is also important in other, more theoretical ways. When John Stuart Mill gives his well-known 'blameworthiness' definition of moral wrongness in chapter 5 of *Utilitarianism*,[3] it is unfortunately not clear whether he is concerning himself with the sentiment or the act of blame. However, inasmuch as he commits himself, in theory at least, to assessing the appropriateness of blame by utilitarian standards, he must be interpreted as referring to the *act* of blame. For utilitarianism is a view about practical reasons, reasons for actions, not about evaluative reasons, reasons for feeling. Insofar as some utilitarians elide this point, they do so because they do not really believe in evaluative reasons, or they assimilate them to practical reasons. In reality, however, when we assess whether the *sentiment* of

---

[3] John Stuart Mill, *Collected Works* (London: Routledge, 1963–91), vol. X, 246.

blame is reason-supported in a particular case, we are not considering the expediency of the *act* of blame. Properly moral judgment is, rather, a special case of our general evaluative capacity to assess reasons for feelings as such. In that respect, the view proposed here is more like Adam Smith's than like Mill's, in that Smith takes the "propriety" of feelings in general to be determined by their objects, not by the utility of the actions they dispose agents to take.[4] This divergence makes a very big difference.

Granted these elucidations, I claim that (1) is true *a priori*. Can it in that case serve as a *definition* of 'morally wrong'? There is a "cart and horse" objection to any proposed definition of moral wrongness in terms of the blame-feeling. Thesis (1), it may be granted, is an *a priori* truth; but it is so by definition of 'blame,' not by definition of 'morally wrong.' Blame in the moral sense is defined as that sentiment which there is reason to feel toward something that is morally wrong. So (1) is true by definition, but by definition of 'blame.' 'Morally wrong' is semantically primitive in the sense that it is indefinable.

I think this makes a correct point about, so to speak, the lexicon of English. But I don't think it shows that the concept of the morally wrong cannot be characterized in terms of the concept of an evaluative reason for blame. We can elucidate a concept by saying what is required for possession of the concept, rather than by the semantic route of explicit definition within the existing resources of a language. What you distinctively need, to have the concept of moral wrongness, is sensitivity to reasons for the blame-sentiment.

On this approach, however, we cannot characterize blame as 'that sentiment which there is reason to feel toward something that is morally wrong.' To be fruitful, this approach must characterize the blame-sentiment without appealing to the notion of moral wrongness. How to do this?

In general, we characterize emotions by the objects that arouse them and the actions which they prompt. We may indicate the objects by showing exemplary cases, and where possible, by stating some general condition on the objects. Thus, we could individuate the blame-sentiment by saying that it is what one is disposed to feel toward an agent in a variety of sufficiently well-described cases—for example, toward someone who steals, who acts cruelly, who shows gross ingratitude. Furthermore, a general condition will be important: the object of the blame-sentiment must be something which the agent had warranted reason not to do, and which the agent could have refrained from doing. (I discuss this further in Section IV.) This is, of course, not sufficient: the nature of the reasons matters. It is the fact that the agent did the thing, despite *those* reasons, reasons of kinds which we exemplify by giving examples, that gives sufficient reason for responding with the sentiment of blame.

---

[4] Adam Smith, *The Theory of Moral Sentiments* (Indianapolis, IN: Liberty Fund, 1984), Part I, section 1, chapter iii, and Part II.

We can also approach the blame-sentiment from another direction—
from the characteristic action which it prompts.

Blame does not prompt an agent to attack (as anger does), or to flee (as
fear does). It is not resentment, because resentment is specifically occa-
sioned by what is taken as injury to oneself. Gratitude and resentment are
agent-relative feelings, constituting the realm of benefits and torts, whereas
the blame-sentiment is agent-neutral and constitutes the realm of right
and wrong. If there is reason for anyone to feel it toward the object, there
is reason for everyone to feel it. Its characteristic behavioral quality is a
chilliness or a shrinking away or withdrawal, rather than aggression. This
is particularly clear in one's own case, in the experience of self-blame or
guilt—which could hardly be resentment directed against oneself, but is
indeed a shrinking from oneself. (The resentment view must make guilt
something different from blame: guilt might be viewed as fear of the
resentment and retaliation of others, for example.)

Blame disposes agents toward *withdrawal of recognition.*[5] To withdraw,
withhold, or refuse recognition is to cut off relations or refuse to enter into
them, to exclude, in however partial and temporary a way; in more extreme
cases, it leads to ostracism, casting out, outlawing. Like fear, blame disposes one to create distance between oneself and the object; but the difference is that the disposition of fear is to flee, whereas the disposition of
blame is to cut off or exclude. Guilt, or self-blame, is the withdrawal of
recognition from oneself. (Hence, "I couldn't live with myself if I did
that.") And it is important that recognition can be restored through a
process of reconciliation that typically involves remorse, repentance, and
forgiveness.

This sketch of the blame-sentiment plainly needs to be filled in. But let
us assume that a fuller account can fix the sentiment clearly enough to
allow the non-question-begging introduction of a term that denotes it: 'β'.
The referent of 'β' is the sentiment that (i) is the appropriate, reason-
supported response to certain paradigms of belief and action, and (ii)
prompts a characteristic type of action, namely, withdrawal of recognition. We then have the following definition:

(1ᵃ) It is morally wrong for x to α = were x to α from the beliefs that
are warranted in x's epistemic state, and without any extenuat-
ing circumstances, there would be sufficient reason to feel sentiment β toward x for α-ing.

Thesis (1) should now be understood in the sense of (1ᵃ). Furthermore,
this definition can be widened into a "sentimentalist" account of moral

[5] Compare T. M. Scanlon, *Moral Dimensions: Permissibility, Meaning, Blame* (Cambridge,
MA: Belknap Press of Harvard University Press, 2008), chap. 4.

concepts in general, that is, a definition in terms of evaluative reasons, reasons for feeling.[6]

IV. MORALITY, BLAME, AND PRACTICAL REASONS

If I blame someone for doing something, I must think he had a reason not to do it. That, though not sufficient, is necessary: if you show that he had no reason not to act as he did, you refute the charge of blameworthiness. There can be no reason to blame someone who *had no reason not to do* what he did.

This is true, but in what sense? As noted in Section II, talk of the reasons a person has is ambiguous. In blaming someone, I am not directly concerned with his warranted reasons; I am concerned with the reasons there would be for him if his factual beliefs were true. Let us call these the agent's belief-relative reasons.[7] Belief-relative reasons are not reasons in either the primitive sense or the warranted sense.

Blame does not follow reasons as such. Suppose you have just inadvertently taken poison. There is reason to ring for an ambulance. But I am not blameworthy for failing to call an ambulance if I have no warranted reason to believe that you have taken poison, and thus fail to believe that you have.

Nor, however, does blame follow warranted reasons. Suppose that I have warrant to believe that you have just swallowed poison, but, failing to recognize that warrant, I fail to believe that you have, and do nothing. In this case, I am not blameworthy unless I could have been expected to recognize that warrant for belief. If my failure to recognize the warrant is negligent, then I may be blameworthy; the blame attaches to the failure to recognize the warrant, not to the failure to help you. Note that this failure is still practical: it is a failure to think carefully enough, for example, about what was in that packet, and that is a failure to do something: "you didn't think." If, however, in the circumstances I could *not* have been expected to recognize the warrant—there was no negligent failure to think—then I am not blameworthy.

In contrast, suppose that I believe, though without warrant, that you have taken poison, and I do nothing. Am I blameworthy? Yes. We could quite naturally say that given that belief, I had reason to call an ambulance, and here the sense of 'had reason' is the belief-relative sense mentioned above: there would have been reason for me to call an ambulance if my beliefs were true.

---

[6] I argue that this is so in my book *The Domain of Reasons* (Oxford: Oxford University Press, forthcoming). The themes of this essay will be developed more fully there.
[7] Note the restriction to factual beliefs. Purely normative beliefs that are false can sometimes excuse or remove a person from blame; however, in the following examples, I am abstracting from such issues.

Next, suppose you administer a drug to a patient, and given your epistemic state, there is warrant for you to think it is a cure. But in fact you don't believe that; you *unwarrantedly* believe it to be a poison.[8] You took yourself to be poisoning the patient; in fact, you cured him. Let us further suppose that other facts that you believe to obtain would not, if they did obtain, give you sufficient reason to poison the patient (for example, you do not believe him to be Hitler, etc.). Are you blameworthy? You are, just because you believed yourself to be poisoning the patient. So either that was what you intended to do, or you didn't care that that would be (as you thought) the effect of your action. Either way, you are blameworthy; yet there was no *warranted* reason for you not to administer the drug. Because blame follows the beliefs under which you acted, it follows neither the reasons there were for you, nor the warranted reasons there were for you, but your belief-relative reasons. In this case, there was belief-relative reason for you not to administer the drug.

Thus we have:

(2) If your α-ing is blameworthy, then if your factual beliefs were true, there would be reason for you not to α.

This feature of blame, its connection to your belief-relative reasons, is inherent in the sentiment itself: one grasps it in understanding the sentiment of blame and thus understanding what can constitute an intelligible object of the sentiment. It makes no sense, lacks reason, to blame people for doing what they had no belief-relative reason not to do (though they may be blameworthy for having the beliefs they have). This is a point about the immanent rationality of feelings: it makes no sense to blame in such cases, in the way that it makes no sense, lacks reason, to resent a good turn without in any way thinking it to be maliciously meant, patronizing, etc. Someone who resents a good turn has to read malice or slight into the other's action, and similarly, someone who feels the sentiment of blame toward the other for what he did must read some belief-relative reason for not acting into the other's state of belief, or some epistemic negligence ("He knew, *really*"; "He *should* have realized"; etc.).

So far, we have been considering blameworthiness, not moral wrongness. Blame connects to belief-relative reasons; thesis (1), however, connects moral wrongness to *warranted* beliefs about the facts.

I submit that the actual beliefs from which an action was done are relevant to its blameworthiness but not, in general, to its moral permissibility or wrongness.[9] Say you administer the drug when there is actually

---

[8] The example is adapted from an unpublished discussion of these issues by Derek Parfit, which I have found very helpful.

[9] If I believe that an action is morally wrong, it does not follow that it is. But, depending on my actual factual and normative beliefs, it may be blameworthy on my part to do it, even

warrant, given your epistemic state, for you to believe that it will cure the patient; but you fail to recognize that warrant and, in fact, give it to him from the *unwarranted* belief that it will poison him, with the intention of poisoning him. In that case, your action is blameworthy (absent extenuation), but according to thesis (1) it is *not* morally wrong. Had your belief been warranted, you would have been doing something morally wrong. In fact, it was not warranted, so although you acted with a blameworthy intention, the action itself was not morally wrong. That remains the case even if, despite the fact that you have warrant to believe the drug will cure the patient, the drug actually kills him. So you intended to kill him, and you killed him: even so—though you are much to blame for what you did—what you did, given your epistemic state, was not morally wrong. Given what you had warrant to believe, it was actually the morally right thing to do.[10]

Moral wrongness turns neither on the agent's actual beliefs, nor on the facts, but on the beliefs warranted in the agent's epistemic state. Although blame, in contrast, is primarily concerned with the actual beliefs under which you acted, there is nonetheless a connection between blameworthiness and warranted reasons, as follows:

(3) If, were x to α from the beliefs that are warranted in x's epistemic state, either x would be blameworthy for α-ing or extenuating circumstances would apply to x's α-ing, then x has warranted reason not to α.

Suppose, first, that x would be blameworthy for α-ing. Then, by thesis (2), x's factual beliefs must be such that, if they are true, there is reason for x not to α. Now suppose those factual beliefs that x has are warranted; then x has warranted reason not to α. We get to this conclusion from the self-determining nature of moral agency: if some facts would constitute a reason for a self-determining agent x not to α, then x can tell by reflection alone that they would. Thus, if he is warranted in believing that those facts obtain, he has warrant to believe that there is reason for him not to α; that is, he has a warranted reason not to α.

Suppose, secondly, that extenuating circumstances apply to x's α-ing. Extenuation exists when an action that would normally be blameworthy is excusable. It may be excusable *either* because you excusably failed to become aware of warranted reasons not to do the action *or* through some excusable failure to act on those reasons, even though you were aware of them (for example, the understandable emotional turmoil you were in).

---

if it is not morally wrong. Furthermore, conscientious conviction can itself affect moral permissibility.

[10] I am grateful to David Copp for very helpful discussion of this point (about which we disagree).

These alternatives cover large categories. The first, in particular, may involve something as simple as the fact that there was a great need for haste and you excusably failed to consider a possible consequence, or something as complex and hard to evaluate as the fact that in the society in which you live, you could not be expected to grasp the reasons not to do what you did. But given that this is the overall shape of extenuation, to say that extenuating circumstances apply to a person's action implies that there *was* warranted reason for that person not to do the action. Thus, we arrive at (3).

From (1) and (3), we conclude:

(4) If it is morally wrong for x to α, then x has warranted reason not to α.

I suggest, further, that (3) can be strengthened. Can there be reason to blame a person who, acting from warranted beliefs about the facts, does what he had warrant to do? Surely not. You cannot be blameworthy for doing what you had sufficient reason to do because you correctly saw that you had sufficient reason to do it: an action done from warrant cannot be blameworthy. This gives us:

(5) If, were x to α from warranted factual beliefs, either x would be blameworthy for α-ing or extenuating circumstances would apply to x's α-ing, then x has no warrant to α.

Thesis (5) seems to me to arise, again, from the nature of the blame-sentiment; like thesis (2), it is a principle internal to the sentiment of blame, a principle governing the intelligibility of that sentiment. How could there be reason to blame you for acting from warrant—doing what you had most reason to do because it *was* what you had most reason to do? What is there for blame to latch onto? You could *reasonably* be blamed only if you could and should have believed that there was more reason for you to do something else, that is, that there was warrant not to do what you did. So, for example, suppose it were true that you always have sufficient reason to do what you warrantedly believe is best for you—as egoism says. Then it could not be *blameworthy* for you to do that.

By a similar argument to the one just given, thesis (5) yields:

(6) If it is morally wrong for x to α, then x has no warrant to α.

Since it is morally obligatory not to α if and only if it is morally wrong to α, we can conclude from (4):

(7) If it is morally obligatory for x not to α, then x has warranted reason not to α.

Likewise, we can conclude from (6):

(8) If it is morally obligatory for x not to α, then x has no warrant to α.

Can we further deduce that x has warrant not to α? If (acting from warranted factual beliefs) you were either blameworthy for α-ing or extenuation applied, you must have had warranted sufficient reason to believe that there was sufficient reason not to α.[11] That is, you must have had warrant not to α. Thus, as well as (8), we have:

(9) If it is morally obligatory for x not to α, then x has warrant not to α.

Thesis (8) and thesis (9), taken together, say that moral obligation is *categorical*, in the sense of being inescapable and supreme.[12] That is, if you have a moral obligation to do something (not to omit doing it), then you have warranted sufficient reason to do that and no other thing. This conclusion is striking: not merely is the categoricity of morality *consistent* with a sentimentalist account of moral concepts in terms of reasons to blame—it actually follows from it. The key to the categoricity of morality lies in the hermeneutics of the blame-sentiment.[13]

My account of moral obligation relativizes it to epistemic states. We can confirm the account, in the first place, by examples. There is the example already mentioned: if I have warrant to believe that you have unwittingly taken poison, then I have a moral obligation to ring for the ambulance. That is so, even if in fact you have not taken poison.[14] In contrast, if you have unwittingly taken poison, but I have no warranted reason to believe this, then I have no moral obligation to ring for an ambulance: I do not act morally wrongly if I do not do so.

Consider now the case of the intended poisoning that cures the patient. Here moral wrongness and blameworthiness intelligibly diverge. Suppose the agent had warrant to believe that administering the drug would

---

[11] That is, not just *insufficient* reason to believe that there was sufficient reason to α (which would also entail absence of warrant to α).

[12] This is David Brink's terminology. See David O. Brink, "Kantian Rationalism: Inescapability, Authority, and Supremacy," in Garrett Cullity and Berys Gaut, eds., *Ethics and Practical Reason* (Oxford: Oxford University Press, 1997).

[13] Moral obligation is categorical, but that is not to say that it is reason-constituting. If you have a moral obligation to α, you have warrant to α; but it is not the fact that you have a moral obligation to α that constitutes that warrant. The moral obligation exists *in virtue of the nature of the warrant*. It is because of the kind of reasons there are for doing the thing that it is morally obligatory to do it. Those reasons are what make it morally obligatory—moral obligation supervenes on them: that is, knowingly to ignore them merits blame.

[14] It is true that, if you do not die, people would not in practice feel the sentiment of blame as strongly as if you had. That is a significant point; however, I think the general view would still be that I had a moral obligation to act and was blameworthy not to have acted.

cure the patient; in that case, I argued, it was not morally wrong to administer it. That conclusion remains true even if the agent nonetheless *unwarrantedly* believed that the drug would poison the patient and was thus blameworthy for administering it, and even if, in fact, the drug did kill the patient. Symmetrically, if the agent had warrant to believe that the drug would poison the patient, it was morally wrong to administer it, even if the agent unwarrantedly believed that the drug would cure the patient and in fact it did. In the first case, we have blameworthiness without moral wrongdoing; in the second, we have blameless wrongdoing.

It is true that if you are offering me moral advice, you might well say to me, "It would be morally wrong to do that," and then mention some facts—which I could not otherwise have known—that (as we would naturally say) *make* it morally wrong. Thus, it seems that what makes an action morally wrong is the facts, not the agent's warranted beliefs about the facts.

But we need to consider the requirements of advice. When I ask for advice about what I ought to do, I *may* be asking what I am warranted in doing in my actual epistemic state. This is so, for example, if I know that you and I are in the same epistemic state. Or if I am in a group of people who share an epistemic state, then my question "What ought we to do?" is the question "What are we *warranted* in doing?" But if I ask someone who knows more, then I am asking for advice in the light of what *he* knows. Thus, in Allan Gibbard's forest example, if I ask a forester what we ought to do to get out of the forest, I ask because I hope he knows the best way. If he does, then it would be wholly inappropriate for him to tell me to take a straight line and stick to it, even though that is what I am currently warranted in doing in my present state of ignorance.[15] He should be helping me by advising me in the light of what he knows, not what I know. Exactly the same applies if your advice is about the moral aspects of my decision. You should be advising me about those aspects in the light of what *you* know, not what I know.

Speaking on the basis of what he knows, the forester might simply say, "This is the best way out," without telling me why. In telling me that, he would not be implying that I already had a warrant for thinking this is the best way out. But at this point a contrast emerges. What if you said, "This is what you have a moral obligation to do," without telling me why? Strictly speaking, that would be true only if I *already* had a warrant for thinking I had that moral obligation. If you were basing your advice on facts I did not know, you should have made that clear.

Suppose, however, that for one reason or another, confidentiality perhaps, you are unable to tell me the relevant facts. What you could still say is, "If you knew the relevant facts, you would have such and such a moral obligation." Next, suppose I am warranted in thinking that you are reli-

---

[15] As Gibbard points out (*Wise Choices, Apt Feelings*, 19).

able. In general, agents have a moral obligation to do that which someone they know to be reliable assures them they would have a moral obligation to do if they knew the facts. The obligation arises because, in virtue of what the reliable person has said, they have sufficient reason to believe that the facts are such as to constitute sufficient reason to do the thing—a reason, moreover, that it would be blameworthy to ignore if they knew what it was. It is surely blameworthy not to act on such a warrant.

For these reasons, it is natural to formulate moral principles in terms of the facts: "If a person has taken poison, you ought to call an ambulance," not "If you have sufficient reason to believe that a person has taken poison, you ought to call an ambulance." When we formulate principles in this way, we are spelling out the reasons which, if you know of them, it is blameworthy on your part to ignore. It is in this sense that moral wrongness supervenes on the facts.[16]

V. Morality, Self-Determination, Autonomy

A survey of our judgments about moral obligation and blame seems to me to tell in favor of the foregoing account of moral obligation. But there is a more general consideration. Moral obligations, like rational requirements, follow warranted beliefs, because we must be able to *act from* them. People must be able to determine reflectively what moral obligations they have in a concrete situation, just as they must be able to determine reflectively what specific warrants they have. Similarly, the connection between failure to comply with a moral obligation and moral criticizability is like that between failure to comply with a warrant and rational criticizability. In both cases, we need to know the actor's warrants, actual beliefs, and excuses. We can ask what a person was either *rationally* or *morally* required to do given the factual beliefs he actually held, and we can ask whether he had warrant for his factual beliefs. We can also ask whether he was rationally or morally required, in the circumstances, to pay more attention than he did to establishing warrants. In short, the notions of moral obligation and rational requirement occupy the same role-position in the pattern of normative assessment.

As I said at the outset, however, we should distinguish between self-determination and autonomy proper. Self-determination consists in recognizing what one has sufficient reason to do relative to one's acceptance of certain normative tenets, and acting from that recognition. I am self-

---

[16] Final elucidation: I have been speaking about moral obligations, not about rights and the corresponding duties of right. The latter should be distinguished from moral obligations. Suppose you are a deceased person's executor, and that person has left a last will. You don't know that: the will is lost but still exists. The will leaves the property to X. In that case, X has a right to the property and you have a duty of right to execute the property in accordance with the will. But you don't have a moral obligation to do so, because you don't know of the will. (You may have a moral obligation to make a search, etc.)

determining if I determine myself by normative tenets which I personally accept, and do not merely "know about" (e.g., as being generally accepted, or dangerous to ignore, etc.). I am self-determining even if I accept those tenets themselves on authority, on trust, or by my own *fiat*, and whether or not I have personal insight into their truth (indeed, even if they cannot be said to *be* true or false). I can determine myself, act from my own assessment of reasons, so long as I am able to audit my epistemic state, determine what reasons I have in the light of my acceptance of certain normative propositions or commitments, and act from those reasons. The same distinction applies in the moral case. I am morally self-determining if I am able to audit my epistemic state, determine the concrete moral obligations I have in the light of my acceptance of certain moral tenets, and act from those obligations. I can have this ability even if I have no personal insight into moral truths, and even if there are no moral truths. What is required for self-determining moral agency is simply that I am able to audit, from within my epistemic state, what specific moral obligations I have in a concrete situation—relative to moral tenets I personally accept.

It is inherent to the very notion of moral agency—with its dimensions of answerability and susceptibility to blame—that it is at least self-determining agency. It follows that the notion of self-determination is present wherever moral concepts are found. In contrast, the idea of moral *autonomy* is stronger. Moral autonomy is more than self-determination; it is self-determination grounded in personal moral insight, that is, in the ability to recognize, by one's own lights, true moral propositions as true. The same can be said of rational autonomy; it is self-determination grounded in personal insight into reason relations as such, that is, the ability to recognize personally the truth of true propositions about reasons.

We have weaker or stronger notions of rational and moral agency, depending on whether we think of these forms of agency as merely self-determining or as requiring full autonomy. The stronger notion, that of autonomy, clearly assumes that normative tenets are indeed *propositions*, whose truth or falsity is knowable by personal insight. I will call the principle of moral or rational insight that is assumed in this notion of autonomy, the (moral or rational) *Insight Principle*. For the moral case, it can be stated as follows:

Insight Principle: Moral agents can know their moral obligations (in all specific, concrete situations) by means of their own insight into them.

For rational autonomy, exactly the same can be said, substituting "rational" for "moral," and "warrants" for "moral obligations." Autonomy in both cases can be a matter of degree, depending on how much insight actors have, and how much control over their acts.

Rational autonomy can furthermore be understood broadly or narrowly. The broad understanding takes rational autonomy to include a grasp of evaluative reason relations. The narrow understanding takes it to include only epistemic and practical reason relations. Since rational autonomy consists (in the ideal case) of first-person insight into *all* reason relations, if we accept that there are evaluative reasons we must understand it in the broad way. Moral autonomy is then a special case of rational autonomy; it calls on broad, not narrow, rationality. It is insight into reason relations, but the reason relations involved include evaluative reason relations. So I agree with Kant that moral autonomy is rational agency. But because Kant did not accept that there are evaluative reasons at all, the difference between the picture of morality sketched here and Kant's picture of it is great.

However, this difference, albeit great, is independent of Kant's master thesis, that moral agency requires autonomy. That could be true on either picture of morality. And this thesis, the thesis that human beings are moral agents only because they are autonomous, has fundamentally shaped modern ethical and political ideas. Particularly influential is an *egalitarianism of autonomy*, according to which all human beings are equally autonomous; and this is especially held to apply to *moral* autonomy. Nothing in the ethical legacy of Kant and Rousseau is more influential than this: the idea that what sets all human beings apart is their equal capacity for moral agency, and that their equal status and dignity as ends in themselves is founded on that capacity.

Kant's moral philosophy brings this idea into unprecedentedly sharp focus. Equal capacity for autonomy is not a question of equal technical or computational skills, or equal experience. What Kant asserts is the equal *normative insight* of all humans, and on that basis their equal positive freedom. This proudly humanist doctrine is protected by Kant's transcendentalism about rational agency. Human beings are set apart from nature by this power. In principle, it seems, Kant's doctrine is that every rational being, through its own inherent spontaneity—through the causality of freedom—has insight into all pure reason relations. Quite clearly, however, what especially matters to Kant is an egalitarianism of pure *moral* insight. It drives Kant's insistence that morality is accessible to everyone, that arriving personally at a correct moral judgment is open to the simplest human being. Every human being merits absolute respect, because every human being has absolute moral insight.

Shorn of the transcendental backing Kant provides for it, however, egalitarianism about moral autonomy is an empirical thesis (though it also assumes a cognitivist moral epistemology). It is a much stronger thesis than the claim that moral agents must be self-determining. It is true that reason relations of any kind can only be known, in the first instance, by personal insight. However, that does not entail that everyone must know them in that way. It may be that some agents, perhaps many, can know, or truly believe, or just more-or-less wholeheartedly endorse reason relations, only through faith, or trust, or on authority, or from a desire to be at one with others. While the very idea of moral agency requires self-determination, it is not obvious that it requires autonomy.

If the capacity for moral insight varies, we are left with three possibilities. The first is to say that the Insight Principle does not apply to everyone, because not everyone is fully autonomous in the way Kant envisaged; people vary in their degree of moral insight. Moral norms, however, *do* apply to everyone; but some people must come to accept them in a less than fully insightful way. Those people are self-determining, but they are not autonomous.

This is a view that has been taken for granted in many societies at many times. The notion that God or the gods tell us the moral law is a version of it. The gods usually have authoritative priestly interpreters; however, if this is to be morality rather than mere command, there must be a spontaneous disposition to accept the moral law implanted in people's hearts. But today even this degree of hierarchy sticks in many people's gullets. There are then two alternative options. Of these, the first, historically very important over the last century or so, subverts the notion of autonomy from within. From the egalitarianism of autonomy it retains only the negative claim that no one is better placed to judge of fundamental normative claims than anyone else is. This, it says, is because we cannot justify the degree of objectivity in moral judgment that talk of greater or less moral insight assumes. This view agrees that your moral obligations are those given by your own judgment of conscience; but it does not claim that conscience is a faculty of knowledge. *Authenticity* of acceptance still matters, but not because authentic as against inauthentic acceptance delivers moral truth. Instead, authenticity, understood as deciding sincerely or "authentically" for oneself as against being led by others, becomes a peculiar, legitimacy-conferring, modern virtue of the person, though bereft of any epistemological foundation. We "respect" the authentic person's moral judgment not because it is "right" but because it is *his* sincere judgment. This is still a strong ideal of self-governance, but it drops autonomy and with it moral objectivity.

The second alternative option preserves autonomy, the Insight Principle, and the unity and objectivity of morality. But it holds that those who lack insight into some moral norm do not have the moral obligations associated with that norm. For—contraposing the Insight Principle—if they cannot tell for themselves that they have a certain moral obligation, then they do not have it. In a specious sense, this point preserves a thesis of equal autonomy: everyone is equally capable of recognizing what reasons and moral obligations there are *for him*. However, not everyone is equally capable of telling what reasons and moral obligations there would be for him if only he were capable of the necessary insight: in that more obvious sense, not everyone is equally autonomous. Furthermore, on this view, not everyone has the same moral obligations. On this view, the standards of moral obligation are higher for the more insightful (and thus more autonomous) than for the less insightful. Thus, while this view preserves autonomy and moral objectivity, it gives up egalitarianism about autonomy: it is the standpoint of moral autonomy *without* egalitarianism.

We can trace the implications of this standpoint for modern moral assumptions further, by bringing together the theses discussed in this and the previous section: the Insight Principle and the categoricity of morality.

VI. AUTONOMY AND THE INSIGHT PRINCIPLE

Morality is linked to reasons for action by the crucial implications stated in thesis (7) and thesis (9) in Section IV. Those implications can be contraposed. If the agent has no warranted reason not to α, then it is not morally wrong for him to α. Thus, a substantive theory of practical reasons can shape one's views of moral obligation. This obviously applies, for example, to egoistic and instrumentalist theories of practical reasons.[17]

A distinctive theory of practical reasons is also a main source of Bernard Williams's critique of morality—as he notes, for example, in the following passage:

> Blame rests, in part, on a fiction; the idea that ethical reasons, in particular the special kind of ethical reasons that are obligations, must, really, be available to the blamed agent. . . . *He ought to have done it,* as moral blame uses that phrase, implies *there was reason for him to have done it,* and this certainly intends more than the thought that we had a reason to want him to do it. It hopes to say, rather, that he had a reason to do it. But this may well be untrue: it was not in fact a reason for him, or at least not enough of a reason. Under this fiction, a continuous attempt is made to recruit people into a deliberative community that shares ethical reasons. . . . But the device [i.e., the "fiction"] can do this only because it is understood not as a device, but as connected with justification and with reasons that the agent might have had; and it can be understood in this way only because, much of the time, it is indeed connected with those things.[18]

In saying "*He ought to have done it,* as moral blame uses that phrase, implies *there was reason for him to have done it,*" Williams is assenting to

---

[17] Egoism holds that what there is reason for you to do wholly depends on what promotes your own good. Instrumentalism holds that what there is reason for you to do wholly depends on the objectives you actually have.

[18] Bernard Williams, "How Free Does the Will Need to Be?" in Bernard Williams, *Making Sense of Humanity* (Cambridge: Cambridge University Press, 1995), 16; emphasis in the original.

something like thesis (7), or indeed thesis (9).[19] Thus, he accepts that the categoricity of the moral is part of our concept of the moral. He then adds his theory of internal reasons, which says that there is reason for x to α only if α-ing will serve a motive that x has, and he notes the contrapositive implication. If α-ing *doesn't* serve a motive that x has, it won't be true that x has a reason to α, and thus it won't be true that x ought to have α-ed, "as moral blame uses that phrase"; that is, it won't be true that x had a moral obligation to α. The fiction we are then led into, Williams says, is that of treating x as though he really *did* have the relevant reasons, the reasons which generate a moral obligation.

We are led into this fiction, he thinks, because we sometimes want to blame people who, by his internalist standards, simply do not have these ethical reasons. We want everyone equally to fall within the scope of blame. But suppose there are people who just don't have certain reasons which we regard as morally salient, because these reasons have no grounding in their motives. In that case, we fantasize that they do have these reasons after all; we imagine that there are reasons that apply to them irrespective of their motives.

I have argued elsewhere that Williams is mistaken in tying reasons to motives.[20] For present purposes, however, we can waive that issue; the relevant point is that an analogous internalist argument can be mounted from the Insight Principle alone. Even if what reasons there are for you does not depend on your *motives*, given the Insight Principle it still depends on something about you: on what reason relations you can grasp by personal insight. If moral agency is autonomous agency, what makes one a moral agent is the capacity to recognize morally salient reasons as such, in the first-person way. Williams presents a motivational form of internalism; the Insight Principle presents a cognitive form of internalism.[21]

Similar issues thus arise. According to the Insight Principle, if a moral agent has a moral obligation, he is capable of personal insight into that obligation. Conversely, then, if an agent cannot know by personal insight that he has an obligation, then he does not have it. Furthermore, to know in the first-person way that he is subject to a moral obligation, he must be able to recognize, in that way, not only the relevant practical reasons but also that failure to act in accord with them will give sufficient reason for guilt and others' blame. A lack of personal insight

---

[19] I say he is assenting to something like these, because he does not discuss whether moral obligation is connected to reasons as such or to warranted reasons.
[20] John Skorupski, "Internal Reasons and the Scope of Blame," in Alan Thomas, ed., *Bernard Williams* (Cambridge: Cambridge University Press, 2007), 73–103.
[21] Williams treats Kant's view as a "limiting case" of internalism (Williams, "Internal Reasons and the Obscurity of Blame," in Williams, *Making Sense of Humanity*, 44, note 3); see also Bernard Williams, "Replies," in J. E. J. Altham and Ross Harrison, eds., *World, Mind, and Ethics: Essays on the Ethical Philosophy of Bernard Williams* (Cambridge: Cambridge University Press, 1995), 220, note 3. I do not think it is quite right to treat Kant as a limiting case of *motivational* internalism, but he certainly is a *cognitive* internalist.

at either point will remove the agent from the scope of answerability and blame.

Thus, the Insight Principle has the implications for morality and answerability that interested Williams. If, as he suggests, our drive is to bring everyone within the scope of answerability, then we must either insist that people have reasons even if they have no insight into them, or insist that everyone has insight into reasons, at least the reasons involved in moral agency. The big difference is that the Insight Principle, unlike Williams's theory of internal reasons, is indisputably a major influence on modern morality, in the shape of characteristically modern doctrines of conscience. No modern theorist of morality as autonomy can set the Insight Principle aside.[22] So that leaves only the second option, that of insisting that everyone has equal, full insight into moral obligations and their underlying reasons.

I doubt whether commitment to equal moral autonomy is solely a result of the wish to make everyone equally answerable, that is, liable to blame. Equal moral autonomy is a modern ideal, closely associated with notions of equal worth, and thus with ethical foundations for liberal democracy that are both philosophically problematic and deeply held. That may explain the fierceness with which people cling to Kant, who surrounds these particular foundations with a formidable *a priori* defensive wall. There is the transcendental armor-plating of the causality of freedom, the idea that the Categorical Imperative can be deduced from autonomy, and the further idea that it provides a criterion of moral obligation which "the most common and unpractised understanding"[23] can apply without difficulty.

In reality, the capacity for moral insight is an empirical capacity. It calls—among other things—on emotional intelligence, the ability to judge evaluative reasons. There is no *a priori* guarantee that it is distributed equally. Nor is it, I have argued, a conceptual truth that moral agency requires a capacity for full first-person moral insight. What it requires is the capacity for self-determination.

How important is this? It is important in that it should shift our understanding of moral judgment and moral agency away from the Kantian model. Yet it need not shift it further, so to speak, than to Hegel's critique

---

[22] J. B. Schneewind, *The Invention of Autonomy* (Cambridge: Cambridge University Press, 1998), recounts how a command model of morality increasingly gave way to a model of morality as self-governance, with Kant's notion of autonomy as a culmination of the process. The striking subsequent history of autonomy remains to be told. (Schneewind takes it that autonomy is implicit in the notion of 'self-governance.' My use of 'self-governance' is somewhat different: self-determination is the basic kind of self-governance required for any moral or rational agency; autonomy is stronger. A *pure* command model would not be morality: it must combine with some notion of inner assent.)

[23] Immanuel Kant, *Critique of Practical Reason*, in Kant, *Practical Philosophy*, ed. and trans. Mary J. Gregor (Cambridge: Cambridge University Press, 1996), 169 (Akademie edition, 5:36).

of *Moralität* (by which he means the standpoint of abstract and individ-
ualist conscience, of which Hegel takes Kant's moral theory to be an
outstanding example) and Hegel's account of modern *Sittlichkeit* (the
broadly accepted moral convictions and practices of a society).[24]

Self-determination, as Hegel profoundly sees, requires the context of
moral community—*Sittlichkeit*. It remains true, however, that between
self-determination and autonomy lies not a chasm but a territory with no
clear-cut frontier. In particular, moral principles are not like positive law.
To determine what to do in accordance with positive law, or external
command, I need to know what that law is. Furthermore, it is an open
question whether I have reason to do what that law requires me to do.
Moral self-determination is not like that. I can know my moral obligations
by reflection on reason relations alone.

Thus, moral self-determination requires that I freely internalize reasons
as reasons—that I accept or assent to them *as* reasons and be capable of
acting on them. On Hegel's view, they should "not merely lay their claim
on" me "as external laws and precepts of authority to be obeyed, but have
their assent, recognition, or even justification in [my] heart, sentiment,
conscience, intelligence, etc."[25]

Moral agency requires at least this much "making them one's own."
Questions remain about the moral psychology of normative assent, about
what elements of thought and feeling ("heart, sentiment, conscience, intelligence") can be involved. We shall still need something like the Insight
Principle, but our way of answering these questions will determine how
we broaden it.

This, in turn, raises issues about the epistemology of moral judgment. Its epistemic bases are, on the one hand, one's own spontaneous
dispositions of feeling and will, and, on the other, recognition of and
critical response to the spontaneous dispositions of others. This involves
the influence of others, which works through much more than explicit
discussion, let alone argument. Still, explicit discussion, including argument, is essential for solid normative knowledge. If there is to be knowledge of reason relations, it must come from pure insight into reason
relations on the part of at least some people. However, that does not
imply a one-way transmission from these knowers to others. Normative knowledge is inherently social. It rests on discussion with others
as well as personal spontaneity—discussion from which no voice is
excluded. The point applies to all normative knowledge, but especially
to moral knowledge, because of its sentimental and practical bases. The
resulting picture of *Sittlichkeit*, moral life, actually provides (to my mind)
a better foundation for democratic ideals than a picture of ourselves as

---

[24] Hegel's most extended discussion of this contrast is to be found in his *Elements of the
Philosophy of Right* (1821). For commentary, see (for example) Allen W. Wood, *Hegel's Ethical
Thought* (Cambridge: Cambridge University Press, 1990).
[25] G. W. F. Hegel, *Encyclopedia of the Philosophical Sciences* (1817), sec. 503.

perfectly autonomous knowers, each equipped with access to a fail-safe procedure for deducing moral conclusions, which we operate in the solitude of conscience.[26]

VII. Conclusion

As I said at the beginning, two deep features of moral judgment should guide our discussion of morality: the first is that moral judgment is rooted in the rationality of the feelings; the second is that moral agency is self-governing agency.

What I hope to have shown is that moral judgment is judgment about evaluative reasons, specifically about reasons to blame. The sentiment of blame can be characterized in a noncircular way by its objects and practical dispositions. Furthermore, it is by virtue of its object (failure to respond to certain reasons highlighted by the sentiment itself) that blame gives rise to the categoricity of moral obligation.

Because moral agency is self-determining agency, I must be able to tell, by reflection on my actual epistemic state, what my moral obligations are, just as I must be able to tell what my warrants are. So moral obligation, like warrant, is relative to epistemic states. As to self-governance, it can be less than autonomy but must be more than authenticity. Yet these latter conceptions of moral agency have a strong influence on our ethical culture. A more realistic conception of self-determining moral agency is something that we greatly need.

Finally, though I have not developed this argument, I believe that the bases of normative knowledge involve an interplay between individual spontaneity and communal discussion: in the case of morality, between individual conscience and the moral sentiments underlying common moral sense. Moral reflection is the "common pursuit of true judgment," and self-governance, however individually insightful, can only count as knowledge, and work properly, within the context of that common pursuit.

Moral Philosophy, University of St. Andrews

---

[26] It would be a one-sided caricature to say that Kant himself propounded this picture, since there is much in his ethics taken as a whole that goes against it. Yet it is also true that Kantian ethics has historically both played to and entrenched the picture.

MAKING ROOM FOR OPTIONS: MORAL REASONS, IMPERFECT DUTIES, AND CHOICE*

By Patricia Greenspan

I. Introduction

The notion of an imperfect obligation or duty, which contemporary moral philosophy takes from Kantian ethics, affords a way of mitigating morality's demands while recognizing moral obligation as "binding" or inescapable, in Kant's terms: something an agent cannot get out of just by appealing to ends or priorities of her own. A perfect duty, as Kant puts it, allows no exception in the interest of inclination.[1] It tells us precisely what we must do, with no option of putting it off until some other occasion. By contrast, an imperfect duty leaves open crucial features of the required act. Understood in this way, as duties of indeterminate content, imperfect duties such as the charitable duty to aid those in need leave leeway for personal choice. We get to choose whom to aid and when and how much. We may be obligated to meet a certain threshold, but we will be exceeding what is required of us if we go beyond that. Imperfect duties therefore allow us authority to shape our own lives, balancing concern for others with our own particular projects and concerns. But imperfect duties interest me, in the first instance, in connection with practical reasons.

The term "practical" here just means "having to do with action." Reasons are understood as facts, not as mental states, and practical reasons are facts that count for or against action, in contrast to theoretical reasons, which concern belief. Similarly, "practical rationality" entails action in accordance with one's overall structure of practical reasons, as distinct from believing what one has reason to believe. The term "practical rationality" can be used for a property of agents, in which case it implies awareness of the relevant reasons, but it also sometimes refers to a system of norms for assessing action in light of reasons, analogous to morality but also including logical and instrumental considerations. On this latter

* Let me express my gratitude to my colleagues Samuel Kerstein and Christopher Morris, the students in my 2008 graduate seminar at the University of Maryland, an audience at the July 2008 meetings of the Australian Association for Philosophy, the other contributors to this volume, and Ellen Frankel Paul, for very helpful comments on earlier drafts of this essay.
[1] Immanuel Kant, *Groundwork for the Metaphysics of Morals* (1785), ed. Thomas E. Hill, Jr., trans. Arnulf Zweig (Oxford: Oxford University Press, 2002), esp. p. 222n. (Akademie edition, vol. 4: 421n.). Below I note some departures from Kant's account, along with other interpretations of imperfect obligation.

use, practical rationality requires, say, taking the means that are actually necessary to one's ends, not just the means one thinks are necessary. Since my concern in this essay is solely with practical reasons and rationality, I often omit the term "practical," taking it to be understood. I treat moral reasons as a subtype of practical reasons, which also include whatever reasons are entailed by pursuit of self-interest or by our particular personal projects or concerns. But the precise import of many of my central terms here—including "reasons," "rationality," and for that matter, "morality"—is the subject of ongoing philosophical debate, so these definitions should be taken merely as rough guides to my meaning in what follows.

Now, on what I take to be the common conception of practical reasons, implicit in much of the literature, they are essentially prima facie requirements of action, possibly overridden or undermined by opposing reasons, but otherwise constraining rational choice.[2] On this account, then, it would be irrational to take some reason as one's strongest and yet make no attempt to act on it. If I have a reason to aid a certain famine victim, say, then I am required to aid him, unless I have just as weighty reasons to aid other victims instead or to do something else with the same resources. A moral reason would yield a binding obligation, on this account, just insofar as it outweighs competitors.

However, in a case where there happens to be some best or most effective way of fulfilling an imperfect obligation, and our reason for a certain option counts as our strongest reason, what happens to our leeway for choice? I mean to be working from objective notions of obligation, and reasons, and of morality and rationality as systems of norms, according to which their content is independent of what the agent knows or is in a position to know. But in that case, when we supplement moral with instrumental reasons, or morality with rationality, there might seem to be particular victims we are required to aid, whether or not we can tell who they are. For surely we have a moral reason to aid any given victim, not just victims generally. So if we can best satisfy our imperfect obligation by aiding certain victims, then we really are required to aid them, in particular, after all.

I have a different interpretation of practical reasons that will let us retain our options for discharging an imperfect obligation, with obligation understood in terms of reasons, and without denying that we have a moral reason to aid each of the needy. I call this the "critical" conception

[2] This view emerges in Charles Larmore, "Reflection and Morality," elsewhere in this volume. Cf. also the "motivation requirement" put forth as a widely accepted starting-point in R. Jay Wallace, "Three Conceptions of Rational Agency," *Ethical Theory and Moral Practice* 2, no. 3 (1999): 217–42, at pp. 217–18; and the account of a similar view as granted by all parties to the current debate about reasons, in Garrett Cullity and Berys Gaut, "Introduction," in Cullity and Gaut, eds., *Ethics and Practical Reason* (Oxford: Clarendon Press, 1997), 1–27, at p. 3.

of practical reasons, or the normative function of practical reasons, since it understands a reason as normative just insofar as the reason offers or answers criticism of some act or other practical option.[3] An obligation or other practical requirement has to be based on criticism of alternatives to the required act, so that mere reasons in favor of action will not be enough to support a requirement, contrary to the common conception.

Elsewhere, in a complex argument whose key points will be explained more fully below (as they apply to imperfect obligation), I maintain that we are rationality permitted to *discount* reasons in many everyday cases: to set them aside, or ignore them, as influences on our choice.[4] We can discount their underlying criticism, for instance, by waiving our objections to a certain action, as when we set priorities for ourselves that emphasize some of our concerns over others. But the reasons that underlie moral obligations are binding on us insofar as they rest on criticism from the standpoints of other persons, which we lack the authority to discount unilaterally.

However, in cases of imperfect obligation, it might look as though we are entitled to discount certain moral reasons: those based on criticism from potential beneficiaries we choose to pass over. I want to argue that there is a better way of describing such cases, in terms of the critical conception, a way that distinguishes our specific moral reasons from the indeterminate critical reason underlying our imperfect obligation. I may have a reason to aid a particular famine victim, say, but if I have done or am going to do enough for others, I am not required to aid that victim. Even if my reason to aid him is stronger than any reasons I have for other ways of satisfying my obligation, but assuming that it does not count *against* those alternatives, my reason does not ground a practical requirement.

The general project from which this essay is drawn is an attempt to defend a conception of practical reasons that I think is better suited than the common conception to deontological morality: the approach to morality that takes "ought" and related notions of right (such as "duty" and "obligation") as basic moral concepts, rather than explaining them solely in terms of the promotion of good consequences or the expression of good

---

[3] Note that "critical," as I use the term, implies no reference to Kant's *Critiques;* cf. the notion of a "critical conception of practical reason," in Onora O'Neill, "Vindicating Reason," in Paul Guyer, ed., *A Cambridge Companion to Kant* (Cambridge: Cambridge University Press, 1992). My plural term "practical reasons" refers to particular considerations for or against action, whereas "practical reason" in the singular, without the indefinite article, refers to a faculty of the mind or a system of norms (sometimes capitalized as "Reason").

[4] See my "Practical Reasons and Moral 'Ought'," in Russ Schafer-Landau, ed., *Oxford Studies in Metaethics*, vol. 2 (Oxford: Oxford University Press, 2007), 172–94. "Discounting" is sometimes used more broadly, to cover any reduction in the weight assigned to a reason, on the model of the temporal "discount rate" for value, as in George Ainslie, *Picoeconomics: The Strategic Interaction of Successive Motivational States within the Person* (Cambridge: Cambridge University Press, 1992). As I use the term, discounting might be seen as the limiting case of this broader notion, with weight reduced to zero.

character ("virtue"). If the fact that something is good gives us a reason for doing what is needed to attain it, the common conception of practical reasons as prima facie requirements would seem to saddle us with a requirement to attain the maximum good. What I want to do in this essay is to show how the critical conception of practical reasons instead can serve to set limits on how much can be required of a particular moral agent.

Nonetheless, I understand the limits on moral obligation to be compatible with the assumption of some of our duties by the state, even though this effectively takes back some of the leeway for choice that morality grants us. In cases of global need such as famine relief, large-scale (and coercive) coordination may sometimes be needed to respond adequately. I will argue later (in Sections V and VI) that this should not be conflated with enforcing fulfillment of our individual obligations, though it does carry a cost in moral freedom. It removes some of the indeterminacy of our imperfect moral duty, at least to the extent of assigning particular contributions to individuals and pinning down the recipients of aid (even if not the recipients of any individual's contribution). For the moment, though, I want to ask how we can make sense of imperfect obligations in the first place in terms of practical reasons.

II. Pinpointing the Problem

Let me first backtrack a bit to bring out more fully the motivation for questioning the reasons behind imperfect obligations such as the duty to give aid. In general, explaining obligation in terms of practical reasons seems promising as a way of demystifying deontological ethics, the ethics of moral duty. It replaces talk of properties on the order of "intrinsic wrongness" with a notion that is clearly essential to our everyday understanding of action. Reasons of the sort that yield moral obligations can then be distinguished as "binding" by denying an agent the authority to set them aside. The distinctiveness of these reasons will thereby be explained not by appeal to metaphysics, but just by appeal to structural features of practical reasoning.

However, the notion of imperfect obligation is important to a common-sense deontological approach precisely as a limitation on morality's binding demands. We need only contribute a reasonable amount of aid to the needy, say—at some vaguely specified level, possibly rather high, but still leaving us leeway to choose when and to whom and how much we contribute, and hence how much we have left over to devote to the pursuit of our optional ends. This is in contrast to extreme versions of utilitarianism—and also to Kant's view—which would have us contribute as much as we can, compatibly with fulfilling other, equally serious practical demands.[5] We seem to have a moral reason, though, to aid any individual who needs aid. In a case where aiding a particular individual happens to be our most effective way of aiding the needy, if our reason to aid that person cannot just be set aside, what happens to our leeway for choice? Though we may not know or be able to determine whom we have most reason to aid, on an objective notion of reasons there may still be such a person—someone starving in a remote area, or perhaps a particular homeless person we pass on the street every day. (More likely, it is a group of people, but let me keep things simple.) Assuming that the suffering we would be alleviating if we acted on the reason is more significant than whatever we would be giving up by doing so, and assuming that our reason to aid that particular person counts as our strongest reason, we would seem to be required to aid him in particular. But this would defeat what I take to be the point of our imperfect obligation. Adding instrumental requirements to moral obligation seems to narrow our options here to one.

Of course, we can grant that it is not morality alone, but only morality in combination with instrumental rationality, that seems to require acting on our strongest moral reason in such cases. Morally speaking, we have further permissible options for fulfilling an imperfect obligation, so we would not be blameworthy for declining to take our most effective option, even when it is clear to us which option that is. But I take it that our common-sense view goes beyond this, to allow us multiple options for discharging our imperfect duties that count as morally *and* rationally permissible. We are not required, simpliciter, to give everything we can to famine relief (or whatever should turn out to be the most pressing charitable concern). Nor are we required to aid some particularly needy famine victim, or the one we can aid most effectively.

Before suggesting a way to get what we want here, let me pause briefly for some further terminological clarifications. There are different ways of interpreting imperfect obligation, some of which come up in my discussion later in this essay, but it should already be apparent that I am working from an interpretation in terms of indeterminate specification. I might add, though, that what is left to the agent's choice is whether or not to satisfy the obligation in a given instance—on a certain occasion, toward a certain person, to a certain degree—not just whether she should satisfy it in a certain way. After all, we can distinguish different ways of satisfying virtually any positive obligation: a borrowed book can be returned in

---

[5] For utilitarian arguments requiring maximal contribution to famine relief, see esp. Peter Singer, "Famine, Affluence, and Morality," *Philosophy and Public Affairs* 1, no. 1 (1972): 229–43; and Peter Unger, *Living High and Letting Die: Our Illusion of Innocence* (New York: Oxford University Press, 1992). Kant's insistence on doing as much as we can surfaces, e.g., in his application of the formula of humanity to the duty to aid those in need (see Kant, *Groundwork*, 231 [4: 430]). The point of imperfect duties, on his account, is apparently just to eliminate the possibility of conflicting obligations.

person or in the mail, say, but that does not make the duty to return it imperfect.[6] We might even think of a prohibition as satisfied in different ways to the extent that different acts might be substituted for the one that is forbidden: firing a gun into the air versus merely twiddling one's thumbs instead of shooting someone, for instance. Though there would be no problem if my suggestions in this essay extended beyond imperfect duties, I think we can draw at least a fuzzy line cordoning them off from duties that leave us only morally insignificant choices.

Note, too, that imperfection in the relevant sense does not amount to a *defect* in an obligation. For another use of the term "imperfect" just to mean "unfinished," consider its use in grammar: "past imperfect" and so forth. The project of shaping our moral lives is ongoing, and the unfinished aspect of imperfect obligation helps to make it so.

I should also mention a logical or semantical feature of the term "obligation" that is obscured by its use to supply the missing noun form for "ought." Unlike "ought," "obligation" does not appear to be closed under logical or causal consequence: strictly speaking, that is, we do not have an *obligation* to do everything required to fulfill our moral obligations, even if we ought to, and even if we have a moral reason to do so that amounts to our strongest reason in a certain case. It is not quite right to say, for instance, that someone who promised to return a book has an obligation specifically to mail it, even when mailing it happens to be the only way of returning it. "Obligation" seems to be tied fairly closely to the description under which an act is required, and mailing was not part of the deal.

Instead, we may say that the agent here has an obligation that *requires* her to mail the book back to its owner. I also follow standard practice in using "obligation" interchangeably with "duty," though there may be some differences here as well. But let us speak of the result of combining rationality with morality to derive something more specific as a *requirement*, rather than an obligation or a duty. We may then think of "binding" force as applying primarily to the moral reasons underlying such requirements.

In a nutshell, then, the question that imperfect obligation poses is how we can see some moral reasons as nonbinding, or optional, even when they outweigh all competing reasons. I think the solution depends on challenging the common conception of practical reasons as themselves prima facie requirements. The usual assumption seems to be that, if I have a reason to do *A*, then I am required to, unless I have at least as strong a reason for doing something else instead. Indeed, that may be part of what makes reasons seem an appropriate basis for moral obligation, as a species of requirement. Along with some other recent authors, though, I

<hr>

[6] Cf. Roderick M. Chisholm, "Supererogation and Offense: A Conceptual Scheme for Ethics," *Ratio* 5, no. 1 (1963): 1–14.

advocate loosening the tie between reasons and requirement, in the first instance to allow for optional nonmoral reasons in everyday cases.[7] But my approach depends on an overall conception of practical reasons in terms of criticism that it can sometimes be rational to discount, or set aside. To allow for imperfect moral obligations, I need to make sense of exceptions to the ban on discounting moral reasons.

III. Reconceiving Reasons

What makes a fact a reason, on the approach I propose, is a relation to criticism: reasons either offer or answer criticism of some act or other practical option. The usual approach starts from a relation of *favoring* action, but the critical conception reverses our normal way of talking about reasons by treating negative reasons—reasons counting *against* action, what we might call "critical" reasons—as primary. One might think of this move as similar to the move in Newtonian physics away from the Aristotelian view (and our intuitive view) of the motion of objects as a departure from a state of rest that requires an outside force to explain it, and toward a view that treats motion as the natural state and coming to rest as what needs explanation. As agents, our natural state is activity: we flail about, doing this and that, often with a motive but with no need to cite a reason in the normative sense featured here (a fact that serves to justify what we do) until we encounter an objection. Reasons in favor of our action then become relevant, in response.

Critical reasons, on my account, represent a possible action (or other practical option) as in some way objectionable, subject to criticism. They offer criticism of various things we might do, rather than serving in the first instance to counter reasons in favor of things we might do. On my account, reasons in favor, positive reasons, are understood primarily as responses to other reasons. They serve in the first instance to *answer* potential criticism, by citing some valuable feature of the act in question. So their primary normative role might be said to be defensive. They may play a more important *motivational* role than critical reasons, as entice-ments toward action, with a commendatory function in cases where they exceed what is needed to answer applicable criticism. But their basic normative function is derivative from that of critical reasons. Critical reasons serve to set up a standard of correctness, ruling out acts that fall short, whereas positive or "favoring" reasons essentially serve to buttress an act against any such attempts to rule it out.

---

[7] For some other attempts to capture optional reasons, see Joseph Raz, *Engaging Reason: On the Theory of Value and Action* (Oxford: Oxford University Press, 1999), 90–117; Jonathan Dancy, "Enticing Reasons," in R. J. Wallace, P. Pettit, S. Scheffler, and M. Smith, eds., *Reason and Value: Themes from the Moral Philosophy of Joseph Raz* (Oxford: Oxford University Press, 2004), 91–118; and Joshua Gert, *Brute Rationality: Normativity and Human Action* (Cambridge: Cambridge University Press, 2004), esp. 19–39 and 62–84.

This reversal of our ordinary way of thinking about reasons will, of course, seem counterintuitive. Its justification will lie in its results: for present purposes, in the way it lets us retain our options for fulfilling an imperfect obligation. At this point, however, before getting to moral reasons, I want to say more to illustrate the general distinction between positive and negative reasons. My aim here is not to motivate the distinction but instead just to spell it out more clearly, making evident rather than minimizing its clash with intuition.

First, as a simple example of a negative or critical nonmoral reason, consider the reason usually cited against smoking cigarettes, that smoking increases the risk of lung cancer. This fact can be said to offer a criticism of smoking—an entry on the "con" side of the ledger, when we assess the considerations for and against taking up or continuing the habit—even though it is stated in positive grammatical form, as a fact about what smoking does, rather than something it fails to do, such as promoting or protecting good health.

Now, perhaps we would be likely to consider reasons against an acquired habit like smoking only if we were antecedently aware of some reasons in its favor, but on the objective notion of reasons featured here, what matters is not our awareness of a reason but just how it bears on some practical alternative, something we might think of doing, whether or not we are likely to do it. Whether or not anyone has an urge to smoke, reasons against it can, in principle, be entered on the "con" side of the ledger before there is anything on the "pro" side: i.e., a positive reason, in favor of smoking, such as the fact that a particular agent who already has taken up the habit would no longer be distracted by the craving for a cigarette if she smoked one. I have purposely stated this positive reason in negative grammatical form, rather than citing the fact that some agent would get pleasure from smoking, to make it clear that what is in question in calling a reason positive also need not be the form of the statement expressing the reason, but rather its bearing on action.

Of course, a positive reason also can be cited without the need to respond to any criticism (meaning any criticism that has been offered or is likely to be offered), but simply to justify one's choice of a particular option. On my account, however, the point of a positive reason is to defend the choice against *potential* criticism: it is well to have an answer to criticism "in the bank." Consider a case of competing positive reasons, reasons in favor of incompatible options. Among the various blazers in my closet, one may be most flattering, even though several others would be reasonable choices too. Green is my best color, let us suppose, but blue looks good enough. Suppose I have no particular need to look my best, and no other factors tip the balance against either choice: both blazers are in good shape, neither has been worn more frequently, and so forth. Then either choice will be rational, in the sense of "rationally permissible," or "within reason." For, by hypothesis, my reason for choosing the green blazer implies no significant criticism of choosing the blue one. Instead, on the present account, it serves in the first instance to defend the choice of green against potential criticism. If no criticism is applicable, it commends but does not require choosing the green blazer.

In cases where we do have a practical requirement, it is likely to be stated in positive grammatical form, though it depends on criticism of alternatives to what is required. In that sense, requirements rest on negative reasons. To avoid confusion, however, I prefer the term "critical reasons" in what follows. Requirements typically also involve positive— or, as I shall now say, "favoring"—reasons, as needed to answer criticism of the required act; but what makes something a requirement rather than a mere recommendation is what it rules out. This point is familiar in connection with moral obligation, which is often explained as applying to acts to which all the alternatives are wrong. If the fact that others need aid, say, gives rise to an obligation to provide them with aid, that fact counts *against* letting them suffer, as well as answering criticism from those with competing claims on our resources: our creditors, our dependents, ourselves.

I have characterized positive or favoring reasons as answering criticism, but they do so in a particular way, by citing valuable features of the act or option in question. There are other ways of answering criticism: by undermining it (for instance, showing that it or some criticism at least as strong also applies to alternative options), or by *discounting* it (setting it aside, or "bracketing" it) as an influence on choice. In the cases on which my defense of optional nonmoral reasons turns, discounting involves appeal to higher-order reasons, reasons ruling out attention to certain first-order considerations—or, to use Joseph Raz's term, "exclusionary" reasons.[8] It is important that discounting in this sense does not involve denying that the first-order considerations count as reasons, or reasons applicable to the agent, though we sometimes talk that way. For instance, T. M. Scanlon cites a higher-order reason for discounting personal considerations in competitive contexts: for not worrying about a friend's hurt feelings if we defeat him in tennis, or for not preferring our friends in assessing fellowship applicants.[9] In such cases, we might well say that friendship is no reason to let the friend win. But if we treat the ban on personal considerations as a higher-order reason, it need not cancel the rational bearing of those considerations on action, but just the assignment to them of any deliberative weight. We would be acting inappropriately, but not irrationally, in these contexts, if we did give special consideration to a friend.

---

[8] Cf. Joseph Raz, *Practical Reason and Norms* (Princeton, NJ: Princeton University Press, 1990)—though Raz's own account of optional reasons in *Engaging Reason* rests, instead, on appeal to the incommensurability of first-order reasons.
[9] See T. M. Scanlon, *What We Owe to Each Other* (Cambridge, MA: Harvard University Press, 1998), 50–55.

My own preferred examples of discounting involve setting optional priorities for oneself. For instance, I might decide to ignore objections to working long hours in order to focus single-mindedly on work—as a matter of personal decision, presumably because of reasons I have for getting work done, but not necessarily because I consider those reasons more important than the objections to overwork, or weightier in some sense independent of my decision. In deciding what weight to *assign* to my first-order reasons, I essentially *declare* some of them more important to me.

Elsewhere I consider a case of turning down a lure of administrative power as a reason to serve on university committees.[10] To sum up the case very briefly: all I am doing, when I decide to turn down the lure of power in order to focus on research, is setting my own priorities, not legislating for relevantly similar moral agents. Nor must I be legislating for agents with the same priorities, or even very strictly for my future self, to the extent that my priorities may be nonstringent, allowing for occasional deviations. I do acknowledge a reason to pursue power—that it would offer me some benefits (or perhaps count as a benefit in itself)— though it may be a reason I do not need to act on, if my current level of power is adequate. The prospect of greater power—and for that matter, my competing ideal of single-minded intellectual focus—here amounts to a reason that can be discounted *without* a further reason, just because I decide to set it aside. As a purely positive or favoring reason, it does not imply significant criticism of alternatives, so action on it is optional: I can simply turn it down.

My defense of optional nonmoral reasons ultimately rests on this idea, of a favoring reason as a reason that serves to answer criticism without implying significant criticism of alternatives. This represents a departure from maximizing conceptions of rationality. A similar notion has been defended in detail in recent work by Joshua Gert on justifying versus requiring roles (or "strengths") of reasons.[11] Gert's notion of a "purely justificatory" reason captures the kernel of what I have in mind by a purely positive or favoring reason, though my terminology and my explanation in terms of criticism are meant to extend to moral reasons. Gert confines moral reasons to a separate domain, whereas, on my account, "criticism" is meant to cover moral criticism as well as prudential and other forms of criticism. Moreover, besides merely justifying action— defending it as permissible, rationally or otherwise—a favoring reason that does more than answer applicable criticism also serves to recommend action.[12] But I share with Gert the denial that strong enough favoring reasons must yield a practical requirement.

---

[10] See my "Practical Reasons and Moral 'Ought'."
[11] See Gert, *Brute Rationality*, e.g., p. 137.
[12] It also might be said to confer merit on the act, and thereby on the agent, to accommodate the notion of supererogation on the kind of account offered by Terry Horgan and

The notion of a purely positive or favoring reason might at first seem to violate the logic of reasons, since any reason could be said to imply a criticism (namely, a criticism of whatever would prevent action on it). However, I count criticism as significant only when it makes out the option in question as itself in some way objectionable. While any reason in favor of action also counts against failing to act, we can treat the negative formulation as trivial where it merely restates information from the "pro" side of the ledger.

Consider again my choice between green and blue blazers. Unless I have some particular reason to look my best, the fact that wearing the blue blazer would keep me from wearing the green one, and hence from wearing my most flattering color, is no real objection to it. As a reason against wearing the blue blazer, the fact that the green one would look better has no serious weight, assuming that the blue one looks good enough. In general, what a favoring reason tells us is that a certain option is permissible (and perhaps even commendable), but not that it is required. We need to apply this notion to moral reasons in order to capture imperfect obligation.

IV. Combining Optionality and Bindingness

Moral reasons of the sort that yield requirements—critical moral reasons—are off-limits to discounting to the extent that they rest on moral criticism issued from personal standpoints other than the agent's. On the critical conception, this is what gives our obligations to others binding force. An agent is in a position to waive only her own criticism, or criticism presupposing her optional ends or evaluative frameworks. But in cases of imperfect duty, we might seem to be entitled to discount criticism from potential beneficiaries whom we decide to pass over.

Insofar as we have moral reasons to benefit particular individuals in such cases, however, I think we should treat them as favoring reasons: nonbinding moral reasons, of a sort that can serve to answer criticism without offering any.[13] Such reasons figure in ascriptions of moral virtue beyond what is required. Similarly, in a case of imperfect duty, aiding a particular individual may be commendable without being required, even if it is favored by one's strongest applicable reason. The reason I have to give some money to a homeless person I pass on the street, say, supplies

---

Mark Timmons, "Untying a Knot from the Inside Out: Reflections on the 'Paradox' of Supererogation," elsewhere in this volume.

[13] One might think my reason for action in such a case would offer a criticism of failure to act, e.g., that a certain potential aid recipient will suffer unless I aid him. But note that this criticism is not really applicable unless no one else is in a position to alleviate the suffering in question. Strictly, the criticism applies to the surrounding community, or to some collective body including myself, which may indeed be subject to requirements in such cases, as will be evident in my later discussion of political issues.

an answer to criticism I might be subject to if I do give him something (e.g., criticism for my failure to give that money to others, or to use it to further other valuable ends). But I am not subject to *moral* criticism for failing to aid that particular individual, even if aiding him was my best option for aiding the needy, as long as I satisfy the general duty to aid the needy in enough other ways. Thus, I need not appeal to a higher-order reason to justify discounting my reason for aiding him, but can do so simply on the basis of (morally unobjectionable) personal preference.

This is not to say that he cannot object to my failure to aid him, but his complaint would not amount to a moral criticism. I would not need to take it into account unless it undermined some further end I happened to have, such as a desire to avoid his resentment. Insofar as it yields only a nonmoral reason, I could legitimately discount it by appeal to higher-order reasons, such as reasons for disregarding personal pressure in distributing aid.

I take moral criticism to be criticism of the sort that grounds blame, as distinct from simple resentment.[14] Where aiding a particular individual is my best option for discharging my general duty, my failure to aid him might instead be subject to *rational* criticism, for failing to take the best means to my morally required ends. But the force of any objection here still depends on reference to an optional end (namely, the end of satisfying my duty most effectively, which is not morally required). Moreover, a charge of rational imperfection would be analogous to what we might say about my failure in the blazer case to choose the color that looks best on me. I am required only to take *some* effective means to satisfying my obligation, not to take the *most* effective means. Falling short of a more demanding rational ideal would be compatible with rationality in the broad sense presupposed here—"rationally permissible," or "within reason"—unless we smuggle in maximizing assumptions.

What yields a requirement in the case of our imperfect duty to aid would seem to be a reason based on *indeterminate* criticism—criticism of an agent's failure to contribute enough to the needy, leaving occasions, recipients, and amounts of aid unspecified. This reason is supposed to be binding in its own terms, though its terms are loose, so that (among other things) it is not tied to the standpoints of particular beneficiaries. The relevant criticism issues from a more general, but still personal, standpoint: at a minimum, the collective standpoint of the needy. What is important is that this standpoint of criticism is independent of the agent's standpoint, so that she is not in a position to discount a reason based on it.

---

[14] Cf. the accounts of moral obligation in John Skorupski, "Moral Obligation, Blame, and Self-Governance," and Stephen Darwall, " 'But It Would Be Wrong'," both elsewhere in this volume. But I would not make the link to emotional blame or other reactive attitudes an explicit part of the definition of moral obligation, if pinning down the relevant sort of practical criticism can do the job. It is essentially criticism that tends to make one unworthy of others' personal regard, or of relationship with others.

This is not to say that an agent has to recognize such a reason—has to accept others' criticisms as reason-giving for her—but only that, if she does recognize both the reason and its basis in an independent personal standpoint of criticism, she cannot consistently think she is in a position to discount it. Note that this interpretation of binding force does not depend on a claim about the comparative *weight* of moral and other reasons. The Kantian position on binding force is often interpreted as a claim that moral reasons necessarily outweigh all others, but we need not suppose that even the slightest moral consideration outweighs personal concerns, however serious. The need to concentrate on completing a manuscript or other important project, say, might be enough to justify paying a bit less attention than one should to others' everyday needs.[15] What it would not justify is a decision to assign their needs no weight in deliberation.

The resulting position on binding force would not satisfy Kant, or a Kantian reading of "inescapable" moral reasons as necessarily conclusive. For that matter, if the explanation of binding force limits the ban on discounting to critical reasons with sources outside the agent's standpoint, it would extend to Kantian "duties to oneself" only if these duties are interpreted as based on criticism from others. Perhaps others in the agent's circle could be seen as adversely affected by a decision to neglect her duties to herself.[16] But one might instead represent such duties as rational requirements, arguing that no higher-order reason an agent could cite would be adequate to justify discounting certain basic criticisms of her own of self-neglect, compatibly with rationality.

In any case, the indeterminate moral reason corresponding to an imperfect obligation to others has to rest on criticism from a personal standpoint besides that of the agent, though not that of a specific beneficiary of obligation. The relevant standpoint can be seen as interpersonal, or personally inclusive, rather than impersonal.[17] Simply alluding to "the moral standpoint" as an impersonal source of criticism would not provide a satisfying explanation of the limits on what the agent can discount, for there are other impersonal standpoints that one can be justified in setting

---

[15] For less everyday examples, cf. esp. the case of Paul Gauguin's pursuit of his art by leaving his family and moving to Tahiti, discussed in Bernard Williams, "Moral Luck," in Williams, *Moral Luck* (Cambridge: Cambridge University Press, 1982), 20–39; and other cases discussed in R. G. Frey, "Goals, Luck, and Moral Obligation," elsewhere in this volume.

[16] I owe this suggestion to Michael Weber.

[17] Cf. Darwall's account of what he calls "impersonal" reasons in "'But It Would Be Wrong'." The term derives from P. F. Strawson's treatment of reactive attitudes in Strawson, "Freedom and Resentment," *Proceedings of the British Academy* 48 (1962): 1–25, where it indicates that an attitude is not a reaction just to a slight to oneself. In application to standpoints of criticism, however, "impersonal" suggests independence of persons generally. I want to distinguish moral reasons from others, such as aesthetic reasons, that might be thought to rest on criticism from an impersonal standpoint. "Interpersonal," in any case, seems a better fit with the interpretation of moral obligation in terms of "second-personal" demands that Darwall advocates, in an account with which I am broadly in sympathy.

aside. I can acknowledge aesthetic criticism of the arrangement of computer equipment on my desk, say, but discount it as irrelevant to my purposes in setting up a computer. If moral criticism is different, we want to be told why.

Besides the collective standpoint of potential beneficiaries, one might suggest that all moral agents are in a position to lodge criticism of the failure of any one agent to fulfill an imperfect obligation. Among their other duties, agents have a perfect obligation of fairness, particularly in cases like the duty to aid, where what is in question is a shared social burden. A shift to the standpoint of the moral community would also extend the ban on discounting to general moral duties that are not owed *to* anyone, such as the duty not to pollute the environment. Even where someone's failure to shoulder a social burden does not actually increase the burden on others, others are in a position to criticize her for doing less than they do. But I now want to turn to questions about what happens when the burden, or part of the burden, is taken over by the state. When the government uses our taxes to provide aid to the needy, is it essentially enforcing the fulfillment of our imperfect obligation? To the extent that the government specifies the amount and recipients of aid, what happens to our leeway for choice?

V. Political Specification of the Duty to Aid

It was Kant's "natural law" predecessor Samuel Pufendorf (1632–1694) who introduced imperfect duties into the modern literature, and he took them to be unenforceable by definition. I have been working from a version of the familiar interpretation of imperfect obligations in Kant's *Groundwork for the Metaphysics of Morals* (1785) as obligations whose content is incompletely specified. The content of an imperfect duty includes a rough threshold of adequacy, I would add, thus allowing for supererogatory satisfaction: donating more to famine relief than duty requires, say. Though Kant did not intend this reading, it fits his reference to imperfect duties as "meritorious," along with his later treatment of them in *The Metaphysics of Morals* (1797) as "duties of virtue."[18] They can be seen as pulling into the realm of duty an ideal of virtue, extending higher than ordinary agents are required to satisfy, as well as involving a motivational component that cannot be compelled. There is also a narrower reading of the notion of imperfect duties, as in John Stuart Mill's treatment of justice in *Utilitarianism* (1863)—and perhaps more familiar in

---

[18] See Immanuel Kant, *The Metaphysics of Morals* (1797), trans. Mary Gregor (Cambridge: Cambridge University Press, 1991), for the treatment of imperfect duties as requiring direct concern for the beneficiary (which for Kant does not entail undergoing a feeling, but just the adoption of an end). I note that John Rawls also holds that duties of virtue include perfect duties that require action for the right reasons; see Rawls, *Lectures on the History of Moral Philosophy* (Cambridge, MA: Harvard University Press, 2000).

rights-based political theory—on which it is particularly the beneficiary of an imperfect duty that is left unspecified, so that no right is correlative to the duty.[19] However, I take an obligation to be imperfect if it simply fails to specify precisely how much is owed to others, even in a case where it is owed to someone in particular.

Consider, for instance, the duty to care for elderly parents or for a child. Here the beneficiary is specified, but the requisite amount of care is not. Such cases also make it clear that our imperfect moral duties may be as stringent as any other duties, if the term "stringent" refers to the seriousness of a violation rather than to the level of required satisfaction. The requirements for satisfying our imperfect duties may be rigorously imposed on us, even if they are only loosely spelled out. But while a duty to "care" entails appropriate concern and thus cannot be enforced by law, sometimes we had better ensure at least a minimum standard of overt action rather than letting individual motivational resources determine what gets done. Thus, the law steps in to enforce child support, even if it cannot thereby force anyone to provide it from the right motives. The resulting legal duty will be perfect insofar as it specifies the requisite level of support, presumably at or around the threshold for satisfying the moral duty.

For famine relief and similar global forms of aid, we may also need to sacrifice some of the moral quality of individual motivation in order to enlist the enforcement powers of the state. Individuals may lack enough control over what is done with their contributions (as well as how many other people join them in contributing) to make a real difference, and sometimes even large-scale voluntary organizations may not be up to the job. However, even apart from worries about individual moral worth— since taxation tends to evoke a grudging attitude rather than love and concern—having the state step in serves to limit the leeway for choice that imperfect duties provide. We may still be able to afford to contribute more on our own after taxes, but we have lost direct control over how the state-mandated portion of our contribution gets distributed: for example, we cannot directly control how much relief goes to victims of famine versus victims of hurricanes, earthquakes, or tornadoes; nor can we directly decide whether to give priority to national disasters, or to disasters that affect a certain subgroup, or to spread our efforts evenly across the world.

I do want to allow for the role of the state in these matters—and also in correcting extremes of poverty via taxation—despite the regard for individual autonomy embodied in my use of the notion of imperfect obligation. Taxation to reduce inequalities in the distribution of wealth is seen by natural rights libertarians as violating our rights where the inequalities are not a result of past wrongs. I focus here primarily on the less controversial case of responding to natural disasters, where the state's use of our

---

[19] See John Stuart Mill, *Utilitarianism* (1863) (Oxford: Oxford University Press, 1998), 94.

tax dollars for that purpose might be seen as limiting our right to decide how to discharge our duty to aid. But since I share the skepticism recently expressed by Thomas Nagel about treating all economic inequalities as instances of injustice, what I say may be applicable, *mutatis mutandis,* to redistributive issues as well.[20] What if we recast non-rectificatory redistribution of wealth as a relief measure, a response to another sort of disaster (or possibly a preemptive response to a foreseeable disaster) for those in poverty, and potentially for society as a whole?

In thinking about this issue informally over the years, I have been inclined to take the state as having duties of its own, insofar as it has resources and powers that individuals or voluntary organizations may lack.[21] After all, institutional entities can be bearers of obligations: a corporation, for instance, has obligations not to pollute the water, to treat its employees fairly, and so on. These are, of course, perfect duties. Even if they ultimately have to be explained in terms of the duties of individuals, they need not have quite the same content: some of the individual duties will involve setting up an institutional structure designed to prevent, detect, and punish violations, often in ways that individuals could not manage or should not attempt on their own. Similarly, the state, even if set up for other purposes, might be said to incur some duties, in virtue of its size and resources, to do more than we could otherwise accomplish in fulfilling our imperfect duties, such as the duty to give aid. We are therefore required to see that the state is endowed with appropriate structures to discharge such duties as can be transferred to it in this manner.

More strictly, perhaps I should speak not of the state but of the community—the collective body whose instrument the state is—as the bearer of obligations, insofar as it is organized by a state. The important point is just that political enforcement of measures that satisfy the imperfect duties we have as individuals need not amount to enforcing their fulfillment by individuals, as in the case of child support. To put it roughly but simply, my suggestion is that the state instead assumes or takes over some of our duties, possibly modifying them in the process—and that the state *should* assume them or take them over, and that we have an obligation to equip it to do so. Instead of forcing us to discharge our duties, the state forces us to participate in a coordinative arrangement designed to accomplish the same ends.

Now note that, in cases involving nearby emergencies, we seem to have a *perfect* duty of mutual aid, or what might be distinguished as a duty of

---

[20] See Thomas Nagel, "Justice and Nature," *Oxford Journal of Legal Studies* 17, no. 2 (1998): 303–21. I should note that my ensuing remarks were written before the various economic disasters of September 2008. I am reminded of a fortune cookie I once got: "Today's philosophy is tomorrow's common sense."

[21] Philip Pettit has done systematic work along these lines. See, e.g., Pettit, "Responsibility Incorporated," *Ethics* 117, no. 1 (2007): 171–201.

rescue.[22] I do not have moral leeway, say, to pass by an accident victim whom no one else is available to help, on the grounds that I have given or plan to give enough aid elsewhere. But the difference in size and scope between individuals and states, along with the duties states have to distribute goods fairly, would seem to mean that some duties of charity *become* duties of rescue, when they are transferred to the state. A tornado in the midwestern U.S. counts as "nearby" from the national perspective, though perhaps not from mine; and for a sufficiently powerful state with global reach, the same might be said of an epidemic in Africa or a tsunami in the Far East.

Thus, the transfer of our obligations to the state will modify some of them, making imperfect obligations perfect, or more nearly so, but not simply by pinning down the level of required contribution, as with child support laws. The larger scale of societal obligations transforms our individual obligations to the point where it no longer makes sense to see the state as enforcing them, as opposed to substituting something else with the same purposes. Besides issues of geographical proximity, a shift to the collective level may mean that there is no one else in a similar position to help some subset of the needy whose relief a particular individual might be justified in leaving to others. There are also further obligations of fairness that apply to a state distributing aid. Within broad limits, an individual is free to give preference to a special subgroup: those she regards as her own fellows or those suffering from misfortunes that move her or simply happen to catch her eye. I might be within my moral rights, for instance, to fulfill my own duty to aid those in need by directing my contributions to organizations aiding women, preferring female victims whose lives are not in danger over males whose lives I might save. I do not need to claim that I am doing more long-term good thereby, or correcting a worse social problem. Nonetheless, of course, we would be indignant if state officials gave preference in relief efforts to some particular subgroup of victims, even without a sexist or racist or other morally objectionable rationale.

In some cases, if the state's greater power and scope turn charity into rescue, it may also have to take *more* from us as individuals than we would otherwise be obligated to provide. From my perspective, donating money to victims of a particular hurricane or tornado may be more than I am morally required to do, but the state may have a perfect duty to use my contributions, pooled with those of others, for particular relief efforts. At this level, we might even grant that a particular victim is *owed* aid— that moral criticism is warranted from his standpoint if the state fails to

---

[22] Proximity affects the stringency of duty, including imperfect duty, in part by helping to set a threshold of minimally adequate virtue: unresponsiveness to perceptible suffering on the part of others is, in general, a worse trait than ignoring distant suffering. Cf. Singer, "Famine, Affluence, and Morality," which denies the relevance of distance, along with degrees of bindingness of obligation.

aid him—contrary to what I argued above with respect to individual agents' imperfect duties.

Thus, assigning some of our imperfect obligations to the state may indeed mean sacrificing something as individuals. According to what I have suggested, this cost is imposed on us by another sort of requirement: to set up the state along lines that enable it to respond to emergencies effectively, when occasions arise in which individual efforts, or the efforts of voluntary groups, are not adequate. This seems to amount to a rational requirement conditional on morally obligatory ends—relocating, to the level of political organization, the combination of rationality and morality that concerned me earlier in application to moral reasons. Instead of being required to aid specific needy individuals, we are required to see to it that the state is in a position to take over some of our duty to aid—with results that may limit our leeway for choice in similar ways.

If we prefer to think of the community as the bearer of our collective obligations, rather than the state, we might speak instead of granting the state a permission—authorizing it—to do what is needed to fulfill community obligations.[23] That might seem to allow us to impose constraints on its authority, by analogy to a private firm set up to distribute our pooled donations to charities of its choosing. The only obligation of such a firm, presumably, would be to use the money we gave it for the purposes prescribed. It would not take on further obligations or permissions in virtue of the size of our pooled resources, and it could discount criticism from needy individuals it passed over, albeit not on morally objectionable grounds. Nor would such a firm be empowered to make us give more—we might even ban it from asking us for more—if unforeseen emergencies arise.

I assume, however, that there are more fundamental constraints in play here. We are required to set up or reform the state to allow for its effectiveness in satisfying our collective charitable duties, as noted. At least where aid to its own citizens is in question, a better analogy might be to a mutual aid society, understood to have as its defining purpose the provision of specified forms of aid to its members, so that it owes aid to those members who need it and should be authorized to charge enough in membership dues to fulfill their needs.

The imperfect duty on which my argument has focused is assumed to be satisfiable via taxation, rather than by enlisting individuals for labor or other nonmonetary contributions, which would raise harder issues of individual autonomy. Some proposals of the latter sort are not unthinkable, at least where they leave adequate scope for individual choice: for instance, the suggestion one occasionally hears that a period of national service should be required of everyone before settling into a career. But

---

[23] This is my restatement of a suggestion made by Christopher Morris, to whom I owe the analogy that follows.

anything more long-term, or demanding more specific forms of service (most notably, military service), would be worrisomely intrusive. Even if governments were in a better position than we are as individuals to decide what jobs we would find most satisfying and would perform most effectively, for instance, it would take more to justify surrendering to governments the authority to choose our careers. It is not inconceivable, though, that we should sometimes have to deal with conflicting obligations arising from our dual status as morally autonomous individuals and members of a political community.

Note that our reasons for authorizing a state to do some of what is necessary to discharge our duty to aid need not rest on the possibility that we will, at some point, need aid ourselves. Rather, we might decide to authorize a state to assume some of our duties because we suspect that we would fail to meet the threshold for satisfying some of our imperfect moral duties if left to do so on our own. Those arguing against taxation to relieve poverty sometimes reproach its defenders for not being more charitable in private contexts themselves, but transferring some responsibility to the state is defensible as a way of ensuring fulfillment of our charitable obligations. At a particular time when aid is urgently needed, I might turn out to be unable to contribute, perhaps because of conflicts of duty that could have been avoided with better planning. Or I may have satisfied my imperfect duty unwisely, giving so much to tsunami relief that I am caught short when a hurricane comes along. What is in question here, once again, is a rational requirement that we have in light of our moral obligations, though in this case it depends on acknowledging tendencies to violate the obligations, unless we take special measures for long-range self-control. If such tendencies were rare, it might be selfish to want to make up for them by transferring our obligations to the state, thereby imposing costs on others; but, of course, such tendencies are quite widespread. By authorizing the state to tax us in order to make up for them, we are essentially letting it tie us to a moral mast. In what follows, I do want to acknowledge grounds for keeping a hand free, but my discussion will also bring out a further reason for assigning this role to the state.

VI. Priorities

Let me now take a further look at some of the moral-psychological issues raised by binding ourselves to morality via the state, from the standpoint of an individual balancing moral and personal priorities, apart from any political commitments or constraints. I hope in the course of a somewhat looser discussion in this section to reconnect my argument to the general view of practical reasons and discounting outlined earlier, pausing to answer some objections to the view. In the end, my discussion will suggest that even our freedom to pursue our personal priorities can be made to speak in favor of the transfer of some of our charitable obligations to the state. For we need the state to put appropriate limits on the level of individual contributions to the satisfaction of large-scale collective obligations, if doing so involves discounting moral reasons in the way my approach suggests. But I want to begin by acknowledging at length some of the moral costs of the transfer. My aim in this area is to seek a sensitive balance between conflicting considerations rather than the elimination of conflict with a single stand pro or con.

Transferring imperfect obligations to the state means losing some of the leeway for personal choice allowed by an imperfect obligation.[24] But we might also be said to lose something that is both morally and personally valuable if we thereby dispose of our moral obligation. While farming a job out to others may take a load off our minds and get the job done better, it also tends to make our own contributions a matter of mere routine. Even if we can discharge the duty to aid without feeling love and concern, the moral worth of what we do presumably depends on some thought about the problems we are alleviating. If nothing else, satisfying an imperfect duty normally at least involves attention to the task of assessing others' needs and figuring out what to do about them. We pay a moral cost, then, if our attention is redirected toward satisfying the tax collector.

For that matter, the value we place on relationships—bonds to particular persons, on the usual understanding—as components of the good life, can also be seen as extending to obligation, as a relationship of being bound to particular goals, tasks, or concerns. Think of the resistance many of us feel to retiring from our jobs. Being obligated means being harnessed, when all goes well, to the good. (Sometimes the relationship is imposed on us, but the same is true of relationships with persons.) It may be just as well, then, if there are limits to how much of this the state can take over.

Of course, an individual would still be free to exceed the threshold required to satisfy the duty transferred to the state, meeting a higher standard of virtue. But the minimum required by a *"duty* of virtue" (to use Kant's later term for imperfect duties) prompts us at least to try on the states of mind that motivate virtuous behavior, in a way that an ideal of virtue, a standard of perfection, may not. In the terms introduced in my initial discussion of reasons, what is at issue here is the difference between a critical reason and a favoring one. An ideal of virtue may inspire greater efforts (when it does manage to inspire), but it is optional, whereas criticism of an agent, for not meeting the threshold set by a duty of virtue,

---

[24] In addition to my own account here in terms of optional reasons, see the argument in Lauren Fleming, "Imperfect Duties, Moral Latitude, and Constructing Moral Agency" (unpublished) that the "strong latitude" involved in imperfect obligations is essential to self-definition and responsible moral agency.

makes a demand on her. I take rationality to require that someone who acknowledges a criticism as legitimate must either answer it or act to avoid it, and the attempt to decide which course to take requires attention. We can get around this in particular cases, cultivating habits of satisfying our duties more or less automatically, but even this typically requires thought, perhaps especially for imperfect duties. Barring conflict, it is only in complex cases such as those that involve questions of fairness that we may have to think at length about how exactly to satisfy a perfect duty—there is no question of *how much* to satisfy the ban on breaking promises, say; nor is there any problem with satisfying it automatically— whereas an imperfect duty provides a nudge in the direction of virtue. This is what we lose if the state assumes the duty, even if we still have the opportunity to do more.

I say all this as someone who is not primarily focused on the aim of helping others. The distinctive feature of imperfect duties, as duties of virtue, is the fact that they do not really require virtue, but rather just a touch of it: a decent amount, not precisely specifiable, perhaps enough to find onerous at times, but clearly short of the ideal. They are thus able to leave room, not just for personal preferences as to *how* to satisfy them, but also for competing nonmoral priorities that we set for ourselves. I am free to contribute to Smile Train, for instance, which finances operations on facially deformed children, rather than giving the same amount to Oxfam for famine relief, but I am also entitled to earmark some of my available funds, beyond the threshold for satisfying my imperfect charitable duties, for contribution to local art galleries, or even just for the development of my own abilities or appreciative capacities, without having to defend my choice as ultimately promoting the good as much as its charitable alternatives.

If I knew I could do the most good by contributing to famine relief, I might be said to be acting against my strongest reason, and hence irrationally, if I instead donated my available funds to Smile Train and the arts. But remember that, on the critical conception, my reasons for satisfying an imperfect duty to aid in particular ways, or beyond the required minimum, are merely favoring reasons: reasons that imply no significant criticism of alternatives, but instead serve to justify action by answering potential criticism. I can discount these favoring reasons simply as a matter of personal preference. On the account I outlined earlier, "less than ideal" does not count as a significant criticism, so either choice may be justified, and either reason may be strong enough to act on, even if one of them counts as stronger.[25] The critical conception thereby removes a kind of pressure toward the best that emerges from the common conception of

---

[25] Cf. Raz, *Engaging Reason*, 102–4; and Joshua Gert, "Normative Strength and the Balance of Reasons," *Philosophical Review* 116, no. 4 (2007): 533–62, for alternative arguments based on comparison of the two reasons in terms of a univocal measure of strength.

practical reasons as prima facie requirements. The comparative strength of reasons no longer dictates rational choice.

In some such cases, my competing nonmoral reason might even have the force of a requirement. In deciding, say, to pursue a certain career, I lay myself open to criticism (if only self-criticism) for failing to follow through. The fact that I have decided to do something yields a critical reason, that is, even if the decision itself is made just on the basis of favoring reasons ascribing value to the activities in question. The answer to criticism for failure to follow through that would be provided by a strong enough *moral* favoring reason would justify the failure to follow through, but would not yield an opposing requirement, even on the assumption that it concerns matters of greater importance or value. I do not have to give up my personal commitments, in short, or even tolerate a distraction from them, in order to save a life, assuming that what is in question is not a duty of rescue but just the fulfillment of an imperfect charitable duty.

A serious enough personal commitment might even outweigh the general moral reason one has to contribute an adequate amount to those in need. I interpreted the latter reason as binding, not because it necessarily outweighs nonmoral reasons, but rather because it would be inappropriate for an individual agent just to set it aside, failing even to raise the question of comparative weights. Note, too, that the comparison will depend on more than how much good one could accomplish by acting on one reason rather than the other: there might be a case, say, where a group of agents would be able to provide enough aid without the help of one of them who would otherwise be prevented from following through on a central project of her own.

As I understand it, the decision involved in the setting of personal priorities essentially *enacts* a critical reason against failure to follow through, a reason that may apply only to the agent but that would seem to be important enough to rational planning and coordination with others, as presupposed by moral agency, that it deserves others' respect. In light of this, one might want to ask whether it is conceivable that *others* could sometimes discount moral criticism on an individual agent's behalf, even if the agent herself is not in a position to do so. I suggested earlier that an appropriate source of criticism for failure to fulfill an imperfect obligation (such as the duty to give aid) might be the broader moral community, including fellow moral agents as well as potential beneficiaries, if we add in an obligation to do one's fair share in satisfying a collective obligation. For that matter, one might say that all moral agents are "potential" beneficiaries of the duty to aid, since anyone could come to be in the situation of those in need. So while an individual may not be entitled to discount others' criticism unilaterally, might there be some sense in which the moral community could do so on her behalf? After all, where an imperfect duty is in question, this will not amount to cancelling the criticism of specific others who would be wronged by a failure to fulfill it. If we see the moral community as the source of criticism, it will just be withholding criticism of its own.

Something like this might be true informally of the moral community as an aggregate of individuals, but it is hard to see what an act of discounting on the part of a community could amount to, except insofar as it is organized by a governing body charged with allocating social burdens. There are obvious risks in allowing the state such discretionary powers, though. We do sometimes let people off the hook in special cases, demanding even less of them than the minimum required of others so that they can concentrate on other activities, presumably activities that are of more than merely personal value, even if they are not morally required. Think of the exemption of students or fathers of young children from the military draft during the Vietnam war. However, to answer concerns about fairness, it is important that an individual's role in fulfilling the collective duty in question make no heavier demands on him than the pursuit of the relevant activities.

Instead of special dispensations for some, one might think we all deserve some relief from charitable duties, just to the extent of having it publicly recognized when we have contributed enough. The price of giving a donation to a private charity, once it becomes a big business using modern marketing techniques, seems to be an immediate and unending stream of appeals for more, replacing with guilt, annoyance, or simple indifference the kind of caring attitude that ideally accompanies meeting the threshold set by an imperfect duty. In giving anything, one risks being made a "mark." To handle these pressures in a caring but untroubled fashion requires a moral personality whose development, while it may be admirable, exceeds our moral duty.

Some might want to object that one *ought* to feel guilt in such cases: it would be morally unworthy, at best, simply to pass by a homeless person or to spurn appeals for charitable funds without a tug of discomfort, even if one has indeed given enough on other occasions. But I have argued at length elsewhere that we can allow for the appropriateness of guilt and similar attitudes in such cases without the corresponding belief that one is guilty of a wrong.[26] Justifying an emotion requires only enough reason for making the corresponding thought an object of discomfort, as is needed to hold it in mind. Such discomfort plays an important moral role as a counter to the tendency to put off fulfillment of an obligation.[27] For that matter, feelings of guilt may sometimes be morally required of us to meet

---

[26] See esp. my *Practical Guilt* (Oxford: Oxford University Press, 1995). Let me thank Bruce Langtry for pressing this objection in discussion.

[27] I argue this in terms of discounting in my essay "Craving the Right: Emotions and Moral Reasons," in C. Bagnoli, ed., *Morality and the Emotions* (Oxford: Oxford University Press, forthcoming).

a minimal standard of virtue.[28] But it does not follow that we are required to *act* as those feelings suggest we should.

We may need the state, then, not just for more effective fulfillment of some of our moral duties, but also to put some systematic limits on how much can be asked of us in their name. Discounting, in the sense I distinguished—depriving certain considerations of weight in deliberation, while still acknowledging them as reasons—would seem to require an agent capable of reflection. While a community may have priorities, it cannot set any, except insofar as it is organized for reflection and action by some sort of governing body.[29] To avoid being completely at the mercy of others' needs (unless I simply harden my heart against them), I thus may have to let the state take some of my leeway for choice off my hands.

VII. Conclusion

Let me sum up very briefly the main lines of my argument in this essay. My primary aim was to use a conception of practical reasons in terms of criticism to make sense of imperfect obligation, a notion that can limit the moral demands on an agent by leaving her leeway for choice. But it was unclear how the relevant reasons could then still supply the binding force attributed to moral requirements. I proposed loosening the tie of reasons themselves to requirements and distinguishing two sorts of reasons by their relation to criticism: (1) reasons offering criticism (including moral and other requirements), and (2) favoring reasons. In the case of our imperfect duty to aid those in need, we have a critical reason against failing to contribute enough to the needy generally. But the reasons in favor of benefiting a specific individual imply no significant criticism of failure to aid him in particular, and in that sense are merely favoring reasons. Both reasons count as moral, but only the critical reason has binding force, as a consideration that the agent has to take into account, to the extent that she accepts it as offering criticism from an interpersonal standpoint that she is in no position to set aside unilaterally. By contrast, even moral favoring reasons, whatever their strength as reasons, are sub-

---

[28] See my "Guilt and Virtue," *Journal of Philosophy* 91, no. 2 (1994): 57–70. Acting on a requirement to feel an emotion would depend on some degree of control over what we feel, but on that point see my "Emotional Strategies and Rationality," *Ethics* 110, no. 3 (2000): 469–87.

[29] Note that not everything we refer to as "setting priorities" involves the sort of discounting of competing concerns that is at issue in my account. Sometimes, "prioritizing" a particular concern just amounts to assigning it priority in our plans to reflect its pre-given weight or importance. I take it that ordinary talk in political contexts of setting social priorities fits this mold and hence is unproblematic on the common conception of reasons as prima facie requirements. In allowing for priority-setting in light of optional reasons, my own account is also meant to accommodate decisions to modify the pre-given weight of one's reasons. I discuss this in application to free will issues in "Reasons, Decisions, and Free Will" (unpublished).

ject to discounting, since their normative role in the first instance is simply to answer criticism.

Sometimes the state may be in a better position than individuals to aid those in need and may tax us for that purpose, but we should not see it as thereby forcing us to fulfill our imperfect duties. Instead, it assumes them; or, more precisely, the community organized by a state assumes them and should authorize the state to do what is necessary to fulfill them, where the state's power and resources put it in a better position to fulfill them adequately. However, transfer to the state will tend to make an imperfect duty less imperfect, by pinning down and sometimes altering the amount of our individual contributions and the beneficiaries of our pooled contributions. The state's larger scope and capacities can turn duties of charitable aid into duties of rescue. Transferring an imperfect duty to the state involves an obvious cost in terms of individual freedom of choice, but there is also a moral cost to individuals in replacing the virtuous motives of charity with those that tend to accompany paying taxes. Nonetheless, I note that, with modern marketing techniques, charity as big business can exert a kind of relentless pressure that also would tend to undermine virtuous motivation. A compensating feature of state involvement is the fact that its more precise demands come with limits.

Philosophy, University of Maryland, College Park

THE OBLIGATION TO BE VIRTUOUS: KANT'S CONCEPTION OF THE *TUGENDVERPFLICHTUNG**

By Paul Guyer

I. Introduction

In his final work on practical philosophy, *The Metaphysics of Morals* (1797), Immanuel Kant employs a distinction between specific ethical duties or obligations and a general obligation to be virtuous. The latter concept might seem redundant or vacuous: it might well seem as if the obligation to be virtuous is reducible, without remainder, to the obligation to fulfill one's particular duties (as happiness may be reducible to the satisfaction of one's particular desires), so that no obligation is being added to our specific ethical obligations by this concept. Kant himself may create this impression when he calls the obligation to be virtuous merely "formal," in comparison to the "material" or presumably substantive duties of virtue. This essay will nevertheless attempt to make Kant's distinction plausible by showing that Kant understands the obligation to be virtuous as calling for efforts to strengthen one's commitment to fulfilling one's particular duties by a variety of means that, in spite of the "formality" of this obligation, are in fact different from the actions taken to fulfill particular duties on particular occasions. Thus, the obligation to be virtuous does call for actions that are not extensionally equivalent to those called for by specific ethical obligations. In my view, Kant has hereby uncovered an important feature of the moral life: he shows that virtue is not achieved simply by attempting to fulfill one obligation after another, but requires a comprehensive effort at the development of moral character.

II. Duties of Virtue and the Obligation to Be Virtuous

In the "Metaphysical Foundations of the Doctrine of Virtue," the second half of *The Metaphysics of Morals,* Kant distinguishes between specific duties of virtue (*Tugendpflichten*), such as the duty to develop one's own talents or to be beneficent to others, and a general obligation of virtue or

* Work on this essay has been supported by the generous award of a Research Prize from the Alexander von Humboldt Stiftung, and by the hospitality of the Lehrstuhl für Deutschen Idealismus of the Institut für Philosophie of the Humboldt Universität zu Berlin.

obligation to be virtuous (*Tugendverpflichtung*).[1] He expresses this distinction by characterizing the latter as "formal" and the former as "material," and he infers the singularity of the general obligation to be virtuous from its formality, and the multiplicity of the specific duties of virtue from their materiality. Kant uses the distinction between "formal" and "material" throughout his philosophy for many purposes, so it is not immediately clear what this means; but as I have already indicated, it could suggest that the obligation to be virtuous is a vacuous addition to our specific duties of virtue. So we must first see what Kant means by this distinction, and then explain why it does not imply the vacuity of the concept of a general obligation to be virtuous.

We can begin to see what Kant means when he first makes the distinction between material and formal duties, and the inference to the plurality of the former and the singularity of the latter, in section II of the introduction to the "Doctrine of Virtue." He starts by distinguishing what he here calls "ethical obligations" (a general term that does not yet distinguish between specific duties of virtue and the obligation to be virtuous) from the juridical obligations or duties of right that have already been discussed in the first half of *The Metaphysics of Morals*, the "Doctrine of Right." He makes this distinction by means of the criterion that duties of right are accompanied with rights on the part of specific persons to coerce their fulfillment,[2] while ethical obligations do not permit coercive enforcement:

> To every duty there corresponds *a* right in the sense of an *authorization* to do something (*facultas moralis generatim*); but it is not the case that to every duty there correspond *rights* of another to coerce someone (*facultas juridica*). Instead, [the latter] duties are called, specifically, *duties of right.* —

But following his dash, Kant then introduces the distinction within the class of noncoercively enforceable ethical obligations with which I am concerned:

> Similarly, to every ethical *obligation* there corresponds the concept of virtue, but not all ethical duties are thereby duties of virtue. Those

---

[1] I borrow this interpretation of Kant's term *Tugendpflichten* from Philip Stratton-Lake, "Being Virtuous and the Virtues: Two Aspects of Kant's *Doctrine of Virtue*," in Monika Betzler, ed., *Kant's Ethics of Virtue* (Berlin and New York: Walter de Gruyter, 2008), 101–21.

[2] I purposely use the vague words "are accompanied with" in order to sidestep the debate about whether the possibility of legitimate coercive enforcement is part of the *concept* of a duty of right or is rather connected with it in a way that counts as synthetic but *a priori*. For my position in this debate, see my "Kant's Deductions of the Principles of Right," in Mark Timmons, ed., *New Essays on Kant's Metaphysics of Morals* (Oxford: Oxford University Press, 2002), 24–64, reprinted in my *Kant's System of Nature and Freedom* (Oxford: Clarendon Press, 2005).

duties that have to do not so much with a certain end (matter, object of choice) as merely with *what is formal* in the moral determination of the will (e.g., that an action in conformity with duty must also be done *from duty*) are not duties of virtue. Only *an end that is also a duty* can be called a *duty of virtue*. For this reason there are several duties of virtue (and also various virtues), whereas for the first kind of duty only one (virtuous disposition) is thought, which however holds for all actions.[3]

The specific duties of virtue are material and plural because they are duties that are also ends, or duties to have and pursue ends: in the first instance, the two comprehensive ends of one's own perfection and the happiness of others,[4] and then the more specific ends that comprise those two comprehensive ends, such as the duties to preserve and cultivate one's own physical and mental capacities (in the first case) and the duties to practice beneficence, gratitude, and sympathy toward others while refraining from arrogance, defamation, and ridicule toward them (in the second case). The ethical obligation that is not one of these material and specific duties, however—or what seems to be the duty to have a virtuous disposition—is formal in the sense that it concerns not what is to be done but, so to speak, how it is to be done, that is, the kind of motivation from which the more specific ethical duties are to be fulfilled. This formal obligation is singular rather than plural because there is only one way to have a truly virtuous disposition, namely, to act "from duty," or out of respect for the moral law itself.[5] Kant emphasizes this point by describing the categorical imperative that is to be the content of virtuous motivation as itself a formal principle: "The concept of duty stands in immediate relation to a *law* (even if I abstract from all ends, as the matter of the law). The formal principle of duty, in the categorical imperative 'So act that the maxim of your action could become a universal law' already indicates this. Ethics adds only that this principle is to be thought as the law of *your* own will and not of will in general."[6] It is something about the will in general that requires us to adopt the specific material ends that are also duties (namely, self-perfection and the happiness of others), but ethics

[3] Immanuel Kant, *The Metaphysics of Morals*, "Doctrine of Virtue," introduction, section II, 6:383; the translation in the text is from Kant, *Practical Philosophy*, ed. and trans. Mary J. Gregor (Cambridge: Cambridge University Press, 1996), 515. In subsequent notes, I provide page references to the translation, abbreviated as "Gregor." All emphasis within quotations is in the original unless otherwise noted.
[4] Kant, *Metaphysics of Morals*, "Doctrine of Virtue," introduction, section IV, 6:385–88.
[5] See Immanuel Kant, *Groundwork for the Metaphysics of Morals*, in Kant, *Practical Philosophy*, ed. and trans. Mary J. Gregor (Cambridge: Cambridge University Press, 1996), section I, 3:400–401; Gregor, pp. 55–56. For a similar emphasis on the formality of the general obligation to be virtuous, see Stratton-Lake, "Being Virtuous and the Virtues," 105.
[6] Kant, *Metaphysics of Morals*, "Doctrine of Virtue," introduction, section VI, 6:388–89; Gregor, p. 520.

adds the obligation that we be virtuous by making the moral law itself our fundamental motivation. This obligation seems to be formal precisely in the sense that it does not require any further specific actions ("matter") of us, but requires only that we fulfill our specific ethical duties from one sort of motivation rather than another. As we will eventually see, however, this impression is misleading.

In a later section of the introduction to the "Doctrine of Virtue" in which he discusses "Concepts Preliminary to the Division of the Doctrine of Virtue," Kant also presents the contrast between the plural duties of virtue and the singular obligation to be virtuous as a contrast between material and formal duties, although here he uses his all-purpose distinction between the formal and the material[7] in two different ways. He first uses it to distinguish all ethical obligations of any kind from duties of right, and only then uses it to contrast the specific duties of virtue with the general obligation to be virtuous. Thus:

> This principle of division must *first*, in terms of what is *formal*, contain all the conditions that serve to distinguish a part of the doctrine of morals in general from the doctrine of right and to do so in terms of its specific form. It does this by laying down 1) that duties of virtue are duties for which there is no external lawgiving; 2) that since a law must yet lie at the basis of every duty, this law in ethics can be a law of duty given, not for actions, but only for the maxims of actions; 3) that (as follows in turn from this) ethical duty must be thought as *wide*, not as narrow, duty.
>
> The principle of division must *secondly*, in terms of what is *material*, present the doctrine of virtue not merely as a doctrine of duties generally but also as a *doctrine of ends*, so that a human being is under obligation to regard himself as well as every other human being as an end. . . .[8]

Here Kant claims that ethical obligations, unlike duties of right, cannot permissibly be coercively enforced, because they are duties to adopt certain ends or policies, such as being beneficent, and therefore they do not specify specific types of actions that must always be performed or omitted, as fulfilling contracts may always be required or expropriating property with-

---

[7] By calling the distinction between formal and material "all-purpose," I mean that every aspect of Kant's philosophy is organized around this distinction; for example, in the constructive theory of knowledge of the *Critique of Pure Reason*, the general distinction between intuitions and concepts is a distinction between the matter and the form of knowledge, but within each sphere the distinction between empirical and pure—between empirical and pure intuition, between empirical and pure concepts—is also, fundamentally, a distinction between matter and form. And so on.

[8] Kant, *Metaphysics of Morals*, "Doctrine of Virtue," introduction, section XVII, 6:410; Gregor, p. 537.

out consent may always be prohibited. Instead, ethical obligations leave open to contextual determination when and how they are to be fulfilled: for example, to whom and in what ways one should be beneficent, since one obviously cannot be beneficent to everybody and in all ways. The crucial difference between duties of right and ethical obligations, in other words, arises from the fact that the former are themselves in a sense formal duties—they arise from the necessity of preserving equal spheres for freedom of external action for all persons regardless of what anyone's particular ends are[9]—while the latter are material duties—they are duties to adopt and promote particular ends. The relative determinacy of the formal duties of justice (that is, the relative specificity of what it takes to preserve equally maximal spheres of freedom of action) may be contrasted with the relative indeterminacy of the material duties of ethics (that is, the relative indeterminacy of what it takes to realize such ends as self-perfection and the happiness of others). And this contrast is at least part of what, in turn, explains why duties of justice are enforceable through coercion, while duties of virtue are not—for specificity is a necessary condition of enforceability. (But it may not be a sufficient condition for coercive enforceability: a moral justification for the coercive enforcement of a duty is always necessary, even if what is required by such a duty is specific enough for the attempt to enforce it coercively to make sense in the first place.)[10]

This argument may seem only to strengthen the impression that all ethical obligations are reducible to the material obligations of duties of virtue. However, in going on to make a third point, Kant now reuses the contrast between formal and material in a different sense, in order to draw the contrast between specific duties of virtue and the general obligation to be virtuous in the same way as he had in section II of the introduction to the "Doctrine of Virtue":

> *Third*, with regard to the distinction of the material from the formal in the principle of duty (of conformity with law from conformity with ends), it should be noted that not every *obligation of virtue* (*obligatio ethica*) is a duty of virtue (*officium ethicum s. virtutis*); in other words, respect for law as such does not yet establish an end as a duty, and only such an end is a duty of virtue.—Hence there is only *one* obligation of virtue, whereas there are *many* duties of virtue; for there are indeed many objects that it is also our duty to have as ends, but there

[9] See Kant, *Metaphysics of Morals*, "Doctrine of Right," introduction, section C, 6:230–31.
[10] For a brief discussion of this issue, see Stratton-Lake, "Being Virtuous and the Virtues," 109–10. Stratton-Lake makes it sound as if Kant sometimes thinks that the specificity of perfect duties is a sufficient condition for their coercive enforceability. However, Kant's inclusion of all perfect duties to oneself, as well as some perfect duties to others, among the duties of virtue, rather than the duties of right, makes it clear that he could not have thought this, as does his attempt to provide a justification for the use of coercion even in the case of those perfect duties to others included in the sphere of right. See Kant, *Metaphysics of Morals*, "Doctrine of Right," introduction, section D, 6:231; Gregor, p. 388.

is only one virtuous disposition, the subjective determining ground to fulfill one's duty. . . .[11]

Again, the obligation to be virtuous is necessarily singular because it is the obligation to act out of a certain motivation, namely, respect for "law as such" or for the moral law, and there is only one such law, while the moral law itself gives rise to a number of specific duties to adopt ends that cannot be coercively enforced. Kant here emphasizes the difference between the general obligation to be virtuous and the specific duties of virtue by remarking that the general obligation to be virtuous could, and in some sense even should, be the motivation for fulfilling duties of right. Nonetheless, of course, while the outward fulfillment of the latter can be coercively enforced, the satisfaction of the requirement to have this inward motivation cannot be: the "virtuous disposition . . . extends to duties of right as well although they cannot, because of this, be called duties of virtue." Kant had also made this point in the general introduction to the whole *Metaphysics of Morals*.[12]

Thus, Kant distinguishes between the general obligation to be virtuous (as the formal obligation to make respect for the moral law one's fundamental motivation) and the specific duties of virtue (as the material obligations to make one's own perfection and the happiness of others one's mandatory ends, and the even more specific requirements for implementing these goals). But this distinction only seems to force upon us the question whether it makes any sense to speak of the former as itself a duty or obligation, that is, whether it makes sense to say that one has a duty to fulfill one's duties in a specific way, out of a specific motivation. It might well seem that it must be either redundant or potentially infinitely regressive to say simply that one has a duty to fulfill one's duties. That is, it might well seem that to describe something—whether juridical, such as the requirement to fulfill one's contracts, or ethical, such as the requirement to be beneficent—as a duty is already to say that one is obliged to fulfill it, and that it would either add nothing or else add a potentially infinite repetition to say that one has a duty to fulfill one's duties (that is, that one has an obligation to fulfill one's obligations). To call them duties is already to say that their fulfillment is mandatory, and there seems nothing more to say. And if there is anything more to say, why not keep saying it?—that is, why not say that if one has a duty to fulfill one's duties, then one has a duty to fulfill one's duty to fulfill one's duties, and so on?

[11] Kant, *Metaphysics of Morals*, "Doctrine of Virtue," introduction, section XVII, 6:410; Gregor, pp. 537–38.

[12] See Kant, *Metaphysics of Morals*, introduction, section IV, 6:219–21; Gregor, pp. 383–85. For further discussion of this point, see Katja Maria Vogt, "Duties to Others: Demands and Limits," in Betzler, ed., *Kant's Ethics of Virtue*, 219–43, at 226–31.

To be sure, Kant is not simply saying that one has a general duty to fulfill one's specific duties; rather, he is saying that one has a general obligation to fulfill one's specific duties *in a particular way,* namely, out of a certain motivation, out of one's respect for the moral law. But is even *that* the sort of thing that can sensibly be called a duty or an obligation? One might object to this, first, out of a certain general picture of motivation and action. That is, one might suppose that it makes sense to talk of duties where there is room to talk of *choice,* and that there is room to talk of choice with regard to our *actions,* but that our motivations are just states that we *have,* not states that we *choose:* motivations are the states on which our choices of actions are based. Thus, one might argue that it makes no sense to say that we have a duty to have a certain motivation, because we cannot choose to have one motivation or another. Kant himself does not limit choice in this way, however: at least by the time he published *The Metaphysics of Morals* in 1797, he had, in his 1793 work *Religion within the Boundaries of Mere Reason,* straightened out earlier confusions in his view about the freedom of choice. In the latter work, he says that our most basic—"radical"—free choice is precisely the choice of whether to make the moral law or self-love our most fundamental maxim and motivation, that is, whether to adopt the principle always to make the principle of self-love subordinate to the principle of morality (and therefore to act out of self-love only when that is consistent with morality) or, vice versa, to make the principle of morality subordinate to the principle of self-love and to act morally only when that is consistent with acting out of self-love.[13] Kant clearly incorporated into *The Metaphysics of Morals* the fundamental distinction that he had to make in order to arrive at this view that we freely choose whether or not to make the moral law our fundamental motivation. This is the distinction between *Wille* or will *simpliciter* as an essentially cognitive faculty that offers us the moral law, and *Willkür* as the faculty of choice or "elective will," the practical faculty that makes the choice between the moral law and self-love.[14] So when he makes the distinction between the general obligation to be virtuous and the specific duties of virtue in this work, Kant does think that we can choose whether or not to make the moral law our fundamental motivation; thus, he thinks that we can choose to adopt specific ends (such as being beneficent to others) out of respect for morality as such or, for example, out of our sense of prudence. Thus, Kant himself would not think it an objection to the idea of a general duty to be virtuous that this duty would make sense only if we had a freedom to choose our motivation that we do not have; in his view, we do have the freedom to choose our fundamental motivation.

[13] See Immanuel Kant, *Religion within the Boundaries of Mere Reason,* in Kant, *Religion and Rational Theology,* ed. and trans. Allen W. Wood and George Di Giovanni (Cambridge: Cambridge University Press, 1996), Book I, 6:36–44.

[14] See Kant, *Metaphysics of Morals,* introduction, section III, 6:226; Gregor, p. 380.

However, it might still be objected that Kant's own conception of "moral worth" conflicts with his idea of a general obligation to be virtuous. In the famous opening section of the *Groundwork for the Metaphysics of Morals*, Kant appeals to what are supposed to be common-sense notions of the good will and duty, "the good will though under certain subjective limitations and hindrances,"[15] in order to arrive at an initial formulation of the categorical imperative that will then be confirmed and amplified from more philosophical premises in the second section and, finally, proved to be binding for us human beings in the third. His strategy is to find indubitable examples of moral worth (not empirical examples, to be sure, but thought experiments), that is, cases in which it is beyond doubt that there is good will or that duty has been done, in order to establish the constraints on any possible candidate for the moral law or categorical imperative.[16] (The categorical imperative is the moral law as it presents itself to creatures, like we human beings, who do not automatically follow it because they have inclinations that compete with the demands of morality. Should there be any purely rational beings who do not have such contra-moral inclinations, the moral law would not present itself to them in the form of an *imperative*.) Kant's argument from the concept of duty to the formulation of the moral law then proceeds in three steps.

His analysis begins from the premise that although agents who are motivated solely by inclination can still, at least under fortunate circumstances, act *in conformity* with duty, only in cases in which agents have no inclination in favor of the actions that duty requires (or in which those very agents who were previously moved by inclination have now lost their inclination but still do what duty requires) *can we be sure* that they are acting *from duty* alone and thus that their actions have what Kant calls "moral worth."[17] The point of this is to show that if we can be sure that an agent demonstrates moral worth only when he acts without inclination, then it must be possible to act on the moral law without inclination, and therefore the moral law cannot be grounded on inclination.[18] Kant then draws the consequences of this premise in the two further steps

[15] Kant, *Groundwork*, section I, 4:397; Gregor, p. 52.
[16] As Allen Wood says, Kant's point in these examples is not "to assert that other performances of duty are devoid of moral value but only to distinguish what is central to morality from what is comparatively peripheral." Allen W. Wood, *Kantian Ethics* (Cambridge: Cambridge University Press, 2008), 149. This interpretation of the point of Kant's examples of the morally worthy performance of duty in section I of the *Groundwork* is also consistent with what Samuel Kerstein has called a "criterial reading" of Kant's derivation of the fundamental principle of morality. See Samuel J. Kerstein, *Kant's Search for the Supreme Principle of Morality* (Cambridge: Cambridge University Press, 2002), chap. 4.
[17] Kant, *Groundwork*, section I, 4:397–98; Gregor, pp. 52–54.
[18] Numerous authors in recent years have argued that Kant's point in these examples is not to present a general theory of the moral evaluation of character, but rather to use indubitable examples of moral worth to derive the fundamental principle of morality or the necessary constraints on it that will, in turn, lead to its derivation. In addition to Allen Wood and Samuel Kerstein, already mentioned in note 16, see also Andrea Marlen Esser, *Eine Ethik für Endliche: Kants Tugendlehre in der Gegenwart* (Stuttgart: Frommann-Holzboog, 2004), 329–

of his analysis of duty, inferring, first, that if moral worth (and therefore
the moral law) is independent of inclination, then the moral law also
cannot concern the objects of inclination and, indeed, cannot concern the
objects of our actions at all,[19] and, second, that moral worth can lie only
in acting from respect for the moral law itself,[20] which, since it cannot
concern inclinations or their objects, can only prescribe that our maxims
have the form of law as such, or be universalizable.[21] The relevance of all
this to our present concern is simply that, in this analysis, Kant presents
"moral worth" or acting *from duty* as something different from and more
estimable than merely acting *in conformity with duty:* acting in conformity
with duty regardless of motive "deserves praise and encouragement but
not esteem,"[22] while only acting from duty merits esteem. And this suggests that even though we can use the absence of any inclination from
these indubitable cases of moral worth to determine the content of the
moral law (because obviously agents who clearly have moral worth must
be acting in accordance with the moral law), there is something supererogatory about actually acting *from* respect for the moral law. The agents
who merely act in *conformity* with the law and who merit praise and
encouragement for so doing are, after all, acting in accordance with the
law. Thus, it seems as if they *are* doing their duty, and as if acting *from duty*
(that is, more precisely, from respect for the moral law) is *doing more than
one's duty* and deserves "esteem" precisely because it is so. Thus, it would
seem, acting in conformity with the moral law is what duty requires, and
acting from duty deserves esteem just because it is more than what duty
requires; and so it seems that if to have a virtuous disposition is to be
motivated to act from respect for the moral law itself, then to have such
a disposition must be more than what duty requires; therefore, it seems
that there cannot be a duty to have a virtuous disposition.

Kant suggests a similar objection to the idea of a general obligation to
be virtuous in the introduction to the "Doctrine of Virtue" itself, by means
of a contrast between "merit" and "demerit." Kant says that the fulfillment of imperfect duties "is *merit* (*meritum*) . . . but failure to fulfill them
is not in itself *culpability* (*demeritum*) . . . but rather mere *deficiency in moral*

30; and Thomas E. Hill, Jr., "Kantian Virtue and 'Virtue Ethics'," in Betzler, ed., *Kant's Ethics
of Virtue,* 29–59, at 36–37.

[19] Kant, *Groundwork,* section I, 4:399–400; Gregor, pp. 54–55. I have argued that the second
step of Kant's argument is formally invalid, since he fails to consider the possibility that the
moral law could be grounded in the value of a *necessary* object of the will rather than on an
object of mere inclination, or that the moral law could command the realization of such a
necessary rather than contingent object. I have also argued, however, that Kant rectifies this
fallacy by the argument that humanity itself is a necessary end of the will that is the ground
of the categorical imperative in the second section of the *Groundwork* (4:427–29). See Paul
Guyer, "The Derivation of the Categorical Imperative: Kant's Correction for a Fatal Flaw,"
Harvard Review of Philosophy 10 (2002): 64–80.
[20] Kant, *Groundwork,* section I, 4:400; Gregor, p. 55.
[21] Ibid., section I, 4:401–2; Gregor, pp. 56–57.
[22] Ibid., section I, 4:398; Gregor, p. 53.

worth . . . unless the subject should make it his principle not to comply with such duties";[23] and he includes the general obligation to be virtuous as well as the specific duties of virtue among the imperfect duties. In fact, he immediately illustrates this claim with the general obligation to be virtuous rather than with a specific duty of virtue: "It is only the strength of one's resolution, in the first case, that is properly called *virtue* (*virtus*); one's weakness, in the second case, is not so much *vice* (*vitium*) as rather mere *want of virtue*, lack of moral strength (*defectus moralis*)." [24] Since there is no actual demerit in not being virtuous (unless one has made it a principle not to do one's duty) but there is special merit in being virtuous (that is, in fulfilling one's particular duties with a virtuous disposition), it seems again as if fulfilling one's duties is one thing and doing so virtuously is another, additional thing, above and beyond duty, and therefore not part of duty.

These reasons are internal to Kant's own account of moral worth and merit, and seem to make his idea that we have a general obligation to be virtuous in addition to our specific duties of virtue problematic. Can his idea be saved? In fact, the ground for an affirmative answer to this question has already been suggested in the last quotation from Kant: by virtue or a virtuous disposition in general, Kant does not just mean being motivated by respect for the moral law alone, but rather the *strength of one's resolution* to be so motivated. This is something that *can be developed* and, indeed, that one *can choose to develop*, as well as something the development of which is, for real-world human beings, a *necessary condition* for the fulfillment of their particular duties in the absence of external, coercive constraints. Thus, it is a necessary condition for the fulfillment of their particular duties of virtue, and, for that reason, it is something that can be demanded of them as itself a duty. Kant makes it clear in two key passages that virtue is not just being motivated by the moral law but rather the strength to be so motivated in the presence of natural inclinations that may be an obstacle to being so motivated in every human being. By means of this strength we may constrain ourselves to the fulfillment of our particular duties. In the first passage, Kant writes:

> *Virtue* is the strength of a human being's maxims in fulfilling his duty.—Strength of any kind can be recognized only by the obstacles it can overcome, and in the case of virtue these obstacles are natural inclinations, which can come into conflict with the human being's moral resolutions; and since it is the human being *himself* who puts these obstacles in the way of his maxims, virtue is not merely a self-constraint . . . but also a self-constraint in accordance with a prin-

[23] Kant, *Metaphysics of Morals*, "Doctrine of Virtue," introduction, section VII, 6:390; Gregor, p. 521.
[24] Ibid.

ciple of inner freedom, and so through the mere representation of one's duty in accordance with its formal law.

All duties involve a concept of *constraint* through a law. *Ethical* duties involve a constraint for which only internal lawgiving is possible, whereas duties of right involve a constraint for which external lawgiving is possible. Both, therefore, involve constraint, whether it be self-constraint or constraint by another. . . . [T]he moral capacity to constrain oneself can be called virtue. . . .[25]

This passage makes it clear that virtue in general lies not merely in being motivated by the moral law in addition to acting in conformity with its mandates, but in having the strength to constrain oneself to have this motivation, a strength that is a necessary condition in us human beings for acting morally because of the obstacles that our natural inclinations can and so often do present. Kant reiterates this conception of virtue in a second passage, under the rubric "On Virtue in General":

Virtue signifies a moral strength of the will. But this does not exhaust the concept; for such strength could also belong to a *holy* (superhuman) being, in whom no hindering impulses would impede the law of its will and who would thus gladly do everything in conformity with the law. Virtue is, therefore, the moral strength of a *human being's* will in fulfilling his *duty*, a moral *constraint* through his own lawgiving reason, insofar as this constitutes itself an authority *executing* the law.[26]

Again, Kant suggests that virtue is not just being motivated by the moral law, thereby possessing the ground of moral worth and merit that goes beyond duty; rather, virtue is the strength of will that is necessary in order to fulfill duty in the face of the obstacles to so doing that are natural to human beings. Thus, virtue is, in this way, a necessary condition for the fulfillment of duty, not something above and beyond duty, and, for this reason, it is something that can be demanded in the name of or as part of duty. For this reason, it seems to make sense after all to say that we have an obligation or duty to be virtuous as well as specific duties of virtue.

No sooner has he led us to this conclusion, however, than Kant seems to undermine it by adding that "Virtue itself, or possession of it, is not a duty (for then one would have to be put under obligation to duties); rather, it commands and accompanies its command with a moral constraint (a constraint possible in accordance with laws of duty)."[27] Here Kant seems to hold that it *cannot* be a duty to have what is a necessary

[25] Ibid., section IX, 6:394; Gregor, pp. 524–25.
[26] Ibid., section XIII, 6:405; Gregor, p. 533.
[27] Ibid.

condition for the fulfillment of particular duties, and perhaps that such a supposition would generate an infinite regress after all. So now it seems as if we are back where we began, and must ask again whether Kant's idea of a general obligation to be virtuous can be saved from what is apparently his own direct criticism of any such idea.

I will argue that Kant himself finally shows us how to defuse this criticism by arguing that even if it may not make sense to say that we have a duty to *have* a disposition that is a necessary condition for any specific obligation, it makes perfectly good sense to say that we have a duty to *cultivate* and *strengthen* a natural disposition that is a necessary condition to the performance of our particular obligations. On Kant's view, this is how the general obligation to be virtuous should be understood: as an obligation to cultivate and strengthen our natural tendency to be moved by the moral law.[28] This calls for acts that are different from the specific acts required to fulfill particular duties of virtue, and thus the obligation to be virtuous is not, in the end, merely formal and is not reducible without remainder to the duties of virtue. Before I make that argument, however, I want briefly to locate Kant's conception of obligation historically, and by so doing to suggest that there is historical precedent for his conception of a duty to cultivate what is a necessary condition for the fulfillment of more particular duties.[29]

III. Two Conceptions of Duty

On one conception of duty with which Kant was obviously familiar, a duty is simply an action required by a law. Thus, in his *German Ethics* (1720), Christian Wolff wrote: "By duty [*Pflicht*] we understand an action that is in accordance with a law.... No law is without obligatoriness [*Verbindlichkeit*]."[30] In a textbook three decades later (1750), Johann Stephan Pütter and Gottfried Achenwall defined moral obligation as

---

[28] Allen Wood succinctly characterizes the response I will offer to the present objection: "It is not a duty to have virtue in general, because only by having some degree of virtue is it possible to be placed under the self-constraint of duty at all. But greater virtue is a perfection of our will, so we have a wide or meritorious duty to improve ourselves in that respect" (Wood, *Kantian Ethics*, 144).

[29] In pursuing this issue about the plausibility of Kant's conception of a general duty to be virtuous, I will sidestep an issue raised by Stratton-Lake, "Being Virtuous and the Virtues"; and Marcia Baron, "Overdetermined Actions and Imperfect Duties," in Heiner Klemme, Manfred Kuehn, and Dieter Schönecker, eds., *Moralische Motivation: Kant und die Alternativen* (Hamburg: Felix Meiner Verlag, 2006), 23–37, esp. 27–29. This is the issue of whether it makes sense to say that one has a general duty to perform imperfect duties, when those duties do not themselves seem to make it mandatory to perform particular actions on particular occasions. I will just assume for the present discussion that it makes sense to think of a particular policy or end (such as being beneficent) as being commanded by a general sense of duty rather than being recommended by prudence; I will not worry about how the obligatoriness of the policy is transmitted to particular actions on particular occasions.

[30] Christian Wolff, *Vernünftige Gedancken von der Menschlichen Thun und Lassen* (1720), 4th ed. (Frankfurt and Leipzig, 1733), section 221.

whatever actions the will should determine to do in accordance with the concepts of good and evil: "That *obligates* [*obligat*] in the most general sense which connects with a spontaneous act a resulting good or evil. . . .The connection of a motive with a free action is called a *moral obligation* [*Obligatio*]."[31] These definitions suggest that whatever is required by a law (in Wolff's apparently deontological formulation) or by a moral conception of good and evil (in Pütter and Achenwall's explicitly teleological formulation) is a duty, and that it would make no sense to look beyond the particular requirements of the moral law or moral ends for a general duty to conform to moral law or seek moral ends. (I say Wolff's "apparently deontological" formulation, because his larger argument is that our duties are to perfect the mental, physical, and external conditions of ourselves and others—as well as to worship God—and thus his moral philosophy, as a whole, is as teleological as they come.)[32] To look for such a general duty would indeed risk generating an infinite regress of duties which does not need to get started in the first place.

A more complex conception of duty, however, and one to which Kant seems to be responding, is to be found in the widely influential, somewhat earlier work of Samuel Pufendorf, whose *Whole Duty of Man and Citizen* (1673) remained influential throughout Europe for a century.[33] Pufendorf makes two moves that are helpful to understanding Kant's conception of duty. First, he not only defines a duty as "human action in conformity with the commands of law on the ground of obligation,"[34] but goes on to define a law as "a decree by which a superior obliges one who is subject to him to conform his actions to the superior's prescript."[35] Thus, he implies that a duty or an obligation is not merely prescribed by a law, or an act required by a law, but is also "introduced into a man's mind by a superior." To this last inference he immediately adds that a superior is "one who has not only the strength to inflict some injury on the recalcitrant, but also just cause to require us to curtail the liberty of

---

[31] Johann Stephan Pütter and Gottfried Achenwall, *Anfangsgründe des Naturrechts* (*Elementa Iuris Naturae*) (1750), ed. and trans. Jan Schröder (Frankfurt am Main: Insel Verlag, 1995), sections 80, 82, p. 39.

[32] As Kant makes clear in his *Critique of Practical Reason*, 5:40; Gregor, p. 172.

[33] This work was an abridgment of Pufendorf's *De jure naturae et gentium libri octo* ("On the law of nature and nations, in eight books") of 1672. The Latin version was widely accessible, and the book was translated into English as early as 1691; the English edition, in turn, went through five editions by 1735. The latter edition of Andrew Tooke's translation has recently been republished as *The Whole Duty of Man, According to the Law of Nature*, ed. Ian Hunter and David Saunders (Indianapolis, IN: Liberty Fund, 2003). A modern English translation of the first edition of the work is Samuel Pufendorf, *On the Duty of Man and Citizen According to Natural Law*, ed. James Tully, trans. Michael Silverthorne (Cambridge: Cambridge University Press, 1991). As the former includes some material not included in the latter, I will quote from both in what follows, distinguishing them by the different titles of the translations.

[34] Pufendorf, *On the Duty of Man and Citizen*, Book I, chap. I, section 1, p. 17.

[35] Ibid., Book I, chap. II, section 2, p. 27.

our will at his discretion."[36] There are thus two elements in Pufendorf's conception of duty: a duty is not merely an action required of agents in accordance with a law for the existence of which there is a good reason; it is also an action required of agents by an authority that has the power to enforce that law. On Pufendorf's account, the primary source of duties is God, who has created us to live sociably with one another and has legislated the laws of nature with the good reason that they are what it is necessary for us to follow in order to live sociably with one another. The secondary source of duties is the civil authority that transforms natural law into civil law and adds whatever further obligations are necessary in order to maintain civil authority itself.

A second aspect of Pufendorf's conception of duty that will turn out to be important to Kant is Pufendorf's conception of the nature of duty to oneself. Pufendorf employs the tripartite division of duties into duties to God, duties to self, and duties to others—a division that would remain canonical in German moral philosophy throughout the eighteenth century.[37] "Perhaps the duties imposed on man by natural law are most conveniently divided in accordance with the objects on which those duties are to be exercised," Pufendorf writes. "On these lines they form three principal divisions. The first teaches, on the basis of right reason alone, how one should behave towards God; the second towards oneself; the third towards other men."[38] Our duty to other men is obviously to live in accordance with the rules that make it possible to live with them sociably (to which we have a natural disposition) by keeping our unsociable impulses (which we also naturally have) in check. Our duty to God is the direct duty to worship him in gratitude for our creation, but we also have an indirect duty to fear him in order to better maintain our society with other men:

> The precepts of natural law regarding others are derived primarily and directly from sociality, which we have laid down as the foundation. The duties toward God as Creator can also be deduced, indirectly, from that source, insofar as the ultimate sanction of duties

[36] Ibid., Book I, chap. II, section 5, p. 28.

[37] Thus, the division of duties into those toward God, toward self, and toward others, was preserved in Alexander Gottlieb Baumgarten's *Initia Philosophiae Practicae* (*Introduction to Practical Philosophy*) published in 1760, and would, in turn, structure Kant's lectures on ethics, for which Baumgarten's book served as the text, at least as late as 1784–85, the date of the notes by Georg Ludwig Collins translated in Immanuel Kant, *Lectures on Ethics*, ed. Peter Heath and J. B. Schneewind (Cambridge: Cambridge University Press, 1997), 37–222. (But note that the Collins transcription is largely identical to earlier transcriptions, such as that by Johann Friedrich Kaehler from the summer semester of 1777, published as Immanuel Kant, *Vorlesung zur Moralphilosophie*, ed. Werner Stark [Berlin and New York: Walter de Gruyter, 2004], and may be a copy of an earlier set of notes rather than a transcription of what Kant actually said in 1784–85.) Of course, as we will see below, Kant denies that we have any duties directly to God.

[38] Pufendorf, *The Whole Duty of Man*, Book I, chap. III, section 13, p. 37.

toward other men comes from religion and fear of the Deity, so that a man would not even be sociable if he were not imbued with religion, and because reason alone in religion extends no further than to religion's capacity to promote the tranquillity [sic] and sociality of this life.[39]

Pufendorf also interprets our duty to ourselves as an indirect duty to cultivate those powers of our mind and body by means of which we may successfully fulfill our duties to others and to God (in the latter case, since our duty to God is already itself, at least in part, an indirect duty, our duty to ourselves is, at least in part, a doubly indirect duty):

> The duties of a man toward himself, however, emanate from religion and sociality together. For the reason why in some matters man cannot dispose of himself at his own absolute discretion, is partly that he may be fit to worship the divinity, and partly that he may be an agreeable and useful member of human society.[40]

The duty that we have with regard to our mind or soul is, in turn, divided into "the right Formation of the Mind and the Heart," that is, the duty to form true opinions about God and society, and the duty to regulate "the Dispositions of our Minds; in reducing and conforming them to the Dictates of right Reason . . . and in one word, in getting ourselves possest [sic] of all those Qualities which are necessary for us to lead an *honest* and a *sociable* Life"[41] and "*To gain the Mastery over our Passions.*"[42] The duty that we have with regard to our body is to "strengthen and preserve the powers of the body with appropriate food and exercise"; "We should not weaken them by intemperance in food or drink or by unseasonable and unnecessary toil or by any other means,"[43] so that our bodies will be fit instruments for the accomplishment of our moral objectives with regard to others in society.

The contents of Kant's own enumeration of our duties to ourselves in the "Doctrine of Virtue" is obviously deeply indebted to Pufendorf, but this is not the point that I want to emphasize. Rather, I want to draw attention to two more general points. First, Kant's account of duty clearly includes Pufendorf's requirement that there is a duty only when there is not just a good reason for the performance or omission that is enjoined, but also a proper authority for the enforcement of that performance or omission. However, Kant changes Pufendorf's conception of the primary

---

[39] Ibid.
[40] Ibid., Book I, chap. III, section xiii, p. 60.
[41] Here I quote from Tooke's 1735 translation: Pufendorf, *The Whole Duty of Man*, Book I, chap. V, section ii, pp. 70–71.
[42] Ibid., Book I, chap. V, section viii, p. 77.
[43] Pufendorf, *On the Duty of Man and Citizen*, Book I, chap. V, section 3, p. 47.

superior for the enforcement of duty from God to our own reason and the strength of our own will. Kant begins his "Discussion of the Concept of a Doctrine of Virtue" with the Pufendorfian premise that "The very *concept of duty* is already the concept of a *necessitation* (constraint) of free choice through the law," but he fundamentally alters the theological foundation of Pufendorf's theory of natural law when he continues that "Since the human being is still a *free* (moral) being, when the concept of duty concerns the internal determination of his will (the incentive) the constraint that the concept of duty contains can only be self-constraint (through the representation of the law alone); for only so can that *necessitation* (even if it is external) be united with the freedom of his choice." [44] For Kant, the idea that our duty to live sociably with other men is imposed upon us by the will of God, and enforced by the strength of God, is the very picture of heteronomy. For Kant, for whom autonomy is the ultimate moral value and the source of all moral obligations, the requirements that we preserve our own freedom and cultivate the means for its successful exercise, and that we live on terms of equal freedom with others, can only be the contents of the moral law suggested by our own reason. Moreover, the freedom that is the ultimate aim of all morality can be imposed upon us only by the strength of our own will if it is not to contradict itself—if it is not to become an imposed freedom that is no longer freedom. For all the similarities in both form and content between Kant's moral philosophy and the Pufendorfian paradigm, this is a fundamental revolution.

The sea-change between Kant's ethics of self-imposed and self-enforced obligation and Pufendorf's theory can also be seen in Kant's revision of Pufendorf's conception of the relation between divine and civil authority. For Pufendorf, our primary duty is the duty to live sociably with others, a duty in accordance with natural law that is primarily enforced by our fear of God, and secondarily enforced by civil authorities in accordance with civil law (but under the authority of God). For Kant, civil or juridical law is typically enforced through the external, aversive constraints of a public penal code, which works upon and is satisfied with our merely prudential motivation for obedience. Yet it is also possible and morally estimable for us to obey the dictates of civil law out of the purely moral motivation of respect for the moral law itself, which is, after all, the source of the requirement that we preserve maximally equal spheres of external freedom in our interactions with others, as well as of the non-coercively enforceable duties to ourselves and others that comprise ethics: "All that ethics teaches is that if the incentive which juridical lawgiving connects with . . . duty, namely external constraint, were absent, the idea of duty by itself would be sufficient as an incentive," and indeed there is a "proof of

[44] Kant, *Metaphysics of Morals,* "Doctrine of Virtue," introduction, section I, 6:379–80; Gregor, pp. 512–13.

virtue" in the observation of juridical legislation only if we "do it even where no coercion may be *applied*."[45] Kant does not see the observation of legal requirements out of fear of the consequences of disobeying them as undermining our autonomy in the way that he sees fulfilling moral requirements generally only out of fear of divine punishment or hope for divine rewards as the epitomy of heteronomy, because he views the institution and maintenance of the juridical authority of the state as itself a product of our freedom. However, he does view the motivation to fulfill even juridical legislation out of our respect for the moral law alone as the fullest expression of our freedom.

My first general point, then, has been that Kant accepts from Pufendorf the requirement that duty must always involve the possibility of constraint by an appropriate authority, but he radically transforms Pufendorf's conception of duty by making the ultimate authority for duty our own reason, enforced by the strength of our own will. My second general point is that Kant accepts from Pufendorf the idea of indirect duty that structures Pufendorf's conception of duty to oneself and even, to an extent, his conception of duty to God. To confine ourselves to the former case, Pufendorf, as we saw, conceives of duty to self as the duty to develop those capacities and powers in oneself that will enable one to satisfy one's duties to others in society. On his account, then, we can have a duty to ensure the existence of the necessary conditions to satisfy other duties, and there is nothing redundant or infinitely regressive in such an idea. We have a duty to develop those capacities in ourselves that are necessary to enable us to fulfill our duties to others, and that is not redundant, because there is a substantive difference in content between the duties to self and the duties to others. Nor is it infinitely regressive, because there is no further duty to fulfill the duties to self that are the necessary conditions for being able to fulfill duties to others, and so on. What I now want to suggest is that Kant uses this structure in his own account of the relation between the general obligation to be virtuous and the specific duties of virtue: the development of the strength of will that is required by the former is the necessary condition of fulfilling the latter (and even of fulfilling the duties of right, if there are cases in which external constraint is either not available or not necessary).

By drawing this parallel, I do not want to suggest that Kant reduces all duties to self to instruments for fulfilling duties to others, either other humans or God, as Pufendorf does. For Kant, we have a duty to treat humanity in our own selves always as an end and never merely as a means—a duty that is on exactly the same plane as our duty to treat humanity in others that way—and we would have that duty to ourselves even if, *per impossibile*, there were no other human beings whom we could affect by our actions.[46] I only want to suggest that Kant exploits the idea of an indirect duty to realize the necessary condition of satisfying other duties that Pufendorf suggests in his account of duties to self. But before we can see how the details of this strategy work, we must face the threat left hanging at the end of the previous section, the suggestion by Kant himself that the possession of "virtue itself" cannot actually be a duty.[47]

IV. THE OBLIGATION TO BE VIRTUOUS AS AN OBLIGATION TO STRENGTHEN ONE'S RESOLVE

As I noted earlier, in *Religion within the Boundaries of Mere Reason* (written before *The Metaphysics of Morals*), Kant had abandoned the view of the *Groundwork* that the moral law is the causal law of the noumenal self[48] and committed himself to the alternative view that we have a free, noumenal choice whether to subordinate the principle of self-love to the moral law or to subordinate the moral law to the principle of self-love. Freely choosing to make the moral law superior to the principle of self-love is a necessary condition for fulfilling any particular duties when doing so is not prescribed by self-love. The whole point of instituting a penal code is to make sure that self-love usually will recommend fulfilling duties of right even if commitment to the moral law does not. Thus, in this case, a virtuous disposition (a commitment to be motivated by the moral law above all else) cannot be demanded as a necessary condition for the fulfillment of duties of right, and, from the point of view of right, a virtuous disposition can indeed be regarded as supererogatory, something whose presence is meritorious but whose absence brings no demerit. But it is not appropriate or even possible to enforce fulfillment of duties of virtue by coercive means. It is not possible because coercion can only bring about the performance of particular actions, not the adoption of an end; and it is neither appropriate nor possible because the duty to adopt an end is the duty to choose an end freely. In the case of duties of virtue, then, firm commitment to the superiority of the moral law over the principle of self-love is a necessary condition for the fulfillment of those duties when self-love does not itself prescribe it, which will sometimes or often be the case. Thus, it seems that a virtuous disposition (commitment to the moral law) can be demanded as the necessary condition of fulfillment of the particular duties of virtue, and is not supererogatory at all, but can be considered a duty, the obligation to be virtuous. This could be

---

[46] Or nearly *per impossibile:* a human child who could be raised by wolves and never have contact with any other human beings is not among the empirical possibilities that have to be considered in a Kantian metaphysics of morals, which derives duties for human beings in the actual empirical conditions of their existence and not in imaginary conditions.

[47] Kant, *Metaphysics of Morals,* "Doctrine of Virtue," introduction, section XIII, 6:405; Gregor, p. 533.

[48] Kant, *Groundwork,* section III, 4:446; Gregor, p. 94.

understood on the model of the two-tiered structure of direct and indirect duty that Kant could have adopted from Pufendorf.

Thus, Kant could have countered his own objection by arguing that "Virtue itself, or the possession of it, is not a duty," but this is not what he does argue. Rather, what he does say (four pages after making this remark) is that "Virtue is always *in progress* and yet always starts *from the beginning.*—It is always in progress because, considered *objectively,* it is an ideal and unattainable, while yet constant approximation to it is a duty. That it always starts from the beginning has a *subjective* basis in human nature."[49] In other words, while it may make no sense to say that *to be virtuous* is a duty, it makes sense to say that *to strive to make progress toward becoming virtuous* is a duty. How does this help save Kant from an objection to the idea that a necessary condition of a duty is also a duty?

One thing this remark could be taken to mean is that to be *perfectly* virtuous cannot be considered a duty, because it is simply not possible for human beings to have a holy will (that is, to be moved only by the moral law and not even be moved by self-love) and because agents have no obligation to attempt to do that which is impossible for them to do. But humans can always have purer motivation than they do, and thus can always make progress toward having perfectly virtuous dispositions, so it is possible for "constant approximation" to virtue to be a duty. However, although Kant makes that point later in the body of the "Doctrine of Virtue,"[50] and we will return to it, that does not seem to be his point here. Rather, his point seems to be something like this. On the one hand, the disposition to make the moral law our fundamental maxim is the necessary condition of the possibility of constraining ourselves to fulfill our particular duties of virtue, so it may not seem to make sense to think of that disposition as itself the object of a duty, precisely because it is the condition of the possibility of being put under an obligation. Unless we had such a disposition, it would not be possible for us to recognize any claims of duty at all, so it does not make sense to say that we have a duty to have that disposition itself—that would start us off on an infinite regress. On the other hand, although we do have a natural disposition to do our duty that makes it possible for us to recognize the claim of (and fulfill) particular duties, that is not our only natural disposition. We also have the disposition toward self-love, and thus our natural disposition to be moral always needs to be strengthened, and our disposition toward self-love weakened and controlled. At the noumenal level, we may simply be able to choose to subordinate the principle of self-love to the principle of morality rather than the contrary, but what doing this requires

[49] Kant, *Metaphysics of Morals,* "Doctrine of Virtue," introduction, section XVI, 6:409; Gregor, p. 537.
[50] Ibid., "Doctrine of Virtue," section 22, 6:446–47; Gregor, p. 567.

of us at the phenomenal level is that we constantly strive to strengthen our natural disposition in favor of morality at the expense of our natural disposition in favor of self-love. Thus, even though it would make no sense to say that we would have a duty to have a disposition in favor of morality (a virtuous disposition) if we did not already have one—because without such a disposition, duties can make no claim on us—it makes perfectly good sense to say that we have a duty to strengthen our natural disposition to morality, because that very disposition itself allows us not only to recognize the claim of duty in general but also to recognize that we may always need to strengthen our moral resolve in order to be able to do our duty in particular cases where self-love tempts us to do otherwise. Thus, the general obligation to be virtuous can be perfectly well understood as a duty to strengthen our natural disposition to be moral.[51]

Kant suggests precisely such a pattern of reasoning in his discussion of "The Mind's Receptivity to Concepts of Duty as Such." In this section of the introduction to the "Doctrine of Virtue," preceding by several pages the remark that "constant approximation" to virtue is a duty, Kant writes:

There are certain moral endowments such that anyone lacking them could have no duty to acquire them.—They are *moral feeling, conscience, love* of one's neighbor, and *respect* for oneself (*self-esteem*). There is no obligation to have these because they lie at the basis of morality, as *subjective* conditions of receptiveness to the concept of duty, not as objective conditions of morality. All of them are natural predispositions of the mind, antecedent predispositions on the side of *feeling*. To have these predispositions cannot be considered a duty; rather, every human being has them, and it is by virtue of them that he can be put under obligation.[52]

Love of one's neighbor and self-esteem are being treated here as particular natural dispositions that make it possible for one to fulfill particular duties of virtue toward others and toward oneself; let us leave them aside and focus on the dispositions toward moral feeling and conscience, which seem to be general conditions for recognizing and fulfilling any claims of duty in the absence of external constraint. Kant's claim is that it makes no sense to say that we have a duty to have these dispositions, because without them we could not be receptive to the concept of duty at all; that is, we could not recognize and be motivated to fulfill the claims of duty. His idea must be that although at the noumenal level we simply choose to prioritize morality over self-love, at the phenomenal level our recog-

[51] Thus can the suggestion made by Wood in the passage cited in note 28 above be expanded.
[52] Kant, *Metaphysics of Morals*, "Doctrine of Virtue," introduction, section XIII, 6:399; Gregor, p. 528.

nition of the superiority of morality manifests itself in our moral feeling and conscience outweighing our equally natural disposition to self-love; moral feeling and conscience are the natural means *through which* our free choice to be made moral is made effective on our actions, which of course take place in the phenomenal world.[53] But Kant does not think that we simply make the noumenal choice to be moral and then, as if by magic, our moral feeling and conscience automatically outweigh any contrary natural dispositions. On the contrary, he thinks that our noumenal choice to be moral leads us to take steps to strengthen our moral feeling and conscience so that they will be effective in particular cases of action. In other words, the first manifestation of our recognition of duty in general will be the recognition that we have the duty to strengthen our moral feeling and conscience. Here is how Kant puts the point in the case of moral feeling:

> Since any consciousness of obligation depends upon moral feeling to make us aware of the constraint present in the thought of duty, there can be no duty to have moral feeling or to acquire it; instead every human being (as a moral being) has it in him originally. Obligation with regard to moral feeling can be only to *cultivate* it and to strengthen it through wonder at its inscrutable force.[54]

Kant does not worry that any human being is simply lacking in moral feeling. "No human being is entirely without moral feeling, for were he completely lacking in receptivity to it he would be morally dead," that is, a mere animal. (Perhaps this is a merely analytical point: if you do not have moral feeling, it would not be possible for you to be moved by the thought of duty, and you would not count as a moral agent—we would have to deal with you under some other conception, as a nonperson who should nevertheless be treated humanely.) Kant believes the same about conscience, which he defines as "practical reason holding the human being's duty before him for his acquittal or condemnation in every case that comes under a law," and which I think we should understand as the

---

[53] I have developed this interpretation of Kant's model of moral psychology at greater length in Paul Guyer, *Knowledge, Reason, and Taste: Kant's Response to Hume* (Princeton, NJ: Princeton University Press, 2008), chap. 4. Once again, Allen Wood puts the point succinctly: "Moral action proceeds from desires produced in us by rational choice" (Wood, *Kantian Ethics*, 183). Mary Gregor also wrote the following concerning "those inclinations which facilitate our fulfilment of duty": "In so far as they have previously been cultivated with a view to this purpose they are, in part, the work of freedom." See Mary J. Gregor, *Laws of Freedom: A Study of Kant's Method of Applying the Categorical Imperative in the "Metaphysik der Sitten"* (Oxford: Basil Blackwell, 1963), 175. But Gregor seems to have had in mind the cultivation of specific feelings such as feelings of sympathy, which Kant discusses under the rubric of duties of love to others, rather than the general moral feeling and tendency to conscience that he discusses in the introduction to the "Doctrine of Virtue."

[54] Kant, *Metaphysics of Morals*, "Doctrine of Virtue," introduction, section XIIa, 6:399–400; Gregor, pp. 528–29.

natural disposition that presents particular situations to our empirical selves as cases calling for moral decision.[55] Kant writes: "So too, conscience is not something that can be acquired, and we have no duty to provide ourselves with one; rather, every human being, as a moral being, *has* a conscience within him originally," but "The duty here is only to cultivate one's conscience, to sharpen one's attentiveness to the voice of the inner judge and to use every means to obtain a hearing for it (hence the duty is only indirect)."[56] Again, while it may make no sense to say that we have a duty to have a predisposition without which we could not have duties at all, it makes perfectly good sense to say that we have a duty to strengthen a natural predisposition through which we can make our choice to be moral in particular cases effective. Kant explicitly says that this duty is "indirect" in the case of conscience: what he most obviously means by this is that conscience is what allows us to recognize that we are in particular circumstances in which a duty needs to be fulfilled, while moral feeling is that which provides the impetus to fulfill it, or transmits the impetus of the noumenal choice to fulfill it into the phenomenal world. But both the duty to strengthen moral feeling and the duty to strengthen conscience can also be regarded as indirect duties in the sense previously suggested; that is, they can be regarded as duties because they are the means to the fulfillment of more particular duties, and indeed the only means to the fulfillment of particular duties of virtue where self-love would do otherwise.

So the indirect duties to strengthen moral feeling and conscience suggest a model for the indirect general obligation to be virtuous. Indeed, I would suggest that the duties to strengthen moral feeling and conscience *comprise* the general obligation to be virtuous, or comprise a large part of it. That is, what we have to do in order to make progress toward being virtuous, which is how we are now understanding the general obligation to be virtuous, is constantly take steps to strengthen our natural disposition to have moral feeling and conscience and by that means to "fight" against the "brood of dispositions opposing the law."[57] It is by strengthening these dispositions that we come to "govern ourselves" and gain control over our feelings and inclinations, and even more so over "*affects*" or "*precipitate* and *rash*" feelings and "*passions*" or "*sensible desire*[s]" that have become "lasting inclination[s]."[58] Kant says that "Virtue Requires, in the First Place, Governing Oneself":

[55] Thus, "conscience" would be Kant's term for the psychological faculty that presents "moral salience" to our empirical selves, to borrow Barbara Herman's term. See Barbara Herman, *The Practice of Moral Judgment* (Cambridge, MA: Harvard University Press, 1993), chap. 4, pp. 73–93.
[56] Kant, *Metaphysics of Morals*, "Doctrine of Virtue," introduction, section XIIb, 6:400–401; Gregor, pp. 529–30.
[57] Ibid., section XIII, 6:405; Gregor, p. 533.
[58] On Kant's distinction between affects and passions, see his *Anthropology from a Pragmatic Point of View*, Book III, section 74, in Immanuel Kant, *Anthropology, History, and Edu-*

Since virtue is based on inner freedom it contains a positive command to a human being, namely to bring all his capacities and inclinations under his (reason's) control and so to rule over himself, which goes beyond forbidding him to let himself be governed by his feelings and inclinations (the duty of *apathy*); for unless reason holds the reins of government in its own hands, his feelings and inclinations play the master over him.[59]

This is the conclusion of the section that immediately precedes the one in which Kant states that constant approximation to virtue is a duty. So the positive command to govern ourselves—the general obligation to be virtuous—can only be understood as the command to constantly strengthen our self-government, and this is, in turn, accomplished in large part by strengthening our natural dispositions to moral feeling and conscience, which are the means by which we counter the attractions of affects and passions.

I say "in large part" because Kant amplifies the steps that we must take in order to fulfill our general obligation to be virtuous a little bit in the main body of the "Doctrine of Virtue."[60] In a characteristic display of his love for architectonic organization of his arguments, Kant divides the body of the "Doctrine of Virtue" into two parts, the first concerning duties of virtue to the self and the second concerning duties of virtue to others;[61]

---

cation, ed. Günter Zöller and Robert B. Louden (Cambridge: Cambridge University Press, 2007), 354. For commentary, see Wood, *Kantian Ethics,* 147–48.

[59] Kant, *Metaphysics of Morals,* "Doctrine of Virtue," introduction, section XV, 6:408–9; Gregor, pp. 535–36.

[60] Philip Stratton-Lake observes that Kant "complicates" his distinction between the general obligation to be virtuous and the particular duties of virtue by including the duty to perfect ourselves—which Kant must be understanding as the duty to perfect our moral being in order to think there is any confusion—among the particular duties of virtue (Stratton-Lake, "Being Virtuous and the Virtues," 105). Stratton-Lake then says that to avoid confusion "we have to distinguish between striving to make oneself virtuous and the state of virtue one is striving to attain." This distinction is not the answer to the confusion created by Kant's inclusion of the duty to perfect oneself (morally) among the particular duties of virtue; instead, as we have already seen, it is Kant's solution to the paradox of how we can have a duty to acquire that which is the condition of the possibility of having duties. The response to the confusing inclusion of the general duty to strengthen our virtue among the particular duties of virtue is rather that, as we will now see, the latter treatment only adds one detail to what we can recognize has already been argued in the introduction to the "Doctrine of Virtue," as long as we interpret the duties to strengthen our moral feeling and conscience there as actually comprising the general duty to approximate to virtue.

[61] Note that Kant has reformed the entire Pufendorfian tradition (represented by Christian Wolff and his followers such as Alexander Baumgarten as well) of a tripartite distinction among duties to God, to self, and to others: Kant has already argued in *Religion within the Boundaries of Mere Reason* that we have no direct duties to God, but only a duty to ourselves and others to join in an ethical commonwealth that may require worship of God as a sort of cement, and he briskly argues in an "episodic section" in the "Doctrine of Virtue" that while we may have a *"duty of religion"* to regard all of our duties *"as if (instar)* they were divine commands," this is not a *"duty to God"* (Kant, *Metaphysics of Morals,* "Doctrine of Virtue," section 18, 6:443; Gregor, p. 564).

he then divides Part I (but not Part II) into two books, the first concerning perfect duties to oneself and the second concerning imperfect duties to oneself; and he finally divides each of these into two chapters, the first concerning perfect or imperfect duties to oneself respectively as "an animal being," and the second concerning those duties to oneself "merely as a moral being." [62] The perfect duties to oneself as an animal being are the prohibitions against suicide, self-abuse, and self-stupefaction,[63] that is, duties to preserve one's body and its efficacy as an instrument of one's free choices. The imperfect duties to oneself as an animal being are the duties to perfect (or adopt the end of perfecting) one's natural powers of "spirit" or reason, "soul" or other mental powers (such as memory and imagination) that can be put to work by reason, and "body" or physical strength and skill, all of which are powers by means of which one's free choices can be made efficacious.[64] One's perfect duties to oneself as a moral being are twofold. First, Kant enumerates prohibitions against lying, avarice, and servility; the prohibition of these vices might seem to be duties toward others, but Kant treats them as duties toward oneself because violating them would undermine one's power to communicate with others, one's power to use nonhuman things for reasonable purposes, and one's dignity in the eyes of others.[65] Second, and what is relevant to our present argument, he lists the "Human Being's Duty to Himself as His Own Innate Judge"[66] as "the *First Command* of All Duties to Oneself," namely, the duty to "'*know* (scrutinize, fathom) *yourself*,' not in terms of your natural perfection . . . but rather in terms of your moral perfection in relation to your duty."[67] Kant then finally adds an agent's imperfect duty to himself as a moral being, the duty "to increase his *moral* perfection, that is, for a moral purpose only."[68]

What Kant actually says about our duties to ourselves as moral beings within this complicated framework is quite simple. First, he says: "Every human being has a conscience and finds himself observed, threatened, and in general kept in awe (respect coupled with fear) by an internal judge; and this authority watching over the law in him is not something that he himself (voluntarily) *makes*, but something incorporated in his being."[69] Kant does not need to add that our duty with regard to this

---

[62] Part II of the "Doctrine of Virtue" is divided more simply, primarily into a section on "duties of love" toward others (the positive, imperfect duties of beneficence, gratitude, and sympathy) and a section on "duties of respect toward others" (the duties not to be arrogant toward them or defame or ridicule them). The latter should no doubt be considered perfect but not coercively enforceable duties; therefore, they are not perfect duties toward others included in the "Doctrine of Right."

[63] Kant, *Metaphysics of Morals,* "Doctrine of Virtue," sections 5–8.

[64] Ibid., section 19.

[65] Ibid., sections 9–12.

[66] Ibid., section 13, 6:437; Gregor, p. 559.

[67] Ibid., section 14, 6:441; Gregor, p. 562.

[68] Ibid., section 21, 6:446; Gregor, p. 566.

[69] Ibid., section 13, 6:438; Gregor, p. 560.

faculty, which is already present within us and by its nature commands our attention, can only be to strengthen it, because he has already said this in the introduction to the "Doctrine of Virtue." This first perfect duty to oneself as a moral being thus does not add anything to the analysis of what is necessary in order to fulfill one's general obligation to be virtuous that has already been provided in the introduction, and its inclusion here among particular duties of virtue may be momentarily confusing but is harmless.

Second, under the command to know oneself, not in terms of one's natural abilities (and thus what sorts of projects one could prudently undertake) but with respect to one's "moral perfection in relation to our duty," Kant adds that one needs to know one's heart. That is, one needs to know one's good and evil tendencies, which is necessary in order "first to remove the obstacle within (an evil will actually present in him) and then to develop the original predisposition to a good will within him, which can never be lost."[70] Kant adds that moral cognition of oneself will "dispel *fanatical* contempt for oneself as a human being (for the whole human race)"; that is, it will dispel the belief that all human beings are necessarily evil, for this moral self-knowledge will also reveal the natural predisposition to a good will. Kant then infers that "Impartiality in appraising oneself in comparison with the law, and sincerity in acknowledging to oneself one's inner moral worth or lack of worth are duties to oneself that follow directly from this first command to cognize oneself."[71] Here Kant does add something to the requirements of strengthening moral sense and conscience as the constituents of the general obligation to be virtuous that have already been provided in the introduction, but what he adds is something that we might suppose is implicit in them, since knowing what we need to do in order to strengthen our moral feeling and conscience and to weaken other feelings and voices within ourselves surely presupposes knowing what states those feelings are currently in and what our current degree of moral worth or lack of moral worth is. (Nonetheless, as Kant famously asserts in the *Groundwork*, we can never be certain of our real degree of moral worth and are constantly tempted to overrate it[72]— all the more reason why we have a duty constantly to strengthen our moral self-knowledge.) Kant does not explicitly state that we must have some natural predisposition to appraise ourselves in comparison with the law and to acknowledge our inner moral worth or lack thereof, and that our actual duty with regard to moral self-appraisal can only be to cultivate and strengthen it, but perhaps that is self-evident.

Finally, under the rubric of our imperfect duty to ourselves as moral beings, Kant does not actually add any new requirement, but only makes

[70] Ibid., section 14, 6:441; Gregor, p. 562.
[71] Ibid., section 15, 6:441; Gregor, p. 563.
[72] Kant, *Groundwork*, 4:407; Gregor, p. 61.

explicit that a human will is never a holy will (a will that is simply not tempted by inclination), so that our duty to strive after moral perfection "remains only a progress from *one* perfection to another,"[73] and thus: "This duty to oneself is a *narrow* and perfect one in terms of its quality; but it is wide and imperfect in terms of its degree, because of the *frailty* (*fragilitas*) of human nature."[74] That is, we do not have a choice whether or not to strive to be virtuous in this situation or that, as we might have a choice whether to cultivate this potential talent or that one; rather, we are always under a general obligation to improve our virtue. But while there is no limit to how much we can strengthen our virtue, there is also nothing that will ever count as completing the task of strengthening our virtue.[75]

What it takes to cultivate and strengthen our general resolve to fulfill our particular virtues, even when we are not externally constrained to do so, has thus already been largely spelled out in the introduction to the "Doctrine of Virtue," and Kant has not really confused the general obligation to be virtuous with the particular duties of virtue that he discusses in the body of the text. What he has done in the introduction is to show that it does make sense to impose upon ourselves a general obligation to cultivate and strengthen our natural disposition to be moral by cultivating and strengthening our natural tendencies to moral feeling and conscience, which both require cultivating moral self-knowledge. He has also shown this general obligation to be one freely imposed on us by our own reason and thus to be an autonomous form of self-constraint rather than a heteronomous form of external constraint. By so doing, Kant has made sense of a general obligation to be virtuous as well as of particular duties of virtue, and any confusions in his account are quite superficial.

V. CONCLUSION

The problem that was raised by Kant's distinction between specific duties of virtue and a general obligation to be virtuous, and especially by Kant's characterization of the former as "material" and the latter as "formal," was that the general obligation to be virtuous might turn out to be redundant, requiring a certain motivation for our fulfillment of particular duties if we want to earn "moral worth," but adding nothing specific for us actually to do beyond fulfilling our particular duties. We have now

---

[73] Kant, *Metaphysics of Morals*, "Doctrine of Virtue," section 21, 6:446; Gregor, p. 566.

[74] Ibid., section 22, 6:446; Gregor, p. 567.

[75] Although she does not directly discuss the obligation to be virtuous, Mary Gregor usefully distinguishes the imperfect character of striving to be virtuous—that there is no upper bound on how much one might strengthen the will to be moral—from the wide latitude of specific duties of virtue, such as the duty to cultivate one's talents. The latter duties leave one choice regarding whether or not to fulfill the duty in some particular fashion on some particular occasion, but cultivating the strength of our virtue is a task from which there is no remission. See Gregor, *Laws of Freedom*, 172–73.

seen that by "virtue" Kant means the strength of will to fulfill our duties in the face of the kind of resistance to doing so that human beings inevitably face. This strength, in turn, can be broken down into strength of moral feeling and strength of conscience, and Kant's view is that there are steps we can take to strengthen these aspects of virtue that are distinct from simply fulfilling particular duties as they might happen to present themselves to us in the course of daily life. Thus, the obligation to be virtuous is not redundant; it requires us to take steps that may be means to fulfilling particular duties, but that are not equivalent to the actions that we perform in fulfilling particular duties. In so arguing, I would conclude, Kant presents an accurate picture of a genuinely moral life: such a life cannot be simply a matter of reacting to obligations that might happen to present themselves to one, merely hoping that one will have the resources necessary to do the right thing when such situations arise, but must surely also involve preparing oneself for such situations, taking steps to ensure, so far as is humanly possible, that one will have the necessary resources. This is what Kant captures with his idea of an obligation to be virtuous.

Philosophy, University of Pennsylvania

A CONCEPTUAL AND (PRELIMINARY) NORMATIVE EXPLORATION OF WASTE*

By Andrew Jason Cohen

I. Introduction

It is often thought that John Locke's famous (first) proviso on property appropriation—the requirement that there must be "enough, and as good, left in common for others"—cannot be satisfied in the modern world.[1] On the other hand, it is usually thought that Locke's waste or spoilage (second) proviso—the requirement that we must "make use of" that which we want to claim as property "before it spoils" if it is legitimately to be our property—is rendered otiose by the existence of a means of exchange (money), because money allows us to store value so that nothing need spoil. C. B. Macpherson, for example, claims that "[t]he spoilage limitation imposed by natural law has been rendered ineffective in respect of the accumulation of land and capital,"[2] and Thomas Lewis claims that the waste proviso is "somewhat superfluous," at least as a "constraint on labour."[3] I think that this is backward and that the second proviso is likely more problematic for the institution of private property than the first (sufficiency) proviso.[4] The reason for this confusion, I suspect, is a

*I am grateful to the Social Philosophy and Policy Center for the impetus to write this essay, the folks at PublicReason.net for much input early on, and the other contributors to this volume for generous comments. Additionally, Andy Altman, Andrew I. Cohen, Bob Fudge, Jim Taggart, Chase Turner, and Matt Zwolinski all read earlier drafts and made very useful suggestions for improvement. Ellen Paul's comments on the penultimate draft helped me to improve the paper significantly. I appreciate all of the input from these and others named throughout.

[1] For indications of this, see David Schmidtz, *The Limits of Government: An Essay on the Public Goods Argument* (Boulder, CO: Westview Press, 1991), 17-20, where he cites several authors making this sort of claim.

[2] C. B. Macpherson, *The Political Theory of Possessive Individualism: Hobbes to Locke* (Oxford: Oxford University Press, 1962), 208. See also Naomi Zack, "Lockean Money, Indigenism and Globalism," *Canadian Journal of Philosophy Supplement* 25 (1999): 31-53, at 33.

[3] Thomas Lewis, "An Environmental Case against Equality of Right," *Canadian Journal of Political Science* 8, no. 2 (1975): 254-273, at 260. See also John Seaman, "Unlimited Acquisition and Equality of Right: A Reply to Professor Lewis," *Canadian Journal of Political Science* 11, no. 2 (1978): 401-8, where he argues that while money does not spoil and so the second proviso causes no problem for those that hoard (money), hoarding nonetheless "violate[s] equality of right" and the "sufficiency constraint of leaving enough and as good for others" that he thinks equality of right requires (ibid., 403). Seaman seems to think the problem will be that there will not be enough and as good land for all (and this is something to which people have a right).

[4] A. John Simmons, *The Lockean Theory of Rights* (Princeton, NJ: Princeton University Press, 1992), notes that the two provisos may conflict and that at II.46 (see note 6 below), Locke

© 2010 Social Philosophy & Policy Foundation. Printed in the USA.   233

lack of clarity with regard to precisely what waste is. One cannot conclusively determine if waste should limit property if one does not have a
clear understanding of waste. Hence, in this essay, I offer a conceptual
analysis of waste. I also sketch an argument for the claim that waste is
immoral, at least in some cases. My purpose, then, is twofold. First and
foremost, I seek to clarify precisely what we mean when we talk of waste.
Second, I suggest why waste might be morally problematic; in this regard,
however, I will be more suggestive than conclusive. I will not spend time
explicating, defending, or rejecting the first proviso, as it has received
extensive attention in the literature.[5]

In Section II, I briefly look at the two provisos Locke places on legitimate appropriation, in order to set the stage for the broader project. In
Section III, I provide my conceptual analysis of waste, largely bracketed
off from normative questions and the question of its relation to property.
I argue that waste is best understood as (a) any process wherein something useful becomes less useful and that produces less benefit than is
lost—*where benefit and usefulness are understood with reference to the same
metric*—or (b) the result of such a process. In Section IV, I use this definition to sketch possible lines of argument for the claim that we have a
moral duty not to waste. I sketch two lines of argument that I do not think
can succeed and then, in more detail, I present a more promising route—
one that I still think has difficulties to overcome, but that is nonetheless
promising. My concluding suggestions are that (W1) if one person needs
something for her preservation and a second person has it, is avoidably
wasting it, and refuses to allow the first to make some greater use of it, the
second *may be* morally wrong, and that (W2) if one person needs something for her preservation, understood according to her metric, and a
second person has it, is avoidably wasting it according to *his own* metric,

---

treats the spoilage proviso as more fundamental than the first (ibid., 282); Simmons also
indicates that the provisos may be consistent (ibid., 283–84). In ibid., 288, he notes that it is
"at best an odd reading of Locke" to think, as many do, that the first proviso is "the most
important limit on property in Locke . . . a limit that renders the waste limit pointless or of
distinctly secondary importance." He also notes others who recognize the correct order of
importance (ibid., 289 n. 164). One of those, Waldron, argues that the waste condition is the
only real restriction on property. See Jeremy Waldron, "Enough and as Good Left for Others," *Philosophical Quarterly* 29, no. 117 (1979): 319-28, at 320–21; and Jeremy Waldron, *The
Right to Private Property* (Oxford: Oxford University Press, 1988), 209-18. See Waldron, *The
Right to Private Property*, 209, for a clear statement that the waste proviso "is not abrogated
or rendered ineffective" by money, but that "it loses the quantitative delimiting character"
it has without money. Waldron thinks the first proviso is "an effect of the early operation of"
the second (ibid., 211). Against Waldron's view, see Gopal Sreenivasan, *The Limits of Lockean
Rights in Property* (New York: Oxford University Press, 1995), 37-40, who treats the waste
proviso as more fundamental than the first (sufficiency) proviso, but thinks the latter also
sets a real restriction (see, e.g., ibid., 34). On Simmons's view, the first proviso sets an
"outside limit of our share," while "our own capacity to use what we appropriate" sets an
"inside limit," and "violating either the outside or inside limit is unjust (wrong)" (Simmons,
The Lockean Theory of Rights, 283; see also 298).

[5] For an argument that the first proviso is not problematic for contemporary accumulation
of property, see the works cited in note 7 below.

and refuses to allow the first to make some greater use of it, the second *is* morally wrong. In both W1 and W2, someone's preservation is imperiled, but only in W2 is it clear that the person who is wasting is wasting according to his own conception of the good. For that reason, only W2 indicates a definite moral wrong. W1 indicates that there may be a wrong, but in any particular case, further consideration will be required to determine if there is a wrong. I do not, in this essay, seek to determine the proper way that waste should be conceived of as limiting legal property. That project must be saved for another occasion.

II. Two Lockean Provisos

The famous Lockean proviso—that there must be "enough, and as good, left in common for others" if what one mixes one's labor with is to count as one's property—has been much discussed.[6] Some believe that this proviso can no longer be met, as there is very little left in common and what remains in a commons is unlikely to be "as good" as what has been appropriated. David Schmidtz and others have shown that this view is mistaken and that the proviso actually demands, in many cases, that we appropriate in order to avoid tragedies of the commons.[7] Appropriated materials—property—tend to be taken care of better than unappropriated materials. Owners tend to work to guarantee that their property will last. Indeed, they tend to use their property to make more (of many things). The natural supply of a particular species of turtles eaten as a delicacy, to use one of Schmidtz's examples, may be depleted if left in common. If the turtles are divided into private property, their owners have an incentive to breed them so as to guarantee future income. Put simply, "private appropriation facilitates the development and the full use of a resource."[8]

Less discussed than the famous (first) proviso is a second Lockean proviso, which Robert Nozick calls simply a "further condition":[9] "As much as any one can make use of to any advantage of life before it spoils, so much he may by his labour fix a property in: whatever is beyond this,

---

[6] John Locke, *Two Treatises of Government* (1689), ed. Peter Laslett (New York: Cambridge University Press, 1960), II.27. All references to this work will be to treatise number (I or II) and section number. I will not be considering Locke's view that it is labor-mixing that makes property possible. That view has been criticized, of course, but I think Simmons's reconstruction and defense of Locke's argument is successful (see especially Simmons, *The Lockean Theory of Rights*, 272–74).

[7] See David Schmidtz, "When Is Original Appropriation Required?" *Monist* 73, no. 4 (1990): 504–18; Schmidtz, *The Limits of Government*, 20–27; David Schmidtz and Robert Goodin, *Social Welfare and Individual Responsibility: For and Against* (Cambridge: Cambridge University Press, 1998), 31–33; and David Schmidtz, *Person, Polis, Planet* (Oxford: Oxford University Press, 2008), 197–98. Cf. Lewis, "An Environmental Case against Equality of Right," 262.

[8] Seana Valentine Shiffren, "Lockean Arguments for Private Intellectual Property," in Stephen Munzer, ed., *New Essays in the Legal and Political Theory of Property* (Cambridge: Cambridge University Press, 2001), 156.

[9] Robert Nozick, *Anarchy, State, and Utopia* (New York: Basic Books, 1974), 176.

is more than his share, and belongs to others."[10] This condition is less discussed, it is safe to assume, because most scholars think it easily satisfied since the advent of money.[11] To use a Lockean-style example, if one has an orchard of apples producing too many apples for one to possibly eat on one's own, one need not let them go to waste but can instead sell them, accumulating money that does not spoil and thus can be saved and used to secure one's future. It is, indeed, fairly easy to satisfy the second proviso in such cases. Nonetheless, I think more needs to be said about this oft-ignored condition.[12] People waste things all the time, and this fact does strike some of us, at least, as morally problematic.

Consider the Misanthropic Apple Farmer. This farmer has been growing and selling apples for years, making a tidy profit. One year, although nothing else changes, he has a change of heart and decides not to tend his orchards. He reinforces his fences, fires his workers, and sits on his porch with a shotgun watching the apples grow and eventually fall to the ground. Workers come to collect the apples, and he informs them that their services are not desired. They offer to collect the apples, sell them on their own, and give him some percentage of the income. He declines the offer and tells them to vacate his premises or he will call the police. They leave. The next day, some passing college students stop and pick a few apples for their dessert. He grabs the apples from them and forces them off "his land." The next day, some five year olds do the same, and again he angrily forces them to leave without apples. There are now apples all over the ground. As time passes, they spoil.[13]

---

[10] Locke, II.31. In II.37, Locke indicates that no one has the right to allow spoilage and that allowing it is against natural law. Locke's argument assumes a theological basis that I do not rely on here.

[11] See Sreenivasan, *The Limits of Lockean Rights in Property*, 35, and Lewis, "An Environmental Case against Equality of Right," 263, for the plausible argument that land becomes scarce because money cannot spoil (so more land can be used to produce, resulting ultimately in storeable money rather than perishable goods). While that is likely both to be correct and to be Locke's view (see Locke, II.47-50), it does not mean that money (or land) cannot be wasted. Of course it can: "throwing money in the sea or melting it down and sprinkling it over the earth might well count as a kind of waste prohibited by natural law" (Simmons, *The Lockean Theory of Rights*, 300 n. 195). See also Benjamin Damstedt, "Limiting Locke: A Natural Law Justification for the Fair Use Doctrine," *The Yale Law Journal* 112, no. 5 (2003): 1179–1221, at 1196, for the view that the invention of money removes (most) worries about waste, but also for the view that the waste proviso is negligible with regard to tangible goods (since they can be sold), but more important for intangible goods (ibid., 1182). Damstedt is worried about wasted intellectual property (ibid., 1212ff.). For related discussion, see Lior Jacob Strahilevitz, "The Right to Destroy," *The Yale Law Journal* 114, no. 4 (2005): 781–854, at 809–812, for an excellent case in patent law; and Shiffren, "Lockean Arguments for Private Intellectual Property," 140 n. 6, for discussion of why "[t]he value of information may be time-dependent."

[12] As I have already indicated, the better Locke scholars do not ignore it. Simmons, Waldron, and Sreenivasan, for example, recognize its importance.

[13] Waldron indicates a wonderful example in John Steinbeck's *Grapes of Wrath* (chapter 25) where oranges are guarded as they rot to prevent anyone from eating them because the owners wish to inflate the price of oranges by limiting supply. This is, Waldron says, a

In this example, Locke's second proviso is, perhaps oddly, satisfied. As written, the proviso reads: "as much as any one *can* make use of . . . before it spoils." Our misanthropic farmer *can* make use of the apples (by selling them), but chooses not to. If we read Locke literally in the *Second Treatise* (II.31), the proviso is satisfied. Reading the passage that literally, though, would be a mistake. Not only would it be right that the proviso is easily satisfied given the advent of money, but it would turn out to be vacuous. It would be impossible to imagine a scenario in which someone would fail to satisfy the proviso—for anything they had *could* be sold, thus not spoiling. The proviso, clearly, has to be read somewhat differently. Indeed, Locke gives what may be a stricter version of the second proviso later in the *Second Treatise*. In II.38, he says:

> [W]hatsoever he tilled and reaped, laid up and made use of, before it spoiled, that was his peculiar right; whatsoever he enclosed, and could feed, and make use of, the cattle and product was also his. But if either the grass of his inclosure rotted on the ground, or the fruit of his planting perished without gathering, and laying up, this part of the earth, notwithstanding his inclosure, was still to be looked on as waste, and might be the possession of any other.

This passage may be read as providing a proviso that is too strict, a proviso according to which one risks losing ownership of anything one holds that one *allows to waste*.[14] The proviso needs to be more carefully formulated. On the one hand, the Misanthropic Apple Farmer is plausibly acting immorally and in a way that threatens his ownership of the apples. On the other hand, the Absent-Minded Gardener, who simply fails to see a ripe tomato in her garden and thus fails to pick it before it rots, is at least clearly not acting immorally. While both may be wasting, one is doing so meanly, the other accidentally.[15]

---

violation of the proviso because someone "accumulates resources purely to beggar his neighbors, to diminish their ability to satisfy their needs" (*The Right to Private Property,* 208).

[14] Consider Lawrence C. Becker, *Property Rights: Philosophical Foundations* (London: Routledge and Kegan Paul, 1977), 82. On Waldron's account (see *The Right to Private Property,* 218–19), spoilage seems only to limit property retrospectively, so that we cannot say until after the apples spoil that they were not the property of the Misanthropic Apple Farmer. This may be so (it fits with the passage from Locke, II.38, just cited), but it seems unlikely. Citing the same section, Simmons indicates that "Locke allows . . . that property in external goods must continue to be used by the owner, else it returns to the common" (*The Lockean Theory of Rights,* 230). I think this is an accurate reading of Locke; if it is correct, it cannot be that the limit is only retrospective, because from a retrospective viewpoint, there is nothing to return to the common (the apples are gone, spoiled). In any case, if there is a moral problem, it begins before the actual spoilage is complete.

[15] I will not here seek to determine if these intuitions are correct; I merely use them to motivate the view that how the proviso is formulated matters. For Locke, I think, the purported owner loses the right to exclude in both cases; that is, both the apples and the tomato cease to belong to the cultivator, and others can permissibly take them.

I do not intend to engage in textual exegesis here to determine the best way to read Locke.[16] Nor do I intend to determine the most plausible spoilage proviso. My concern, instead, is to begin the prior conceptual and normative work—determining what waste is and whether there is a moral failing involved in wasteful behavior (i.e., whether there is a duty not to waste). It is a separate (and, I think, conceptually later) project to determine if waste should limit property. Here I note only that the first version of the waste proviso mentioned is too weak to limit property and that the second version is too strict. The first version leaves the proviso vacuous, while the second allows for a far more intrusive governmental system than most would be comfortable with: any spoilage at all would leave ownership in question and thus would invite state interference and coercive redistribution.[17] What is important for my purpose is to recognize that the waste proviso—and, by extension, waste itself—deserves more attention than it has traditionally received.

For a reasonable property system to treat the waste proviso seriously, the proviso must be understood in some more sophisticated way—with a clearer understanding of what waste is—than that already discussed. I do not offer such a revised proviso here, but I begin the work necessary to prepare for such an undertaking. In the next section, I attempt to determine the best way to understand waste (which should be how a Lockean should conceive of waste in the waste proviso). In Section IV, I sketch an argument that waste is immoral (and that we have a moral duty not to engage in certain sorts of wasteful behavior).

III. Waste: A Conceptual Analysis

A. Preliminaries, especially on waste as inversely related to need[18]

Edward McCaffery discusses possible definitions of waste from the classical literature (especially William Blackstone and Thorstein Veblen),

---

[16] As I have already indicated, I do not seek to determine if Locke's argument *for* property, as opposed to his view that waste limits property, is sound. See Becker, *Property Rights*, 32–56, and Simmons, *The Lockean Theory of Rights*, 236–77, for excellent discussions of that argument. Becker includes helpful discussion of J. S. Mill's reconstruction of Locke's argument (in Mill's *Principles of Political Economy*, Book II, chapter 2, section 6).

[17] This would be *intrusive* because it is not part of a system that one could become accustomed to. Taking "holdings" (or "possessions") as a broader category than property, so that one may have a holding with or without full property rights in the item, we can say that a system wherein property was more-or-less a life-long lease on holdings need not be intrusive. (Michael Otsuka, *Libertarianism without Inequality* [New York: Oxford University Press, 2005] argues for such a system.) It would, at any rate, be no more intrusive than our current income tax system. By contrast, stepping in to take anything allowed to go to waste would require constant vigilance of all citizens, who would constantly worry that something they (take themselves to) own would go to waste and thus be confiscated.

[18] For a discussion of the historical definitions of waste, see Pierre Desrochers, "How Did the Invisible Hand Handle Industrial Waste?" *Enterprise and Society* 8, no. 2 (2007): 348–74, at 349–51.

but none, I think, captures the core notion. McCaffery is clearly right to mark a distinction between dissipation ("pure loss of value," with not even pleasure gained from the loss) and extreme frivolity ("selling the farm for a sack of beans"), and he is also right that they are related.[19] One seems to waste if one burns dollar bills or if one lets them loose in the wind. John Simmons marks another distinction: "waste includes not only holding without using, but frivolous destruction."[20] I am looking, in this section, for what makes these and all forms of waste related— that is, for the core notion. "Non-urgent, frivolous or excessive consumption"[21] won't do, since dissipation is none of these and since vacations, for example, are (usually) non-urgent but nonetheless not (necessarily) wasteful. Dissipation (or destruction) also cannot be the core notion, because excessive and useless consumption is not dissipation, because destroying fuel (etc.) is *how it is used* and thus not wasteful, and because destroying something that has no value cannot be a waste.[22] Nor is simple non-use[23] the core notion since, as we will see in Section III.B, there are things we do not use but do not thereby waste.

Intuitively, we tend to think of waste as related to need. The idea is clear: if we did not waste, there would be less need. There is a positive correlation: more waste usually makes more need. While this is true, it does not mean that waste is "unmet need," "a failure to meet a need," or "the failure to use X to satisfy a need."[24] There must be conceptual space between the unneeded and the wasteful. We might not need to take a family vacation, yet taking the vacation does not seem wasteful

---

[19] Edward McCaffery, "Must We Have the Right to Waste?" in Stephen Munzer, ed., *New Essays in the Legal and Political Theory of Property* (Cambridge: Cambridge University Press, 2001), 76–105, at 85–87.

[20] Simmons, *The Lockean Theory of Rights*, 285. While the second item in Simmon's distinction is McCaffery's "dissipation," the first is something distinct from either item in McCaffery's distinction—perhaps a type of hoarding.

[21] McCaffery, "Must We Have the Right to Waste?" 86.

[22] Waldron claims that "[t]he terms of the Spoilation Proviso . . . are not breached unless the goods in question actually perish" (*The Right to Private Property*, 218–19). I doubt this is Locke's final view (Waldron convincingly cites II.46), but textual exegesis is not my concern. It seems likely to me that things can be wasted without actually perishing. Strahilevitz uses "destruction" and "waste" interchangeably, but does not take the former to mean complete perishing. See Strahilevitz, "The Right to Destroy," 792.

[23] McCaffery, "Must We Have the Right to Waste?" 88–89.

[24] These were suggested by Gordon Hull. In his analysis, presented in Hull, "Clearing the Rubbish: Locke, the Waste Proviso, and the Moral Justification of Intellectual Property," *Public Affairs Quarterly* 23, no. 1 (2009): 67–93, you only have waste if "(a) there is irrevocably unmet demand, (b) the goods to satisfy that demand already exist," and "(c) property claims prevent satisfaction of those demands." I am inclined to think, though, that the product of a great musician is wasted if there is no demand for the work because existing persons are too unsophisticated to appreciate it or because it is simply unknown. In neither case would there be an irrevocably unmet demand, and in neither case would it be property claims interfering. Hull's analysis has the virtue of providing a direct relation of waste to property. My account, by contrast, leaves that for a later stage.

in itself.[25] Moreover, needs may go unmet because of genuine scarcity rather than waste; and even when what is needed is present, there may be good reasons not to use it to satisfy the need.

That waste and need are (often) related seems clear, and will be an important consideration later. Even single persons can be said to waste things when they need them: for example, perhaps Harry is lost in the wilderness, freezing, and uses his last match to light a cigarette instead of lighting a fire to keep warm. Nonetheless, not all waste is a failure to satisfy a need. I can waste things I don't need (destroying the umpteenth car in my extensive collection for no reason), and it may be that no one needs what I waste (say the cars are all old clunkers). At the same time, it seems there are things we have that *no one* needs and that don't seem like a waste at all (Picasso paintings, for example) as well as things we have that no one needs that are a waste ($150 running shoes, for example, especially when it has been shown that they don't help as much as less expensive variants). Simply put, we can waste even when there is no need. There can even be waste on the proverbial island deserted but for one inhabitant.[26] Even if the island produces more food than its one inhabitant can eat, some of us have the intuition that the inhabitant would be wasting foodstuffs if he carried them to the top of a cliff and tossed them into the ocean in a weighted bag so that they sank to the bottom.[27] Something's being needed (by someone) seems not to be a necessary condition for its (possibly) being wasted.

Just as something might be wasted though it is not needed by another, something might be wasted though no one has an intention to waste it. That this is so can easily be seen. I may foolishly believe that I should invest all my extra money in the production of carcinogenic pills, believing that the return on my investment will be substantial. I would be wrong and will have wasted my money, without intending to do so. (Recall, though, that whether there is a moral injunction against such an act of waste is a distinct question.) That I do not intentionally waste my money does not mean that I do not waste it. In such a case, I am wasteful, even though it is not my intention. Indeed, not only can I waste without intending to, but I can also waste even when I have no intention what-

[25] Matt Zwolinski indicated this; I appreciate it. Working out the relation between need and waste would also entail an analysis of need (as opposed to want); I cannot offer such an analysis here.

[26] Andrea Scarantino pushed me on this question.

[27] Some people apparently do not think there is waste in the case as I specified it, since (I think) the food would go unused in any case. This strikes me as mistaken as a conceptual issue. I agree that the act of destroying the excess food might not be immoral in this case (or in a case where food arrives as manna from heaven), but the act still seems accurately described as waste. If the definition I endorse below is correct, it is waste. Importantly, I will note shortly that the food might "go to waste" without the interference of the inhabitant, but this would not be the waste of the inhabitant (it would be nature's waste).

soever. I can waste time,[28] for example, by failing to form any intention whatsoever. This is not unusual. If I watch in shock as my car rolls to the edge of a cliff and I form no intention, it will be true that I wasted time I could have used to try to prevent the car from falling over the cliff.

B. Waste as nonuse or underusage

Simmons and others note the importance of use in Locke's conception of property.[29] Given that clear importance, we get a better start in defining waste by thinking of it as "the nonuse of something." [30] The intuition here is clear: when the apples spoil because they are unused, there is waste. Of course, we are not close to an adequate definition yet; there are many things we do not use that are not wasted. We don't use some rocks, for example, but we don't say we waste them.

Perhaps we should take care not to limit considerations of use to *our* use. The rocks may be used by insects as homes, for example. I think we can exclude such worries here; if we include use by insects (and bacteria, etc.), then there is likely nothing that is unused on the earth, and so this definition would not do, as there would be nothing wasted, which seems clearly false.[31] As I have already indicated, even if we exclude such considerations, this definition will not work, since there are things we do not use that we do not waste.

Perhaps I have already been too quick. After all, we sometimes hear people say that nature itself can be wasteful.[32] We might say the biological nature of humans is wasteful, for example, given the existence of spontaneous abortions. In such cases, it seems like the biological material that is the fetus is wasted.[33] If an animal kills another animal but does not eat or otherwise use the whole carcass—as indeed happens—there is also, plausibly, waste. I think such claims are correct: nonhuman animals can waste, and, plausibly, nature as a whole can waste. My final analysis can

[28] See James Michener, "On Wasting Time," *Reader's Digest* 105, no. 631 (October 1974): 193–200, in which he argues for the value of wasting time. I don't disagree with his basic sentiment, but I suspect that what he describes as wasting time is not actually *wasting* time. It is more like usefully passing time in a way that allows one to refresh.

[29] See, e.g., Simmons, *The Lockean Theory of Rights*, 282–98. For Sreenivasan, the spoilage condition "actually imposes a due-use condition on nonmonetary goods, in addition to the requirement that one not allow one's possessions to spoil" (*The Limits of Lockean Rights in Property*, 101).

[30] This is likely the first intuitive definition of waste. For Damstedt, "[w]aste occurs where a unit of a product of labor is not put to any use" ("Limiting Locke," 1194), but he also indicates that the waste proviso is violated when there is a combination of nonconversion (into money) and nonuse (ibid., 1183).

[31] Nonetheless, I do not think we should simply ignore the uses made of various objects by nonhuman creatures—this is the view that nature only exists for us, which strikes me as an impoverished view of nature.

[32] Jessica Berry suggested I consider this possibility.

[33] I am inclined to think this is often also a confused way to speak or a shortcut for something different: disappointment with the loss.

accommodate such claims, but it is worth temporarily bracketing such thoughts.

The concern with waste as a moral issue suggests that wasting is an action done by an agent.[34] Someone may waste paper, for example, but it is not the wasted paper that is of moral interest; it is the fact that the paper *is wasted by someone.*[35] The waste we are interested in, then, seems to involve an *agent's* nonuse of something. But as we have already seen, it cannot be simply "an agent's nonuse."

We might consider waste to be "an agent's nonuse of something *designed to be used.*" This avoids the problem of including things in the category of "waste" that are unused but which we have no use for (like some rocks). But this definition is not much of an improvement. At most, this is a *type* of waste, for we do use things that are not *designed* to be used (absent a theological story)—like wood from trees—and we may use them *in such a way that seems wasteful.* It seems wasteful, for example, to chop down a tree to enable planting a different tree one has a minimal preference for, and to simply burn the first tree (not for heat, but just to get rid of it). But, since the tree was not designed to be used (again, absent a theological story), this would not count as waste if this definition were correct.

A further attempt to refine the definition is to say that waste is "an agent's nonuse of something *useful.*" This improves upon the last definition, since something designed to be used is presumably useful, but the category "useful" includes more than just things *designed* to be used. There are two problems, though. The first is that it will be unclear how to determine if something is useful. A boulder in the wilderness does not seem useful, but if it could be made into gravel for a driveway, it might be useful. We would not want to say that our failure to use the boulder (as raw material for gravel) is wasteful. The second (related) problem is that something useful (whether designed to be used or not) can be used in multiple ways, and some ways will seem wasteful by comparison to others.[36] Turning the boulder into gravel is one thing; using it in my backyard as a paperweight (say, to hold down a piece of paper with the number of my house on it) is another. This is not nonuse, but it seems wasteful. Sometimes using something in certain ways is wasteful.

The first problem just mentioned takes us from "an agent's nonuse of something useful" to "an agent's nonuse of something she *should* use." The second problem takes us from that to "the agent's nonuse *or underusage* of something she *should* use." This version of the definition, I think, is

[34] Marcel Weber suggested this. As I suggested in the last paragraph, I reject this claim in my final analysis. If this view were correct, nature could not waste (unless it were taken to be an agent).

[35] This may not be the only moral concern. If the thing wasted is of moral value, its wasting is of moral concern, and this is distinct from the moral concern with the agent who does the wasting. Jim Taggart pointed out the need for this qualification.

[36] Bernard Baumrin, "Waste," *Journal of Social Philosophy* 24, no. 3 (1993): 5–18, at 7–8, notes that waste may be a comparative term.

promising (though I will ultimately reject it).[37] Since nonuse of something the agent should use is a form of underusage, the latter includes the former, so that this definition of waste is more simply written as "an agent's underusage of something she should use." For further simplicity, we can say that waste is "the underusage of something one should use," understanding implicitly that the underusage is that of an agent.

The definition of waste as "the underusage of something one should use" accords with Simmons's view that "Locke's real concern . . . must be with *productive use* (and waste), *not* [mere] spoilage."[38] It also captures part of the intuition behind Bernard Baumrin's claim that "to be wasted it [i.e., any object] needed to be made unavailable to others who might have made use of it," and that "[t]o be made unavailable to others . . . a kind of thing (e.g., apples) must become so transformed as to cease to exist as a thing of that kind and with it all its possible uses as a thing of that kind [must cease to exist]."[39] If an object is unavailable for use, it is underused. That others might have used it implies that there is a use for the thing (and thus plausibly implies that it should be used).

An objection might be raised here. Imagine wanting to use a tin can as a hammer to drive in a nail that has come loose on a cupboard shelf. This is not *underuse*, though it may be *misuse*.[40] Some might nonetheless think it is a waste (or a wasteful use)—thereby arguing against the present definition. I think this is a mistake. I do not think we should say this nonstandard use of the tin can is a waste, even if we do want to say there is something wrong with it. What, after all, is wrong with it? One possibility is that the can used as a hammer might break open, spilling its contents, which would then be wasted. But the fact that the contents might be wasted with the nonstandard use of the can does not make that use a waste. Perhaps the nonstandard use of the can would, upon spillage of its contents, become a part of the wasteful act that is the spilling of the can's contents, but that does not mean the nonstandard use of the can is itself a waste. If the nearest hammer is in the garage and would take precious time to retrieve, then use of the can as a hammer might actually be efficient. Of course, storage of tools closer by may be more efficient, and leaving them in the garage may seem wasteful. This suggests what is intuitively accurate: waste and efficiency are (at least close to) ant-

[37] Note that if this definition were correct, our deserted island inhabitant would not be wasting when he tosses foodstuffs into the ocean in a weighted bag, if the island produced so much that he should not use (eat) it all. If this were correct, we could say that nature wastes here, but not that he does. Those who think these conclusions are correct may disagree with my rejection of this definition. Thanks to Bob Fudge for pointing this out.

[38] Simmons, *The Lockean Theory of Rights*, 285 (emphasis in the original).

[39] Baumrin, "Waste," 6-7. See also note 22 above.

[40] Lewis seems to consider waste to be only misuse: "Waste, meaning a misuse of property, is excluded as a possible constraint because it is inconsistent with the initial assumption of freedom to govern oneself" ("An Environmental Case against Equality of Right," 260). Against this view, see the final paragraph of this subsection.

onyms.[41] This also supports the idea that waste is "the *underusage* of something one should use." Underusage, I suggest, is a type of inefficiency.

Let's consider an example. A very rich athlete has built a large home for himself with an extremely large closet in it.[42] There are, I think, different ways that waste can be involved here. It may be that the closet itself is underused by the athlete. This is plausibly waste: the athlete may have another, smaller closet that he overuses instead of storing stuff in this larger closet. (Perhaps it is further from where he usually is with stuff that he normally stores.) He may think to himself, "I should use the large closet more—it is far better designed for storage," but he may not work up the will to bring the stuff to the large closet. (Perhaps he could end this waste by being more strong-willed.) Alternatively, the athlete may be extremely organized and efficient and may realize that the small closet suits his purposes better; he may think that there is a different use of the space the large closet takes up that would be significantly better than the current use (as a large closet). Under this alternative description, what is really wasted is the space in the home and not the closet itself. (Perhaps he could end this waste by redesigning this area of his home so as to create an office or entertainment room for himself.)

I suspect, though, that what many people consider waste in this scenario is different from either of the two possibilities just discussed. I suspect it is not the waste of the closet itself or of the space in the house, but the waste of the *resources used* to build the closet that is most disturbing. That is, I suspect that when some people consider the closet "a waste," they are speaking indirectly; they really mean that it was a waste of resources to make a closet like that for one person. The real concern is that the resources used to build the closet could have been better used— perhaps to build a small home for an impoverished homeless person.

Consider, now, the closet example with reference to our working definition of waste: "the underusage of something one *should* use." If this definition is right, the athlete could be speaking correctly if he claimed the closet was a waste because he could not make good use of it—it would be underusage of something (the closet) he should use.[43] The athlete could also be speaking correctly if he claimed the space used for the closet was wasted—it would be underusage of something (the space in his home) he

---

[41] Helga Varden thinks that "trying to produce tomatoes in the north of Finland (an environment naturally hostile to successful tomato farming)" is wasteful, and that we cannot maintain a distinction "between waste and inefficiency when the inefficiency is so great as to call into question the rationality of the alleged 'productive' activity." Helga Varden, "Locke's Waste Restriction and His Strong Voluntarism," *Locke Studies* 6 (2006): 127–141, at 135. This captures, I think, the normal intuition that even successful activities can be wasteful if the success is contingent upon great inefficiency.

[42] The example was suggested by Ari Kohen.

[43] This would be true even if he literally *could not* use it. In such a case, we might not say he shouldn't waste it (as he cannot fail to do so), but that does not mean it wouldn't be waste.

should use. What about the final claim of waste—the possible waste of resources to make such a large closet for one person? The question is whether there is underusage of those resources. Is it underusage to build such a closet? I am sympathetic with those who say yes, but I am not certain. Another example will push the intuition.

Consider the rich heiress who buys a $3,000 dress, wears it once, then hangs it in her closet to be forgotten and buys another for the next occasion, and repeats the process indefinitely.[44] We might say here that the heiress is underusing the dress and also that the resources that went into creating the dress were underused. Again, I am sympathetic with those who would say such things and would thus say there was waste here. What should be clear from both this example and the parallel use of waste in the previous example (the waste of resources in building the closet) is that the normativity in the definition of waste now under consideration is not only in the second part, where we explicitly say that the item in question is something "one *should* use." (I take it to be obvious that whether one should use the building materials to create the closet is a normative question.) The normativity is also in the first part, where we reference "the *underusage* of something." If that is an accurate understanding of waste, we will need some standard to determine if a particular use is *under*usage, or *proper* usage, and this standard will be normative.[45]

Our current working definition of waste is "an agent's *underusage* of something she should use." There is an obvious worry about this sort of definition: it says nothing about the agent who is doing the wasting. If I underuse an apple, letting it spoil, I am the one wasting it. If I run water for no reason (or for the mild pleasure of hearing it), I am the one wasting the water. In other situations, though, it may be that the one underusing an item is not the one doing the wasting. Put differently, the agent causing the underusage may not be the same as the agent who could make more or better use of the resource in question. If, for example, my leaving my water faucet on causes you to be unable to use water (to clean something, say), it may be *your* underusage (or the combination of my minimal use with your complete lack of use) that is the problem, though *I* am the cause of it. In such cases, I am the one who wastes—by making it so that you cannot act to use the water. Clearly, you do not do anything wrong in this scenario. Equally clearly, you do not waste the water—you do not even

---

[44] This example and the water-running example below were suggested by Simon Cabulea May.

[45] Richard Chappell suggests that this is just the same normative element repeated twice, since "whether it's 'under-usage' depends on how much it *should* be used." He thus thinks this definition might be reworded, so that waste would be "using something less than one should." I think, by contrast, that it may be helpful, in various cases, to recognize that whether something should be used, and how much it should be used, are distinct questions. Running water, for example, should be used, but how (or how much) it should be used is a separate question. (I think we can identify some ways it should not be used: for example, for one's listening pleasure.)

have the *chance* to waste the water, because of my act. The conclusion to be drawn here is that waste cannot be simply "the *underusage* of something one should use," though it could be "the *causing* of the underusage of something one should use." While it is ordinarily the case that the agent underusing X is the agent who causes the underuse of X, they need not be the same agent.[46]

There is a final and, I think, fatal problem in much of the foregoing approach to defining waste. I have been discussing waste as underusage, but there are clearly times when *overusage* is as problematic as underusage and seemingly for the same reasons.[47] Simple examples will make this clear: someone who shampoos her hair five times a day uses too much shampoo; someone who never writes a word using less than two inch lettering uses too much paper; someone who pours so much balsamic vinegar on her salad that a half inch remains in the bowl when the salad is gone uses too much vinegar; and so on. In all of these cases, the issue is overuse. It is tempting to reply that these are actually cases of underusage of the money needed to buy the items in question (shampoo, paper, balsamic vinegar)—since the agents involved could have gotten more for their money with better use—or that they are cases of underusage understood in a more detailed way (the balsamic vinegar remains in the bowl, perhaps, because it is underused; in all cases, less value is gotten from the uses than could be gotten). While there is something right about such a reply, it is ultimately unpersuasive. Perhaps money was underused when the shampoo was purchased, for example, but the shampoo itself was wasted and *not* underused. It seems like we would say both that the person involved wasted her money and that she wasted the items specified—and not because she underused what she poured (say) but because she overused. So the current definition of waste cannot be right.

One further refinement of the current definition is possible to try to improve it: waste may be "the causing of the *improper* (under- or over-) use of something one should use." This may be thought of as an improvement over the previous definition, as well as an improvement over another definition we noted in passing: simple misuse. Neither strikes me as acceptable. They both simply push the difficult question back. Instead of asking "What is waste?" we ask "What is misuse?" or "What is improper use?" and the difficult work returns to haunt us. To some extent, the same is true of all definitions based on underusage, though the question with

---

[46] It may be tempting to take a different tack here. The benefit of this new definition is that it would always allow us to say, should waste be blameworthy, that *the agent who wastes* is blameworthy (even when the waste involves someone causing someone else to underuse). It might be thought that this can be accomplished while maintaining that waste is simply "the *underusage* of something one should use." We can have blame in the appropriate place, on that view, if waste itself is not morally blameworthy but the *causing of waste* is. I will not dwell on this objection here.

[47] Brandon Turner originally suggested this, but it did not become fully salient for me until a discussion with Donna Cohen.

these is at least somewhat narrower (that is, "What is underusage?" is narrower than "What is misuse?" since the latter includes the former and more). "Misuse" and "improper use" are simply too vague. So we try a different path.

C. Waste as a process or the result of such a process

Recall that Locke tells us that "if either the grass of his inclosure rotted on the ground, or the fruit of his planting perished without gathering, and laying up, this part of the earth, notwithstanding his inclosure, was still to be looked on as waste" and thus possibly not the property of the one who allowed it to perish. Causing the fruit to be underused is waste. But notice that if we define waste that way, when we say "the apples are wasting" we can only be speaking derivatively, since the apples are not causing their own underusage. Speaking precisely, we can say only that they are the product of waste. This is not really worrisome, but it suggests that we should extend the definition to include not only the *act of waste* but also the *product*. For reasons that will be apparent momentarily, we also do well to talk of the *process* of waste rather than the *act* of waste.

Suppose we define waste as "(a) any process wherein something useful becomes less useful[48] or (b) the result of such a process." Such a process would *usually* be caused by an agent, but it need not be usefulness to the causing agent that matters, and there might be some cases where no agent (or no moral agent) is causing the process—all three points of which are in accord with things said earlier. Some such processes are natural, requiring no intentional being for their initiation. Nature can thus be wasteful (consider spontaneous abortions, as mentioned earlier). This definition also handles the last problem raised in the previous subsection—that of overusage. When our over-shampooer washes her hair five times in a day, she is engaging in a process wherein the useful shampoo becomes less useful. The fifth shampoo of the day simply does less good than the first (or is neutral or even bad, making the hair and scalp less healthy than they were), and the emptier shampoo bottle is less useful than it was with more shampoo in it.

That this definition handles overusage so well may provoke some worry about how it handles underusage. Consider our athlete's closet. We specified three ways that waste may be involved there: it may be that the *closet itself* is wasted by the athlete; it may be that the closet is a waste of *space*; or it may be that what is wasted are the *resources used* to build the closet. These are all handled straightforwardly. That the closet is a waste is clear: it is the result of a (building) process wherein some things—the space and the materials used—become less useful than they were; they would have been more useful if used to make a better-designed house or to build a

---

[48] This includes becoming *useless*, ceasing to be useful.

small home for a homeless person. The same is true of the space misused in the home. Finally, the resources themselves were wasted because they were made into something (the overly large closet) less useful than they themselves were; again, they could have been more useful in a better design. Note also how this works in simple cases: if you absentmindedly throw away a perfectly good apple (or pharmaceutical, etc.), you initiate a process whereby something useful becomes less useful. The contaminated apple is now useless.

Of course, as currently formulated, this definition will not do. Most things we use *well* go through a process wherein they become less useful (or cease to be useful).[49] When I eat my dinner, the foodstuffs are no longer useful (they no longer *are*). If I wear my favorite shirt often enough, it begins to form holes, becoming less useful. Presumably I am not wasting in either case. What matters in the sort of processes that we do consider wasteful, I think, is that potential is lost.[50] When a useful drug is accidentally dropped into a toilet, it is a waste, because the drug had the potential, say, to cure an illness—and that potential is lost. When I wear my favorite shirt for the thousandth time, its potential is not lost; it has been used to its fullest (since its purpose is to be worn).

Not all lost potential is a waste. It may be that I had the potential to be a great salesperson, but chose to pursue philosophy instead. Even if I am not as good a philosopher as I could have been a salesperson, it would be odd to say that I wasted my salesperson-attributes. Nothing was wasted, because although I did not actualize one potential, I did actualize another in a way that offsets the loss. So what seems to matter is that potential is lost in a way that is not offset.[51] We must thus improve on the current definition of waste as "(a) any process wherein something useful becomes less useful or (b) the result of such a process." We can do so by incorporating a clause about the overall loss of potential (and in this way we can address the worry, noted above, about normal usage making an item less useful). We can say that waste is "(a) any process wherein something useful becomes less useful *and that produces less benefit than is lost,* or (b) the result of such a process."[52]

---

[49] Simon Cabulea May reminded me of this.

[50] Kristin Nelson Jones suggested this.

[51] This may be thought to push back to the previous definition, "the causing of the underusage of something one should use." "Underusage" is lost potential that is not offset. We rejected that definition, though, because it did not handle cases where overusage was wasteful. If we refined it to "the causing of lost potential without offsetting gain," it would be similar to the first part of the definition I propose here. We could make it closer still: "(a) any process that results in potential being lost without offsetting gain, or (b) the result of such a process." I assume this could also be refined further to match the final definition I provide below, but I see no advantage in doing so.

[52] I should note that something that *seems* like waste might result from a process that produces more benefit than is lost. This would not, on this technical definition, be waste. I would call it a "remainder" or a "by-product." The intuition against calling it waste is simply that it was part of a process that created value and that could not (we assume) have

It may be thought that this latest definition can be shortened to "(a) any process that produces less benefit than is lost or (b) the result of such a process."[53] This is a mistake. I assume that we do not waste trees deep in the Amazon rainforest when we leave them untouched. As Benjamin Damstedt indicates, "one does not violate the waste prohibition by removing too little out of the common."[54] If the shortened version of the definition were correct, we would have to say we waste the trees—for there is (at least plausibly) a process in the rainforest example that produces less benefit than is lost (while there is no process wherein something useful becomes less useful). Granted, such a process is a *negative* process—the process of (or initiated by) our not using the trees—but this is arguably a process. What is produced from such a process (nothing)[55] is, at least plausibly, of less benefit than what is lost (by not harvesting the trees, for example). Hence, without a clause indicating that such processes are excluded, the shortened definition will not do. Adding such a clause may make the definition satisfactory, but will also make it lose its advantage (brevity) over the unshortened version. To clarify the advantage of the longer version of the current definition over the shorter one: on the longer version, the trees are not wasted simply because they do not become less useful when we do not use them. The first clause—"any process wherein something useful becomes less useful"—is thus needed.

We have already seen that the current definition handles the athlete's closet case and the case where food or pharmaceuticals are thrown away. Consider now the case of the $3,000 dresses. The materials used to make the dresses were wasted, according to this definition, if they could have been used to create something from which more use would have been gotten—as seems likely. The dresses themselves would only count as wasted if, while they hang in the closet, their use value decreases. If it does not, they are not wasted—but, again, the resources used to make them were. The current definition also appropriately han-

---

created such value without it. This is like the destruction of gas in the use of a motor that is necessary for some benefit—not a waste, but proper use. Of course, *this by-product could be wasted once it is produced* (by being subject to another process that produces less benefit than is lost and wherein it becomes less useful), or it could be used productively.

[53] Or shortened even further to "any inefficient process or the result thereof." I believe this fails for the same reasons discussed in this paragraph and for the reason discussed in the penultimate paragraph of the next subsection (III.D).

[54] Damstedt, "Limiting Locke," 1198. It may be, as Pat Greenspan suggested in correspondence, that the trees *go to waste* even if *we* don't waste them, or it may be that *nature* wastes the trees. If so, we might ask whether we have a responsibility to prevent the waste, but we would not, I think, say *we* waste. Finally, it may be, as Matt Zwolinski suggested in correspondence, that *we waste an opportunity* by not using the trees. Still, we are not *wasting the trees*. The case is a bit harder when we discuss things like wind and sun power. As Jim Taggart suggested in correspondence, it might seem that we *do* waste when we do not take advantage of them to help with our energy needs. Still, even here, I am inclined to think that what we waste (directly) is an opportunity.

[55] At least if we ignore the benefit of oxygen production and the like.

dles the case of normal usage—by means of the second clause, "produces less benefit than is lost." The favorite shirt worn over and over (until it wears out) and the meal eaten are not wasted on this definition: far more benefit (the years of wear, or the nutritive value) is gained than is lost (say, usefulness as a rag, or as insect bait), so the process involved is not wasteful.

Throughout this section, I have been assuming that there are objective facts about use-value, and this warrants further comment. Unfortunately, I can only give the most rudimentary indication here of the objectivity of use-value.

I admit (for present purposes) that raw materials have no essential use. Hence, the objective use-value cannot come from the object itself. Some might suggest that if the value is not in the object itself, it must come from the individual who uses the object (presumably, but not necessarily, the owner) and that the use-value must therefore be subjective. On such a view, it might be said that the compulsive shampooer is not wasting shampoo, but merely satisfying her preferences. But we can admit that she is satisfying her preferences and still argue that she is wasting the shampoo, when we recognize that her preferences are not rational.[56] What matters is that there is an objectivity to use-value even though the object has no essential use. On my own view, the objective use-value of an item is relational, determined by how well it could serve the purposes of moral agents. This means that if I use the dollar bill in my pocket as kindling for my fireplace on a warm summer's day (when the fire does me no good), I am getting less value from the dollar than I should—for it could serve the purposes of moral agents in significantly better ways. I might use it, for example, to pay my overdue electricity bill, or to buy (part of) a meal for a homeless person.[57]

Importantly, the fact that there are objective facts about use-value (if I am right) does not mean that interference will be warranted to attain that use-value. When such interference is warranted is a normative question I begin to address below (in Section IV).

[56] Moreover, if it is assumed that revealed preferences can never be wrong, there are worse difficulties than the (likely) fact that no one would ever be said to be wasting. (For more on these difficulties, see my "On Hard-Headed Economics Capturing the Soft Side of Life," manuscript, section V.) From the other side, discounting revealed preferences does not mean giving priority to some governing body that is meant to decide what is best for everyone. I thank Andrew I. Cohen for prompting here, and Ellen Paul for prompting on the entire question of the objectivity or subjectivity of use-value.

[57] The purposes of moral agents are not merely those things that particular moral agents happen to want; they are objectively good for those agents (whereas agents may want things that are not good, and may even be bad, for them). I cannot, of course, offer a full explanation of objective purposes here, and, hence, cannot give a full explanation of the objectivity of use-value. I suspect that a eudaimonist account, perhaps an Aristotelian one, would be the best way to approach this question. In any case, it may be that the best way to understand the objective value of the various possible uses of an object requires counterfactuals of the following sort: if item X had been used as Y, it would have served purpose P for a moral agent. But I leave this question to the side.

D. A concern, three objections, an advantage, and a final refinement

There is an interesting concern about the current definition (indeed, it may apply to all of the definitions thus far considered). When Locke's less sophisticated followers largely ignore the spoilage proviso, it is because they think it too easily satisfied to be of concern. It is supposed to be easily satisfied because things can be sold, and money saved, so that there is no spoilage. Of course, once money can be saved, the possibility arises that it can be hoarded.[58] Those who believe that resources were wasted in building a very large, and largely unused, closet for our athlete above may also believe that hoarding money is morally problematic. If some hoard money, after all, others may (supposedly) have to do without. Thus, hoarding, like waste, seems to be correlated with need—and thus is perhaps the same as waste.

I sympathize with, but do not accept, the view that a billionaire wastes her money if she merely lets it earn interest and does no (other) good with it. The problem with that view is simply that it seems she doesn't *waste* it at all—after all, the process it is involved with is that of earning interest and thus becoming *more* useful. I think this ambivalence is both common and sensible.[59] I suspect some hoarding is waste and some is not. If the billionaire simply stuffs her cash in her mattress, it would be wasteful, since her action not only makes something unavailable that could be used but also results in the item hoarded being less useful (since, without interest, the value of the cash does not keep up with inflation). Such hoarding is thus wasteful according to the definition now on offer. However, other hoarding is not: if the billionaire puts her money into high-yield investments, thereby increasing its value, it does not become less useful. (Moreover, it is not *unavailable* in any real sense—it is invested, and thus available to those who can pay an acceptable return. That it is not available to you or me because the billionaire has access to better-paying borrowers is irrelevant.)

It might be objected that we should not consider only the billionaire's needs. It might be suggested that the money could be used to produce shelter for the homeless, to feed the starving, and to educate the illiterate, and that all of this clearly amounts to lost benefits that are greater, at least socially, than the interest she earns. There is some-

---

[58] Paul Gowder raised this concern.

[59] I suspect the ambivalence is present in Locke's thought. He seems, after all, to think that the Europeans' taking of land from Native Americans in his day was acceptable, since the latter were "wasting" the land by not using methods of agriculture available in Europe (see II.45; cf. Zack, "Lockean Money, Indigenism, and Globalism," 32). Surely the Native Americans were not destroying the value of the land or even making it worth less—they were simply not increasing its value. They were, it might be said, hoarding it. Indeed, "land can be wasted (e.g., by the idle rich) by lying unused" (Simmons, *The Lockean Theory of Rights,* 286–87). Yet "Locke quite explicitly allows accumulation for comfort and convenience not just need-satisfaction" (ibid., 285, referring to M. Seliger, *The Liberal Politics of John Locke* [London: Allen Unwin, 1968]).

thing right about this, especially if we (foolishly, to my mind) ignore the fact that her investment is an *investment* and so enables something productive to be done that might be a greater benefit (suppose it is an investment in improved agriculture). What this shows is that what is wasteful will be indexed. What might not be wasteful to an individual may be wasteful to a society, and perhaps vice versa. In the current sort of case, the hoarding may be wasteful from a societal perspective, but not from the individual's perspective.

The idea that what is wasteful will be indexed fits well with the view, expressed at the end of the last subsection, that the objective use-value of an item is relational. The maximum objective value achievable with any item will be that which best satisfies the most purposes of moral agents. Of course, individuals will have their own purposes, some of which can only be satisfied if someone else's are not—even when the other's purposes are (in some sense) more important or more extensive. Given that, an individual may rightly think that someone else's use of an item is wasteful while the other person rightly thinks it is not. In each case, the purposes considered are one's own, leading to opposing conclusions about the sort of value created. Consider this example. It is perfectly reasonable for me to think Thelma wastes the filet mignon when she feeds it to her dog Fido—because my purposes (and those of others) are more important to me than Fido's. Still, Thelma might rightly think she does not waste the steak, since her purpose is to make Fido happy and she fairly weights that purpose more heavily than my purposes.

A different example might help make the indexing point clearer.[60] Consider the destruction of a great work of art by a collector who somehow gets tremendous joy from the destruction.[61] Such destruction is not wasteful from the perspective of the collector (who gets great benefit), but it is wasteful from the perspective of the society that loses the artwork with no benefit. The point is simply that whose purposes are taken as primary will determine what is considered wasteful, and, in many cases, there are reasonable differences regarding whose purposes are primary. To say that "waste is indexed to P" is to say that P's purposes are taken as primary in that evaluation. That waste is indexed, though, does not mean that it is subjective. In the art destruction case, it would be an objective fact that, indexed to the art collector/destroyer, there is not waste, and it would be an objective fact that, indexed to (the rest of) society, there is. It may also be that one of these perspec-

---

[60] The billionaire example is problematic, since it assumes we should ignore the value of the investment *as an investment that allows other productivity*. As I have said, if we do not ignore that, the billionaire does not seem to be wasting at all; she is, rather, making money available—in the form of capital to be borrowed—to others who can put it to more directly productive use than she can herself.

[61] See Joseph L. Sax, *Playing Darts with a Rembrandt: Public and Private Rights in Cultural Treasures* (Ann Arbor: University of Michigan Press, 1999).

tives is objectively more important than the other, or that one is of no moral value (or is of disvalue).

Recognizing that waste is indexed allows us to answer another objection: namely, that when I supposedly waste money, it does not itself become less useful and so I cannot be actually *wasting it*. If I spend, say, $300 on an ordinary umbrella, the storekeeper has $300 which is not less useful than it was before I (mis)spent it. Hence, it might be said that there is no waste. Yet surely I did waste.[62] What we should say, I think, is that, indexed to the shopkeeper, there is no waste, but indexed to me, there is—I could have gotten far more for the $300 than the umbrella. (Alternatively, we can say that I wasted my resources—which includes, but is not identical to, the $300.) Importantly, though, we can also say that it is (or is not) wasteful from an *all-things-considered* perspective. That is, all things considered, (a) a process wherein something useful becomes less useful to all who could possibly make use of it, and that produces less benefit (to all of them) than is lost (to all of them), or (b) the result of such a process, is wasteful from the broadest possible perspective.[63] None of this, I think, is problematic for the conceptual issue; it may raise worries for the moral issue.

There is one final objection to my conceptual analysis worth considering here. A critic may want to say that for an item X to be such that it can be wasted, it must be that X can rightfully be used.[64] Including such a condition allows us to say that trees deep in the Amazon are not being wasted (even if we otherwise adopt the definition discussed in Section III.B above; as I have already indicated, on the current definition they are not being wasted whether or not we include a clause about rightful use). The trees are not being wasted, the critic would presumably say, because no one has a right to use them. I think this is misguided. It is certainly clear that I can waste something I have a right to use. I have a right to use the dollar in my pocket, but I can tear it up and drop it in a sewer drain, for example. It is also clear, though, that I can waste some-

---

[62] This is not to say that any interference with my purchase is warranted. Perhaps it would even be wrong for most people to even remark about the waste. Yet surely a close friend would be justified in asking if there was some special reason I would make such an oddly expensive purchase, and, of course, there may be special circumstances that make the purchase more beneficial than it appears. Perhaps the shopkeeper is someone I wish to help out but who would not accept the money unless I purchased the umbrella. Still, absent such circumstances, I do not believe we should shy away from the judgment that I would be wasting my money, even if it gave me satisfaction.

[63] According to Waldron, Locke believes that "[a]n owner is not entitled to decide to allow his goods to perish uselessly in his possession (II. 46). In Locke's view, such a decision is tantamount to an abandonment of exclusive property in the goods. But what counts as use and what counts as useless destruction is for *the owner* to decide: briefly, anything he takes to be useful to himself counts as a use of the object however wasteful it may be to someone else" (Waldron, *The Right to Private Property*, 161). Recognizing Waldron's implicit recognition that waste is indexed, I think the moral claim would reverse Waldron's final point: if waste is immoral, it must be so understood from the broader perspective, not the narrower.

[64] This objection comes from Justin Weinberg.

thing I have no right to use. I can steal your car and use it as a doorstop, say. Clearly a waste. I can go into the Amazon rainforest and burn trees for fun. Again, clearly a waste.

How does the current definition fare with regard to the sort of case just mentioned? If waste is "(a) any process wherein something useful becomes less useful and that produces less benefit than is lost, or (b) the result of such a process," then it is clear that I can waste your car (to which I have no right)—perhaps by blowing it up for fun, thereby making it into a useless charred wreck. The same is true of the trees in the Amazon. It is also the case that according to the current definition, nonuse of trees deep in the Amazon is not a waste—for, as previously noted, the trees are not becoming useless or less useful. (This is perhaps comparable to the nonwasteful sort of hoarding.) Perhaps if we allowed a tree disease to destroy all of the trees, it would be a waste, but that is a different matter (perhaps comparable to the wasteful sort of hoarding).[65]

The current definition has, it should be noted, another advantage over the previous definition—"the *causing* of the underusage of something one should use." That definition (and its immediate predecessor) was doubly normative: determining what *under*usage is and determining what we *should* use are both normative issues. The current definition—"(a) any process wherein something useful becomes less useful and that produces less benefit than is lost, or (b) the result of such a process"—by contrast, only involves normativity, if at all, in determining usefulness. The usefulness of an item might be determined in economic terms, perhaps by drawing on talk of opportunity costs and cost/benefit analyses. Alternatively, as I have already suggested, usefulness may be understood in terms of how much the item aids human flourishing or pursuit of the good.[66]

Exactly how to flesh out the usefulness of an item is, I think, of the utmost importance. I also think, though, that how it is fleshed out will depend on who is doing the fleshing. This brings us back to our recognition that waste is indexed. When the art collector destroys the work of art for pleasure, he obtains a benefit: his own pleasure. From his perspective, his destruction of the painting is not a waste. For society at large, by contrast, there is a great loss: the sum of the pleasures others would have had if the work had not been destroyed, along with the educational value (and the like) that is sacrificed. Given all of that value, a museum might offer to buy the painting to prevent its destruction (which would be a waste from the societal perspective). The public might be asked to contribute funds to aid the effort to prevent the destruction. The collector, though, may so value the pleasure he receives by seeing the painting

[65] Whether this counts as *our* wasting (since we do not interfere) or nature's wasting, I will not try to determine.
[66] The opportunity-cost idea was suggested by Mark LeBar; the idea about aiding pursuit of the good was suggested by Kristin Nelson Jones.

destroyed, that no monetary amount would alter his choice.[67] There are other cases like this.

Consider a sacred object or place, such as Shiprock in northwestern New Mexico, which plays a special role in Navajo culture. What Shiprock is good for—its usefulness according to Navajo cosmology—is precisely to play this special role. Using it for any other purpose, or at least any purpose incompatible with or destructive of that role, would be a waste indexed to the Navajo. For example, if it were discovered that uranium (or a chemical that cured cancer) was abundant within this distinctive rock formation, there would surely be a move to mine it. From the Navajo perspective, mining Shiprock would be a waste, since it would destroy this sacred site and no other benefit compares to what would be lost.[68] By contrast, from the perspective of those eager to gain from mining, the only waste (if any) would be to leave the formation untapped. Certainly, indexed to them, mining is not a waste: it would be a process wherein something basically unused becomes very useful and a process that produces tremendous benefit with little loss (to put the point more extremely than it need be put).

I do not pretend to know how to determine, from an all-things-considered perspective, whether there is waste in such cases or not. I think it is clear, though, that we would not be warranted in simply assuming that the benefit to be gained from mining outweighs the loss incurred by doing so. Such an assumption would entail that waste is simply inefficiency, something like "the production of less benefit than is lost"[69] (where benefit and loss are understood in a purely instrumental or economic sense).[70] Throughout this essay, though, I have been trying to clarify the concept of waste in a value-free way, without endorsing any particular substantive claims as to whether this or that activity (e.g., mining or not mining Shiprock) amounts to waste. To

---

[67] Perhaps the values are incommensurable, but this need not be the case, since it could simply be that, *as it happens*, no monetary amount that could be raised in the situation at hand would alter his choice.

[68] I do not know that any actual member of the Navajo tribe believes this or that the tribe as a whole would endorse it. (But see Peter Nabokov, *Where Lightning Strikes: The Lives of American Indian Sacred Places* [New York: Viking Penguin, 2006], esp. chap. 6.) The issue is not pertinent to my point, since surely there could be other examples where some person or group did think this way about an object or place that others had a very different (and perhaps merely monetary) appreciation for. One thinks of the Great Pyramids, the Western Wall, the Dome of the Rock, Stonehenge, etc., but more mundane cases exist, as I will discuss below (see note 99 and the surrounding text). I owe the example of Shiprock and prodding about the point (and help in phrasing it) to Jim Taggart.

[69] I mean this to be neutral between various ways of understanding efficiency and inefficiency in economics.

[70] This sort of assumption may have been behind much of Locke's thought on this matter. His failure to remain neutral with regard to the values considered arguably helps explain the limitations of his account of waste and the lack of contemporary interest in it. That is, Locke's account is likely biased toward the view of waste as nothing but inefficiency (i.e., something productive of less benefit than is lost in a purely economic sense).

simply assume that instrumental monetary value should carry the day violates this goal. We should thus refine the definition of waste one last time.

I shall understand waste as "(a) any process wherein something useful becomes less useful and that produces less benefit than is lost—*where benefit and usefulness are understood with reference to the same metric*—or (b) the result of such a process." This refinement of the previous definition merely makes clear that the indexing matters and that we should not build into our definition of waste any prejudice in favor of one metric of usefulness (or value) over others. In the case of Shiprock, the metric used by the Navajo would be that of the sacred, blessed, consecrated, spiritual, etc., while the metric used by those believing it should be mined would be that of money or energy (or, best-case scenario, medical cures and promotion of life). Given the different metrics used, there is no surprise that the two groups come to different conclusions about the question of waste.[71] Fortunately, in many cases we actually face, we have a common metric with which to consider the question.

IV. The Duty not to Waste: A Preliminary Analysis

I began this essay by discussing Locke's provisos. Turning now to the morality of waste, let us consider the second proviso again briefly. Damstedt writes: "The penalty associated with a violation of the waste prohibition is the loss of exclusionary property rights in the good, but the prohibition does not create an affirmative duty to prevent waste."[72] While Damstedt indicates that a duty to avoid waste would not necessarily follow from the fact that violation of the proviso means loss of property, it is equally the case that having a duty to avoid waste does not necessarily mean that the proviso indicates a real limit to property. I discuss only the morality of waste in the rest of this essay. Here, I am not seeking to determine if the penalty should be loss of exclusionary property rights. My far more modest goal is not even to conclusively determine if there is an affirmative duty not to waste, though I would like to offer such an argument. Instead, I will sketch out possible routes someone might take to argue that waste is immoral. I begin by discussing two possible routes that might be thought fruitful in defending a duty not to waste (though they will ultimately prove to be unsuccessful). I then spend more time on the route I think actually works and propose two normative principles indicating when waste is immoral.

---

[71] To be clear, I take a metric to be related to a conception of the good, such that when one measures benefit, usefulness, etc., against a particular metric, anything that helps attain that good is positive, and anything that hinders it is negative.
[72] Damstedt, "Limiting Locke," 1195.

A. Dismissing two lines of argument

First, it might be suggested that waste is immoral because it involves some sort of harm to oneself.[73] The idea here is that if I waste my resources, I will be less able to preserve myself or advance the pursuit of my goals. While I think there is something important in this line of reasoning, I do not think it can be the full story, for several reasons. First, whether it is true that waste makes me less able to preserve myself is contingent upon circumstances. If I happen to be born super-rich, my waste will not cause me harm (unless it occurs on a tremendous scale). The rich can waste with ease because they have much more than they need. Second, it is not clear to me that there is such a thing as "harm to self." Following Joel Feinberg,[74] I would admit that I can hurt myself (i.e., I can set my own interests back), but not that I can *harm* myself (i.e., I cannot *wrongly* set my interests back). Since non-wrongfully setting back someone's interests is not immoral, this argument can only provide a prudential reason not to waste. It is a prudential reason I take to be of obvious importance—wasting (often) makes life worse for oneself—but is also of limited domain. (This prudential reason is unlikely ever to be of import to the super-rich.)[75]

A second route that might be pursued is what we might call the "disgust argument."[76] Watching a gluttonous super-rich individual slothfully remain idle while using resources in wasteful ways strikes many of us as disgusting. Some might want to take such a feeling—or the fact that humans have always had such visceral reactions—to suggest that wasteful behavior is immoral. The problem with this sort of argument is familiar. Historically, people have found many perfectly moral things disgusting. Some wanted miscegenation to be illegal because they thought it a disgusting practice and thus immoral. Homosexuality and same-sex marriage are more contemporary examples, as is cloning. Arguments against these practices tend to be of the sort that "we must recognize that we feel disgust for a reason," without providing much in the way of fleshing out what such a reason would be.[77] I take such arguments to be of no moral value with regard to those questions, and thus I give them no weight when it comes to waste. Nonetheless, I share the visceral reaction against waste. Therefore, I move now to what I take to be a more promising argument.

---

[73] Chase Turner provided the idea here as well as some of the objections.

[74] I also follow Feinberg's approach below. See note 85 and the accompanying text.

[75] A Kantian approach defending duties to oneself may fare better. I suspect, though, that a direct route here could at best defend an imperfect duty not to waste. Nonetheless, in the last paragraph of section IV.D below, I make use of this sort of approach (in more Lockean terms) as part of the argument I think fares best for showing waste to be immoral.

[76] Bob Fudge provided the idea here as well as some of the objections.

[77] See, for example, Leon R. Kass, "The Wisdom of Repugnance," in Leon R. Kass and James Q. Wilson, eds., *The Ethics of Human Cloning* (Washington, DC: AEI Press, 1998), 3–60.

B. Framing the discussion in terms of toleration

In his *Two Treatises* (II.31), Locke says that "nothing was made by God for man to spoil or destroy," but at I.39, he says that "a right to destroy anything by using it" is "the utmost property man is capable of." These two statements seem initially inconsistent, but if we read the first as "nothing was made by God for man *merely* to spoil or destroy," the inconsistency vanishes. On this reading, the first statement means that we have no right to destroy anything *by wasting it;* the second means only that we can destroy property if doing so is part of (non-wastefully) *using it.* This is how John Simmons interprets Locke; he explains that "the right to destroy what one has property in is at least often a constituent part of property, but this is not a right to destroy the thing frivolously. We have a right to destroy things we own only in our *use* of them for 'the comfortable preservation of (our) beings' (I, 87)." [78] This seems the best reading of Locke. It also seems plausible in its own right.

Recall that we have defined waste as "(a) any process wherein something useful becomes less useful and that produces less benefit than is lost—where benefit and usefulness are understood with reference to the same metric—or (b) the result of such a process." Although there may be some normativity built into this definition—in the metric of benefit and usefulness—most of the normative work is left to be done. It is not obviously or necessarily the case that waste is always immoral, so normative work is needed. Moreover, in cases where there are competing metrics, determining which metric should control will require extensive normative work.

One way to pose the bigger question here is in terms of *jus abutendi—the right to waste.* [79] If property includes *jus abutendi,* then just as I can practice throwing knives in my own yard, so long as I am not throwing them at you, I can practice throwing them at my wall even if doing so will destroy them. Similarly, our Misanthropic Apple Farmer might insist that since he is harming no one and the apples are his, no one has a right to interfere with his letting them rot, his sinking them in a weighted bag in the ocean, or his using them as fuel for a giant and useless bonfire. Yet some of us want to at least consider if interference is permissible here. [80]

One way to frame the normative question, then, is in terms of toleration: When should we tolerate waste, and when should we not? This way

---

[78] Simmons, *The Lockean Theory of Rights,* 233.

[79] I assume the term is better translated "a right to abuse" or "*just* abuse," but from Roscoe Pound (1939) forward, it has been deemed a right to destroy, injure, or waste. The sixth edition of *Black's Law Dictionary* (1990), for example, talks of an owner as one who has a right "to spoil or destroy" property (this is interestingly dropped in the seventh edition of 1999). See Strahilevitz, "The Right to Destroy," 783.

[80] We might want legal interference to be permissible (on Lockean grounds), claiming that such waste—the farmer's allowing the "fruit of his planting" to perish—is *such a waste* that the apples "might be the possession of any other." We might want to say, that is, that the farmer's property right is limited by his waste. I will not discuss this here.

of framing the normative question about waste sits between two other ways that are perhaps more popular: When is there a moral duty not to waste? And when does waste limit property? The question of toleration is related to the first of these others since, arguably, we should tolerate when people satisfy their moral duties, and we can only question whether we should not tolerate when a duty (e.g., not to harm another) is not being met. The question of toleration is related to the second alternative way to frame the normative concern since, arguably, when we do not tolerate waste, we effectively limit property. If someone wastes her own goods, and we allow the state to interfere with (not tolerate) the waste, we effectively say, "You do not have the right to waste what you own," which means ownership is limited and does not include the right to waste (*jus abutendi*). The question of toleration is not equivalent to either of these other questions, however. It is not equivalent to the question about a moral duty not to waste, since sometimes we do tolerate when duties are not met. It is not equivalent to the question regarding property for two reasons. First, the limitation of property involves only questions of waste with regard to what one owns (or otherwise takes oneself to own), and the question of toleration, here, is broader: Should we tolerate your waste of your own goods, your waste of unowned goods, and your waste of other's goods? Second, the moral question of toleration is also broader in a different way: it includes not only concern with what government may justifiably interfere with, but also concern with what individuals and nongovernmental groups may justifiably interfere with—and, presumably, it is only justifiable governmental interference that sets a conceptual limit to property. That is, where property is a legal institution, it is law that sets its limits, not actions by other individuals. If a child takes her sibling's radio because she cannot tolerate the music he plays, she does not limit what counts as his property but only limits his use (i.e., the radio still belongs to him). By contrast, when the government makes cocaine illegal, it makes it the case that no one can have property in the narcotic (i.e., when the police officer confiscates it, the holder is not wronged). Similarly, then, my decisive failure to tolerate your waste may involve taking something from you, but it leaves the taken item your property (I legally wrong you), whereas if the government decisively (and justifiably) fails to tolerate waste, it sets a legal limit on what can be held as property.[81]

My use of toleration to frame the normative question is not accidental. I use it because I *am* interested in the possible property-limiting nature of

[81] The point here is that within a legal system, that system determines the conception of property within the society (cf. Waldron, *The Right to Private Property*, 31). This is not to say that property is only a legal construct. On my own view, property is a moral concept, but legal systems flesh out the concept to form the conception of property within their societies. In doing so, they greatly influence the resulting property schemes, so that, for example, cocaine is not (conceptually) property (whether or not it should be legal). Any particular property scheme, of course, may be immoral, but this is a question of the morality of the legal system. I thank Andrew I. Cohen and Jim Taggart for pushing me to clarify this point.

waste, as well as the broader question of when toleration is required (though I consider neither at length here). I also use it because it provides a ready model within which to consider when waste is most problematic. In particular, it provides a model to determine when interference with an individual's waste is permissible and when it is not—even if waste is bad in the latter sort of case.

An initial possibility to consider in determining when interference with an act of waste is permissible is economic: interference might be thought permissible when the waste involves a substantial economic loss for society. This is, in large part, the path Lior Jacob Strahilevitz takes.[82] On his view, when there is only minor economic loss, even postmortem waste should be permitted (he discusses the ritual burying of the dead with jewelry). As an argument for including a limited *jus abutendi* in property, I think Strahilevitz's argument is quite persuasive. It does not, though, settle the question of when nongovernmental interference is permissible or whether toleration is required. That is, it does not answer the question about the morality of waste (nor was it intended to).

As I have discussed elsewhere,[83] interference is morally permissible when harm is done or credibly threatened. This is John Stuart Mill's basic view, his harm principle:

> [T]he sole end for which mankind are warranted, *individually* or collectively, in interfering with the liberty of action of any of their number is self-protection. . . . [T]he only purpose for which power can be rightfully exercised over any member of a civilized community, against his will, is to prevent harm to others.[84]

Following Feinberg, I understand a harm to be a wrongful setting back of interests.[85] The question I now address, then, is when waste constitutes a wrongful setting back of someone's interests. If we define waste as "(a) a process wherein something useful becomes less useful and that produces

---

[82] See Strahilevitz, "The Right to Destroy," 803, 854. Strahilevitz also considers ex ante arguments (ibid., 808-21), but even these are based on the total economic value (fairly narrowly understood) that would be produced by allowing or disallowing the wasteful act.

[83] Andrew Jason Cohen, "What the Liberal State Should Tolerate within Its Borders," *Canadian Journal of Philosophy* 37, no. 4 (2007): 479-513.

[84] John Stuart Mill, *On Liberty* (1859), ed. Elizabeth Rapaport (Indianapolis, IN: Hackett Publishing, 1978), 9 (emphasis added). The harm principle is a moral principle about both individual and legal action. It indicates not only what sorts of justifications for state interference with individuals are legitimate, but also what sorts of justifications are legitimate for anyone to thus interfere. Here, I deal only with the broader category.

[85] See Andrew Jason Cohen, "What the Liberal State Should Tolerate within Its Borders," 482. Feinberg writes: "For the purposes of the harm principle, we must think of harming as having two components: (1) it must lead to some kind of adverse effect, or create the danger of such an effect, on its victim's *interests;* and (2) it must be inflicted wrongly." Joel Feinberg, *Freedom and Fulfillment* (Princeton, NJ: Princeton University Press, 1992), 3-4 (emphasis in the original).

less benefit than is lost—where benefit and usefulness are understood with reference to the same metric—or (b) the result of such a process," then when does waste wrongfully set back someone's interests? The basic idea is that if a specific instance of waste violates the harm principle,[86] it exceeds the normative limits of toleration and thus makes interference morally permissible. We can then say that people are not at liberty to act in that way—they have at least a prima facie duty not to act in that way. But when is that?

C. Getting the question straight

The question of toleration that we are concerned with here is threefold: must others tolerate (1) your waste of your own goods, (2) your waste of unowned goods, and (3) your waste of others' goods? The third part of the question is easily dismissed: if you have permission to waste someone else's goods, the question is the same as if you owned the goods yourself; if permission is not present, theft is involved and takes precedence. In any case, what is wrong with wasting someone else's goods without her consent is as obvious as what is wrong with stealing: it wrongfully sets back her interests in maintaining her property. Hence, the question of toleration here really centers on two subquestions. The first question is whether (i) ownership includes *jus abutendi* in such a way that it cannot be immoral to waste what one owns, or (ii) such waste is immoral but must be tolerated, or (iii) interference in such waste is permissible. Answering this question requires determining when the presence of waste overrides the presumption that a person may do with his belongings as he wishes without interference. When, to put the point bluntly, is the *jus abutendi*—the right to destroy or waste—morally overridden?[87] The second question is about the waste of unowned goods (perhaps unownable goods) and can be dealt with along with the first.

What is wrong with wasting one's own goods or unowned goods (whether the goods are in an unclaimed natural state or whether they have been discarded by their previously rightful owners) is far less obvious than what is wrong with wasting someone else's goods. Some will insist either that one cannot (i.e., by definition) waste one's own goods or that one has a right to waste one's own goods, so that it cannot be wrong to do so. If the definition of waste I have offered is accepted, the first objection falls away. It is obviously conceptually possible to waste what

---

[86] Or a correlated principle like my Principle T (see Andrew Jason Cohen, "What the Liberal State Should Tolerate within Its Borders," 494).

[87] Here I simply assume for the sake of argument that there is such a right in a just legal regime. If there is not, then interference with waste of one's own goods is more likely to be morally permissible. This suggests that if there is no moral justification for a legal *jus abutendi* in property, there is more likely to be a duty not to waste. It does not imply, though, that there is no such moral duty if *jus abutendi* is part of property.

one owns if my definition is correct. One might, for example, light one's last match and forget to use it to ignite a much-needed lantern, allowing the match to burn out as one watches in a daze. Surely, this is a process wherein something useful becomes less useful and that produces less benefit than is lost (with benefit and usefulness understood with reference to the same metric). Wasting one's own goods is thus conceptually possible. Can it be wrong to do so? Here, it might help to remember that saying it is wrong to do something does not mean either that it is illegal to do it or that it should be illegal. It is not the case that the government should interfere in every moral wrong (for example, the government should not interfere when one person lies to another, unless the lying constitutes fraud). It is moral wrongness alone that we are discussing here, not legal wrongness or the morality of the law. With that qualification on the table, it should be easier to see that it is at least plausible to say that one can wrongfully waste goods that one owns—even if one has a right to waste those goods. It is not, after all, always good or morally neutral to exercise one's rights; nor is it the case that one never has a right to do what is wrong.[88] Upon leaving a restaurant, one might have a right to pour ammonia on one's leftovers in front of a starving homeless person, but it is surely at least plausibly immoral to do so.

D. The answer (?)

The Millian-Feinbergian framework of analysis easily explains the wrongfulness of wasting others' goods (as I have already indicated). It may also help us deal with the possible wrongfulness of wasting one's own goods. In the rest of this section, I sketch what I take to be the most plausible line of argument to defend the immorality of waste.

The argument begins by recognizing that it is bad if a person starves.[89] In some cases, of course, it might be the all-things-considered best thing if one person starves (say, rather than a hundred people starving), but that does nothing to alter the fact that it is bad if a person starves.[90] This follows from what we can call "the suffering principle": suffering is bad (analytically true) and prima facie justifies interference (to thwart it).

---

[88] For more on this, see Jeremy Waldron, "A Right to Do Wrong," *Ethics* 92, no. 1 (1981): 21–39; Robert Audi, "Wrongs within Rights," *Philosophical Issues* 115 (2005): 121–39; and Andrew I. Cohen, "Famine Relief and Human Virtue," in Andrew I. Cohen and Christopher Wellman, eds., *Debates in Applied Ethics* (New York: Blackwell Publishers, 2005), 326–42, at 330 33.

[89] I do not want to say that the starving person has a right to food. While I am not prepared to deny such a claim, I also have no defense to offer in its favor. This is somewhat unfortunate, since if the starving person did have a moral (claim) right to food, waste would clearly be immoral in any instance where it prevented satisfaction of that right.

[90] Ending suffering is not the sole goal of a moral life. As Schmidtz notes, we could end all suffering by making the world uninhabitable to sentient life (see Schmidtz, *Person, Polis, Planet*, 155). There are other moral values.

Though the "prima facie" in the principle is important and the warrant to intervene is defeasible, Peter Singer would claim that "if it is in our power to prevent something very bad from happening, without thereby sacrificing anything morally significant, we ought, morally, to do it."[91] Failing to do so is, on his view, a wrong. The intuition behind this sort of view is clear: it is bad if people suffer; it is not bad if we save them; thus, if we can save them without moral cost, we ought to. While this view rests on a plausible and perhaps obvious claim—that suffering is bad—it has difficulties, and I reject it below in favor of the Millian-Feinbergian line. What does that view tell us here?

Clearly, when people starve, their interests are set back (from the baseline of not starving, which they clearly have an interest in). Thus, if we allow them to starve, we allow their interests to be set back. What remains an open question is whether *allowing their interests to be set back* is morally comparable to setting them back oneself or is in some other way wrongful. In short, the question is whether an omission of this sort is wrongful.[92] Only if it is, would we have a case of a harm and thus a case where interference is permissible according to this analysis.

James Rachels presents a persuasive case that, at least in some instances, allowing suffering is morally equivalent to causing it.[93] His examples make the point. In the first example, Smith drowns his baby cousin in order to inherit a sum of money, while Jones merely lets his baby cousin drown (when he can easily save him) in order to inherit money. Jones seems blameworthy in much the same way that Smith does, even though Jones "merely" lets the cousin die. In another example, a Down's syndrome baby with an intestinal blockage is allowed to die after birth; the blockage could be easily removed to save the baby, but the parents decline to have this simple procedure performed because they only want a "normal" child. The parents seem no less guilty than if they refused to allow the child nutrition. Feinberg discusses another case, wherein B has a heart attack and reaches for medicine that would save him; in one version, A pushes the medicine out of B's reach, and in another version, he simply refrains from pushing it within B's reach (because he wants B to die).[94] While some may quibble with Rachels and Feinberg about the judgments made in these cases, the general point stands: at least sometimes, it is as bad—and wrongful—to allow someone to suffer or die as it is to cause them to suffer or die. The case where we choose (perhaps extreme) waste

[91] Peter Singer, "Famine, Affluence, and Morality," *Philosophy and Public Affairs* 1, no. 2 (1972): 229–243, at 231.

[92] For Feinberg's discussion of how omissions can be understood as causes of harms, see Joel Feinberg, *Harm to Others* (New York: Oxford University Press, 1984), 171–86. See also Patricia Smith, "Legal Liability and Criminal Omissions," *Buffalo Criminal Law Review* 5, no. 69 (2002): 69–102.

[93] James Rachels, "Active and Passive Euthanasia," *New England Journal of Medicine* 292 (1975): 78–80.

[94] Feinberg, *Harm to Others,* 167. Feinberg attributes the example to Thomas Grey.

rather than saving the starving person is arguably of this sort. Pouring ammonia over perfectly edible leftovers, rather than letting the starving person eat them, seems to be like this. That is, it seems to be an *allowing to suffer* that is as blameworthy as a *causing to suffer*. In this sort of waste, at least, there seems to be moral wrongness. Of course, this is an extreme case, and other instances of waste may not be wrong.

Remember that to waste something is to begin a process wherein something useful becomes less useful and that produces less benefit than is lost—where benefit and usefulness are understood with reference to the same metric. If one wastes food or the resources to buy food, one makes the food or resources less useful than they could be. The food would be more useful if we gave it to the starving person, thus preventing him from starving; other wasted resources would be more useful if we used them in a better way, so that we had more ability to provide food for the starving. The fact that more or better use could be gotten from the resources, however, does not mean that there is immorality here.

Importantly, there are times when preventing waste involves significant cost. I may occasionally have to throw out spoiled food. This does seem wasteful: I engage in a process (say, leaving the food in the refrigerator instead of the freezer) wherein something (the food) becomes less useful and where less benefit is produced than is lost. Nonetheless, there are costs to the sort of vigilance that would be necessary to prevent every instance of such waste. In such cases, it is hard to imagine that the waste is such that interference is permissible—even though there are starving people who could have used the food. This is nothing unusual; it follows simply from the fact that "ought" implies "can." That I cannot always prevent the waste means that I am not obligated to do so.[95] Of course, there are cases of waste that we can avoid. Such cases, wherein one wastes one's own goods but could (easily) avoid doing so, would presumably be of the sort that the avoidance of the waste could allow for the prevention or cessation of the suffering of another. Such cases are at least plausibly immoral.

In order for a particular case of waste to be immoral, it is clearly not enough merely that someone claims there is waste. So too, and more importantly, it is not enough that the instance be one of waste indexed to someone other than the actor.[96] The art museum cannot simply claim that the art collector is wasting the Picasso painting when he sets out to destroy it and expect the mere claim to justify interference. Nor is such destruction immoral or interference-warranting simply because the art museum is correct that, indexed to it, the destruction would be an instance

---

[95] As Matt Zwolinski pointed out in correspondence, this is actually too quick. That I cannot always prevent waste means that I am not obligated to always prevent waste. I may still be obligated to prevent any particular instance of waste. The point in the text is that there are some occasions of waste I cannot avoid and so am not obligated to avoid.

[96] I thank Jim Taggart for pushing me to discuss this.

of waste. Similarly, when the restaurant patron pours ammonia on his leftovers rather than offering them to the homeless person, it is not enough that the homeless person claims there is waste or that he is right that there is waste indexed to him. The art collector's interest (no matter how perverse) in destroying the painting may matter. Similarly, if the restaurant patron gets joy from contaminating his food, that joy may matter. I also think it should matter in both cases that the actors have the characters they do—characters lacking in virtue. I will not pursue that line of inquiry here, but because the perversity of the characters may make these examples less illuminating for our purposes, I will use another.

Consider, again, Shiprock. Suppose Big Pharma wants to mine the formation for the cancer cure it holds. It stands to profit financially; cancer victims stand to profit medically. The benefit gained from both perspectives is clear; indexed to Big Pharma or to cancer victims, mining the formation is not waste. Indexed to the Navajo, though, it may well be. We cannot simply assume that the value of mining to Big Pharma or to the cancer victims outweighs the value of not mining to the Navajo, or that the former value matters in a way that the latter does not. Surely, if we are going to say that there is an immorality here, it should be that there is waste from the all-things-considered perspective. That is, if waste is to be considered immoral, it must be waste that is (a) a process wherein something useful becomes less useful to all who could possibly make use of it, and that produces less benefit than is lost (again, to all of them)—*where benefit and usefulness are understood for each of them with reference to their own single metric*—or (b) the result of such a process.[97] As I have already indicated, in cases such as Big Pharma versus the Navajo, determining whether there is waste all things considered will be a difficult task. This does not change if we assume that Big Pharma owns the formation.[98]

Unfortunately, there will be cases of waste significantly like Big Pharma versus the Navajo. Someone might, for example, want her house destroyed when she dies because she cannot bear the thought of anyone else living there,[99] but her neighbors and township may want the house sold and left standing to maintain the community. Indexed to the owner, there may not be waste in the destruction of the house; indexed to the others, there may be. These cases will all be difficult if we remain neutral between the

[97] As I have already indicated, none of this implies subjectivism. The metrics involved would be objective facts about the parties. See notes 56 and 57 and the accompanying text.

[98] Some might think that, in the real world, since the Navajo Nation owns (or, as an independent nation, has sovereignty over) Shiprock, its metric is the controlling one. Others might think that, given the life-saving potential, that view is mistaken. I imagine more people will think that if Big Pharma rightly owns the formation, the questions we are asking here are irrelevant—that if Big Pharma owns the formation, it can do with it as it likes, even destroy it. But that has yet to be established: it is the question of whether waste limits property (a question for another essay).

[99] The example is from Strahilevitz, "The Right to Destroy," 784 n. 7. See *Eyerman v. Mercantile Trust Co.*, 524 S.W.2d 210, 217 (Mo. Ct. App. 1975).

parties and their metrics (as I think we should). I cannot here offer a means of adjudication. However, cases where there is a single metric for all of the involved parties (some of which cases may involve only one party) should be somewhat easier to adjudicate. In those cases, if there is waste from the all-things-considered perspective—taking into consideration the loss that would be incurred if the waste were avoided—it is plausibly immoral.

If one accepts that it is morally wrong to allow suffering (which is also a setback of interests), then what was said above is as true of wasting unowned goods (when such is easily avoided) as it is of wasting one's own goods (when such is easily avoided). If I find a stash of canned foods in an abandoned 1950s-era bomb shelter (supposing the food still maintains its nutritional value), and I decide to blow up the cans for some minimal amount of fun, I waste the food. I take the presumably unowned food (assuming the abandoned shelter has no legitimate owner)[100] and use it in a process that removes its usefulness and produces less benefit (in the explosion I create) than is lost. The lost (nutritional) usefulness could be used to save a starving person.

There is, in the foregoing discussion, an empirical claim that should be made explicit: the claim that there are starving persons. Given this empirical claim, the conclusion is limited: so long as (1) there are starving persons, and (2) allowing starvation when one can easily stop it is wrong, it follows that easily avoidable all-things-considered waste which results in an inability to prevent starvation is morally wrong. Since there are starving persons, the conclusion that we have a duty to avoid waste should be accepted if one accepts that we are blameworthy if we let someone suffer in this way. Indeed, if avoiding the waste is costless and the saving of the starving person immediate, there would seem at least as much of a duty not to waste (in such cases) as there is to save the mythical child drowning in the pool that can be saved with a turn of the arm.

Obviously, what has been said thus far supports, at best, only a limited duty not to waste. If there were no starving people (or people otherwise in need of help that could be provided were it not for waste), there would be no duty not to waste, according to the above argument. More importantly, in a case where one was not blameworthy for letting someone starve when one could prevent it, there would be no duty not to waste. This happens more regularly than might be thought. For example, I could eat half of my dinner and give the rest to the homeless person outside the restaurant, but I choose to eat it all (not quite, but almost, gluttonously). Some might think that in a case of that sort, there is a duty not to waste and, indeed, a duty to provide half the meal to the homeless person. After

---

[100] Plausibly, this taking is akin to an original acquisition. When I take the unowned food, it plausibly becomes my property. If it does, the question of wasting unowned goods reduces to the question of wasting one's own goods.

all, Singer might suggest that doing so does not require "anything morally significant" compared to the very bad thing that can be prevented.

Others have shown significant difficulties for Singer's view.[101] The challenge has to do with incentives and unintended consequences. The basic idea, put starkly, is this: If we aid those who are starving, we provide an incentive for others to appear to be starving. Worse, if we aid those who are starving now, we may encourage the birth of more people into conditions of starvation.[102] Providing for those who are starving has moral hazards. Of course, it may be insisted that we cannot avoid having "dirty hands." Still, if providing for those who are starving now is likely to bring it about that there are twice the number of starving people later—an empirical question—that would be a bad thing. In that case, wasting foodstuffs (or other resources that can be turned into foodstuffs) may be a *better* option than saving these things in order to provide for those who are starving. While this clearly does not support a *duty to waste*, it does disallow the hoped-for support for a *duty not to waste*.

While Singer's principle seems mistaken once one considers the broader impact of following it, Rachels's claim about *allowing* sometimes being as wrong as *doing* seems to stand. The claim, modified for this discussion, is that sometimes one is as morally blameworthy for *allowing* another to suffer (by starving, for example) as one is for *causing* another to suffer. Even assuming that the possible unintended consequences of preventing the suffering could not in any way be bad (because of a decree from God, say), this claim is of limited help with regard to a duty not to waste. While we likely agree that one must save the mythical drowning child when one is sunning poolside and can almost effortlessly reach over to pull him out of the water, cases of waste will not (usually) be that costless or that immediate. At best, then, Rachels's claim only helps support a substantially limited duty not to waste.

A fuller argument for my Millian-Feinbergian analysis would require a discussion of the proper baseline from which to consider whether one sets back the starving person's interests. That is, we would need to determine what level of interest-fulfillment counts as the starting-point from which our action or inaction is judged to have set back the interests of the suffering (starving) individual. Four possibilities suggest themselves: (a) where the person is now—starving; (b) a minimally acceptable level of

---

[101] See Schmidtz, *Person, Polis, Planet,* 145–64, esp. 148–49, and Andrew I. Cohen, "Famine Relief and Human Virtue," for discussions of the limits of the principle Singer offers. Given those discussions, I think Singer's principle needs to be understood differently than Singer himself does if it is to be accurate, but I will not discuss this here.

[102] Garrett Hardin, "Lifeboat Ethics: The Case Against Helping the Poor," *Psychology Today* (September 1974): 38–43 and 124–126. Hardin's point is originally about the morality of government intervention; Schmidtz's point (see the previous note) is more general. In any case, I think both points can be applied to individuals. Nonetheless, as Matt Zwolinski suggested in correspondence, it is clear that moral hazard arguments more easily justify institutions that allow waste than they justify waste by individuals.

welfare; (c) where the person would be if not for the fact that he is now starving; and (d) where the person would be if not for the way the world is set up. I suspect the relevant baseline is (a). If that is right, though, when I waste and thereby refuse to help alleviate the suffering of the starving person, I do not set his interests back: he simply is in a bad way to begin with, through no action of mine. I do not harm him by not helping, and thus I have no duty to refrain from wasting so that I can help him.

Let us briefly consider the other candidate baselines. Option (d) is of no help here, since there is no way to tell how well off the suffering person would be if the world were set up differently. The world could be set up in a variety of ways that would leave more people suffering (and suffering in worse ways than those who now suffer). Option (c) is also of no help, since it merely asserts that the baseline is "not where we are" without indicating anything more: it says what the baseline *is not*, not what it is. Option (b) is obviously the best hope for strengthening an argument for a less limited duty not to waste, but it is an unlikely baseline from which to consider if one sets back another's interests. If (b) *is* accepted as the appropriate baseline, then even helping someone can be seen as harmful if it does not bring him above the accepted minimum; any action, even one that helped the other person, would "wrongfully set back interests" if it resulted in the other's rising to anything less than the minimum.[103] In such cases, we would have to say there was both help and harm, and while it may be that one act can be both helpful and harmful, we would then need further discussion to determine what combinations of help and harm are acceptable. The fact that the help and harm are, as it were, on the same scale, though, seems to make such judgments unnecessary; if one fails to bring the sufferer above the accepted minimum, one harms him (or leaves him in a harmed condition), and that justifies interference. This simply leaves too much room for interference. Perhaps further argument could show that this view is mistaken, but to me it seems sound.

Progress in defending a less limited duty not to waste may be possible. Talk of starving *others* may obscure a central fact we considered earlier: waste is correlated to need. This is not a conceptual necessity, as we saw in Section III.A, but it is an important consideration nonetheless. What is obscured, then, in considering *others* is that it is need in general that may go unmet when we waste, not just the need of others. Indeed, it may be *our own need*. Most of us accept that we have a moral duty to preserve ourselves when possible, but even if this is not accepted as a genuine moral duty, it is surely a matter of prudence. We should not waste because when we do, we risk our own preservation. Indeed, "the waste restriction is a natural complement to the principle of self-preservation [since] . . . [i]f we waste the resources we have appropriated, then we are not investing labour in them to preserve ourselves."[104] As others have indicated, Locke argues that we have a moral duty to labor, and he surely would not encourage wasteful labor over productive labor.[105] Helga Varden, for example, indicates that "the spirit of the waste restriction is that labour subject to the proviso gives us an enforceable right and duty towards one another to pursue *productive uses* of the resources."[106] Being productive rather than wasteful has clear instrumental value in aiding self-preservation.[107] Intrinsic moral value might also be aided in being productive rather than wasteful.

If one adopts John Simmons's Lockean view that labor should be understood as "a kind of purposive activity aimed at satisfying needs or supplying the conveniences of life,"[108] one is led to conclude that waste is morally unacceptable. On that sort of view, Locke is concerned to prevent property from causing harm. (Indeed, he tells us that "it would always be a sin, in any man of estate, to let his brother perish for want of affording him relief out of his plenty.")[109] Hence, Locke's first proviso forbids appropriation that leaves others worse off than they would be without that appropriation because it is wrong to leave others in a harmed condition.[110] Of course, there are different sorts of harms; as I have previously suggested,[111] some harms are only infringements of autonomy, while others include theft or battery. Infringing upon autonomy, which is intrinsically valuable, is interfering with an agent's purposive activity, infringing upon her right to self-government. This can be done in various ways,

[104] Varden, "Locke's Waste Restriction and His Strong Voluntarism," 128.

[105] For the view that Locke intends the waste proviso to be an "imperative to labour," see Lewis, "An Environmental Case against Equality of Right," 260; cf. Shiffren, "Lockean Arguments for Private Intellectual Property," 147ff. See Simmons, *The Lockean Theory of Rights*, 101, for a defense of the view that while we must labor, we can productively do so in ways that fit into our own plans.

[106] Varden, "Locke's Waste Restriction and His Strong Voluntarism," 133.

[107] Hence, for Locke, "Productive labor . . . is virtuous and God-fearing; while idleness is sinful as well as anti-social" (Waldron, *The Right to Private Property*, 147). Locke is against both the idle able poor and the idle rich; indeed, it is idleness per se he opposes (Sreenivasan, *The Limits of Lockean Rights in Property*, 47). He opposes idleness because it is a form of waste that is particularly pernicious (for the reasons I discuss in the text).

[108] Simmons, *The Lockean Theory of Rights*, 273.

[109] Locke continues: "As justice gives every man a title to the product of his honest industry, and the fair acquisitions of his ancestors descended to him; so charity gives every man a title to so much out of another's plenty, as will keep him from extreme want, where he has no means to subsist otherwise" (I.42). Locke seems to recognize no conflict between the two conjuncts. In any case, my own worry about Locke's view of charity here is that he makes it too much like a perfect duty, depriving it of the element that would seem to make it *charitable*. (Of course, it is not unreasonable to think that Locke treats charity as a third proviso on property.)

[110] Cf. Clark Wolf, "Contemporary Property Rights, Lockean Provisos, and the Interests of Future Generations," *Ethics* 105, no. 4 (1995): 791–818, where the first proviso is read as a harm principle (esp. 803–9).

[111] Andrew Jason Cohen, "What the Liberal State Should Tolerate within Its Borders," 485 n. 9.

including not allowing her what she needs to self-govern—including subsistence.[112] Hence, on the Locke-Simmons line, our treatment of our property "must do no 'harm' or 'prejudice' to others,"[113] which it does if it "denies others an opportunity equal to one's own for self-preservation and self-government."[114] Put more simply, "If I waste what others would otherwise use, I deny them the opportunity of productive use (and show that I do not respect them or their projects). Since their right is to make property by their labor in whatever fair share of the common they choose, I infringe their right by precluding their choice of the goods I waste. . . . Waste harms others, even in conditions of relative plenty."[115] As just discussed, the argument here is not only about the instrumental value of productivity (especially as opposed to waste) for self-preservation; it is also about disallowing hindrances to the intrinsic moral value of autonomy. Of course, there is no denying the instrumental disvalue of waste where self-preservation is concerned: "[W]aste is clearly contrary to the best (i.e., most efficient) preservation of humankind."[116]

E. Suggested normative principles

What we should conclude now is that the moral problem with waste (if there is such a problem) is related to need (generalizing from the need for food). Taking need to be that which is required for the preservation of life (or, perhaps, for a minimally decent life), need is, prima facie, something that should be met where possible. In other words, it is bad that people live in need. Because (some) waste can cause or exacerbate need (when it could be avoided without sacrifice), it is morally problematic. Truly wasteful activity, activity that results in waste all things considered (see Sections III.D and IV.C), seems to be of this sort. Still, whether there is a moral duty not to waste is unclear. This is because it is unclear if an agent sets another's interests back by not satisfying a need the agent did not cause. Even given this difficulty, we must admit that waste is a problem since it is not conducive to the preservation of others and ourselves.

Clearly, we are not responsible for preventing all bads that are in our power to prevent. Returning to a previous example, the fact that I could forgo my family vacation and use the money instead to pay for other

---

[112] On Sreenivasan's Lockean view, property ends where there is not "*enough and as good direct means of subsistence . . . available for others*" (Sreenivasan, *The Limits of Lockean Rights in Property*, 55).

[113] Citing Locke's *Two Treatises* (e.g., I.37; II.33, 36, 37), Simmons (*The Lockean Theory of Rights*, 292) is talking about appropriation, but the same presumably holds for what is done after appropriation. Indeed, on Simmons's view, there are four types of duties that are the content of natural law (see ibid., 51, 60): duties to preserve oneself, to preserve others, not to 'take away the life' of another, and not to do what 'tends to destroy' others.

[114] Simmons, *The Lockean Theory of Rights*, 292.

[115] Ibid., 286.

[116] Ibid., 284.

people's needs is not enough to show that I have done something wrong when I take my family on vacation. I propose that my failure to alleviate someone else's need (when she cannot alleviate it herself) is a wrong at most when my failure includes easily avoidable waste of something that could satisfy her need. Hence, *if one person needs something for her preservation and a second person has it, is avoidably wasting it, and refuses to allow the first to make some greater use of it, the second may be morally wrong.*[117] (I call this principle W1.) Since I do not waste my resources when I take a vacation with my family, my action is not counter to any duty.[118]

How wrong would a violation of W1 be? This will be difficult to determine. If a person is wasting an item, he is treating it in such a way that it becomes less useful. The less useful the item is made, the more good is forgone and so, presumably, the worse (morally) the act of waste. If instead of alleviating a child's starvation, I burn the extra money in my wallet, it is surely worse than if I stuff it under my mattress. Per our earlier discussion, cash becomes less useful when stored in a mattress, but not as much less useful as when it is burned. Moreover, in the mattress-stuffing case, there is a possibility that the waste will end. We can add that if there are no hungry individuals to eat his apples, the Misanthropic Apple Farmer is less bad than he would be if there were—partly because his misanthropy has no effect on others. No harm is done or can be done, since there is no one to be hurt. Similarly, if the worst that occurs because of my wasteful burning of cash is that a child gets one less toy than she would have gotten, it is not as bad as if someone starved. The interest that is set back matters; if the interest that is set back is an interest in a need, it is worse than if it is an interest in a mere want. I will say no more about this here.

Given our discussion of varying metrics of usefulness and benefit, W1 will be somewhat unsatisfying as a normative principle, since we want to know if the waste is waste according to the metric of the one doing the (supposed) wasting or the metric of the one in need (or according to the conjunction or disjunction of the two).[119] Fortunately, we can alter W1 to gain an additional principle that is more definitive (because it is less inclusive). I thus propose principle W2: *If one person needs something for her preservation, understood according to her metric, and a second person has it, is*

---

[117] Some might suggest that we need to qualify the moral claim with intentionality, such that "if one person needs something for her preservation and a second person has it, is *intentionally* wasting it, and refuses to allow the first to make some further use of it, the second may be morally wrong." I do not think the qualification is needed. One can act immorally unintentionally—this is acting negligently by not forming an intention one should.

[118] I will simply assume that family vacations are at least sometimes morally permissible. In any case, at least some vacations are not wasteful. My family gains significant beneficial shared experiences and relaxation when we take vacations. Of course, in some cases, those benefits should give way to others—imagine, for example, that either we take our vacation or a bomb kills a million innocent civilians.

[119] I owe thanks to Andy Altman for pushing me to clarify this issue.

avoidably wasting it according to his own *metric, and refuses to allow the first to make some greater use of it, the second is morally wrong.* The item suspected of being wasted must be something needed by the first person according to *her* metric (not the metric of the person doing the wasting), but the waste must be measured by the metric of the second person (the one supposedly doing the wasting). Presumably, in many cases, these over-lap: we all need food and water for self-preservation, after all. In some cases, though, they may diverge. A member of the Navajo tribe, to return to that example, might claim he needs the Shiprock for his self-preservation *as a Navajo.* Let us take that claim at face value. Even if it is true, it is not necessarily the case that Big Pharma acts immorally when it mines the formation for the cancer cure—because according to its metric and that of those with cancer, the mining is tremendously beneficial and not at all wasteful. As I have said, I do not know how to adjudicate such a case to determine if the mining is waste all things considered. But if there is waste according to the metric of the one doing the wasting—that is, if the one doing the wasting gets less benefit from the process than is lost in the process—then there is simply no excuse for not providing the item to the other party. Both parties would gain—the one who would waste would have less loss by providing the item to the other instead of wasting it, and the other would have her need satisfied—and only mean-spiritedness could stand in the way of the clearly better outcome. Principle W2 indi-cates a definitive wrong, but may only be helpful where the metrics of the parties overlap (or are identical). In cases where they do not overlap, I suspect that the persons accused of waste will be able to truthfully indi-cate how what might be waste if indexed to another is not waste when indexed to them. Still, W2 will be helpful in a significant, though limited, range of cases.[120]

To the conclusions expressed in principles W1 and W2, I would add only that waste is worse the less useful it makes the item wasted, and is worse when an interest in a need is set back than when an interest in a mere want is set back. Put simply, waste is morally worse when it entails more forgone good and when it entails a failure to meet more important interests. Perhaps none of this is surprising.

V. Conclusion

I have defended the view that waste is best understood as (a) any process wherein something useful becomes less useful and that pro-duces less benefit than is lost—where benefit and usefulness are under-stood with reference to the same metric—or (b) the result of such a

[120] W2 is narrower than W1. I take all violations of W2 to be violations of W1. In cases where violations of W1 are violations of W2, there is a definitive wrong. There may be other violations of W1 that are not violations of W2 but that are definitively wrong.

process. I have used that definition to sketch possible lines of argument for the claim that we have a moral duty not to waste, including a line of argument based on harm to self and one based on disgust. Both of these were addressed briefly and rejected. After reframing the question, I offered a Millian-Feinbergian line of argument for a duty not to waste that I take to be promising. That argument begins with the plausible "suffering principle"—suffering is bad (analytically true) and prima facie justifies interference to thwart it—and the additional idea that, sometimes, allowing an evil is as morally wrong as doing an evil. The argument requires further discussion of baselines for determining when interests are set back, but is strengthened by considering how waste impairs purposive activity. If the argument goes through, then (W1) if one person needs something for her preservation and a second person has it, is avoidably wasting it, and refuses to allow the first to make some greater use of it, the second may be morally wrong; and (W2) if one person needs something for her preservation, understood according to her metric, and a second person has it, is avoidably wasting it according to his own metric, and refuses to allow the first to make some greater use of it, the second is morally wrong. Two projects remain: to determine if the argument just sketched can be strengthened to avoid the problems mentioned, and then to determine if property ought to be limited by a proviso against waste.

Philosophy, Georgia State University

THE DUTY TO SEEK PEACE

By Bernard R. Boxill

I. The Duty to Seek Peace

Immanuel Kant declared that "seeking the state of peace" is "a matter of unmitigated duty." [1] He also maintained that "the argument that something has until now been unsuccessful" does not "justify abandoning" a "morally obligatory" intention unless its "attainment is demonstrably impossible." [2] Therefore, he must have believed that the attainment of peace was not demonstrably impossible.

There were prominent philosophers well known to Kant whose work seemed to imply that peace might be impossible—notably, Thomas Hobbes and Jean-Jacques Rousseau. Hobbes's work, the main inspiration for present-day Realists, strongly suggested that, barring a world state which would be practically impossible to establish, the best we could hope for was a stand-off between countries deterred from attacking each other out of fear of devastating retaliation—a situation which was still a state of war. [3] Rousseau seemed to agree. According to Rousseau, barring a world of poor, backward, and isolated states—which might once have been possible, but was impossible in his time, as it is in our own—our best hope was the stand-off suggested by Hobbes's philosophy, though Rousseau seemed to believe that the balance of power on which this stand-off depended was liable to be much more unstable than Hobbes's work had implied. [4] But although Kant drew considerably from the work of both these philosophers, he made no attempt to directly rebut their arguments about the prospects for peace, presumably because such an attempt, even if it was successful, would not imply that peace was not demonstrably impossible. Yet Kant evidently felt that he had to do something to allay worries that someone might prove that peace was impossible, since such a proof would imply that we have no duty to seek peace. He took up this task in *Perpetual Peace*. In that book, he set out an elaborate set of arguments purporting to show that nature had given us a "Guarantee of

[1] Immanuel Kant, *Perpetual Peace*, in Ted Humphrey, ed., *Immanuel Kant: Perpetual Peace and Other Essays* (Indianapolis, IN: Hackett Publishing Company, 1983), 116.
[2] Immanuel Kant, "On the Proverb: That May Be True in Theory, But Is of No Practical Use," in Humphrey, ed., *Immanuel Kant: Perpetual Peace and Other Essays*, 87.
[3] Peter Caws, ed., *The Causes of Quarrel: Essays on Peace, War, and Thomas Hobbes* (Boston: Beacon Press, 1989).
[4] Stanley Hoffman, ed., *The State of War: Essays on the Theory and Practice of International Politics* (New York: Praeger, 1965).

Perpetual Peace," and he declared that nature enables us to predict peace from a "practical" point of view and that it "makes it our duty to work toward bringing about this goal (which is not a chimerical one)."[5] Since Kant says that his arguments about nature "make" it our duty to seek peace, he must have believed that they showed that the attainment of peace was not demonstrably impossible, presumably because they showed that peace was possible.

If Kant's arguments in *Perpetual Peace* show that peace is possible, we are entitled to ask about the sense of "possible" in which they show this. The word "possible" is ambiguous; things can be logically or conceptually possible, physically or causally possible, or practically possible, for example. In *The Metaphysics of Morals,* Kant claimed that we have a duty to act in conformity with the idea of a moral end, "even if there is not the slightest theoretical likelihood that it can be realized, as long as its impossibility cannot be demonstrated either."[6] This claim implies that peace need be only minimally possible to make seeking it a duty. Certainly, it must be conceptually or logically possible or perhaps also consistent with the known laws of science. But for seeking peace to be a duty, the possibility of peace cannot be required to be much greater than that; for example, it cannot be required that establishing peace must be consistent with known historical trends. If this were required, there would be considerably more than the slightest theoretical likelihood of peace being realized. But the arguments in *Perpetual Peace* that Kant says make it our duty to seek peace appeal to historical trends that Kant claims to discern. Consequently, even if these arguments "make" it our duty to seek peace by showing that peace is possible, we are entitled to suspect that Kant meant them to play some *further* role.

In the next section, I will argue that the further role Kant wanted his arguments to play was to cultivate a hope for peace that would support the duty to seek peace. In succeeding sections, I will argue that he tried to cultivate this hope by showing that there was a good chance that we would eventually establish peace because historical trends suggested that opportunities would arise for well-placed moral politicians to implement his plan for peace. However, current trends, especially the trend toward globalization, suggest that such opportunities are likely to become increasingly rare, and consequently that we can no longer rely on Kant's way of cultivating a hope for peace. Another way to cultivate such a hope would be to apply Kant's way to current trends and thereby devise a new plan for peace that such trends suggest we will have opportunities to implement. In the meantime, however, we need to sustain our hope for peace. Otherwise, we may not even be able to come up with a feasible plan for

---

[5] Kant, *Perpetual Peace,* 125.
[6] Immanuel Kant, *The Metaphysics of Morals,* in Mary J. Gregor, ed. and trans., *Immanuel Kant: Practical Philosophy* (Cambridge: Cambridge University Press, 1996), 491.

peace. One way to do this would be to reflect on the great value of peace, for hope is sustained not only by a belief that its object is likely, but also by the conviction that its object is valuable. In the final sections of the essay, I ask why Kant did not use this way to cultivate a hope for peace and why he never supposed that fear of war, and compassion for the victims of war, could be cultivated to support the duty to seek peace. I argue that he deliberately ignored these possibilities of securing peace because considering them could have endangered the establishment of what he took to be a peace worth valuing and hoping for—namely, not merely the absence of war, but the full and complete development of human talent. I conclude that clarity on these issues should persuade us to firmly set aside Kant's strategies to secure peace, and to rely more on compassion and perhaps a little fear to support the duty to seek peace.

II. Supporting the Duty to Seek Peace with the Hope for Peace

In this section, I argue that Kant wanted his arguments in *Perpetual Peace* to encourage a hope for peace that would support the duty to seek peace; that was the further role he wanted these arguments to play, besides establishing that there was a duty to seek peace. Consider the following passage, which comes at the very end of *Perpetual Peace:* "If it is a duty to make the state of public right actual," and "if at the same time there is a well founded hope that we can do it," then "perpetual peace" is no "empty idea," but a "task" that "steadily approaches its goal. . . ."[7] The passage says that if our duty to establish public right exists "at the same time" that we also have a well-founded hope that we can do it, then we will steadily approach the goal of peace. It suggests that Kant was committed to two claims. The first is that as we approach the goal of public right, we will also steadily approach our goal of establishing peace. This claim suggests that Kant must have believed that public right and peace are so closely related that approaching public right provides considerable assurance that peace is also being approached.[8] In that case, Kant's implication that he had given us a well-founded hope that we could establish public right implies that he also believes that he has given us a well-founded hope that we could establish peace. The second of the two claims in question suggests that the duty to do something and the hope to do it can work together to assure the goal of the duty. I say this because Kant writes as if the duty to establish public right, and the well-founded hope

---

[7] Kant, *Perpetual Peace*, 139.
[8] Kant describes public right as "a system of laws for a people . . . which, because they affect one another, need a rightful condition under a will uniting them." See Kant, *The Metaphysics of Morals*, 455. The concept is discussed fully in Arthur Ripstein, "Kant on Law and Justice," in Thomas E. Hill, Jr., ed., *The Blackwell Guide to Kant's Ethics* (Oxford: Blackwell Publishing, 2009), 161–78.

that we can do it, must occur "at the same time" to justify the inference that public right is being approached. But the idea that a hope to do something and the duty to do it can work together to assure the goal of the duty suggests that the hope to do something can usefully and legitimately support the duty to do it.

Attributing such a view to Kant may seem odd. On a standard view, Kant believed that emotion could not support duty. This standard view concedes that he allowed that the emotions sometimes motivate us to act in *accordance* with duty, but it maintains that he thought this merely accidental because even in these cases the emotions never motivate us to act *from* duty. Moreover, the view maintains that the emotions are unreliable because they cannot always be summoned up when needed, and they often motivate us to act wrongly. Recently, however, many leading Kantians have challenged this standard view.[9] These philosophers admit that some passages in Kant's *Groundwork for the Metaphysics of Morals* especially might make the view appear to be sound, but they insist that a broader study of his works shows that while he always disapproved of relying on the emotions as a guide to dutiful action, his considered view was that they could be cultivated to play important *supportive* roles in morality. Thus, in *The Metaphysics of Morals,* Kant states that we have an "indirect duty" to "cultivate the compassionate natural ... feelings in us, and to make use of them as so many means to sympathy based on moral principles and the feelings appropriate to them," and he goes on to maintain that it is "therefore a duty not to avoid the places where the poor who lack the most basic necessities are to be found but rather to seek them out, and not to shun sick-rooms or debtors' prisons and so forth in order to avoid sharing painful feelings one may not be able to resist. For this is still one of the impulses that nature has implanted in us to do what the representation of duty alone would not accomplish."[10] The last sentence in this passage suggests that Kant believed that the compassionate feelings can sometimes motivate us to act in accordance with certain duties if we ever find ourselves unable or unwilling to perform those duties for the sake of duty, and that we should cultivate the emotions for this reason. Some commentators prefer to read Kant as saying that sympathetic feelings are not themselves "directly motivating factors" but, rather, enable us to act from duty by negating inclinations that tempt us to violate our duty. I will not pursue the issue any further. Suffice it to say that contemporary Kantian scholarship indicates that it is at least possible that Kant intended his argument in *Perpetual Peace* to show that there were good grounds for hoping that

---

[9] See, for example, Nancy Sherman, *Making a Necessity of Virtue: Aristotle and Kant on Virtue* (Cambridge: Cambridge University Press, 1997).

[10] Kant, *The Metaphysics of Morals,* 575, 576.

we would succeed in our duty to secure peace, and that we could use this fact to cultivate a hope for peace that would support the duty to seek peace.

III. CULTIVATING THE HOPE FOR PEACE

How can we cultivate a hope for peace? If hopes can be well founded, then presumably they may not be well founded. What distinguishes well-founded hopes from those that are not well founded?

On a common view, hoping for something involves a belief that there is a "good chance" that what one hopes for will be realized.[11] The expression "good chance" is somewhat vague, but I think it safe to take it to mean that what one hopes for is likely. For example, if my friends are scuttling their plans for a picnic tomorrow because of bad weather reports, I will probably not start them hoping that they can have their picnic by persuading them that it is conceptually and logically possible that tomorrow will be sunny. A much better way to start them hoping for a sunny day tomorrow would be to persuade them that the meteorologists have changed their forecasts and now predict that there is better than a 50 percent chance that tomorrow will be a sunny day. But the common view cannot be that hoping is possible only if the "good chance" of the hoped-for event occurring is more than 50 percent. It must allow for the obvious fact that we can and often do hope for tails (or heads) when a fair coin is flipped even if we believe that the chance of tails (or heads) is exactly 50 percent. But people do not only hope for tails when a coin is flipped, they often hope to win the lottery when they have only one ticket and they know that their chance of winning is infinitesimal.

Although the common view must therefore be rejected, a qualified version of it seems defensible. We can begin by noting that there is something odd and even a little foolish about hoping to win the lottery when one has only one ticket and literally millions of tickets have been sold. There is nothing the least bit odd about describing hopes as foolish. Hope is an emotion and, like most emotions, it can be described as rational or irrational and as foolish. We speak routinely of foolish fears and foolish anger and also, accordingly, of foolish or unreasonable hopes, and even of wise hopes, and of good and evil hopes.[12] Presumably, we say that hoping to win the lottery is foolish because the chances of winning are so small. Hoping for something involves an outlay of time, energy, and sometimes even resources. Someone who hopes to win the lottery may very well buy expensive things on credit that he cannot afford, expecting to be able to pay off his debts after he wins the jackpot. At the very least,

[11] Martha Nussbaum, *Upheavals of Thought* (Cambridge: Cambridge University Press, 2001), 28.
[12] John Deigh, "Cognitivism in the Theory of Emotions," in John Deigh, ed., *Emotions, Value, and Law* (New York: Oxford University Press, 2008), 39–71.

he will spend some time and energy making plans about what he will do with the money or just imagining what he will be able to do with it. And the more he hopes, the more and more time and energy all this planning and imagining will absorb. One may therefore conjecture that hoping for very unlikely things like winning lotteries is foolish, given what it costs and given that it will almost certainly come to nothing. The hoper, as we say, is setting himself up for disappointment and frustration.

If hoping to win the lottery is a foolish or at least unreasonable hope because its chances of being realized are so small, it seems that reasonable hopes are hopes with somewhat greater chances of being realized. In the case of reasonable hopes, we may plausibly say that we have good grounds for hoping, and when the chances of getting what we hope for are especially good, we may also plausibly say that our hope is well founded. If these considerations are persuasive, then it seems that when Kant implied that our hope for peace was well founded, he must have meant that we had reasons to believe there was a good chance that peace would one day be established.

Attention to some detailed considerations confirms this conclusion. As we saw earlier, Kant believed that the duty to seek peace presupposes only that peace is barely possible. He may also have believed that this possibility was enough to sustain a hope for peace. As we saw earlier, we *can* hope for things even when the chances of securing these things are very small. Of course, the example I used to make this point (people hoping to win the lottery with one ticket, although they know that their chances of winning are infinitesimal) does not show that the possibility of peace necessary to support a duty to seek peace suffices to support a hope for peace. As I have allowed, Kant may have believed that a duty to seek peace implies only that peace is conceptually or logically possible, and winning the lottery is more than only logically or conceptually possible. But even if Kant believed that the possibility of peace necessary to support the duty to seek peace could also support a hope that peace will be established, it does not follow that a hope for peace is well founded just because we believe we have a duty to seek peace. The passage cited earlier from the end of *Perpetual Peace* suggests that having a duty to establish public right and having a well-founded hope that public right can be attained are different and separate things. In other words, the passage suggests that it may be possible to have duties to secure ends even though we do not have well-founded hopes that we will succeed in securing them. Consequently, when Kant suggested in that passage that we have a well-founded hope for peace, he must have believed that the possibility of establishing peace was greater than the possibility of establishing peace that follows from the fact that we have a duty to seek peace.

Of course, it still does not follow that he believed that he was giving us reasons to believe that there was a "good chance" of establishing peace. There need not be a "good chance" of establishing peace just because the possibility of establishing peace is greater than the possibility of peace necessary to show that we have a duty to seek peace; after all, the latter possibility may be merely that peace is conceptually or logically possible. So we need another argument to show that when Kant claimed that we had a well-founded hope for peace, he meant that he had given us reasons for believing that there was a "good chance" for peace. I noted earlier that hopes generally become more reasonable as the chances of securing what is hoped for become greater. Hopes also generally become stronger and more intense as the chances of securing what is hoped for become greater.[13] The fact that hopes can vary in strength should come as no surprise. Hope is an emotion, and like other emotions (fear and anger, for example), it may be more or less intense. The fact that hope is generally strengthened as the chances that it will be realized become greater does not mean that a hope can be very strong only if the chances of its being realized are great. Since we can hope for something that we believe is very unlikely, our hope for it may conceivably be enormously strengthened if we come to believe that it is a little less unlikely. Consequently, I grant that Kant could conceivably enormously strengthen our hope for peace by showing us that peace is barely more than just logically or conceptually possible. And I grant too that, generally, the stronger the hope, the greater the motivation to try to establish what is hoped for and, consequently, the more likely that the hope will be realized. It still does not follow, however, that Kant was entitled to believe that we would approach the goal of peace, just because he had enormously strengthened our hope for peace. The fact that people hope intensely for some outcome does not necessarily justify an assurance that they will come close to achieving it. Strong hopes and strenuous strivings do not assure success. Indeed, they are fully compatible with almost certain failure. Success does not depend only on hope. It depends on how things are independently of hope. We can have some confidence than our hopes will not be frustrated only if there is some good likelihood of achieving what we hope for, independently of our hopes for it. Consequently, when Kant says that he can predict that we will approach our goal of peace because we have well-founded hopes that we will secure that goal, he can only mean that we have a "good chance" that peace will be established, independently of our well-founded hopes for peace.

Kant's argument can therefore be summarized as follows: We have a duty to seek peace; this duty implies that peace is possible; and possibility of peace may be enough to support a hope for peace. But our hope for peace is well founded; that is, there is actually a good chance that peace will be established. If we reflect on the fact that our hope for peace is well founded because we have a good chance to establish peace, our hope for

<hr>

[13] I do not mean that strong or intense hopes are the same as reasonable hopes. Strong or intense hopes may also be very unreasonable hopes.

peace will be strengthened. This strengthened hope for peace will energize our search for peace, and given that there is already a good chance for peace, this assures us that we will approach the goal of peace.

We have already agreed that hope can be intensified by reflecting on the fact that its object is probable. Now we must consider the claim that intensified hope energizes the search for the object of the hope. This claim is not always true. If a meteorologist tells me that tomorrow will be a sunny day and I believe him, I will believe that there is a "good chance" that tomorrow will be sunny; and if I want tomorrow to be sunny, his news will start me hoping that tomorrow will be sunny, or will strengthen my hope that tomorrow will be sunny. But it will not motivate me to do anything to make tomorrow a sunny day, because I can do nothing to make tomorrow a sunny day. Similarly, hoping to win the lottery with one ticket will not motivate me to do anything to increase my chances of winning the lottery. It may motivate me to buy more tickets, but then I would not still be hoping to win the lottery with one ticket. In other words, hoping to win the lottery does not improve one's chances of winning the lottery. If John and I each have one ticket in a lottery, the fact that I hope to win and he does not, does not make me more likely to win than he is. In contrast, when it is possible to do something to increase one's chances of securing what one wants, hoping to secure it may very well increase one's chances of securing it. Suppose John and I are equally fit and are given one month to prepare to race against each other. If I hope to win and he does not, then even if we both want to win, my chances of winning are greater than his, all else equal, because my hope to win will motivate me to train harder than he is likely to train. Generally, when initiative and effort can increase the chances of establishing some desired state, hoping for it motivates us seek to establish it more effectively, and consequently increases the chances that we will establish it. Kant seemed to hold this view. In the course of repudiating Moses Mendelssohn's pessimistic conception of history, he wrote that "hope for better times, without which an earnest desire to do something that benefits the general good would never have warmed the human heart, has always influenced the work of the well-intentioned."[14]

IV. Kant's Blueprint for Peace

If we grant that Kant has strengthened our hope for peace by showing us that this hope is well founded, the next question to ask is whether he has provided room for our strengthened hope to motivate us to act effectively to secure peace. The answer seems to be that he has. His arguments in *Perpetual Peace* seem to tell us exactly what we must do to secure peace: we must establish the three institutions he lists in the three "Definitive

[14] Kant, "On the Proverb: That May Be True in Theory, But Is of No Practical Use," 86.

Articles" of *Perpetual Peace:* namely, a republican constitution for *every* state; a pacific federation of *all* states; and a Cosmopolitan Right that entitles individuals to *visit* foreign countries and to attempt interactions with the natives, but also entitles the natives to turn them away, at least if this can be done without destroying them.[15] Kant seems to present these institutions as a blueprint for establishing peace. Consequently, he seems to imply that we can do our duty to secure peace by doing what we can to help establish them.

Unfortunately, however, Kant sometimes writes as if the best thing we can do to help ensure that these institutions are realized is to leave it to nature. "Nature," he proclaims, guarantees peace through the "mechanism of man's inclinations," which he appears to identify as our unsocial sociability, our prudence, our greed, and our fear.[16] These passions, along with the intelligence that they stimulate to grow ever more subtle and acute, will, without any help from morality, eventually drive human beings to set up the three institutions. In none of his arguments concerning these institutions does Kant show us people acting *from* duty. At best, he shows us people acting *in accordance with* duty (for example, defending themselves against others), but mainly he also shows us people acting *against* duty (for example, making war for profit). Thus, he argues that the natural nonmoral inclinations involved in competition (clearly, greed and pride) can spread republicanism through trade.[17] And he also argues that war will eventually become so devastating that we will be driven (presumably by prudence, fear, and material self-interest) to "enter into a federation of peoples."[18] Finally, he maintains that nature drives human beings to use the intelligence and understanding they have acquired as a result of competition to design a state that directs the forces within it against each other in such a way that the one "hinders or nullifies the destructive effects of the other," leaving everyone free. Such a state is republican, of course, and his statement that selfishness and intelligence alone (without morality) can set it up is famous: "[T]he problem of organizing a nation is solvable, even for a people comprised of devils (if only they possess understanding)."[19]

V. IMPLEMENTING KANT'S BLUEPRINT FOR PEACE

We should not infer that Kant meant that to establish the institutions that will establish peace, we should always follow our selfish inclinations

[15] Kant, *Perpetual Peace*, 112, 115, 118.
[16] Ibid., 120–25. By "unsocial sociability" Kant refers to the tendency of human beings to enter society, but to want to dominate others once in society.
[17] Immanuel Kant, *Idea for a Universal History with a Cosmopolitan Intent*, in Humphrey, ed., *Immanuel Kant: Perpetual Peace and Other Essays*, 36–38.
[18] Ibid., 34–36.
[19] Kant, *Perpetual Peace*, 124.

intelligently, even if this means acting wrongly. Such a view would contradict his whole moral philosophy. It would not even work to establish peace, since it falls easily before Rousseau's argument that if the passions drive the intelligence to become ever more subtle and powerful, they will drive it to subvert any institution it designs to contain them.[20] Thus, the view is no better than the Realists' view that only a balance of power can establish peace. Since Kant dismissed that view derisively, we should conclude that he understood its fatal flaw and, consequently, would take care to keep that flaw out of his own argument.[21]

He kept that flaw out of his own argument by supposing that at some point in the interdependent development of intelligence and passion, intelligence will design institutions that will free it from its subservience to selfishness. The point of these institutions would not be to stymie intelligence in its efforts to subvert the institutions, for intelligence will never be stymied in this way while it continues to be driven by selfishness. The point of the institutions would be to educate a faculty already present (but dormant) that will prevent selfishness from driving intelligence to subvert all barriers to selfishness. That faculty is, of course, morality. Kant's idea seemed to be that if intelligence and selfishness alone can indeed, at some point, eventually enable people to design institutions that keep them at peace, then *if these institutions are also just,* they will educate people to pay greater attention to the reasons why the institutions *ought* morally to be secured, and, consequently, will educate them to restrain their selfishness from its usual practice of driving their intelligence to subvert all obstacles that stand in the way of its satisfaction.

Thus, in *Perpetual Peace,* Kant claimed that "a people's good moral condition" would follow from "a good constitution," adding (significantly) that "a good national constitution cannot be expected to arise from morality." [22] His point, I take it, is that it should not be expected that the great mass of the people would design and establish a good constitution from moral considerations, although these same people would support it from moral considerations once they were educated by it.

But if the people cannot be expected to establish a good constitution from moral considerations, and nature won't, how will such a constitution ever be established? Although Kant did not believe that nature alone could produce a good constitution, he supposed that it could do something much less implausible and demanding, namely, produce a constitution that very roughly approximates a good constitution. Or, to weaken the argument even more drastically, he supposed that the trends he discerned suggested that nature will produce *opportunities* that morally moti-

---

[20] Jean-Jacques Rousseau, *Discourse on Inequality,* in Victor Gourevitch, ed. and trans., *Jean-Jacques Rousseau: The First and Second Discourses Together with Replies to Critics and Essay on the Origin of Languages* (New York: Harper Torchbooks, 1990), 117–90.

[21] Kant, "On the Proverb: That May Be True in Theory, But Is of No Practical Use," 89.

[22] Kant, *Perpetual Peace,* 124.

vated politicians and ordinary people—if they are vigilant, imaginative, alert, and well placed—can use to establish a good constitution, or at least to nudge extant institutions closer to such a constitution.[23] It is not even necessary that the institutions produced should be rough approximations of good constitutions. All that is necessary is that intelligence and selfishness can possibly help produce institutions that sufficiently imaginative and moral politicians can use to establish good constitutions. Further, if such politicians are resourceful, they just may be able to keep a good constitution in existence long enough so that the people are educated to support it.[24]

This is the possibility of peace that I think Kant believed his arguments established, and the possibility of peace that he also believed would cultivate a hope for peace. He did not believe, and had no good reason to believe, that natural processes alone could make peace even *possible*. The arguments that they could are implausible and are undone by Rousseau's argument. In addition to being implausible, they encourage moral passivity, as we have already seen. Kant's argument, the argument just presented in the previous paragraph, is that natural processes may bring about opportunities for moral politicians if they are alert and well placed to establish a just constitution and keep it in existence long enough for its educative effects to take hold.

Unfortunately, Kant's defenses of the idea that these three institutions will each make a special contribution to peace—and that together they would secure peace—seem perfunctory. For example, he argued that republican states would contribute to peace because they would go to war only if their citizens authorize it, and their citizens will generally not do so, knowing that they would have to bear the costs of war. This argument seems to fail if we assume that a majority of the citizens of a republic can often shift the costs of war onto a minority. Kant's argument for the contribution that a Cosmopolitan Right makes to peace is similarly perfunctory. It suggests that once states are able to trade freely with one another, they will see that their greed is more effectively satisfied by trade than by war. But this suggestion falls easily before Rousseau's argument, as is amply confirmed by history, including contemporary history. For history tells us that trade can actually lead to war because it disposes states to become dependent on raw materials or commodities that other states control, and that, once dependent on those things, states will be willing to go to war against the states they depend on to keep those materials or commodities flowing steadily, and may even be disposed to take over such states to guarantee their supply. Finally, the case for a federation of states is also far from conclusive. Basically, it seems to rely

[23] See Paul Guyer, "Nature, Morality, and Peace," in Paul Guyer, ed., *Kant on Freedom, Law, and Happiness* (Cambridge: Cambridge University Press, 2000), 418–22.
[24] Kant, *Perpetual Peace*, 127–31.

on the assumption that wars break out only because the states concerned have not talked long enough about how to resolve their disputes peacefully. But of course this assumption is empty because it is logically invulnerable to refutation. It can always be argued that a war would have been avoided if the belligerents had talked a little more.

These considerations suggest that if Kant wanted to show that the three institutions he described in his three "Definitive Articles" are *sufficient* for securing peace, he did not succeed in showing this. His failure is, however, not a catastrophe for his position. Possibly more elaborate arguments may show that it is quite plausible to suppose that the three institutions are together sufficient to secure peace. For example, the so-called Democratic Peace Theorists have urged a battery of interesting and cogent arguments to show that although democracies are not in general peaceful, as Kant surmised, it is nevertheless true that democracies never fight other democracies, at least when they recognize each other as democracies.[25] And these theorists support their arguments with the contention that history has no record of two democracies fighting each other when each democracy recognized the other as a democracy. Even if the considerations raised by the Democratic Peace Theorists are not altogether compelling, they do suggest that further investigation may fully support Kant's view that the three institutions he proposed may be just about sufficient to secure peace.

VI. The Problem of Globalization

More worrisome than the possibility that Kant's three institutions are not sufficient to ensure a just peace is the possibility that his arguments in *Perpetual Peace* do not show that the hope for peace is well founded. As we have seen, he tried to show that such a hope was well founded by arguing that historical trends are likely to create opportunities for moral politicians to realize his blueprint for peace. But according to many authorities, a new trend, globalization, is making such opportunities less and less likely, because it is steadily undermining the sovereignty of states that Kant's blueprint supposes is a condition for securing peace.

Our prospects for peace would therefore be very grim if Kant had proved that his blueprint set out the *only* way to secure a just peace. But he did not prove this, and he did not believe that he had. If his arguments were meant to show that a world of republics, a federation of states devoted to securing peace, and a Cosmopolitan Right are *sufficient* to establish peace, they were not meant to show (and they certainly do not show) that these institutions are *necessary* for peace. Kant's story of how peace could be established, given the historical trends he thought he discerned, was an imaginative reconstruction of one out of the many

---

[25] Michael Brown, ed., *Debating the Democratic Peace* (Cambridge, MA: MIT Press, 1996).

possible future worlds that intelligence and self-interest could have brought
into being, starting out with the facts as he saw them. As he said himself,
although nature guarantees perpetual peace, it "does not do so with a
certainty sufficient to prophesy it from a theoretical point of view." [26] In
other words, the particular future he chose to describe has no predictive
validity whatsoever. He did not predict that history would forever create
reasonable opportunities for moral politicians to set about realizing his
blueprint for peace. If history did once create these opportunities, it seems
now to be embarking on a course in which opportunities to realize Kant's
blueprint are becoming steadily slimmer.

It is possible, however, that history's new course will provide opportunities for moral individuals to establish peace using institutions that
are *very different* from the ones Kant described. I suspect Kant would
not be surprised at such an outcome. In the fifth and sixth theses of his
Idea for a Universal History with a Cosmopolitan Intent, he declared that
the problem of achieving a "universal civil society administered in accord
with right" requires the "correct concept of the nature of a possible
constitution," and "great experience," and consequently is the "hardest
and last [problem] to be solved by the human species." So difficult did
Kant take this problem to be that he claimed that a "perfect solution is
impossible" and that if even an "approximation" is ever found, "it will
only be very late, and after many futile attempts." [27] Given that the
problem Kant describes here is part of the problem of setting out the
conditions for universal peace, it seems highly unlikely (and if not
unlikely then certainly presumptuous on his part) to claim that the
institutions he described in his three "Definitive Articles" were the only
solution to that problem.

Consequently, there is no reason to give up hope for peace. If the
anachronism of Kant's blueprint reduces our hopes for peace, it should
not extinguish them. If Kant could design a blueprint for peace that the
historical trends of his period seemed likely to offer moral politicians
opportunities to realize, we can follow in his footsteps and design a
blueprint for peace that the historical trends we now see emerging are
likely to give us opportunities to realize.

VII. ANOTHER WAY TO CULTIVATE A HOPE FOR PEACE

If we designed such a blueprint, we would be following Kant's way of
trying to cultivate an energizing and motivating hope for peace by dem-
onstrating that there were good grounds for believing that there was a
good chance of peace being established. But there may be another way.
Recall the fact noted earlier that many people seem to hope to win the

---

[26] Kant, *Perpetual Peace,* 125.
[27] Kant, *Idea for a Universal History with a Cosmopolitan Intent,* 33–34.

lottery; it implies that hope is possible even when the hoper believes there is only a very small possibility that his hope will be realized. If this is indeed the case, and if we can discover what makes it possible for people to hope for very unlikely things, we may be able to cultivate a hope for peace even if we cannot demonstrate that our hope for peace is well founded and have no grounds for believing there is a good chance that peace will eventually be established. In particular, we may be able to cultivate a hope for peace even if we have not yet been able to duplicate Kant's feat of producing a blueprint for peace that historical trends are likely to create opportunities for us to realize.

A critic may object that although it is possible to hope for very unlikely things, such hopes are unreasonable; and he may remind me that I myself admitted that hoping to win the lottery with only one ticket is unreasonable. He may also object that hope for very unlikely things is useless in the sense that it does not motivate the hoper to do anything to establish what he hopes for; and, again, he may remind me that I admitted that hoping to win the lottery with only one ticket does not motivate the hoper to do anything to help him win the lottery. Such a critic may conclude that, for these reasons, cultivating a hope for peace when peace is believed to be very unlikely is pointless, and that to support a duty to seek peace, we need a hope for peace that motivates reasonable people to search for morally permissible ways to secure peace.

In response, I emphasize first that the objection does not challenge the very possibility of hoping for things believed to be very unlikely. It only challenges the reasonableness and usefulness of such hopes. But consider the following two examples: (1) very sick patients who accept their doctors' prognoses that they are very likely to die, but who nevertheless keep their hopes for recovery high; and (2) the parents of a very sick child who continue to hope for the child's recovery even if they believe the experts' prognosis that the child has virtually no chance to recover. The hopes of such people are not useless. They powerfully motivate the hopers to search for cures, sometimes with notable success; and they help the hopers to live better lives even when these individuals do not find what they seek. Finally, since such hopes have such good consequences, we should hesitate to dismiss them as unreasonable, though I shall have more to say on this point. If we can explain what makes their hopes possible and also both useful and reasonable, we may be able to discover how to cultivate an energizing hope for peace despite not having yet designed a blueprint for securing peace that we believe current historical trends will create opportunities for us to realize.

For convenience, let us focus on my second example: the hopeful parents and the experts. One large and obvious difference between them is that the parents love the child a lot more than the experts do. I will argue that this difference explains why they continue to hope for the child's recovery even though the experts do not.

BERNARD R. BOXILL

Reflection suggests that in every case of hope, the hoper loves, desires, or positively appraises or evaluates what he or she hopes for.[28] Of course, people can seem to hope for something they acknowledge to be bad: for example, the death of a competitor. But it can be argued that in such cases they are really hoping that the competitor's death will redound to their advantage, which they conceive of as good. The view that hope involves a desire for or a positive evaluation or appraisal of what is hoped for fits with hope's being an emotion. On a widely accepted account of emotion, evaluations or desires are always parts of emotions.[29] So to our earlier finding that hope always contains a judgment about the likelihood of what is hoped for, we can add that hope also always contains a desire for or a positive evaluation of what is hoped for.[30]

We have seen that, like other emotions, hope can vary in strength or intensity. In particular, we saw that it tends to grow stronger as the hoper comes to believe that the probability of its being realized grows higher; and that it tends to grow weaker as he comes to believe that the probability of its being realized falls. We can now add a few refinements. As a hoper comes to believe that the probability that the object of his hope will be realized falls, not only does his hope tend to fall, it also tends to change to despair, and to disappear altogether if his belief in the probability of its object being realized falls to zero. And as a hoper comes to believe that the probability that the object of his hope will be realized rises, not only does his hope tend to rise, it also tends to change to another emotion, this time to confidence, and to disappear altogether if his belief in the probability of its object being realized rises to certainty. *Up to a point,* hope varies in a somewhat parallel way when its other component varies. Thus, hope tends to grow weaker the less the hoper values or desires what he hopes for, and to disappear altogether if he stops wanting it or comes to believe that it has no value; if someone does not want or value something, he won't hope for it. And hope tends to grow stronger the more the hoper values or desires what he hopes for, as long as its realization is neither impossible nor certain. An airline pilot's hope that his plane is in good condition is stronger than his hope that his television at home is in good condition because he values his life and the lives of his passengers more than he values watching the big game.

But here the parallelism ends. Increasing a person's desire for what he hopes for, or persuading him to value it more highly, will not cause his

---

[28] This view is widely endorsed. See, for example, J. Day, "Hope," *American Philosophical Quarterly* 6, no. 2 (1969): 89–102.

[29] Deigh, "Cognitivism in the Theory of Emotions."

[30] I am not reducing hope to these two components of it. See Philip Pettit's warning against doing this in Philip Pettit, "Hope and Its Place in Mind," *The Annals of the American Academy of Political and Social Science* 592 (2004): 152–65. As I have indicated, hope involves various imagining, planning, and motivation, and perhaps a lot more. For further discussion, see Luc Bovens, "The Value of Hope," *Philosophy and Phenomenological Research* 59 (1999): 667–81; and Ariel Meirav, "The Nature of Hope," *Ratio* 22, no. 2 (2009): 216–33.

hope for it to disappear, as long as its realization remains uncertain. Christian believers place incredible value on the beatific vision, and desire it as much as it is possible for people to desire anything; but as long as they live, they never stop hoping for it. If they do stop hoping, it is because they are no longer believers. Further, if the object of hope is valued enough, hope for it never changes into another emotion, however the hoper's estimation of its probability varies. As long as she lives, the saint hopes to be saved, and is never either confident of it or despairing of it. Similarly, the pilot's hope for the safety of his passengers never disappears or changes to something else, perhaps to confidence, no matter how highly he estimates the safety of his plane, as long as it is not parked on the ground and all the passengers have left it.[31] And his hope for the safety of his passengers will remain constant and will motivate him to save the plane even if it seems very likely to go down.

These considerations persuade me that the decisive factor determining the strength of hope is the desire for the object of hope, or the value that is placed on it. If the object is desired enough or valued highly enough, hope for it will remain strong and motivating no matter how small the probability of realizing it seems to be. Because the believer desires salvation or values it highly, he hopes for it and is motivated to seek it, no matter how small its likelihood seems to him to be. His desire for it accounts for the strength of his hope for it, and if he is right about its possibility and value, his hope is reasonable too.

If all this is more or less correct, it seems that we have our explanation for the parents' hope for the recovery of their sick child: they love him too much to give up hoping that he will recover. And their hope is reasonable, not because they love him so much (for the intensity of their love explains the strength of their hope, not its reasonableness), and not only because their hope sometimes leads them to discover how to cure him and makes their lives better, but because parents are right to love their children that much.

If we apply these considerations to the hope for peace, we do not need to follow Kant's example and speculate on historical trends and blueprints for peace in order to cultivate a hope for peace. Hope for peace may motivate us to indulge in such speculations, and if our speculations are plausible they may strengthen the hope for peace a little, but they are in the first place the results of this hope, not its cause. Once peace is established to be possible, the strength of our hope for it depends on the

---

[31] Michael Quinn seems to go even further, claiming that a captain of a ship can hope for its seaworthiness even if he is *certain* that it is seaworthy, given the magnitude of the consequences if he is mistaken. Though the truth of Quinn's claim depends on the special meaning he gives to the word "certain," he is absolutely right that hope remains high if what is hoped for is highly valued or greatly desired, as long as its non-occurrence cannot be absolutely ruled out. See Michael Quinn, "Hoping," *Southwestern Journal of Philosophy* 7, no. 1 (1976): 55.

strength of our desire for it, or on the value we place on it. If we can strengthen that desire and establish that peace is of supreme value, we can cultivate an energizing and motivating hope for it, even if we cannot demonstrate that there is a good chance of establishing it.

VIII. Supporting the Duty to Seek Peace with Fear and Compassion

If the foregoing conclusion is sound, the following question is inescapable: If Kant wanted to help us to have an energizing and motivating hope for peace, why did he embark on his conflicted and implausible speculations about historical trends and blueprints for securing peace? Why did he not stick to something he could probably have done a whole lot better, namely, expounding on the value of peace? To answer this question, we must first answer another one.

That other question begins with a complaint about the examples I used to urge that an energizing hope is possible even if realizing its object is very improbable. The complaint is that the examples beg the question. Consider the case of the very sick patients who believe that they are very likely going to die, but who are still sometimes motivated to seek cures for their illnesses. The complaint is that I simply assume that they are motivated by a hope to live, when they may just as easily be motivated by the fear of dying.

Although I continue to insist that the patients may hope to live despite their doctors' prognoses, I concede that they may be motivated to seek a cure by a fear of death rather than by a hope to live. This is because of the way hope is related to fear. We tend to fear the absence of what we hope for. Because we hope to live, we therefore tend to fear dying. To see why these claims are justified, note that fear resembles hope in having two parts: a judgment about the likelihood of its object, and an evaluation of its object. But whereas the object of hope is valued, the object of fear is disvalued.[32] If something is valued, presumably its absence will be disvalued. In particular, if the patients value living, they must disvalue dying. Consequently, if the patients hope to live because they value living, they must fear to die if they disvalue dying in an appropriate way. Accordingly, if I affirm that the patients may hope to live, I must concede that they may also fear to die, and may be motivated by that fear to seek cures for their illnesses.

This possibility raises the following interesting question: Kant tried to support our duty to seek peace by strengthening our hope for peace. Why did he not try to support the duty to seek peace by strengthening our fear

---

[32] Although we disvalue what we fear, we do not fear everything we disvalue. Disvalued things can be disvalued for different reasons. When we fear something, we disvalue it because we think it is dangerous or somehow bad for us. But we need not fear things that we disvalue because they are ugly, disgusting, or contemptible, for example.

of war? The fear of war is likely to motivate us to seek peace. War increases our risk of dying violently, and most of us fear dying violently. Hobbes saw this very clearly, and indeed he listed fear first among the passions that incline us to peace, well ahead of hope, which he placed third and last after the desire for well-being: "The passions that incline men to peace, are fear of death; desire of such things that are necessary to commodious living; and a hope by their industry to obtain them."[33] So if both hope and fear incline us to seek peace, and Kant was prepared to use a hope for peace to support the duty to seek peace, why was he not prepared to use the fear of war to support that same duty?

As I noted earlier, Kant did use the fear of war and its perils to support his argument that we had good grounds to hope for peace. He suggested that our fear of war and its perils will eventually motivate us to seek peace, and that this motivation is among the factors that give us grounds to hope for peace.[34] But of course this use of the fear of war does not suggest that we use such fear directly to support the duty to seek peace.

Kant may have been wary of using the fear of war to support the duty to seek peace because he thought that there were strict limits on how much the fear of war can be cultivated. When Hobbes argued that the fear of war motivates us to seek peace, he was referring to the war of every man against every other man. In that war, as Hobbes took great care to emphasize, everyone has reason to fear violent death because *everyone* has a high risk of being violently killed.[35] Wars between states do not similarly affect everyone. While they may raise everyone's chances of dying violently, they may not raise everyone's chances of dying violently high enough to ensure that everyone fears such wars. Kant saw this point as it applied to kings. He reasoned that they made so many wars because they themselves did not need to be imperiled by war and, consequently, did not need to fear it.[36] But Kant seemed to think that in republics everyone would be sufficiently imperiled by war to ensure that everyone would fear war; he apparently failed to see that even if decisions to go to war are made democratically, a majority—or those who control the majority— may be able to shift the burdens and dangers of war onto a minority, and consequently that republics may be as liable to make war as kingdoms. Perhaps Kant could defend his position on the ground that people can fear dangers to others (people can fear *for* others, as the point is usually put), especially if they care for these others. Thus, if we suppose that the citizens of republics care for each other—a supposition that is entirely consistent with the claims republicans make about the virtues of their favored kind of state—then all citizens of such states will fear war, some

[33] Thomas Hobbes, *Leviathan*, ed. Michael Oakeshott (London: Collier Books, 1962), 102.
[34] Kant, *Idea for a Universal History with a Cosmopolitan Intent*, 34.
[35] Hobbes, *Leviathan*; see esp. chapter 13.
[36] Kant, *Perpetual Peace*, 113.

because the war endangers them personally, and others because the war endangers those they care about.[37]

This argument could help to vindicate Kant's faith that republics tend to be peace loving, while allowing him to argue that fear cannot be relied on as a general motivation to seek peace—for most states are, of course, not republics. But it is not entirely satisfactory, since it may still be possible to encourage citizens of nonrepublican states to fear for their fellow citizens even when they are not themselves endangered. Be that as it may, there are other emotions besides fear that seem capable of supporting a duty to seek peace: for example, compassion. Aristotle describes compassion as a painful feeling directed at others who are suffering serious and undeserved misfortunes.[38] But war always has many victims, namely, the people that it causes to suffer serious and undeserved misfortunes. Even citizens who are not among the victims of war may therefore appropriately direct their compassion at the victims of war. Further, since compassion is partially constituted by or at least normally accompanied by a desire to alleviate and prevent the misfortunes that arouse it, and since establishing peace seems an obvious way to do this, it follows that cultivating compassion for the victims of war should encourage a desire to establish peace that should help to support the duty to seek peace.

This possibility of using compassion to support the duty to seek peace is all the more intriguing because Kant himself suggests the general possibility of using compassion to support duty. As we have already seen, Kant said that compassion is "one of the impulses that nature has implanted in us to do what the representation of duty alone would not accomplish." Consequently, it does not seem inconsistent with his teaching to suppose that nature has implanted compassion in us to do what the bare "representation" of the duty to seek peace "would not accomplish." Further, if as Kant observed we have a duty to cultivate compassionate feelings and to use them "as so many means to sympathy based on moral principles," it seems that we have a duty to cultivate compassionate feelings in a similar way to support the duty to seek peace. Indeed, in the eighteenth century (that is, in Kant's own lifetime), as David Brion Davis observes, many Europeans were trying to arouse sympathy for the victims of European imperialism, who were, of course, victims of war. Even before that, as Davis notes, compassion had been effectively used to support the duty to abolish slavery, another

---

[37] I am referring, of course, to classical republicans like Rousseau. See Jean-Jacques Rousseau, *The Social Contract or Principles of Political Right*, in G. D. H. Cole, ed. and trans., *The Social Contract and The Discourses* (New York: Everyman Library, 1992). Although Kant referred to his favored state as a republic, it differed significantly from what Rousseau and other classical republicans referred to as a republic. Kant's so-called republic is more akin to what we would today call a liberal democracy.

[38] George A. Kennedy, *Aristotle on Rhetoric* (New York: Oxford University Press, 1991), 1385b13.

ancient scourge of the human race.[39] The antislavery movement, he writes, gained strength from the popularization of the idea of the "power of sympathy" urged by philosophers like Francis Hutcheson and Adam Smith; and he adds that Montesquieu not only argued that Negro slavery violated moral principles, but also tried to arouse sympathy for the slaves by "encouraging the imaginary experiment of a reversal of roles in a world turned upside down."[40]

It may be objected that, like the fear of war, compassion for the victims of war cannot be aroused widely enough to reliably support the duty to seek peace. Thus, it may be argued that while Kant allowed that compassion could support duties in a domestic context, he might well have doubted that it could be effectively used to support duties that involved global considerations. Perhaps he had been persuaded by Rousseau's argument that the advance of reason and the artificial and powerful passions engendered by European competitive society had undermined our capacity for compassion, and that national differences so assiduously cultivated by politicians had exacerbated the problem, making it almost impossible for people of one country to feel compassion for the suffering of those of another. But Kant's enthusiasm for the "universal yet disinterested sympathy" for the French revolutionaries that was expressed by people throughout Europe, "even at the risk that this partiality could be of great disadvantage to themselves," suggests that he allowed that compassion could cross national boundaries.[41] Further, if sympathy for the French revolutionaries showed that commitment to republican ideas was spreading, compassion for the victims of European imperialism showed that the same ideas were spreading, in particular, the idea that all people have a right to govern themselves without the interference of outside powers.

We can still ask, then, why Kant urged the hope for peace—rather than compassion for the victims of war and of European imperialism, or simply the fear of war—as a way to support the duty to seek peace. To answer this question, we must seek a better understanding of fear and compassion.

I noted earlier that we can hope to live and fear to die, and we can hope for peace and fear war. This would not be possible if we feared only dangers we considered likely and if we hoped only for goods we considered not very unlikely. If that were the case, and if we feared war, we could not hope for peace. But as we saw, we can hope for goods that we consider very unlikely. Consequently, we can hope for peace though

[39] David Brion Davis, *The Problem of Slavery in Western Culture* (New York: Oxford University Press, 1966), 411.

[40] David Brion Davis, *The Problem of Slavery in the Age of Revolution, 1770–1823* (Ithaca, NY: Cornell University Press, 1975), 45.

[41] Immanuel Kant, "The Contest of Faculties," in H. S. Reiss, ed., *Kant: Political Writings* (Cambridge: Cambridge University Press, 1991), 182.

we fear war because we consider it very likely. How does this explain why Kant wanted to support the duty to seek peace with a hope for peace rather that with a fear of war?

Consider again the patients who believe that they are likely to die, and both fear death and hope to live. Though they experience both emotions, it does not follow that they are motivated by both emotions, and it makes a difference which emotion motivates them to seek a cure. It may be objected that it can make no difference, since in both cases the same thing, a cure, is sought. But the word "cure" here is ambiguous. It could refer to something that prevents a patient from dying, or it could refer to something that enables him to return to a normal life. If the patients are motivated simply by a fear of death, they may be satisfied with a cure that only prevents them from dying. That is, they may he satisfied with a cure that keeps them from dying, but leaves them in a vegetative state or severely handicapped. If they are motivated by a hope to live, however, it is natural to think that they would not be satisfied with being in a vegetative state or severely handicapped. They will want instead to live normally, perhaps even to flourish. Very similar comments apply to the parents of the very sick child. They fear his dying, of course, but they will not be satisfied with a cure that leaves him in a vegetative state or severely handicapped. They hope that he lives, and thus they will want a cure that enables him to flourish and to realize at least some of the wonderful possibilities they have been imagining for him.

The foregoing discussion helps to explain why Kant did not think of using the fear of war to support the duty to seek peace. The fear of war motivates us to find a way to prevent it; that is, it motivates us to ensure its absence. But the absence of war is perfectly compatible with a condition in which (as Kant saw it) nothing very valuable or even very interesting ever happens. It is compatible, for example, with a condition in which there is only a mediocre development of human talents. Kant not only saw nothing valuable in such a condition, he actually despised it. His rhetorical question to Johann Gottfried von Herder about such a condition drips with contempt. "Does the author really mean," Kant wrote (referring to Herder), "that, if the happy inhabitants of Tahiti, never visited by more cultured nations, had been destined to live for thousands of centuries in their tranquil indolence, one could give a satisfying answer to the question why they exist at all, and of whether it would not have been just as good to have this island populated with happy sheep and cattle as with human beings who are happy merely enjoying themselves?" [42]

When Kant was thinking of peace, he was not thinking only of the absence of war. He was thinking also of the full development of human

---

[42] Immanuel Kant, "Review of J. G. Herder's Ideas for the Philosophy of the History of Humanity, Parts 1 and 2," in Gunter Zoller and Robert Louden, eds., *Immanuel Kant: Anthropology, History, and Education* (Cambridge: Cambridge University Press, 2007), 142.

talents that he believed the absence of war would make possible. But he could not have believed that the mere absence of war would make the full development of human talents possible. After all, he seemed to believe that the Tahitians might well live in "tranquil indolence" for "thousands of centuries." In his mind, the absence of war would make the full development of human talents possible only after, and as a result of, thousands of centuries of war. As he put it himself, "war is an indispensable means for bringing" culture "to a still higher stage."[43]

This should make it clear why Kant did not want to rely on the fear of war, or compassion for the victims of war, to support the duty to seek peace—*as he understood peace*. These emotions would not support the duty to seek peace, because they would motivate us to seek the end of war, a goal that is very different from the goal of the duty to seek peace—as Kant understood peace. Think of Kant's idea of peace: the absence of war and the full development of all human talents. Compare it with the absence of war secured by a fear of war, perhaps a Hobbesian state or a Hobbesian balance of power. Whether or not these arrangements can end war, they certainly suppress the development of human talents; for example, they use up resources that could be used to develop talents, and they require the sovereigns of states to impose a rigid censorship that suppresses and confines the imagination.[44] Or compare the Kantian idea of peace with a peace motivated by compassion. Compassion motivates us to put an end to suffering, not to make the full development of human capabilities possible. Or, finally, compare the Kantian idea of peace with a Rousseau-ian peace secured by the isolation of states from one another. In Kant's opinion, these small, self-sufficient, isolated, homogeneous societies would achieve nothing of value beyond the absence of war.

IX. CONCLUSION

As a leading member of the Enlightenment, Kant naturally supposed that the full development of human talents was of very great value. This supposition was correct, of course. But it is not really at issue. At issue is whether a world at peace, and in which human talents are fully developed, though at the cost of thousands of years of war, is more valuable that a world at peace and without that long history of war, but in which human talents are much less fully developed. Given that Kant very highly valued peace—understood not only as the cessation of war, but also as the development of human potentialities—it follows that if the conception of hope I have defended is correct, he could hope for peace despite the low probability of its ever being realized, and despite the high probability that

[43] Immanuel Kant, "Beginning of Human History," in Humphrey, ed., *Immanuel Kant: Perpetual Peace and Other Essays*, 58.

[44] Hobbes, *Leviathan*, 241, 242.

war would very likely continue for a very long time. If he had been confident that he could persuade the rest of us to agree with him, he could have focused on cultivating in us a better appreciation of the great value of peace as he understood it. Instead, he embarked on his obscure, implausible, and conflicted argument apparently aimed at showing that we have a good chance to secure peace. This was a diversion, whether he intended it to be or not. Without it, he would have had to admit to us that there was a path to peace other than the one he recommended, namely, a path created by compassion and perhaps a little fear and aimed at the goal of ending war as soon as possible. Of course, he did not try to do this. Why?

One possible answer is that he believed that such a path was already closed off by world history. The peace envisioned by Rousseau, Kant might have argued, was no longer possible, given historical events. But this answer is not open to Kant. Specifically, it begs the question. As he put it himself, we have a duty to act in conformity with a moral end "even if there is not the slightest theoretical possibility that it can be realized, as long as its impossibility cannot be demonstrated." In other words, to dismiss a peace secured by compassion is already, *without any argument,* to have dismissed it as unworthy. Perhaps, however, Kant argued for peace in the way he did simply because he was confused. He accepted the common idea that hoping for something required that we think it probable, and concluded that to cultivate in us a hope for peace, he had to show us that peace was probable. A darker possibility is that he understood the controversial nature of the value of the kind of peace he sought, and knew that few would be persuaded to agree with him about its value. Better, he might have thought, to let everyone think that the peace he sought was the peace everyone yearned for, the ending of the suffering and killing of war. He might have hoped that no one would notice that if that was indeed his end, he failed to use the obvious means to support the duty to seek it: namely, compassion.

Philosophy, University of North Carolina at Chapel Hill

GOALS, LUCK, AND MORAL OBLIGATION

By R. G. Frey

I. Introduction

We have goals, and they form an important part of our lives. Indeed, so important can they be for us that they can come to form part of our very identity. How do we weigh them in our lives? How do we come to take them into account? In particular, how do we take them into account if they cut against some of our moral obligations? To many, obligation is the very essence of morality, and the only thing that can outweigh an obligation is another, more powerful obligation. I want to discuss this issue of goals and obligations in the context of some of the claims we have come to associate with Bernard Williams's writings on moral philosophy.[1] I think Williams is right to see as important to our lives projects and goals that do not themselves take a moral turn and that are not easily viewed through a moral prism.

II. Dispensing with Localized Moralities

In the final chapter of *Ethics and the Limits of Philosophy* (1985),[2] entitled "Morality, the Peculiar Institution," Williams, somewhat surprisingly, presents his case for dispensing with morality. His views in this chapter are sometimes likened to those of Friedrich Nietzsche and to the latter's doubts about (Christian) morality, but this seems to me to miss just how much Williams was preoccupied with moral philosophy and with the question of how we shall live.[3]

What Williams seems concerned to reject, in our terms, is particular conceptions of the nature and importance of morality and the role morality should play in our lives. We know from *Utilitarianism: For and Against* (1973),[4] and a host of other writings, that he found utilitarianism a rad-

---

[1] I have in mind here particularly Bernard Williams, *Problems of the Self* (Cambridge: Cambridge University Press, 1973); Williams, *Moral Luck* (Cambridge: Cambridge University Press, 1981); Williams, *Making Sense of Humanity* (Cambridge: Cambridge University Press, 1995); and other works by Williams referenced below. I do not in this essay make use of his work on reasons for action, arguably his most important contribution to moral philosophy.
[2] Bernard Williams, *Ethics and the Limits of Philosophy* (Cambridge, MA: Harvard University Press, 1985), 174–96.
[3] In his naturalization of moral psychology, Williams sees himself as following in Nietzsche's footsteps. See Bernard Williams, "Nietzsche's Minimalist Moral Psychology," in Williams, *Making Sense of Humanity,* 65–78.
[4] J. J. C. Smart and Bernard Williams, *Utilitarianism: For and Against* (Cambridge: Cambridge University Press, 1973).

ically impoverished account of morality, and his work is filled with examples of how wrongheaded utilitarianism seemed as a guide to how we
should live our lives. We know from the final chapter of *Ethics and the
Limits of Philosophy* that he found Kantianism impoverished as well. Indeed,
his indictment of it and what we might think of as the ethics of obligation
is severe, at least according to what he took Kantianism to be, which
others have disputed. Moreover, no form of egoism was for Williams a
plausible account of how we should live our lives, and it is clear also from
the final chapter of *Ethics and the Limits of Philosophy* that he did not think
W. D. Ross and his talk of prima facie duties represented insight of the
deepest character into ethics.[5] Famously, Williams in general thought well
of the moral writings of the ancients, as he made clear in a number of
places (especially in *Shame and Necessity*),[6] but no small reason for this
was because he found in those writings a rejection of what he thought of
as the particularly egregious faults of modern moral philosophy, one of
which I am concerned to notice in this essay. Of course, Williams distinguishes between ethics or (roughly) moral philosophy, on the one hand,
and these committed strategies of how we should live, on the other,[7] and
the former, of which he was a distinguished practitioner, remained for
him a viable and valuable subject, whereas the latter strategies, which he
thought of as "localized moralities," represented, in essence, dead ends.
They simply amounted to deeply impoverished accounts of how we should
live. There is much that is important to a life that utilitarian or Kantian
accounts of the moral life cannot capture.

I shall not rehearse the many particular faults that Williams found with
modern moral philosophy or the various reasons that some have found
for resisting his claims. Entire literatures have been spawned with respect
to each of these. Again, I shall not summarize all of Williams's claims in
the final chapter of *Ethics and the Limits of Philosophy*; indeed, it would
consume too many pages to do so. I shall simply locate my discussion in
the context of this chapter and proceed with that discussion. It concerns
the matter of luck and goals or projects in a life.

III. Luck and Obligation

Part of Williams's complaint against modern moral philosophy is that
it leaves no room for luck in a life. In a postscript to his well-known essay

[5] I think it follows from his doubts about Ross that Williams would find fault with
particularism, or the claim that what we gain insight about is not so much general moral
principles as particular moral judgments in particular cases.
[6] Bernard Williams, *Shame and Necessity* (Berkeley: University of California Press, 1993).
[7] See Williams, *Ethics and the Limits of Philosophy*, chap. 9; and Williams, "Moral Luck: A
Postscript," in his *Making Sense of Humanity*, 241–47. Williams's preoccupation with dispensing with particular conceptions of morality can be found in virtually all of his works in
ethics.

"Moral Luck,"[8] Williams writes of using the term "morality," as opposed to "moral philosophy," for "the local system of ideas that particularly emphasizes a resistance to luck."[9] This resistance is, in turn, founded upon other characteristics that modern moral philosophy has, namely, "its insistence that the conclusions of moral reasoning should take the form of obligations."[10] What then follows is a whole series of considerations about obligations, including, most importantly, the thought that the only thing that can outweigh a moral obligation is another moral obligation. It is this central thought that explains the appeal of Ross, who held that we determine our ultimate duty in a particular situation by determining which of the conflicting prima facie duties is most stringent in the circumstances.[11] What most who objected to Ross seized upon was that he did not say by what principles we were to determine stringency in the circumstances,[12] so that we were unable to determine what our actual duty was. What Williams seizes upon, however, is the thought that Ross seems to believe that moral considerations alone are relevant to this determination. Ross never seems to consider whether nonmoral considerations could decide this issue of stringency; he never seems to consider, that is, whether something which was not itself a moral obligation could determine what we should do in a particular situation. For him, the only thing that can outweigh one moral obligation is another moral obligation, and our task as moral reasoners, deciding how we should live, is to try to determine, among the conflicting moral obligations that characterize the situations in which we find ourselves, which is the weightiest of these obligations.[13]

In essence, Williams's objection to Ross's picture is that it simply fails to take into account those features of our lives and experience which themselves do not take the form of moral obligations and are not themselves moral in character. Williams discusses these features under the heading of "importance," thinking of them as things that are important to a life. All kinds of things can fit this description, including things over which we have no control; they can make our lives worthwhile, yet they themselves take no particularly moral form. He distinguishes importance from deliberative priority: if you find something important, then that will

---

[8] Williams, "Moral Luck: A Postscript." This paper initially appeared in Daniel Statman, ed., *Moral Luck* (Albany, NY: SUNY Press, 1993), 251–58.

[9] Williams, "Moral Luck: A Postscript," 251.

[10] Ibid., 251–52.

[11] Situations were described as consisting of such conflicting duties, so that ultimately what was one's actual duty was the one which was the most stringent duty in the circumstances.

[12] Ross was an intuitionist, and this posed a certain difficulty, in the absence of principles for determining stringency in the circumstances, for those who were not intuitionists.

[13] Williams constantly invokes a moral/nonmoral distinction without always saying in what the distinction consists. But what he has in mind becomes clearer as he begins to contrast moral obligations with reflections on what is or may be important in a life, as I try to indicate below.

affect your life in one way or another, and so affect your deliberations; but those effects do not have to be found directly in the content of your deliberations.[14] Yet, in Ross's picture, how do these things get into your deliberations? And if they do not get into your deliberations, how does his picture of how we shall live capture them at all? Unless Ross can turn whatever is in question into a moral obligation, how does his picture of assessing the weight of conflicting moral obligations capture these considerations at all? For Williams, the mistakes here are to think (i) that only obligations can flesh out what is important to a life, and (ii) that only a moral obligation of greater weight can override a moral obligation. For Williams, a person's projects and commitments will ultimately figure into this broader picture of what is important to a life, and pursuit of these projects and commitments can come to weigh against and even to outweigh some of the person's moral obligations. Williams's famous fictionalized example of the painter Gauguin is supposed to capture this fact.[15]

Should Gauguin continue to honor his obligations to his wife and children and live out the life of a businessman? Or should he seek to become the great artist he thinks he can become and so go off to devote himself to his painting? Of course, there is an obvious difficulty here: it will typically only become apparent how (and to what extent) one's projects and commitments weigh in a life after a period of time elapses. At the time when he must decide whether to abandon his wife and children in order to pursue his project to become a great painter, the fictionalized Gauguin does not *know* either that he has it within him to become a great painter or whether he will in fact become such a painter. Williams therefore introduces the notion of rational justification, which is an after-the-fact kind of justification, carried out in the light of how Gauguin's career has transpired and whether he has in fact achieved his goal. At the time of deciding whether to abandon his family, no such justification is available to Gauguin; but, afterwards, it is, and Williams's point is that what transpires in Gauguin's pursuit of his career is partly a matter of luck. How his career develops and unfolds is not entirely within Gauguin's control, though such things as how seriously he devotes himself to his goal and how he otherwise structures his life may well be. Still, if he achieves his goal, he can, Williams thinks, offer a rational justification of the abandonment of his family. That justification turns not merely on the presence of good fortune in the pursuit of his career as an artist but also on the project he has of pursuing such a career; neither of these things appears to be a consideration of the sort that Ross's picture demands.

Is this right? Can one rationally justify breaking one's obligations and abandoning one's family? Though Williams never says exactly what is

---

[14] Williams, *Ethics and the Limits of Philosophy*, 181ff.
[15] See Bernard Williams, "Moral Luck," in his *Moral Luck* (Cambridge: Cambridge University Press, 1981), 20–39.

involved in rationally justifying setting aside one's moral obligations, and never portrays exactly how Gauguin deliberates about the matter after the fact, it seems to me right that there is a way that luck enters into this kind of discussion and can (arguably) justify what is done.

IV. Luck and Responsibility

That luck plays a role in responsibility seems clear. (I should perhaps refer to a certain kind of discussion of responsibility. Different approaches to the subject are on offer today, such as one featuring appeal to reactive attitudes, such as praise, blame, and shame, as opposed to one featuring, as here, appeal to what one causes.)

Suppose two men set out to assassinate the president. Both buy weapons, practice, take up positions in windows of the School Book Depository, and fire. The bullet of the first assassin strikes home, while the bullet of the second, as the result of a puff of wind, is blown astray and harmlessly dents the pavement. Assassin 1 is responsible for the death of the president and a killing; Assassin 2 is not. Assassin 1 is a murderer; Assassin 2 is not. Legally, there seems to be a way in which Assassin 2 benefits from luck, whereas, morally, I suppose many will want to suggest that they do not want him to benefit. Can we use the charge of attempted murder to deny him this benefit?

Suppose a pickpocket plies his trade at Heathrow Airport, and suppose he puts his hand into a man's pocket which turns out to be empty: this individual cannot be guilty of theft because he takes nothing. According to English law, however, neither can he be guilty of attempted theft,[16] since attempts require that it be possible to complete the offense, and if there is nothing to steal, the offense cannot be completed. Our friend, therefore, is not guilty of theft, since he did not take anything; and he is not guilty of attempted theft, since he could not have taken anything. Of course, we may want to discourage his sort of behavior, so we may charge him with creating a public nuisance or, if we want to be especially hard on him, with assault, at least if he touches the man into whose pocket he puts his hand. But he is not a thief and is not responsible for a theft. He benefits from the fact that the pocket is empty.

Famously, something similar can be true in the murder case. Suppose that Smith is about to stab Jones, but the latter dies of a heart attack the moment before Smith's knife strikes home. Smith cannot be guilty of murder, since it is impossible to murder a dead person, and he cannot be guilty of attempted murder, since one can only attempt to murder a living person. Once again, what one is (legally) responsible for is, in part, determined by luck.

---

[16] See Alan White, "Attempting the Impossible," in R. G. Frey and Christopher Morris, eds., *Liability and Responsibility* (Cambridge: Cambridge University Press, 1997).

Many find it tempting, in order to make clear their moral disapproval in these cases, to make some claim about the characters of the agents involved. In the case of the two assassins, for instance, many may claim that both have an equally black character, thereby making plain that they do not want Assassin 2 to benefit from luck. But claims about character are quite beside the point, since the issue here is one of what one is causally responsible for. Let both men have equally black characters: Assassin 2 is not a murderer and has not killed anyone; he is not responsible for a death. In terms of what he is responsible for, his position is quite different from Assassin 1's. Equally, the pickpocket is not responsible for a theft, though his character may be as black as pitch.

V. Intention and Responsibility

Elizabeth Anscombe tries to deal with Assassin 2. She introduces a distinction between moral and legal murder[17] and thus wants to say of our assassins that, while Assassin 1 is guilty of legal murder, Assassin 2 is guilty of moral murder. Legal murder involves, for example, a dead body; moral murder, for Anscombe, need not. Assassin 2, after all, kills no one. So one can be guilty of murder for Anscombe though one has killed or murdered no one. She wants it to be true that moral murder is a case of having one's will compromised; it is a matter of intention.

President Jimmy Carter is said to have remarked that he had committed adultery "in his heart." We might say of our assassins that they committed murder "in their hearts." Are they not then, morally speaking, guilty of murder? They are guilty only if one can be guilty in this regard by intention alone. Our case of Assassin 2 is a bit misleading, because for Anscombe it is not necessary that this individual do anything by way of carrying out his intention.[18] Suppose he intends to assassinate the president but oversleeps on the morning when he is to perform: if his will is compromised, if he really does intend to perform, he is for Anscombe, morally speaking, a murderer, even if he takes no overt steps to realize his intention. There is no need to deal with this point, however, since Anscombe's distinction between moral and legal murder does not deal with the point about responsibility.

This is the case because we are responsible for more than we intend. Suppose Jack is out for a morning stroll with Jill. As they both move forward, they spy simultaneously, lying on the path before them, a wallet

---

[17] G. E. M. Anscombe, "Moral and Legal Murder," in W. Stein, ed., *Nuclear Weapons: A Catholic Response* (London: Burns and Oates, 1961), 43–62.

[18] This cannot be true of all cases, at least if we are to individuate intentions by what they are intentions to do. Notice that, for Anscombe, so to speak, "trying" to murder the president is not what Assassin 2 is doing: he intends to murder the president but he is not "trying" to do so, if he does not act. I am not ultimately concerned with the distinction between *mens rea* and *actus reus* here, though, obviously, the law is.

bulging with money. They both begin to trot toward it, then they begin to rush, then they begin to run. As they are running, they bump into each other, and on one of these occasions, Jack bumps Jill sufficiently hard to send her flying off the path into a tree, and she dies. Jack does not intend to kill Jill, but if she dies Jack seems clearly responsible for her death. This is why, in after-the-fact judgments of responsibility, we do not focus upon who intended what; rather, we are interested in what actually occurred, and in this, luck can play a part. (Put differently, what you cause lies beyond any mere concern with what you intend.)

I turn now to a more indirect case, one in which I benefit from luck but where I am free from any taint that may arise from anything like putting my hand in another person's pocket. Suppose I love my rich uncle, who has raised me and whose heir I am. It is his birthday this week, and I know he likes to read in bed at night. I send him as a gift the Oxford English Dictionary (OED), all twenty-six volumes. He is delighted with his gift. I realize, of course, that he receives parcels downstairs and his bedroom is upstairs, and that, if he begins to carry the various volumes upstairs, he could have a heart attack and die. (I might, as a good nephew, send him a note that reads, "Uncle, please do not carry these books upstairs in order to read them in bed.") Sure enough, he carries the books upstairs, and on one of these trips has a heart attack and dies. I inherit. In sending my uncle the OED, I neither kill him nor murder him. I do not intend his death. If one is a deontologist and accepts that the intention/foresight distinction is morally significant, then while I foresee that my uncle may carry the OED upstairs, I neither intend his death nor intend that he carry the volumes upstairs and so die as a result. True, I have supplied the means of death, but then so have the car manufacturer who supplies the engine that gives off carbon monoxide and the knife manufacturer who supplies kitchen knives for the home.

Am I, morally speaking, responsible for my uncle's death? I do not think so, even though that death is to my advantage and even though I realize that my uncle may well carry the books upstairs to read them in bed. After all, his decision to carry them upstairs intervenes. One must be careful here, for it may appear that, as a result of my uncle's decision to carry the books upstairs, I am not the cause of my uncle's death, and that it is this notion, causation, that carries the weight in Anscombe's discussion of being, morally speaking, this or that. But this is not the case. Assassin 2 is thought by Anscombe to be, morally speaking, a murderer, but Assassin 2 is not the cause of anyone's death. For Anscombe, one can be a moral murderer without being the cause of death, grievous bodily harm, or injury. For her, causation is not what is crucial here.

But neither, contra Anscombe, is intention what is crucial. Suppose everything in my uncle's case is the same except that I intend my uncle's death when I send him the OED. I am still not responsible for my uncle's death; I still have killed no one. My uncle's decision to carry the volumes upstairs still intervenes, a decision over which I have no control. I may or may not be a good person, but responsibility for an outcome does not track a person's goodness or what a person intends. Just as Jack can be responsible for Jill's death, as they dash together in their race for the bulging wallet, even though Jack does not intend that death, so one can fail to be responsible for things that one does intend, as I am in the revised example of my uncle's case.

Nor must we overlook how extraordinary occurrences can intersect this picture. Suppose that my friends and I set out to play football on a field which, if five games of football are played on that field in a single day, will be irreparably damaged, and suppose further that it has never been the case before that more than one game of football has been played on the field in a single day. I neither know nor believe that the field will be damaged, nor do I have any reason to suspect that it will be damaged or to predict that it will be, to even a minor degree of likelihood. Certainly, I do not intend that the field be so damaged. Still, if four additional games of football are played on the field today, I am (partly) responsible for the damage to the field. My intention that it not be damaged has nothing to do with the matter. Bad luck has overtaken me.

Finally, we must not discount how extraordinary occurrences can intersect the picture and make us hesitant about what to say, though not over intention. Suppose that all the conditions that you require for a killing to be a suicide are met: the individual intends to die, proposes to take steps to bring about his death, takes such steps, buys a massive insurance policy for his family, and dies. The case, it might be thought, could not be clearer. Suppose, however, that Baker, who wants and intends to die, decides to buy a ticket on a regularly scheduled flight across the Atlantic: he does so and then takes his seat and awaits his death. Of course, to most people, taking a regularly scheduled flight is just not risky enough to be thought of as a plausible way of killing oneself. But Baker proceeds and there he sits. Amazingly, and quite unrelated to anything that he or anyone else does, the plane once aloft bursts into flames and goes down, condemning all the passengers and crew to a fiery death. Has Baker committed suicide? He wants and intends to die, takes steps to bring about his death, boards the plane, and, most importantly, dies in just the way he contemplated and thought he would. Surely, however, the temptation here is to say (over causation) that Baker is not a suicide or a self-murderer; rather, even though his death is intended and he dies in the way he contemplated, his death is a product of good (or bad) luck (depending upon how you look at it). Is he responsible for his own death? I think that there is a strong case for saying that he is, though we know, as we have seen, that luck can play a part in determining what he is responsible for. Nor is there anything odd about saying that one can be responsible for one's death, yet not be a suicide, even in a case where one intends to die. Luck takes a hand in producing the death.

The foregoing discussion shows that luck plays a role in our lives. Now I want to develop this discussion further, with respect to the goals and projects lives exhibit and the way these goals and projects can come to weigh against our obligations.

VI. GOALS AND IMPORTANCE

Anscombe's distinction between moral and legal murder also fails to cut more deeply in another and perhaps more telling respect. It might be thought that what Anscombe's claim of moral murder enables us to do is to know, as we decide what to do, what the morality of our act is. We can know this if (i) we (roughly) restrict the determination of the morality of the act to the intention with which we act, and (ii) we know what our intentions are. With these two conditions met, no ground is permitted for luck to intervene. Anscombe already knows which intentions are permissible and which are not; she has a list of these, derived from somewhere — perhaps from her faith.[19] She has this list in advance of acting or intending to act. As we know from her book *Intention*,[20] different descriptions can be offered of what one does (or intends to do). What she then does is to run over in her mind the different descriptions under which what the agent proposes to do may fall, and she mentally checks to see whether the intention with which the agent proposes to act in this case figures on her list of impermissible intentions. Thus, under one description, what the agent proposes to do is (for example) to pump water into the house; under another description, it is to poison the inhabitants of the house. Intending to take the life of innocent people figures on Anscombe's list of prohibited intentions. If it so figures, then the act which exhibits that intention is wrong, no matter what the consequences.

The point here has nothing to do with consequentialism or with whether we know what our intentions are (I assume that we do); it has to do with the thought that we need to know, at the time of acting or deciding what to do, what the morality of our act is, with the result that we need to be able to restrict what is to determine the morality of our acts to that which can be known in advance. It is this last bit that matters. In this discussion, why must we restrict what can affect the morality of our acts to that which can be known in advance? As we saw with judgments of responsibility, why cannot what transpires afterward, so to speak, affect the decision we make? Some of what transpires afterward is, while not moral in character,[21] yet important to our lives, and includes things which we could not know in advance and over which we have little, if any, control.

---

[19] The items on this list are of the sort that one might expect: Don't murder; Don't steal; Don't lie; and so on.

[20] G. E. M. Anscombe, *Intention* (Oxford: Basil Blackwell, 1957).

[21] See below for a discussion of how the moral/nonmoral distinction may be drawn in such a case.

None of this would figure on Anscombe's list of proscribed intentions, and none of it need take the form of prima facie obligations, so as to get into Ross's picture of moral life. In such cases, one is not presenting some further moral claim that other parties to the debate have overlooked, but one is presenting some further claim about importance to a life that other parties have overlooked. The issue here revolves around how one's goals and projects mold and shape one's life and lead one to live out a certain kind of life. As will be seen, I think Williams is right to stress this kind of issue.

Suppose Robert is on his death bed and asks to see his son Alex, a philosopher, one final time. Robert has long admired Alex, and he asks Alex to promise that he will continue his life as a philosopher, work hard at living out this conception of the good life to the best of his ability, and strive to make a contribution to his chosen specialty within philosophy. Alex promises. It is hard to imagine a more dramatic instance of a death-bed promise or an episode in a life more definitive of whom one takes oneself to be; the obligation involved can, I imagine, seem almost over-powering. Now suppose I am Alex's best friend, know him very well, and have had long discussions with him about my own life and his. On the fifth anniversary of his father's death, he asks me what advice I can give him about how he should continue to live his life, and he urges me to be candid and honest with him. In fact, Alex is terrible at philosophy. He has been unable to publish, and all his efforts have been returned by editors with notes urging him to burn his work. He has had to be removed from the classroom, both because he is incompetent as a teacher and because the students in despair have threatened to burn down the university. He has no administrative skills whatever and has lost all the paperwork with which he has ever been entrusted. He has asked for the truth, and I give it: he must, as an urgent matter, give up his career as a philosopher. But what then, he asks, is he to do? Giving him my best judgment, and weighing his talents, I advise him to become a bouncer in a pub. He takes my advice and is now on his way in a new career. He breaks his promise to his father to live the life of a philosopher.

Now there may be technicalities by which one might try to evade the thrust of the example. It might be argued that keeping his promise to his father for five years has discharged his promise and relieved him of the obligation involved. This is not the place to argue about time limits on promises and obligations. It might be argued that the death of his father relieves Alex of promises and obligations to him. This is not the place to argue about the extinction of promises and obligations. In the absence of such technicalities, however, it seems to me that Alex is right to break his promise and to set aside his obligation, that what makes this right is not some further moral feature of Alex's case but rather the mess to which his life has been reduced by living out the life of a philosopher, and that the mess to which his life has been reduced is not something that could have figured on Anscombe's list of prohibited intentions or on Ross's list of prima facie duties. Yet, in terms of rational justification, it certainly seems like something that weighs against Alex's obligation (to live out the life of a philosopher) and justifies setting it aside. How Alex's life turns out, how his career as a philosopher fails to prosper, is not something over which he has complete control.

Very little about Alex's life becoming a mess could be known in advance or could be said to be something that should have been known in advance. It may not have been something that could have been foreseen or ought to have been foreseen. Yet it certainly appears to be something that weighs against his obligation to his father—something, obviously, that seems very much a part of what Alex considers as important to his life. Whether it should have been known in advance seems irrelevant to whether Alex's life becoming a mess should weigh against his obligation. To be sure, Williams does distinguish between extrinsic and intrinsic luck,[22] where the puff of wind blowing the bullet astray is extrinsic; and there need be nothing of this sort that makes Alex's life a mess. But I think this discussion can amount to a distinction without a difference, if, for example, we were to construe Alex's lack of philosophical ability as so multifaceted as to explain various unexpected failures in his life apart from directly philosophical ones.

It might be argued that Alex was right to make the promise to his father and ultimately right to break it; in this way, we might try to treat his life as if it were compartmentalized into a series of separate though not unrelated discrete decisions, each to be seen in its own terms and each quite explicitly moral in character. But the point at issue is not about whether life involves a series of decisions to be engaged in their own terms but about whether something other than another contending moral obligation can weigh against and ultimately triumph over Alex's moral obligation (to live out the life of a philosopher). I think we must answer in the affirmative. This does not mean that Alex should not perhaps feel regret at having to break his promise, but it would, I think, be quite wrong to suggest that he should feel remorse. That would imply that he thinks breaking his promise was wrong, and he does not think this.

VII. Goals, Importance, and Living Out a Life

As I have noted, we must be careful to guard against making it appear that we are talking about Alex's decision now about how to live his life and not about his earlier decision. This can be brought out rather clearly in an example with a slightly different stress—a real case, though I have altered it quite a bit to disguise the people involved.

During the many years I lived in England, I became friendly with a man whose chosen career was that of a pianist. He had immense talent,

[22] Williams, "Moral Luck," 35ff.

a prodigious practice and training schedule, and contact with many of the world's great pianists. Over time, he did indeed turn himself into one of the world's great concert pianists, with performances in all the great musical centers of Europe, Asia, and the United States, with radio and television broadcasts all over the world, and with recordings that are distributed wherever classical music is loved. In the early years of our friendship, we would go on tours through Yorkshire, the Lake District, and the Cotswolds; in later years, of course, his concert schedule made this impossible. On these trips, he would describe the seriousness of his purpose, and I would occasionally get a glimpse of the massive drive that lay behind this purpose. He was aiming at the top, and he had been told by those in a position to know (and so was convinced) that he had the ability to turn himself into one of the world's great concert pianists. To speak of him eventually in the same breath as the great British pianist Alfred Brendel, to compare his virtuosity with that of the great Canadian pianist Glenn Gould only seemed to inspire him further.

I remember one point early in his career, long before he became famous and took his place on the world stage, when it was deemed by him and his advisers that it was absolutely imperative that he should go study with one of the great master teachers of piano. His earlier instructors had helped him enormously, but he had now outstripped their accomplishments and what they could teach him. At an Indian restaurant in Whitfield Street in London, he talked over the two names that had risen to the top of his list. I still remember my astonishment when I heard how much these men would cost, and I counted up the pounds as I realized that he was contemplating spending three years with one of them. Soon the discussion came down to money. He had a little that his father had left him, but he needed much more. It turned out that his mother had been saving money over many years for her old age, specifically, in order to allow her to stay in her own home, without having to go into a nursing home or a home for the elderly, which she would not like at all. Coincidentally, the amount of money she had saved, together with the money that would come from the sale of her house, was more or less the same amount, when added to what he had, that he needed. Subsequently, he took his mother's money (I believe he asked for it, in a conversation in which he pointed out the kind of career that was before him), hired one of the master teachers, and did indeed go on to become a concert pianist of the highest order, of whom his mother was very proud. The demands of his concert schedule became very heavy, and he did not get to visit his mother in her home for the elderly as much as he would have liked before she died, though he always managed, I think, to visit twice a year. I do not know whether he could have reached the level he did without having studied with a master teacher, though other friends doubt it. Nor do I know if there were other sums of money he could have drawn on or how feasible it was to defer his career and earn money in some other way, in order to afford the teacher. I have not been privy to all of the family's financial details and thus cannot say how much money this man subsequently gave his mother or whether he had repaid her by the time of her death. (Any full consideration of the case, one might think, would arguably require that we know these and other things.)

Could this man justify what was done in his mother's case? Could he justify setting aside this most intimate obligation he had with respect to the care of his aged mother? I shall not bother to mount the case in his favor, as it parallels that in Alex's case, except that in this case the brilliance of the performances, the broadcasts, and the recordings are there for people all over the world to see and hear. In Alex's case, failure in his life led him to rearrange it; in the pianist's case, success in living out the conception of the good life he had chosen for himself, and living it out in a dedicated and hardworking manner, led him to the production of musical performances that are there for all of us to study, learn from, and enjoy.

We are not compartmentalizing this man's life but asking a question about his decision to take his mother's money: Could the brilliant performances and the extraordinary career have made his taking the money right? No, someone says, because his taking the money involves a violation of a moral obligation to his mother. But then we begin to mount after-the-fact rational justifications of his setting aside this obligation, thereby moving to meet the point that his taking the money was wrong in the first place because it involved the violation of a moral obligation to his mother. Here, too, the pianist feels regret, as, indeed, anyone would who saw what befell the mother as a result of the decision to take the money; but he does not feel remorse, since he does not believe that the setting aside of the obligation to his mother cannot be justified. When asked what he appeals to, the pianist cites what is important in his life; the conception of the good life that he has chosen for himself and has tried in a dedicated and hardworking manner to live out; the numerous performances, broadcasts, and recordings that are there for all now and in the future to enjoy; and the presence in him of regret for what befell his mother. But, importantly, to say that he can appeal to *none of this* because it is not essentially moral in character, or because it cannot be known or guessed at in advance, or because it does not take the form of countervailing moral obligations that outweigh the obligation at issue, just seems to emphasize this more limited notion of morality that does not capture the full panoply of considerations that go to make up how we shall live. Williams rightly, I think, sees these broader considerations of how we shall live as important to a life, whether they take a narrow utilitarian or Kantian or Rossian form (or some other form altogether).

One may, of course, argue that this picture of rational justification is self-serving, that all it does is to license one in doing something immoral in the guise of, so to speak, fulfilling one's goals or projects. In a sense, the picture *is* self-serving: in determining how I shall live, the things to be considered are not restricted to those things that fall out on, say, Rossian lines as moral. Nor are those things that fall out as moral arguably the crucial ones or the most important. To our concert pianist, living out the life of a concert pianist appears to be something of immense importance to him, and this living out comes to play a role in his life and thinking that no mere list of prohibited intentions or prima facie duties captures. This is not, as such, to denigrate such lists, but it is a mistake to think that they exhaust or even centrally capture ethical experience, let alone what is important to a life. And this, most importantly, is what is being put into the balance against moral obligation.

VIII. GOALS THAT ARE MORE QUESTIONABLE

In the foregoing discussion, I have focused upon goals or projects— living out the life of a philosopher, becoming a concert pianist—that one may think favorably of, before starting out upon rational justifications of what is done in their name. But what of more questionable projects?

In all the biographies of J. Robert Oppenheimer,[23] much is made of his massive importance to the Manhattan Project, to the success of Los Alamos, and so to the effort to develop an atomic bomb by which to end World War II. When General Leslie Groves, overall head of the Manhattan Project, appointed Oppenheimer as scientific director of the project, Groves did not know Oppenheimer very well, had had limited contact with him, and so had no basis upon which to determine that Oppenheimer possessed the skills needed to make a success of the project (though he knew that Oppenheimer was regarded as brilliant). Certainly, Groves had no firm reason to think that Oppenheimer could recruit to Los Alamos a mighty pantheon of the world's physicists. In all these respects, Oppenheimer succeeded.

There occurs early on in his tenure at Los Alamos an incident that is much discussed: Oppenheimer is asked by an intelligence officer for the Army a question to which he responds with a lie. He had associated himself with left-wing causes in the past, had contributed money to left-wing organizations, and had a number of left-wing associates and graduate students. He lies to Army intelligence about who it is that has approached him about his work for the Army. (Eventually, this lie will play a central part in the removal of Oppenheimer's security clearance in 1953, and this removal will put an end to Oppenheimer's role as a scientific adviser to the government.) In fact, Oppenheimer had been told by a friend that if he, Oppenheimer, ever wished to pass along information

---

[23] See, for example, Peter Goodchild, *Oppenheimer* (London: BBC, 1983); R. Rhodes, *The Making of the Atomic Bomb* (New York: Simon and Schuster, 1986); P. Stern, *The Oppenheimer Case* (New York: Harper and Row, 1969); Abraham Pais, *J. Robert Oppenheimer: A Life* (New York: Oxford University Press, 2006); and Edward Teller, *The Legacy of Hiroshima* (New York: Doubleday, 1962).

about the project of which he was in charge to the Soviets, there was an individual nearby who could do so. In response to a question about the episode, Oppenheimer lies to Army intelligence. (The tale gets enormously complicated after this, so I shall just leave it here.)

Now I can imagine several things that might have gone through Oppenheimer's mind. To come forward with the truth would require him to betray a friend, for something which, since nothing came of the business, could seem minor. Again, to say anything that might indicate that he had been approached by the Soviets might cost him the support of Groves and thus his directorship. What's more, while he is just beginning to get his legs under him in his post, he has already realized that he is crucial to the success of the Manhattan Project. And the project does succeed: Oppenheimer turns out to have been a brilliant choice on Groves's part; and he and Groves, together with the many illustrious physicists around them, combine to bring success to the project. Groves thinks of himself as lucky to have chosen Oppenheimer, and says so in public.

In many of the histories of the Manhattan Project and World War II, Oppenheimer's success as director of Los Alamos colors the lie he told to Army intelligence. Even his political enemies, such as physicist Edward Teller, concede Oppenheimer's crucial role at Los Alamos, and the lie to Army intelligence is seen as incidental to the general war effort. But the project on which Oppenheimer was engaged, of course, was the designing and engineering of the atomic bomb. True, Harry Truman made the ultimate decision to use the bomb, and Anscombe holds him firmly to account for this;[24] but Oppenheimer was the enabler, providing the completed bombs, both uranium and plutonium, for use by Truman. Oppenheimer brought the scientific project to a successful close, but that close was not simply the winning of the war but the winning of the war by the dropping of atomic bombs on Japanese cities. (Serving on the targeting committee for use of the bombs, Oppenheimer did not denounce the selection of cities as targets but acquiesced in that selection, and acquiesced as well in the first use of the bomb without warning.)

Subsequently, Oppenheimer opposed the development of the hydrogen bomb, and he later appeared to be highly ambivalent about the use of atomic weapons in war altogether. At one point, he yelled out, in Truman's presence, "I have blood on my hands." (Truman was scornful; after all, he, Truman, decided to use the bombs.) Returning to our question, then, can appeal to a deadly project and his role in it provide Oppenheimer with a rational justification of his breaking of his obligation to tell the truth to Army intelligence? Or does the deadly nature of the affair remove any possibility of this kind of thing? It is not accidental, I

[24] G. E. M. Anscombe, "Mr. Truman's Degree," in *The Collected Philosophical Papers of G. E. M. Anscombe*, vol. 3 (Oxford: Blackwell, 1981), 62–71.

think, that nearly all writers portray Oppenheimer favorably, where his success as the wartime director of Los Alamos colors any lie that may have been told along the way to immense scientific achievement. The claim here is not that this is the case, but only that it arguably could be, which makes the point about what considerations can weigh in a life other than a view of one's moral obligations.

IX. Extrinsic and Intrinsic Luck

As for Williams's distinction between extrinsic and intrinsic luck, I do not think it works the way he thinks it does, as if we get different judgments about luck depending upon whether the luck is extrinsic or intrinsic. Suppose a soccer player loses a leg: this piece of extrinsic luck is pretty devastating. We speak of him as having undergone a tragedy or as having suffered a grave misfortune. But consider Alex: no such "out of the blue" incident has befallen him, yet what happens to him is also a tragedy and a grave misfortune. The temptation, I think, is to treat what befalls the soccer player as fate and what befalls Alex as his fault, and, indeed, his fault in two senses. First, one might be tempted to say that Alex should have known in advance that he had no talent for philosophy and thus should not have chosen for himself as he did. Alas, people do not usually know this sort of thing in advance; what happens is that they go along, studying philosophy, and slowly discover over time that they are making little headway in the subject. Second, and more importantly, it is tempting to think that people who work hard at a subject and who come to immerse themselves in it "make their own breaks" and thus enjoy an earned form of intrinsic luck. Alex must not be immersing himself in his subject and must not be devoting himself seriously to being a philosopher, else he would be "making his own breaks" and thus "getting ahead" in philosophy. But making your own breaks is not given to everyone, and it does not follow simply from hard work. True, you may have a good memory and may learn ideas and arguments in philosophy, but there is no certainty that you will be able to come up with ideas and arguments on your own, or in any event ones that survive scrutiny. Thus, Alex seems to me to be someone who is down on his extrinsic luck and has little or no intrinsic luck, as a philosopher. I do not see that one form of luck is more meritorious than the other. They just occur.

X. Goals and Achievement Versus Obligation

Accomplishment in the pursuit of one's projects and goals is an important part of life, one that partly explains why we strive so mightily to live out lives of our own choosing. For while it is true that others may share our projects and goals, it is more often true that they do not; and if our lives are molded and shaped by these others, it is more likely than not that our lives will not be molded and shaped in such a way as to pursue rigorously our projects and to seek strenuously our goals. But to recognize the importance of our projects and goals to ourselves is not yet to tell us exactly how (or how much) to weigh them or how far we may go in pursuing them. Localized moralities, as Williams calls them, or what we may think of as general views of morality such as Kantianism or Rossianism, will often demand that all projects and goals must be scrutinized through them, so that they must be approved by the dominant Kantianism or Rossianism in question and must be pursued in ways that the dominant morality approves and to the extent that the dominant morality allows. In this way, the localized or dominant morality asserts itself as the fundamental vantage point from which projects and goals are to be assessed, since they are the fundamental vantage point from which the projects and goals that make up those lives must be viewed. But why must these projects and goals be seen from a Kantian perspective (or, for that matter, from a Rossian, egoistic, or utilitarian perspective)? Why must we take, say, obligation in the way that Kant and Ross imagine? Why can we not allow other things that are important to our lives, and which are not themselves obligations, to weigh against those things which are?

A case that brings out these strands of thought is that of the English alpinist George Mallory.[25] In the early 1920s, Britain mounted two expeditions to Mount Everest. The first had ended in failure, and the second—this time undertaken with portable oxygen tanks—was heading in the same direction. On June 6, 1924, George Mallory and Andrew ("Sandy") Irvine departed camp on the North Col, and if we are to believe photographic evidence of one of their party several days later, they were seen moving forward high up on the mountain above 28,000 feet. They never returned. From this point onward, it is hard to separate fact from fiction, for their tale has been romanticized and their deaths mythologized—brave young souls going forward into the unknown and coming to a tragic end.

Mallory's case is very interesting for our purposes. He was on his second expedition to Everest; he knew it would almost certainly be his last. He was older now and, while he was in peak condition, the aging process was taking a toll on his climbing skills. He was now married with a young family. If he failed this time, it was not certain that he would be asked on another expedition, or that the British would even undertake another expedition. He had set heart and soul upon climbing Everest and was determined not to come down the mountain this time without hav-

---

[25] For recent work on Mallory, see David Breashears and Audrey Salkeld, *Last Climb: The Legendary Everest Expeditions of George Mallory* (Washington, DC: National Geographic, 1999); and Jochen Hemmleb, Larry A. Johnson, and Eric R. Simonson, *Ghosts of Everest: The Search for Mallory and Irvine* (Seattle, WA: Mountaineer Books, 1999). These books summarize the state of play with respect to the search for Mallory and Irvine up to the discovery of Mallory's body in 1999.

ing reached the summit. He had trained rigorously and had made himself
into arguably the leading high-altitude climber in Europe (and, indeed,
the world).[26] On this latest expedition, he now had oxygen, of which
Irvine had been put in charge. Mallory's last chance to climb the mountain and achieve his goal thus came to him on June 6, 1924. At dawn, he
set out accompanied by Irvine; he took a camera in the hope of recording
their reaching the summit. Nothing was heard from them again.

Part of the fascination of Mallory's case is that it permits us to speculate
on two matters. While we do not know that a decisive point was reached
in the climb, a point at which Mallory had to decide whether to continue
or not, speculation on whether such a point was reached has been rife. If
it was reached, two matters loom large. First, while Mallory was a leading
alpinist of the day, Irvine was not. He was relatively inexperienced (judged
by levels attained by Mallory). If Mallory decided to go forward, he
placed Irvine's life at considerably increased risk. The upper reaches of
the north face of Everest, especially above 28,500 feet, are treacherous
indeed, and even if Mallory could get up them, it was by no means certain
that Irvine could. And even if he could get up the mountain, could Irvine
have gotten back down? Now, at some point, a decision to go ahead puts
Irvine's life at a substantially increased risk. Every indication we have of
Mallory's character[27] is that he was a good, decent man, so many climbers have speculated that he would not have put Irvine's life at such a risk.
Yet we know that Mallory was determined to succeed this time and to put
everything he had into the effort. How could he not go forward? Yet if he
did go forward, he would do so in the face of his obligation to his friend
Irvine not to take substantial chances with his life.

Second, Mallory was a family man, with obligations to his wife and
children. To go forward beyond a certain point placed these obligations at
substantial risk, well beyond the risk endured through attempting a dangerous climb in the first place. No one believes that Mallory would have
said to himself that he was now prepared to die in the attempt to climb
Everest; he valued his own life and those of his wife and family. But no
one is prepared to believe either that he would have given up the struggle, even in the face of terrific odds against him. Again, no one believes
that, if it turned out there was not enough oxygen for both men to climb
the mountain and to get down, Mallory would have asserted his seniority
and taken what oxygen there was. He was not that sort of man. Moreover,
no one is prepared to believe that Mallory would have reasoned that
climbing the mountain was what mattered, not getting back down; this
would have cost him his own life as well as Irvine's, and he does not

---

[26] I put the matter this way in order to allow for the fact that the Sherpas of Nepal may
well count as the finest high-altitude climbers in the world.

[27] For good accounts of Mallory the man, see David Robertson, *George Mallory* (London:
Faber and Faber, 1969); and David Pye, *George Leigh Mallory: A Memoir* (Oxford: Oxford
University Press, 1927).

appear to have been this sort of man either. Nor was he neglectful or reckless with respect to life; after all, he had turned back on the mountain before.

As I have said, part of the fascination of Mallory's case is that, had a decisive point of the sort I have imagined come to pass, Mallory would have had to decide between his obligations to his family and friend and the pursuit of his goal to climb the mountain. The interest for us lies not in how he would have made this decision (though that is interesting) but in its parameters: his obligations, or his goal. Everything we know of the man (which can be separated from the myths surrounding him) leads one to believe that he would not have taken his obligations lightly; yet everything we know of the man who had made climbing Everest a major and abiding goal of his life leads one to believe that he did not take accomplishment of this goal lightly. For us, the interest lies in his choosing between his obligations and his project or goal, and in whether, if he chose the latter, he could rationally justify his breaking the obligations in question. His project or goal represents a contending force against his obligations, and a picture of the moral life that fails to capture this contending force fails to give an account of (nonmoral) things important to a life.

I do not believe we can treat the case as one of a choice between an obligation to himself and his obligations to others. Despite Kant, I do not think there are any obligations to oneself. Besides, inserting such talk is merely a way of trying to make the case conform to the Kantian/Rossian rubric according to which the only thing that can outweigh a moral obligation is another moral obligation.

Nor do I think one can dismiss the case because one thinks that mountain climbing is not in itself important enough to warrant breaking obligations to family and friends. What makes something important in this discussion is whether one adopts it as a goal and the part that the goal plays in one's life; in Mallory's case, one cannot explain his life—indeed, one cannot explain in some sense who he is—while ignoring his goal of climbing Everest. This is partly the point: who Mallory is is in part determined by this goal of his. For he has shaped and molded his life to achieve it, and he lives out the life so molded and shaped.

One final point. All the best evidence today suggests that Mallory did not succeed in climbing Everest; it suggests that he fell on the way up (and not on the way down). He did not achieve his goal. His body was found by the American climber Conrad Anker in 1999, mummified on the north slope of Everest at 27,000 feet. Mallory had fallen from a height above, though not from the summit, and Anker and others tried to reconstruct what happened to him based on his body's position, the evidence of fractured limbs, and so on. Anker sets all this out in his book *The Lost Explorer: Finding Mallory on Mount Everest,* and sets out as well why he believes Mallory would have been unable to climb the north face very far above 28,000 feet.[28] Does Mallory's failure to achieve his goal (unlike, say, my friend the concert pianist, or Oppenheimer) affect our ability to offer rational justifications in his life for his setting aside certain obligations in order to pursue his goal? I do not see why success, as opposed to the effort to succeed, matters here. For suppose that today we were to discover the camera that Mallory took with him and in it a negative that the cold had preserved of a scene from the top of Everest: would this fact in any way alter how we try to assess the choice between his obligations and his goal?

XI. CONCLUSION

What matters in a life is not confined to morality. But neither is it the case that what is important to a life has to be viewed through the prism of a localized or selected morality such as Kantianism or Rossianism. Indeed, it is difficult to view a life in this way, for our projects and goals themselves do not have to take a moral turn. One can seek to be a philosopher, or a concert pianist, or a physicist, or a mountain climber—conceptions of the good life that are not themselves moral in character. And the ways lives are shaped and molded in order to live out these conceptions of what one wants to do with one's life do not take a particularly moral turn either. Yet any account of morality that ignores or trivializes these projects and goals of lives seems to leave out items that seem crucial to understanding those lives. And that is the central plight of modern moral philosophy, if Williams is to be believed: modern moral philosophy seizes upon some such notion as obligation (or utility) and then flattens out our lives as it views those lives though this notion it has seized upon as important.

Philosophy, Bowling Green State University

---

[28] Conrad Anker and David Roberts, *The Lost Explorer: Finding Mallory on Mount Everest* (New York: Simon and Schuster, 1999).

MORAL OBLIGATION AFTER THE DEATH OF GOD: CRITICAL REFLECTIONS ON CONCERNS FROM IMMANUEL KANT, G. W. F. HEGEL, AND ELIZABETH ANSCOMBE

By H. Tristram Engelhardt, Jr.

I. The Obligatoriness of Moral Obligation in a Secular Age

Doubts about the absolute claim or compelling character of morality absent God are a cardinal[1] element of G. E. M. Anscombe's famous observation that the absence of God recasts the significance of morality. As she notes, once God is removed from the understanding of morality, it is "as if the notion 'criminal' were to remain when criminal law and criminal courts had been abolished and forgotten."[2] Moral discourse may still have the sense that moral obligations are real and should trump prudential or self-interested concerns, but the traditional ground of morality's compelling character is gone. There is no guarantee, absent God as the Enforcer[3] of morality, that one will always be worse off for acting immorally. Immanuel Kant saw this point before Anscombe, when he argued for the practical necessity of affirming God's existence.

Granted, even without God there remains a sense that acting immorally means that, from a particular moral perspective, one has acted against the right and/or the good. That is, within a framework of right-making conditions of the sort that is supported by a Kantian commitment equating morality with a particular account of acting rationally, one is blameworthy, not worthy of happiness, if one acts immorally—although one's immoral actions may make one very happy. So, too, one can be held to have acted immorally if by one's actions one does not maximize the greatest good for the greatest number, as understood within a particular utilitarian account of morality (whether act- or rule-utilitarian, preference-satisfaction-oriented, etc.)—although one may have maximized the good for all those to whom one is most intimately committed. Once the existence of a God Who reliably rewards and punishes is no longer recognized, the question arises as to why moral obligations should always be

---

[1] In this essay, the term "cardinal" is used in the first sense given in *Webster's New Collegiate Dictionary* (2d ed., 1960): "of basic importance; main; chief; as, *cardinal* principles."

[2] G. E. M. Anscombe, "Modern Moral Philosophy," *Philosophy* 33 (January 1958): 6.

[3] For ease in identifying references to God, and following traditional usage, pronouns and other terms referring to God are capitalized.

decisive, especially when there appear to be compelling prudential grounds to act immorally. Why ought one to act morally, when acting immorally will lead to great benefit to oneself and to those with whom one is most closely associated, while acting morally will lead to great harm to oneself and to those with whom one is most closely associated?

The problem is that when the God Who reliably rewards the virtuous and punishes the guilty is no longer acknowledged, the general priority of morality over prudence is brought into question.[4] Or, to phrase matters in a more Kantian idiom, absent a necessary connection between acting rightly and the achievement of happiness, the rationality of morality will be brought into question in a range of cases. These cases are those in which the commitment to act rightly (or even to achieve the greatest good for the greatest number or to have the character of being virtuous) will be plausibly outweighed by the substantial nonmoral costs (to oneself, to those to whom one is most closely bound, and to one's particular community) of acting morally, as well as by the significant benefits of acting immorally. The question is how to determine which among the many normative viewpoints one should invoke to secure the proper priority of morality over prudence. This highlights a further problem of moral pluralism. Absent something like the unique perspective of God, the unity of morality is also brought into question by an in principle irresolvable plurality of moral perspectives.[5] The loss of a God's-eye perspective that would establish the canonical morality has wide-ranging implications for morality. Absent a canonically authoritative moral sense (as endorsed from the perspective of God), there is also the question of what standards one should use to rank cardinal human goods and right-making conditions so as to establish a particular morality.

One way to cut through these puzzles is by affirming that the moral point of view—the ground and perspective for the justification of morality—is that perspective that canonically specifies the content of morality and unites being and morality, such that there is no way to escape due punishment for one's immoral actions, as with an appeal to the perspective of the God Who created and ordered all, and Who will

---

[4] In this essay, "prudence" is used to identify seeking one's own welfare and the welfare of those for whom one is most concerned. As Kant puts it, "Skill in the choice of means to one's own highest welfare can be called prudence in the narrowest sense." Immanuel Kant, *Foundations of the Metaphysics of Morals,* trans. Lewis White Beck (Indianapolis, IN: Bobbs-Merrill, 1959), 33 [Akademie edition, IV.416].

[5] Much has been written addressing the issue of moral pluralism. See, for example, Gilbert Harman, *Explaining Value and Other Essays in Moral Philosophy* (Oxford: Oxford University Press, 2000); David B. Wong, *Moral Relativity* (Berkeley: University of California Press, 1986); and David B. Wong, *Natural Moralities: A Defense of Pluralistic Relativism* (Oxford: Oxford University Press, 2006). For my early arguments on this matter, see H. T. Engelhardt, Jr., *The Foundations of Bioethics* (New York: Oxford University Press, 1986); and H. T. Engelhardt, Jr., "Can Ethics Take Pluralism Seriously?" *Hastings Center Report* 19 (September 1989), 33–34.

punish the wicked and reward the just.[6] If one makes this affirmation, then one has in principle identified at least a possible canonical perspective from which to address these puzzles.[7] In such circumstances, the genesis, justification, and compelling character of morality have an ultimate unity. Much more would need to be said if one embraces this option, but at least in terms of such a theological appeal, one can in principle envisage a defining and compelling perspective: the point of ultimate unity and enforcement of morality that has played a central role in Western thought. The loss of such a final perspective, God's perspective, as an ultimate unity and grounding of morality, marks a rupture in Western culture. After that rupture, the force of moral obligation changes.

As controversial as invocations of God may be, it seems relatively uncontroversial that a theological appeal played a central role in framing the sense of moral obligation that was articulated by European culture after the establishment of Christianity. A distinctly Western culture, church, morality, and moral philosophy came into existence with Pope Leo III's crowning of Charles the Great (December 25, 800) and Pope John XII's crowning of Otto the Great (February 2, 962), along with the establishment of the regal papacy with Pope Nicholas I (858–867) and Hildebrand (Pope Gregory VII, 1073–1085).[8] Western moral reflections were set within a dominant culture where morality received a grounding that was partially theocentric but also reflected the Western European synthesis of faith and reason. Against this background, the taken-for-granted character of morality changed when the theocentric grounding was no longer accepted. The Enlightenment moved the West away from a theocentric moral culture and to the contemporary secular culture—a culture that acts as if the universe were ultimately without meaning (e.g., acts according to a principle of methodological atheism). And once this move was made, the taken-for-granted unity of morality—along with the harmony of being and morality, and therefore the unity and obligatory force of morality—was brought into question.

---

[6] "And His righteousness is to children's children, to such as keep His covenant" (LXX Psalm 102:17–18).

[7] For a recent defense of the rationality of affirming the existence of God, see Richard Swinburne, *Faith and Reason*, 2d ed. (Oxford: Clarendon Press, 2005).

[8] The crowning of Charles the Great created a distinctively Western cultural domain set off against that which had previously constituted a united Christian empire and culture. The crowning was a historically momentous event. "The coronation of Charles is not only the central event of the Middle Ages, it is also one of those very few events of which, taking them singly, it may be said that if they had not happened, the history of the world would have been different." James Bryce, "The Coronation as a Revival of the Roman Empire in the West," in *The Coronation of Charlemagne*, ed. Richard E. Sullivan (Boston: D. C. Heath, 1959), 41. The coronation was followed by the excommunication in A.D. 867 of Pope Nicholas I by St. Photios the Great of Constantinople. Subsequently, a stronger Western empire and a stronger papacy emerged when Pope John XII crowned Otto the Great. The "reforms" of Pope Gregory VII solidified a Western viewpoint nurturing cultural grounds for what became the Western European synthesis of Christian thought and philosophy.

After the secularization of Western culture through the Enlightenment—and especially following the French Revolution and Napoleon's victory at the Battle of Jena on August 6, 1806, which ended the Western empire—a post-traditional culture emerged unanchored in God. Among the consequences was the recognition, however implicitly, that philosophical reason could not substitute for a God in Whom the dominant culture no longer believed. The expectation of a single, canonical, content-full morality was radically brought into question. Moreover, the expectation that moral concerns should trump concerns of prudence and self-interest was also brought into question. This circumstance and its implications for the force of moral obligation have been addressed, in various ways, by Immanuel Kant (1724–1804), G. W. F. Hegel (1770–1831), and G. E. M. Anscombe (1919–2001). This essay explores these implications, discussing how they bear on the possibilities for a general, secular understanding of the unity of morality and the force of moral obligation.

II. Moral Pluralism

As I have already noted, there is the problem of the unity of morality, of establishing which among the many possible moral points of view is canonical and then showing why morality should always trump prudential concerns. Without a defining perspective as provided by God, the coherence of morality will be threatened by an irreducible plurality of moral perspectives, a diversity of moral rationalities, a moral pluralism grounded in different rankings of cardinal values and right-making conditions. These different rankings will presuppose different basic moral premises and rules of evidence, and there will be no canonical perspective by which to choose among them. This state of affairs has momentous implications for the philosophical appreciation of morality. After all, Western European thought from the beginning of the second millennium presupposed that philosophical reflection could establish the proper moral perspective, so that there ought, in principle, to be one common global morality. As the contemporary Italian philosopher Gianni Vattimo puts it, "Atheism appears in this light as another catastrophic Tower of Babel...."[9] Vattimo recognizes that without something like the Divine perspective, one faces the challenge of specifying a canonical moral point of view, with its canonical ranking of cardinal values and right-making conditions, to which one can appeal in order to resolve moral pluralism.

The problem is that there is no one moral perspective to substitute for the perspective of God. Once the deep unity of morality and reality is no longer assumed, establishing as canonical any particular perspective requires establishing as canonical the perspective of a particular hypo-

---

[9] Gianni Vattimo, *The End of Modernity*, ed. Jon Snyder (Baltimore, MD: Johns Hopkins University Press, 1988), 31.

thetical, rational decision-maker, a particular set of rational contractors, a particular ethic of discourse, a particular, rational, game-theoretic perspective, etc. To specify such a perspective, one must first determine how one ought to order cardinal right-making conditions and values, such as liberty, equality, prosperity, harmony, and security. To do this, however, one must already possess a normative standard to determine which basic moral premises and rules of moral evidence should determine the canonical ranking. The difficulty is that all attempts to achieve a canonical perspective from nowhere turn out to require endorsing a particular perspective from somewhere in order to acquire content (that is, the perspectives end up presupposing a particular thin theory of the good and particular rules of moral evidence). As a consequence, one cannot in a principled fashion choose among the competing somewheres without begging the question, arguing in a circle, or engaging in an infinite regress. That is, one must first concede basic axioms and rules of evidence.

Appeals to philosophical reflection do not settle the issue but, indeed, complicate matters. One must choose through philosophical reflection among substantively different philosophical approaches to (and accounts of) the nature and substance of morality. One must choose, for example, between a Kantian deontological and a Benthamite teleological approach, as well as among various competing accounts of the proper ordering of right-making conditions and primary human goods. In different accounts, the force and content of morality are different. For example, in Kant's view, one ought never to lie no matter what the consequences. In contrast, in Jeremy Bentham's (1748–1832) view, all moral concerns, including the morality of lying, depend on whether the action will generally maximize pleasure over pain. At stake is the problem of determining the proper content of moral obligations, and of establishing the canonical ranking of cardinal human goods and right-making conditions—matters about which there is foundational disagreement. De facto, one is confronted with a plurality of substantially different moralities and different accounts of moral obligation. This must be the case, for if one means by a morality a generally coherent set of settled judgments about what it is to act rightly, what good one should pursue, and what it means to be virtuous or have good character, then we do not share such a morality.

This is the case because moralities are more discordant, the more they support different views about the central elements of human life, such as different views about when it is obligatory, permitted, or forbidden to take human life, have sex, or redistribute property. Moralities are distinguished by moral and metaphysical disagreements regarding such issues as the moral propriety of abortion, homosexual acts, social-welfare states, physician-assisted suicide, and capital punishment. For instance, depending on how one regards the moral authority of householders, one will endorse a Texan moral vision that affirms (and indeed celebrates) the prompt shooting of trespassers after dark who cause householders to fear for their lives and/or bodily integrity, or a moral vision that holds that such intruders should be dispatched only as a last resort (or perhaps never at all). Depending on one's view of the importance of retributive justice and the obligation to render it, one will celebrate capital punishment and without embarrassment read Moses Maimonides' (1135–1204) account of the four ways pleasing to God to execute the guilty, or one will regard such views as shocking and immoral.[10]

The point is that philosophical reflection cannot provide a surrogate for a God's-eye perspective that could, in principle, give a canonical unity to morality. Moralities remain different, even if different moralities share the same values but merely rank them differently. Common moral values are not enough to constitute a common morality. For example, depending on how one orders the importance of liberty, equality, prosperity, and security, either one will endorse a social-democratic morality and polity, or one will endorse elitist, capitalist-Confucian polities, such as that in Singapore. Differences also turn on disparate views regarding right-making conditions and their ranking. There is, for example, a growing Confucian bioethical literature that reflects a Confucian morality and affirms the family as the proper locus of authority in medical decision-making. The adherents of this morality seek to replace individual consent with family consent, and affirm a gradation in moral obligation that gives priority to concerns for family, friends, and associates over concern for others.[11] As one would expect, across the world one encounters different moral points of view and philosophical accounts of these views, because there is a plurality of views regarding understandings of the proper ranking of cardinal values and right-making conditions. There are also different lists of such conditions, as well as different understandings of the nature of morality, human flourishing, and the character of the virtuous life.[12] One

[10] "Four types of execution were given to the court: stoning, burning, decapitation with a sword, and strangulation." Moses Maimonides, *Mishneh Torah*, Hilchot Sanhedrin V'Haonshin Hamesurim Lahem 14.1 (New York: Moznaim, 2001), 104.

[11] As an example of the salience of moral pluralism, one should note that the place of individually oriented consent in medical treatment is not unchallenged, even within "Western" bioethics. Indeed, within Western health care policy, a larger role for family authority exists than might at first blush have been expected, given the widespread surface endorsement of respect for individual autonomy and choice as a right-making condition. See, for example, Mark Cherry and H. T. Engelhardt, Jr., "Informed Consent in Texas: Theory and Practice," *Journal of Medicine and Philosophy* 29, no. 2 (2004): 237–52. For an introduction to East Asian perspectives on such matters, see Yali Cong, "Doctor-Family-Patient Relationship: The Chinese Paradigm of Informed Consent," *Journal of Medicine and Philosophy* 29, no. 2 (2004): 149–78; Ruiping Fan and Benfu Li, "Truth Telling in Medicine: The Confucian View," *Journal of Medicine and Philosophy* 29, no. 2 (2004): 179–94; Ruiping Fan and Julia Tao, "Consent to Medical Treatment: The Complex Interplay of Patients, Families, and Physicians," *Journal of Medicine and Philosophy* 29, no. 2 (2004): 139–48; and Ruiping Fan, "Which Care? Whose Responsibility? And Why Family? A Confucian Account of Long-Term Care for the Elderly," *Journal of Medicine and Philosophy* 32, no. 5 (September–October 2007): 495–517.

[12] A sampling of contemporary moral diversity at the level of both community life and philosophical reflection on morality is offered by East Asian moral reflections that differ

is constrained to recognize that moralities are disparate, and that moral pluralism is real. De facto, there is no common human morality.

That our moral diversity cannot be set aside by sound rational argument has been well recognized since Clement of Alexandria (155–220), who observed that one cannot argue one's way beyond a pluralism of philosophical views, given that disagreement is grounded in different foundational assumptions. "Should one say that Knowledge is founded on demonstration by a process of reasoning, let him hear that first principles are incapable of demonstration; for they are known neither by art nor sagacity." [13] Agrippa, a third-century philosopher, summarized this state of affairs in terms of five ways of showing that philosophical argument cannot bring rational closure to foundational philosophical and moral disputes. His point was that, since seven hundred years of philosophical analysis and argument had not resolved the disputes at hand, one should not have much hope for the future. Moreover, since disputants argue from their own perspectives, they will always speak past each other and not resolve their controversy by sound rational argument. In addition, absent common basic premises and rules of evidence, disputants will always argue in a circle, beg the question, or engage in an infinite regress, again precluding resolution by sound rational argument.[14]

Faced with the problems that Agrippa summarized, one can retreat to a form of morality grounded in the will. That is, one can settle with merely giving permission or authorization to a particular framework for cooperation, thus creating a common world of moral authority for those who agree to collaborate. This will allow persons to act together with common agreement and therefore common authority. Such a default procedural morality does not require any particular substantive understanding of the good. Nor can one say that it is good, right, or obligatory to act in this way, outside of the inherent "rightness" found within and defining the practice itself. In the process, claims to a canonical moral content must

---

among themselves and from dominant European and North American moral perspectives. See, for example, Angeles Tan Alora and Josephine M. Lumitao, eds., *Beyond a Western Bioethics: Voices from the Developing World* (Washington, DC: Georgetown University Press, 2001); Julia Tao Lai Po-wah, ed., *Cross-Cultural Perspectives* on the *(Im)Possibility of Global Bioethics* (Dordrecht: Springer, 2002); H. T. Engelhardt, Jr., and L. M. Rasmussen, eds., *Bioethics and Moral Content: National Traditions of Health Care Morality* (Dordrecht: Springer, 2002); and Ren-Zong Qiu, ed., *Bioethics: Asian Perspectives* (Dordrecht: Springer, 2004). See also Ruiping Fan, *Reconstructionist Confucianism: Morality after the West* (Dordrecht: Springer, 2009).

[13] Clement of Alexandria, "The Stromata," Book 2, chapter IV, in *Ante-Nicene Fathers*, ed. Alexander Roberts and James Donaldson (Peabody, MA: Hendrickson Publishers, 1994), vol. 2, p. 350.

[14] For an overview of Agrippa's *pente tropoi*, his five ways of showing that controversies, such as those regarding the canonical content of morality, cannot be resolved by sound rational argument, see Diogenes Laertius, *Lives of Eminent Philosophers*, Pyrrho 9, 88–89. See also Sextus Empiricus, "Outlines of Pyrrhonism," I.15.164–69.

be abandoned.[15] In a world regarded as being without ultimate meaning, a world without a unique and final canonical moral perspective, moral pluralism becomes in principle intractable. In summary, one has good grounds for holding that a definitive choice among competing, content-full moral viewpoints cannot be made on the basis of a conclusive, secular, sound rational argument.

The matter of moral pluralism is compounded by the circumstance that any empirical attempt to account for the phenomenon of reality as a biological or sociobiological phenomenon will favor recognizing a further ground for moral pluralism. Insofar as one considers morality an expression of an adaptation that has maximized inclusive fitness, one should presume that, as with other phenotypic characteristics with a genotypic basis, there may be a plurality of forms of adaptation. As with blood types, for example, it is likely that there will be a plurality of moral inclinations and dispositions to "moral intuitions" that have arisen, given different selective pressures in different environments. It is likely that different environments will favor different balances among genetically based moral proclivities to particular moral inclinations and intuitions, as on the model of balances between homozygotes and heterozygotes, as with sickle-cell anemia and thalassemia. For example, in different ecological niches, one would presume that natural selection would favor different balances between altruistically and egoistically inclined individuals, between those who act honestly and those who act prudently, though hypocritically. Insofar as morality has a biological basis, one would not expect a single, common, pretheoretic set of moral inclinations or intuitions. One would expect that, as biological phenomena, moral inclinations and intuitions would be plural, and one would expect different balances among such inclinations to be favored in different environments.[16] This observation does not involve endorsing the naturalistic fallacy. Instead, it suggests a likely divergence of proclivities to moral inclinations and intuitions prior to any judgment as to which inclinations or intuitions are morally to be affirmed or condemned. All of this is to say that Anscombe is right: the loss of a theocentric grounding for morality

---

[15] A moral framework grounded in permission can, by default, function as a practice into which moral agents can enter independently of any particular content-full morality (i.e., without affirming or assuming a particular ordering of primary goods). Such a moral framework underlies the market. This moral framework, anchored in actual permission, functions as a transcendental framework. It provides the necessary conditions for a general human practice that allows participants to act with an authority derived from their common agreement. This practice will thus implicitly include the agreement only to use each other with permission. Permission, in the sense of authorization, creates a web of moral authority. But this perspective does not establish an obligation to enter this practice based on the goodness or the rightness of always acting morally in this way. Only "within" the practice is there a sense of rightness and wrongness. See H. T. Engelhardt, Jr., *The Foundations of Bioethics*, 2d ed. (New York: Oxford University Press, 1996).

[16] For a classic overview of the biological basis of moral inclinations, see Edward O. Wilson, *Sociobiology* (Cambridge, MA: Belknap Press, 1975), chap. 5.

radically changes the character of morality in a way that cannot be remedied by an appeal to a philosophically constructed rational perspective.

An appeal to God surely does not, in itself, resolve the problem of moral pluralism, especially given the plurality of accounts of God and of what God requires. Yet the possibility of a God's-eye perspective offers the possibility of a canonical moral perspective and of a reliable enforcer of morality. In addition, an appeal to God lies in the background of Western European moral philosophy, which assumed the existence of one God and one morality, and which then, with Kant, assumed a rational perspective from which one can establish a canonical morality. A theocentric appeal does at least envisage the possibility, in principle, of an authoritative perspective: a unique Judge Who can determine the canonical ranking of goods and right-making conditions. This is the case, whether one regards God as *the* authority Who fully knows how properly to rank cardinal human goods and right-making conditions, or whether God is simply regarded as in authority to do the ranking, or both.[17] The Enlightenment attempted to substitute a canonical view of reason or rationality for the perspective of God. The difficulty is that there is, in principle, a plurality of senses of moral authority and moral rationality, so that morality becomes in principle plural.

III. MORALITY, PRUDENCE, AND THE EXISTENCE OF GOD

The loss of the appeal to God's perspective also has the effect of undermining the claim that moral considerations should always trump prudential considerations, as I have already noted. To appreciate the force of this change, one might elaborate the fictive binary and inescapable choice suggested earlier. The first option in this fictive example is to act morally in the sense of never using others as means merely, and maximizing the greatest good for the greatest number (however one would hold the latter should be calculated). This option produces high nonmoral costs to oneself, including (let us say) the prolonged physical violation and painful death of oneself and one's family, friends, close associates, and community, along with the destruction of the nonmoral interests of oneself and

[17] The issue in the background is not just whether God approves of the good because it is good or whether the good is good because God approves of it (the issue that Plato raises in the *Euthyphro*). The matter is more complicated, because there is the further question as to whether the correct ranking of the good is the one endorsed by God because it is the correct ranking, or whether it is correct because God affirms it as correct. Then there is the more profound question as to whether, given an omnipotent Creator God, one can make adequate sense of the good, the right, and the virtuous without reference to this God. Is it possible, absent reference to the Holy (that is, to God) to make sense of a dependent, created universe, including the morality that should structure relationships within such a universe, without reference to the Creator? See H. T. Engelhardt, Jr., "The *Euthyphro's* Dilemma Reconsidered: A Variation on a Theme from Brody on Halakhic Method," in *Pluralistic Casuistry*, ed. Mark Cherry and Ana Iltis (Dordrecht: Springer, 2007), 109–30.

one's family, friends, etc. The second option in the example involves violating a minor right-making condition, such as using persons in a minor fashion as means merely, while also acting to lower slightly the average and total amount of benefits over harms for persons generally (that is, choosing this option would decrease the greatest good for the greatest number). This option avoids the terrible consequences to oneself and one's family, friends, close associates, and community, while also leading to the security, immense prosperity, pleasure, and general flourishing in nonmoral ways of oneself and one's family, friends, etc., all without one's family, friends, close associates, and community actually being formally involved in any immoral activity or one's immoral choice (that is, without their consenting to or affirming one's immorality). They would not be involved in formal cooperation with the immoral act. The first of these two options would, in the usual sense, be the moral choice. It would be what one is obliged to choose in the usual sense of acting morally (in that it would honor right-making conditions of respect for all persons qua persons, and/or it would maximize benefits over harms for the greatest number), but it would be personally very costly. The second option would be an immoral choice in the sense of using others as means merely and diminishing the amount of good for the greatest number, but it would be highly advantageous for oneself and one's family, friends, close associates, and community.

In a universe considered to lack any necessary connection between worthiness of happiness and actual happiness, there is a strong sense in which, in such circumstances, acting morally would be irrational: it would involve acting contrary to very important personal interests. In contrast, acting prudently would be rational, in the sense of being in accord with very good grounds for action. One might attempt to contain the threat to morality posed by circumstances in which acting prudently rather than morally would appear more rational, by creating within morality a basis for such exceptions. Thus, one might attempt to argue that it would be morally allowable to preserve very important interests of oneself and one's family, friends, close associates, and community, as long as the moral costs to other persons are not very high, and the costs of not so acting would be very high to oneself and one's family, friends, close associates, and community. The result would be a sort of Confucian moral principle of graduated love, in terms of which it would be appropriate in certain circumstances to give precedence to one's own good and that of one's family, friends, close associates, and community, where there would otherwise be great harm to oneself and one's family, friends, close associates, and community, but only minor immoral use of others and/or only a small diminishment of the greatest good for the greatest number.[18] The

---

[18] A traditional interpretation of Confucian moral thought requires one to weigh one's obligations to the good of one's family, friends, close associates, and community higher than

question then arises as to how one could establish and then limit the governance of such a principled *de minimis* condition for immoral actions—a condition that permitted one (held that one was allowed and/or obliged), at least in some cases, to be partial to oneself and one's family, friends, close associates, and community as long as prudential concerns were significant and the moral costs were not too high. The point is not so much how exactly to answer the question about the correct balance of the claims of morality and the concerns of prudence in particular circumstances, but to recognize that no definitive answer is possible, once God is out of the picture as the arbiter and enforcer of morality. There is no canonical answer regarding who gets the final say, and by what standards, when weighing moral obligations against the claims of prudential rationality.

IV. God for the Sake of Morality: Kant's Account

Kant attempts to address the problem of balancing the claims of morality and prudence by establishing the absolute force of moral obligation. He does this by making the idea of God central to his understanding of morality, all without acknowledging God's existence. At the end of the eighteenth century, there remained a general acceptance of the special metaphysics of natural theology that often included proofs for the existence of God.[19] Kant's theological reflections, in rejecting the possibility of knowing whether a God exists, represent a substantive break from the antecedent philosophical tradition that had shaped Western European culture. Kant does retain, for epistemology and morality, an indispensable place for the idea of God and a basis for postulating God's existence. Yet Kant's failure actually to affirm the existence of God should come as no surprise, not just given the character of his epistemology, but because, as Manfred Kuehn indicates in his biography of Kant, it is very likely that "Kant did not really believe in God."[20] The idea of God remains central for Kant after the publication of *The Critique of Pure Reason* (1781), even if the actual existence of God is no longer recognized.

In his critical works,[21] Kant develops an implicit distinction between (1) acting as if God existed in order to guide empirical study and (2) affirming what he terms a pure practical postulate of God's existence as a basis for moral action. In the latter case, one acts in a way that affirms

one's obligations to distant and especially anonymous others. See, for example, Ruiping Fan, "Which Care? Whose Responsibility? And Why Family?"

[19] Alexander Gottlieb Baumgarten, *Metaphysik* (Stoughton, WI: Books on Demand, 2004).

[20] Manfred Kuehn, *Kant: A Biography* (Cambridge: Cambridge University Press, 2001), 391–92; see also 3–4.

[21] The critical works of Kant refer to those published beginning with the first edition of *The Critique of Pure Reason* in 1781, which critically bring into question what had been the taken-for-granted understanding of epistemology, metaphysics, and morality in Western European philosophy.

the postulate's truth. As to matters epistemological, Kant invokes God as an idea that can warrant one in acting in empirical investigations *as if* reality will always have a fine-grain intelligible unity. In the appendix to the transcendental dialectic of *The Critique of Pure Reason*, Kant develops his account of God as a regulative ideal in order to "guide the empirical employment of *our* reason [so] as to secure its greatest possible extension — that is, by viewing all objects *as if* they drew their origin from such an archetype." [22] Kant recognizes that, if one acted as if the universe were surd in its origins, one would lack a necessary basis for always looking for the richness of the unities and affinities that had been assumed when the universe had been recognized as the creation of God Who established its physical regularities. Kant presupposes that he can maintain the plausibility of looking for a deep intelligible unity in empirical reality by an appeal to a regulative idea of God, but without claiming the actual existence of even a deistic God. [23]

Kant, however, does not explicitly recognize the challenge of moral pluralism that becomes salient once a God's-eye perspective is lost. Nor does he explicitly appeal to God to set moral pluralism aside, although this appeal is present implicitly in his regulative employment of God in investigating the coherence of empirical reality. The idea of God implies that reason, including moral reason, is united in its character. An appeal to God to vindicate the unity of morality is also implicitly present in Kant's account of the kingdom of ends in *The Foundations of the Metaphysics of Morals* (1785). [24] There Kant, by characterizing God as having a holy will, which is necessarily in unison with the law, creates the assumption that there is but one rationally defensible morality. In *Opus Postumum* (1804), Kant does speak of God as the Law-giver, and therefore as the source of the unity of the moral law. As Kant puts it:

> There exists a God, that is, one principle which, as substance, is morally law-giving. . . . [T]he concept of duty (of a universal practical principle) is contained identically in the concept of a divine being as an ideal of human reason for the sake of the latter's law-giving. [25]

The coherence and unity of morality is secured by the role of the idea of God.

As I have already noted, Kant's view is also that the force of moral obligation will be undercut without a God Who guarantees the harmony

---

[22] Immanuel Kant, *Immanuel Kant's Critique of Pure Reason,* trans. Norman Kemp Smith (London: Macmillan, 1964), 553, A672=B700. Emphasis is in the original unless otherwise noted.
[23] Ibid., A675=B703.
[24] Kant, *The Foundations of the Metaphysics of Morals,* Akademie ed., IV.414.
[25] Kant, *Opus Postumum,* ed. Eckart Förster, trans. Eckart Förster and Michael Rosen (Cambridge: Cambridge University Press, 1993), 204, 22:122-23. (The text breaks off after "law-giving.")

of happiness with the worthiness to be happy. Kant's point is that an important element of the rationality of the priority of morality over prudential concerns is undermined in the absence of a God Who coordinates happiness with worthiness of happiness. Kant's account is more subtle than Anscombe's point, noted above, that without God the very character of morality changes, because it is "as if the notion 'criminal' were to remain when criminal law and criminal courts had been abolished and forgotten."[26] Anscombe's view is straightforwardly that the compelling character of moral obligations presupposed an omniscient and omnipotent God Who enforces morality through eternal rewards and punishments. In contrast, Kant's point concerns the challenge to the rationality or coherence of moral obligation, absent a coordination of happiness with worthiness of happiness. Kant's position is not about conforming to morality in order to avoid God's punishment. Such a motive, for Kant, would be a heteronomous consideration (i.e., it would involve acting motivated by a fear of being punished for one's misdeeds), rather than an appropriate moral motive (i.e., that of acting out of respect for the moral law).[27]

In *The Critique of Practical Reason* (1788), Kant stresses this point while advancing his moralized account of Christianity:

> The Christian principle of morality is not theological and thus heteronomous, . . . it does not make the knowledge of God and His will the basis of these laws but makes such knowledge the basis only of succeeding to the highest good on condition of obedience to these laws; it places the real incentive for obedience to the law not in the desired consequences of obedience but in the conception of duty alone, in true observance of which the worthiness to attain the latter [i.e., the consequences of obedience] alone consists.[28]

Kant recognizes that in the absence of a coordination of happiness with worthiness to be happy, there would be a deep irrationality in affirming the obligation to give precedence to morality over prudential concerns—an affirmation he takes to involve also affirming the idea of happiness being in proportion to worthiness of happiness.

In the "Canon of Pure Reason" at the end of *The Critique of Pure Reason*, Kant underscores the necessity of the postulates of God's existence and of immortality in order to secure what he terms the ideal of the supreme good (the coordination of happiness and worthiness of happiness):

> The idea of such an intelligence [God] in which the most perfect moral will, united with supreme blessedness, is the cause of all hap-

[26] Anscombe, "Modern Moral Philosophy," 6.
[27] Kant, *Foundations of the Metaphysics of Morals*, Akademie ed., IV.433.
[28] Immanuel Kant, *Critique of Practical Reason*, trans. Lewis White Beck (Indianapolis, IN: Bobbs-Merrill, 1956), 133–34, Akademie ed., V.129–30.

piness in the world—so far as happiness stands in exact relation with morality, that is, with worthiness to be happy—I entitle the *ideal of the supreme good*. It is, therefore, only in the ideal of the supreme *original* good that pure reason can find the ground of this connection, which is necessary from the practical point of view. . . .[29] Thus without a God and without a world invisible to us now but hoped for, the glorious ideas of morality are indeed objects of approval and admiration, but not springs of purpose and action. For they do not fulfil in its completeness that end which is natural to every rational being and which is determined *a priori*, and rendered necessary, by that same pure reason.[30]

Because Kant holds that we cannot avoid thinking of ourselves as moral agents, and because Kant also holds that morality cannot be fully coherent, absent our representing the right and the good as ultimately in harmony, he finds himself required to affirm God and immortality. For Kant, if the rational priority of morality is defeated, the rationality of morality itself is defeated, a point he also stresses in *The Critique of Pure Reason*. Again, for Kant, this affirmation of God does not involve a theoretical claim—that is, an epistemic claim that God exists. Instead, the claim concerns the coherence of moral conduct: it is the practical claim that it is morally necessary to affirm God's existence in order coherently to maintain the rationality of the absolute claims of morality over prudence.

In *The Critique of Practical Reason*, Kant develops this point further through his solution to the antinomy of pure practical reason. As in *The Critique of Pure Reason*, where Kant presents a pair of propositions, both of which appear to have a claim to truth while both are in tension (are antinomies), so, too, in *The Critique of Practical Reason*, he addresses an apparent antinomy in morality. He examines the proposition that by seeking happiness one can achieve virtue, and the proposition that by being virtuous one will necessarily be happy. The first proposition he holds to be inadmissible because it would render virtue an effect of the allure of happiness, not an autonomous choice. This proposition is incompatible with what Kant holds to be morality. The second proposition he holds to be false "only if I assume existence in this world to be the only mode of existence of a rational being."[31] Thus, Kant is able to hold that being virtuous will lead to happiness in proportion to worthiness, and he is able to save the rationality of moral obligation by affirming his postulates of pure practical reason:

These postulates are those of immortality, of freedom affirmatively regarded (as the causality of a being so far as he belongs to the

---

[29] Kant, *Immanuel Kant's Critique of Pure Reason*, 639, A811–12=B838–39.
[30] Ibid., 640, A813=B841.
[31] Kant, *Critique of Practical Reason*, 119, Akademie ed., V.115.

intelligible world), and of the existence of God. . . . The prospect of the highest good, necessary through respect for the moral law and the consequent supposition of its objective reality, thus leads through postulates of practical reason to concepts which the speculative reason only exhibited as problems which it could not solve.[32]

The requirement that God's existence be affirmed in the practice of morality is so serious for Kant that he affirms it not merely as an *as-if* existence; instead, he affirms the existence of God as a necessary postulate for moral action. God is recognized as integral to the ideal of the supreme good, although God's actual existence is not affirmed.

In this fashion, Kant completes his recasting of natural theology. In *The Critique of Pure Reason,* he argues that natural theology as a project aimed at metaphysical knowledge fails. For Kant, whether God exists or not is a matter that lies beyond theoretical or empirical knowledge. Nevertheless, ever ready to restore the elements of his pre-critical landscape to a post-critical standing, Kant invokes God to guide scientific inquiry and to provide coherence to morality, thus maintaining the force of moral obligation. At the same time, this allows Kant's moralization of religion, his reduction of religion to its moral significance. Kant's position permits him to maintain a moral attitude and a sense of moral obligation that is in continuity with the moral-philosophical views that emerged with the Renaissance and the Reformation, views that had their roots in Western Christendom's synthesis of faith and reason, though they became shorn of their metaphysical foundations.

V. THE STATE AS A SURROGATE FOR GOD: MORAL OBLIGATION WITH THE FORCE OF REASON, CUSTOM, AND LAW

Hegel seeks to give an account of the nature of moral obligation that contrasts with Kant's account, both in terms of the force of moral obligation and in terms of the significance of religion and theology. Although Hegel obscures the significance of his project in a theological language disengaged from traditional theological commitments, his focus is on creating a post-Christian, post-metaphysical perspective.[33] His use of theological language is not disingenuous: Hegel regards himself as disclosing (and perhaps also effecting) a profound shift in Western European culture. He seeks to maintain, while nevertheless recasting, traditional theological language so as to allow him to recognize (as he assumes) how

---

[32] Ibid., 137, Akademie ed., V.133.
[33] Hegel's reference to the death of God is not without controversy. For some further reflections on the matter, see Gabriel Amengual, "Nihilismus und Gottesbegriff," in *Hegel-Jahrbuch* (Berlin: Akademie Verlag, 2003), 38–44; and William Franke, "The Deaths of God in Hegel and Nietzsche and the Crisis of Values in Secular Modernity and Post-Secular Postmodernity," *Religion and the Arts* 11, no. 2 (2007): 214–41.

332   H. TRISTRAM ENGELHARDT, JR.

religious concerns have become a dimension of his post-Enlightenment culture.

To begin with, Hegel lodges morality fully within a dimension (or what Hegel terms a "moment") of *Sittlichkeit*. Hegel contrasts what he calls *Moralität* (morality as it can be understood, as the universalization of intention and will) with *Sittlichkeit* (a form of morality that is, for Hegel, framed by established moral custom). Morality for Hegel must be understood and realized within the framework of customary morality, the highest category of *Sittlichkeit*, which includes the state.[34] It is within the state that there is the political or legal enforcement, the actual realization, of moral norms.[35] Hegel also introduces *Sittlichkeit* as a way of identifying a moral perspective in terms of which contingent, normative content can be given to morality. Hegel notes that it is only in *Sittlichkeit* that morality gains its full content. Hegel's category of *Sittlichkeit* is meant to overcome the one-sidedness and incompleteness of Kant's account of morality. First, Hegel wishes to moderate Kant's claims regarding the right's priority over the good: "[R]ight is not the good without welfare (*fiat iustitia* should not have *pereat mundus* as its consequence)."[36] Unlike Kant, Hegel does not hold that one should do what is right, if this will have significantly bad consequences. Second, Hegel diagnoses the source of Kant's inability to derive concrete moral guidance from his appeal to universalizability, his appeal to the categorical imperative: "Kant's further form—the capacity of an action to be envisaged as a *universal* maxim—does yield a more *concrete* representation of the situation in question, but it does not in itself

[34] G. W. F. Hegel, *The Philosophy of Right*, secs. 258–60. "Category" in this essay is used in the first sense given in *Webster's New Collegiate Dictionary* (2d ed., 1960): "an ultimate concept or form of thought; one of the primary fundamental conceptions to which all knowledge can be reduced." Although the state is the highest category of *Sittlichkeit*, the highest category of the state is world history, that is, the transition to Absolute Spirit within which philosophy is the highest category.

[35] In his account of moral categories, Hegel begins with an abstract account of rights claims and then shows that this discourse is one-sided and incomplete without an account of the good that he addresses under the rubric *Moralität*. Hegel then creates a distinction between *Moralität* and *Sittlichkeit*, thus fashioning a new terminology for his moral philosophy. As Michael Inwood notes, "All three German words for 'morality' derive from a word for 'CUSTOM': *Ethik* is from the Greek *ethos*, *Moralität* from the Latin *mos* (plural: *mores*), and *Sittlichkeit* from the German *Sitte*. But only in the case of *Sittlichkeit* ('ETHICAL LIFE') does Hegel stress this genealogy: *Ethik* has little significance for him, but is occasionally used to cover both *Sittlichkeit* and *Moralität*. *Moralität* is regularly used for 'individual morality', especially as conceived by Kant." Michael Inwood, *A Hegel Dictionary* (Oxford: Blackwell, 1992), 191.

The difficulty that *Moralität* poses and that *Sittlichkeit* solves is the problem of establishing canonical moral content. *Moralität* seeks but fails to establish particular content-full moral obligations as canonical. The content of morality, Hegel argues, is necessarily contingent, sociohistorically conditioned. As with all actuality, for Hegel there is a necessary dimension of contingency. Abstract right and *Moralität* must therefore be understood within the particularity and contingent content of *Sittlichkeit*, which takes shape within a family, a civil society, and a state.

[36] G. W. F. Hegel, *Elements of the Philosophy of Right*, ed. Allen W. Wood, trans. H. B. Nisbet (Cambridge: Cambridge University Press, 1991), 157, sec. 130. The Latin derives from the famous phrase "*Fiat iustitia, et pereat mundus*" ("Let there be justice, though the world perish").

contain any principle apart from formal identity and [the] absence of contradiction."[37] Kant fails to derive concrete moral guidance, on Hegel's view, because actual moral obligation presupposes the contingent content supplied by an existing moral community:

> In an *ethical* community, it is easy to say what man must do, what are the duties he has to fulfil in order to be virtuous: he has simply to follow the well-known and explicit rules of his own situation. Rectitude is the general character which may be demanded of him by law or custom. . . . In an existing ethical order in which a complete system of ethical relations has been developed and actualized, virtue in the strict sense of the word is in place. . . .[38]

The necessity of the contingency of *Sittlichkeit*'s content involves the claim that the content needed for the moral life comes from the moral life's sociohistorical embeddedness. Hegel thus radically rejects Kant's attempt to ground morality in universalizability and rationality alone, thereby providing a new account of moral norms.

Through his postulates of pure practical reason, Kant appeals to God in order to ensure the coordination of happiness and worthiness of happiness, but for Hegel it is the state, not God, that provides the basis for the harmonization (as far as possible, given sociohistorical circumstances) of morality with happiness. It is a particular culture, framed by its civil society and realized through law, that affirms and establishes one among the plurality of constellations of moral norms. The state, as Hegel contends, is "the march of God in the world [*Es ist der Gang Gottes in der Welt, dass der Staat ist*]." The state is the "actual God [*der wirkliche Gott*]," the category of reality within which moral rights become fully actual by being politically realized. It is within the state that the moral status of persons is secured through law.[39] Through the rule of law, as well as through welfare interventions,[40] the state for Hegel can achieve the harmony of the right and the good, insofar as this is possible in a particular sociohistorical context. Moral norms, and the force of moral obligations, take on a more concrete substance by being enforced through laws that can punish crime and reward virtue. In this way, the state becomes the actual agent for achieving happiness in proportion to one's worthiness to be happy, insofar as this is possible within the limits of place and history. Where Kant seeks to retain the idea of God so as to secure the absolute priority of morality over prudence, Hegel seeks no such abstract absolute priority at the normative level. For

[37] Hegel, *Elements of the Philosophy of Right*, 162, sec. 135.
[38] G. W. F. Hegel, *Hegel's Philosophy of Right*, trans. T. M. Knox (Oxford: Clarendon Press, 1952), 107f., sec. 150.
[39] Hegel, *Elements of the Philosophy of Right*, 279, sec. 258 Addition.
[40] Hegel, *The Philosophy of Right*, secs. 244, 247.

Hegel, *Sittlichkeit* will generally specify the appropriate balance between the good and the right. Hegel thus meets Anscombe's concerns with an affirmation of actual criminal courts, laws, and punishments as integral to the *Sittlichkeit* within which morality receives its concrete significance, and within which moral obligations are concretely realized and enforced. Hegel does not reduce the moral to the legal. Instead, Hegel's position is such that a morality not realized through law is only an abstract wish. It is within this cultural realm that the rational force of moral norms is supplemented with the force of custom and law.

Hegel is committed to eschewing the absolute claims of Kant's ahistorical morality and instead accepting the foundational recasting of moral obligation in the absence of a recognition of the transcendent God to which both Kant and Anscombe refer. Hegel takes this approach because, for him, in contrast with Kant, there is no legitimate idea of God as fully transcendent. God has become a category fully integral to Hegel's speculative reason, but is no longer to be thought of as transcendent. For Hegel, the truth of God is fully realized as Absolute Spirit, which is simply the standpoint of philosophy, a moment of *Geist*, of culture philosophically conscious of itself. As a transcendent noumenal entity, God for Hegel is thus dead. Hence, Hegel's observation concerning "the feeling that 'God Himself is dead'"[41] is set within a complex categorial recasting of religion within philosophy. The possible transcendent space of which Kant spoke (when affirming the practical postulate of God's existence in bolstering moral obligation) is rendered explicitly immanent to thought. God is no longer to be considered a Being in a noumenal beyond.[42] Hegel seeks to reconceptualize and immanentize the noumenal, which had been understood as a domain of existence to which one could refer beyond the bounds of possible experience. The appreciation of God as transcendent is deflated, and God is reconstrued as a way of envisaging the meaning of reality as a whole.[43] In the pro-

[41] G. W. F. Hegel, *Faith and Knowledge*, trans. Walter Cerf and H. S. Harris (Albany: State University of New York Press, 1977), 190 [414]. The number in square brackets refers to the critical edition of Hegel's work: Hegel, *Gesammelte Werke*, ed. Hartmut Buchner and Otto Pöggeler (Hamburg: Meiner, 1968).

[42] The nonmetaphysical account of Hegel's project, which this essay embraces, understands Hegel's mature project as an attempt to appreciate categorial thought, to understand how one can think about thinking about being. Hegel's project is the examination and ordering of the ways that thought apprehends being and being is for thought. This account underlying this essay is deeply indebted to the work of Klaus Hartmann. See, for example, Klaus Hartmann, "On Taking the Transcendental Turn," *Review of Metaphysics* 20, no. 2 (1966): 223–49; Klaus Hartmann, ed., *Die Ontologische Option* (Berlin: Walter de Gruyter, 1976); Klaus Hartmann, "Hegel: A Non-Metaphysical View," in *Hegel*, ed. Alasdair MacIntyre (Garden City, NY: Anchor Books, 1972), 101–24; and Terry Pinkard, "What Is the Non-Metaphysical Reading of Hegel? A Reply to F. Beiser," *Bulletin of the Hegel Society of Great Britain* 34 (1996): 13–20. See also H. T. Engelhardt, Jr., and Terry Pinkard, eds., *Hegel Reconsidered* (Dordrecht: Kluwer, 1994).

[43] For an introduction to some of the controversies regarding what Hegel really meant about God, see Klaus Brinkmann, "Panthéisme, panlogisme et protestantisme dans la

cess, the force of moral obligations as grounded in a transcendent God is likewise reconstrued.

Hegel takes this position early in his career. Already in 1802, there is no longer a "beyond" for Hegel—beyond what we know, beyond what can be compassed in categorial thought within the horizon of the finite and the immanent. For Hegel, "being and thought are one,"[44] and thus, in his criticism of Kant even in this early period, Hegel already rejects Kant's reflections on the transcendent.[45] In this way, Hegel seeks to render religious reality, including God, into a philosophical category in which being is fully comprehended by thought. Hegel's foundational critique of Kant's view is that Kant wrongly construes the thing-in-itself and God as possible existents beyond the horizon of possible experience. For Hegel, both the thing-in-itself and God are immanentized and brought within the sphere of experience and categorial knowledge, so that God is rendered an immanent reality within culture. The most consistent account of Hegel's philosophical project in light of his *Phenomenology of Mind* (1807), *Philosophy of Right* (1821), *Science of Logic* (1812, 1813, and 1816), and *Encyclopedia of the Philosophical Sciences* (published in three editions in 1817, 1827, and 1830) is that he sought to frame a categorial, nonmetaphysical account of reality that requires no reference to the noumenal, to the fully transcendent. Hegel's accounts of reality and of morality are not anchored in any understanding of being that cannot be exhaustively categorially compassed in human thought. Hegel contends that being, insofar as it is, must in principle be fully for thought and that thought can fully apprehend being because there is nothing coherently to be thought about being (such as Kant's *Ding-an-sich*) beyond the bounds of thought. For Hegel, being has been rendered immanent and thought is sovereign. Hegel denies that there is noetic knowledge of the noumenon, knowledge of any being independent of and beyond human thought.[46] Hegel is right in his claims if there is no noumenon. Hegel is also right for practical purposes, if no

---

philosophie de Hegel," in *Les Philosophes et la question de Dieu*, ed. Luc Langlois (Paris: Presses Universitaires de France, 2006), 223–38; William Desmond, "Hegel's God, Transcendence, and the Counterfeit Double: A Figure of Dialectical Equivocity?" *Owl of Minerva* 36, no. 2 (2005): 91–110; William Desmond, *Hegel's God: A Counterfeit Double?* (Aldershot: Ashgate, 2005); Peter C. Hodgson, "Hegel's God: Counterfeit or Real?" *Owl of Minerva* 36, no. 2 (2005): 153–63; Stephen Houlgate, "Hegel, Desmond, and the Problem of God's Transcendence," *Owl of Minerva* 36, no. 2 (2005): 131–52; Quentin Lauer, *Hegel's Concept of God* (Albany: State University of New York Press, 1982); James Kreines, "Between the Bounds of Experience and Divine Intuition: Kant's Epistemic Limits and Hegel's Ambitions," *Inquiry* 50, no. 3 (June 2007): 306–34; Craig M. Nichols, "The Eschatological Theogony of the God Who May Be: Exploring the Concept of Divine Presence in Kearney, Hegel, and Heidegger," *Metaphilosophy* 36, no. 5 (October 2005): 750–61; and Alan M. Olson, *Hegel and the Spirit* (Princeton, NJ: Princeton University Press, 1992).

[44] Hegel, *Faith and Knowledge*, 109 [413].

[45] G. W. F. Hegel, "Glauben und Wissen," *Kritisches Journal der Philosophie*, Band 2, no. 1 (Tübingen: Cotta, 1802) [325].

[46] "Noetic" is used in the adjectival form of the second sense given in *Webster's New Collegiate Dictionary* (2d ed., 1960): "cognition, esp. through direct and self-evident knowledge."

one has the capacity for noetic experience of any being whose nature is not fully compassed in human sensible experience and speculative reflection.[47]

Hegel's final standpoint, Absolute Spirit, as a result becomes, for him, the realization of philosophy, in the sense of philosophy reflectively appreciating the order and rationality of philosophy's major categories. Absolute Spirit is *thought categorially thinking about the unity of being and thought.*[48] Philosophy asks and answers all general rational questions (now set within the horizon of the immanent), so that there is no rational standpoint beyond its standpoint. Philosophy is therefore final or absolute. As Peter Kalkavage puts it, "Hegel's critique of the supersensible Beyond" is the central defining characteristic of his philosophical project.[49] As a consequence, the Kantian support for the authority of moral obligation that was anchored in God collapses. There are good grounds in terms of Hegel's personal views, not just his theoretical commitments, to conclude that Hegel was far from a traditional believer.[50] He was not even a believer for the sake of the rationality of morality, as was Kant.[51] Hegel is quite

[47] See H. T. Engelhardt, Jr., "Critical Reflections on Theology's Handmaid," *Philosophy and Theology* 18, no. 1 (2006): 53–75.

[48] At the close of his *Encyclopedia of the Philosophical Sciences,* in the third part ("The Philosophy of Mind") in the section on "Philosophy," Hegel states: "This notion of philosophy is the self-thinking Idea, the truth aware of itself. . . ." G. W. F. Hegel, *Hegel's Philosophy of Mind,* trans. William Wallace (Oxford: Clarendon Press, 1971), 313, sec. 574. Hegel considers philosophy to be the esoteric study of God (ibid., sec. 573). Indeed, Hegel's point is that philosophers philosophizing are God. Here Hegel recasts, shorn of metaphysical foundation, Aristotle's account of the life of the unmoved Mover, God, which is the life of thought thinking itself: "And thought in itself deals with that which is best in itself, and that which is thought in the fullest sense with that which is best in the fullest sense. And thought thinks itself because it shares the nature of the object of thought; for it becomes an object of thought in coming into contact with and thinking its objects, so that thought and object of thought are the same. For that which is *capable* of receiving the object of thought, i.e. the substance, is thought." Aristotle, *Metaphysics,* in *The Complete Works of Aristotle,* ed. Jonathan Barnes (Princeton, NJ: Princeton University Press, 1984), vol. 2, 1695, 1072b18–22.

[49] Peter Kalkavage, *The Logic of Desire: An Introduction to Hegel's Phenomenology of Spirit* (Philadelphia, PA: Paul Dry Books, 2008), 455.

[50] Walter Kaufmann, *Hegel: A Reinterpretation* (Garden City, NY: Anchor Books, 1966); Horst Althaus, *Hegel: An Intellectual Biography,* trans. Michael Tarsh (Cambridge: Polity Press, 2000), 254.

[51] On this point, Kaufmann quotes Heinrich Heine's (1797–1856) report about an evening with Hegel:

> I, a young man of twenty-two who had just eaten well and had good coffee, enthused about the stars and called them the abode of the blessed. But the master grumbled to himself: "The stars, hum! Hum! The stars are only a gleaming leprosy in the sky!" For God's sake, I shouted, then there is no happy locality up there to reward virtue after death? But he, staring at me with his pale eyes, said cuttingly: "So you want to get a tip for having nursed your sick mother and for not having poisoned your dear brother?"—Saying that, he looked around anxiously, but he immediately seemed reassured when he saw that it was only Heinrich Beer, who had approached to invite him to play whist. . . .
>
> I was young and proud, and it pleased my vanity when I learned from Hegel that it was not the dear God who lived in heaven that was God, as my grandmother supposed, but I myself here on earth. (Kaufmann, *Hegel: A Reinterpretation,* 367)

willing to approach morality without Kant's practical postulate of God's existence, because for Hegel God does not exist even as an idea of a transcendent or noumenal reality to be thought beyond the bounds of the immanent, and because morality itself has been recast so that Kant's assumptions regarding the unity of morality and his claims regarding the priority of the right over the good have been categorially domesticated. Hegel can accept both moral pluralism and the deflation of the force of moral obligation. The importance of God has also been deflated for Hegel. In Hegel's *Encyclopedia*, religion is placed as the penultimate category and is speculatively relocated as a moment within philosophy's reflections. The idea of God has become a way of picturing the wholeness of being. In "The Philosophy of Mind" at the end of his *Encyclopedia*, Hegel states: "God is God only so far as he knows himself: his self-knowledge is, further, a self-consciousness in man and man's knowledge *of* God, which proceeds to man's self-knowledge *in* God."[52]

Hegel recognizes that his proposal is radical. The death and resurrection of God of which Hegel speaks are meant to identify God's death as a metaphysical entity and His resurrection as a cultural entity by and in philosophy. The result is that theology has been fully placed within the demands of philosophy. As Hegel sees the matter, his account is meant to "re-establish for philosophy . . . the absolute Passion, the speculative Good Friday in place of the historic Good Friday. Good Friday must be speculatively re-established in the whole truth and harshness of its God-forsakenness."[53] For Hegel, God as traditionally understood in Western European Christianity dies as metaphysically existing, but is resurrected as Hegel's philosophically domesticated God.[54] The idea of God, as Kant understood it, is transformed so as to be rendered a category of cultural

---

For a slightly different translation of this passage, see Heinrich Heine, *Heinrich Heine's Memoirs from his Works, Letters, and Conversations*, ed. Gustav Karpeles, trans. Gilbert Cannan (London: Heinemann, 1910), 114.

[52] Hegel, *Hegel's Philosophy of Mind*, 298, sec. 564.

[53] Hegel, *Faith and Knowledge*, 191 [414].

[54] Western Christianity began its journey to Hegel's philosophical domestication and recasting of God when, from the early second millennium, it began to presuppose an analogy (i.e., an *analogia entis*) between what human moral rationality could know about created being and the being of God. This move allowed Western culture to assume that philosophical accounts of natural law and discursive accounts of philosophical rationality could substitute for the perspective of God. For an account of how different this Western position was from that of the original Christianity, see David Bradshaw, *Aristotle East and West* (New York: Cambridge University Press, 2004). Philosophy was assumed to be able to discover and lay out a moral perspective that was the same as the perspective of God. In time, this led to recasting God in terms of philosophy's interests. For an account of the quite different original Christian epistemology, grounded in a noetic experience of God, see H. T. Engelhardt, Jr., *The Foundations of Christian Bioethics* (Salem, MA: Scrivener Press, 2000); Engelhardt, "Sin and Bioethics: Why a Liturgical Anthropology Is Foundational," *Christian Bioethics* 11, no. 2 (August 2005): 221–39; Engelhardt, "What Is Christian about Christian Bioethics? Metaphysical, Epistemological, and Moral Differences," *Christian Bioethics* 11, no. 3 (December 2005): 241–53; and Engelhardt, "Critical Reflections on Theology's Handmaid."

reality appreciated in philosophical reflection. Hegel renders God fully immanent, while relativizing the priority of the right over the prudent. In the process, the meaning of moral obligation is foundationally recast.

In all of this, it is important to note that Hegel is not directly developing particular morally normative claims. Hegel is not immediately interested in how, within particular circumstances, moral claims can be defeated by prudential concerns. Instead, Hegel is offering a categorial ordering of various levels of normative concerns or discourse. This categorial ordering is aimed *inter alia* at domesticating the noumenal (e.g., God) along with moral norms by placing them all inside the horizon of the immanent. The result is that all is rendered transparent to categorial thought, to philosophical reflection on how being can be for thought, and how thought can apprehend being. Hegel's moral concerns, including his concerns for the nature and force of moral obligation, are situated within this systematic epistemological and ontological project. The force of moral obligation is to be understood within the sociohistorical character of a particular realization of *Sittlichkeit*, a particular sociohistorically realized morality. The force of moral obligations is thus contingent and sociohistorically situated.

VI. Conclusion: Moral Obligations in a World without God

Today we still confront the concerns raised by Kant and Anscombe regarding the compelling character of moral obligation apart from God as the unifier, judge, and enforcer of moral norms. Granted that there are important senses in which it is wrong simpliciter to engage in immoral acts, nevertheless one can still ask whether morality should always trump prudential rationality in the decisions of actual individuals in particular circumstances. If there is a God Who sufficiently punishes the wicked and sufficiently rewards the virtuous into eternity, then it will never be prudentially rational to act immorally. If there is no such God, the question remains as to why it would always be rational to favor moral rationality over prudential rationality. It will not be enough, following Mill, simply to appeal to a feeling of obligation or a feeling of guilt associated with the violation of moral norms as a sanction to dissuade immorality.[55] One can always critically bring feelings of obligation and guilt into question, so as to redirect one's feelings in terms of what one judges appropriate within particular understandings of morality and of prudential rationality, and then redirect one's behavior.

Hegel's categorial account holds that morality is the higher truth of the perspective from which one can understand the full significance of merely prudential choices. Within the sphere of moral norms, one has, for Hegel,

---

[55] John Stuart Mill, *Utilitarianism*, chap. 3, "Of the Ultimate Sanction of the Principle of Utility."

stepped beyond the encounter that generates the master-slave relation-ship.[56] But this does not mean that one is always, in all particular cir-cumstances, acting rationally by giving priority to moral considerations over prudential considerations.[57] After Hegel has settled the matter regard-ing the categorial ordering of domains of normative concern, the question still remains: Why should one necessarily give precedence, in a particular circumstance, to moral rationality over prudential rationality, in the absence of the God Who punishes and rewards, especially in circumstances in which the state is unlikely to punish or reward effectively? The matter of the ordering of moral considerations over prudential considerations will be settled by local *Sittlichkeit* and its appreciation of custom and law. However, there will remain the noncategorial but nevertheless pressing normative question, in particular circumstances, of the priority of moral considerations over prudential considerations, even after Hegel has fin-ished his categorial ordering of normative realms.

Absent a transcendent point of reference, all will develop and change over time. For Hegel, because being and thought are one, as categories change, reality and morality themselves change.[58] This is a point appre-ciated in part by Anscombe in less radical terms, when she recognizes that across Western cultures there has not been one practice of morality. In that, for Hegel, there is no beyond, beyond the horizon of the finite and the immanent, the full sense of moral norms, of what one can coherently say about morality, will be found within the fullness of *Geist*, a fullness that encompasses moral diversity. There can be disparate histories, as long as there can be a history of these histories. Hegel can also recognize different *Sittlichkeiten*, as long as he can philosophically characterize or comprehend this diversity. Hegel can allow a post-modernity, a plurality of moral accounts, as long as this plurality is located within a categorial account of that moral pluralism. Hegel is able to live with a categorially comprehensible moral pluralism, on the condition that he can categorially place and understand that moral diversity.

---

[56] Hegel, *Hegel's Philosophy of Mind*, secs. 430–37. In his treatment of "Phenomenology of Mind" in the *Encyclopedia* (he also treats the issue in his book *The Phenomenology of Mind*), Hegel examines the struggle for recognition under an encounter that initially leads to a master and a slave, but that culminates in the emergence of a universal self-consciousness, a step on the way to morality.

[57] Hegel, *Hegel's Philosophy of Right*, sec. 130.

[58] Hegel put the matter of categorial change in this fashion: "All cultural change reduces itself to a difference of categories. All revolutions, whether in the sciences or world history, occur merely because spirit has changed its categories in order to understand and examine what belongs to it, in order to possess and grasp itself in a truer, deeper, more intimate and unified manner." G. W. F. Hegel, *Hegel's Philosophy of Nature*, trans. Michael John Petry (London: George Allen and Unwin, 1970), 202, sec. 246 Addition. For Hegel, when categories change, reality changes, because there is no independent perspective beyond our categories, save our categorial reflections on the categories (which thought about thought is Absolute Spirit), that could serve as an independent and objective standard. Hegel with malice aforethought has attempted to deflate any acknowledgment of the existence and perspective of the transcendent God, so as firmly to place reality within his categorial account.

The question that Kant and Anscombe present to us is whether, after the Enlightenment, we are still in possession of a sufficiently robust account of moral obligation. It is surely the case that a significant change in the meaning of morality and moral obligation occurs, once God is no longer recognized as the source of the unity and enforcement of morality. If one embraces an atheistic or agnostic methodological postulate, morality remains in principle plural, and the claims of morality cannot always rationally trump the claims of prudential rationality. If reality comes from nowhere, is going nowhere, and serves no ultimate purpose, then the only final perspectives from which to order cardinal moral goods, as well as establish the priority of moral concerns, are provisional, finite, sociohistorically conditioned perspectives articulated within particular cultural understandings. For Kant, God provided at least a basis for denying moral pluralism and for asserting the priority of morality over prudence. Hegel marks the abandonment of a recognition of such a grounding for the unity of morality and the loss of a fully reliable source for the enforcement of moral obligation. In comparison to what had generally been accepted in Western culture prior to the Enlightenment as the force or compelling character of moral obligation, the force of moral obligation is now deflated. The loss of the recognition of the existence of God—the death of God of which Hegel speaks—is no mean loss.

Philosophy, Rice University

INDEX

Absolute Spirit, 334, 336
Accountability, 148–50
Achenwall, Gottfried, 217
Acts, and omissions, 262, 267
Action, 9–10, 66, 138, 159–60, 165, 212, 241; supererogatory, 29–30, 32, 35–37, 57, 61
Agathon, 130
Agency, 48, 58, 69, 72, 158–59, 168, 173–75, 179–80, 212, 330; self-governing, 159, 162–63, 175, 177, 180
Agent-neutrality, 130, 165
Agents, 71, 80, 84, 155–56, 190, 242, 245, 250
Agrippa (third century philosopher), 323
All-things-considered perspective, 253, 266
Alphonse-and-Gaston routine, 133
Animals, 241
Anker, Conrad, 315
Anscombe, Elizabeth, 302–3, 305–7, 311, 317, 320, 324, 329, 334, 338, 340
Appropriation, 269
Aristotle, 129–32, 144, 292
Atheism, 319–20, 340
Attitudes, moral, 137, 139–41, 144
Austin, J. L., 130
Autonomy, 13, 14, 22, 57, 99, 159, 162, 173, 174, 176, 178, 180, 221, 228, 269–70, 330

Baumrin, Bernard, 243
Being, 335–36, 339
Beliefs, 4, 9–11, 14–15, 66, 70, 74, 76, 80, 83–91, 93–97, 99, 101, 108–9, 140, 159–60, 165–66, 168; luminous, 84; mistaken, 84, 91, 97–98, 103–5; non-normative, 103, 106; reasonable, 106–8; and warrant, 166–72. *See also* Theoretical reasoning
Beneficence, 32, 35–36, 60, 131
Benefit, 248–49, 262, 266, 268, 272
Benevolence, rational, 129
Bible, 22
Blackstone, William, 238
Blame, 48, 69, 70, 73–74, 83, 89, 96, 97, 99, 109 n. 74, 110, 142, 143, 148–50, 154–59, 163–67, 169–70, 172–73, 176–78, 180, 192, 263–64, 266–67
Brandt, Richard, 142
Brendel, Alfred, 308
British idealism, 113

Broad, C. D., 64, 114
Butler, Joseph, 129

Capacities, 208
Carritt, E. F., 117, 121
Carter, Jimmy, 302
Categorical imperative, 113, 120, 127, 178, 213
Causation, 223, 303
Censorship, 295
Character, 22, 206, 215–17, 220, 302. *See also* Virtue
Charity, 35, 43, 197–98, 200–3, 205
Charles the Great (Charlemagne), 319
Christianity, 88, 289, 297, 329, 331, 337
Clement of Alexandria, 323
Cloning, 257
Coercion, 207, 209–11, 218, 222, 238, 259
Compassion, 290, 292–93, 295–96
Confidence, 288
Confucianism, 326
Conscience, 180, 225–29, 232
Consequentialism, 24, 27, 112, 114–19, 122, 127–28, 147–48, 305
Constitutions, 282–84, 286
Contracts, 209
Cosmopolitanism, 282, 284–86
Cost/benefit analyses, 253–54
Critique of Pure Reason (Kant), 327–31
Culture, 295

Damstedt, Benjamin, 249, 256
Dancy, Jonathan, 116
Darwall, Stephen, 25–26
Davis, David Brion, 292
Decision guides, 74, 105, 108
Deliberation, 299–301
Demerit, 214–15
Democracy, 178, 285
Democratic Peace Theorists, 285
Deontology, 24, 31, 53–54, 61–62, 66, 112, 114, 118, 122, 129, 137, 183, 303, 321
Descartes, Rene, 123
Desire, 3, 10–11, 19, 22, 89, 119, 122–23, 140–41, 143–45, 158, 288–90
Disgust, 257
Doctrine of Right, 207
Doctrine of Virtue, 207, 209–10, 214, 220, 224–25, 228, 230–31